READING

Basic | Intermediate | Advanced | Expert

LISTENING

Basic | Intermediate | Advanced | Expert

Informative passages

HACKERS APEX READING includes informative and interesting passages on a variety of topics, such as science, art, and history.

Useful online study materials

HACKERS APEX READING provides access to quality online study materials at HackersBook.com. These include streaming audio recordings of all passages accessible through QR codes in the book.

HACKERS

APEX READING for the TOEFL iBT®

Advanced

HACKERS

Preface

Preface

Thank you for purchasing HACKERS APEX READING for the TOEFL iBT Advanced. The TOEFL iBT is a highly challenging exam, so it is important to select an effective study guide. All of us at Hackers Language Research Institute are confident that this publication will be an invaluable resource as you prepare for the TOEFL iBT.

HACKERS APEX READING for the TOEFL iBT is a series of comprehensive study guides for students planning to take the TOEFL iBT or for those wanting to improve their general English reading skills. This series includes four books that progress in difficulty. Students can begin at the level that matches their current abilities and then move on to the higher ones. All of the books in this series provide step-by-step question-solving strategies for every TOEFL question type. These are based on thorough research and years of instructional experience. Each book also includes informative and interesting passages that enable students to improve their English reading skills and expand their background knowledge at the same time. Furthermore, students will receive access to quality online study materials that are designed to help them get the most out of the books in this series. Key features of HACKERS APEX READING for the TOEFL iBT books include:

- Detailed explanations and question-solving strategies for all TOEFL Reading question types
- A large number of high-quality TOEFL Reading passages and questions
- Two full-length TOEFL Reading tests
- Vocabulary exercises to review essential vocabulary that appeared in the passages
- An answer book with Korean translations and lists of key vocabulary
- Access to streaming audio recordings of all passages through QR codes
- Access to supplementary study materials online (www.HackersBook.com)

Thank you again for choosing HACKERS APEX READING for the TOEFL iBT Advanced, and we wish you all the best whether you are preparing to take the TOEFL iBT in the near future or simply hoping to develop your English reading skills overall.

Table of Contents

How to Use This Book

1 Understand the Question Type

Each chapter includes an Overview page that provides essential information about the featured question type and key strategies for answering it. Make sure you fully understand the strategies before moving on to the Example section, which provides a short passage with up to three questions to apply the key strategies to.

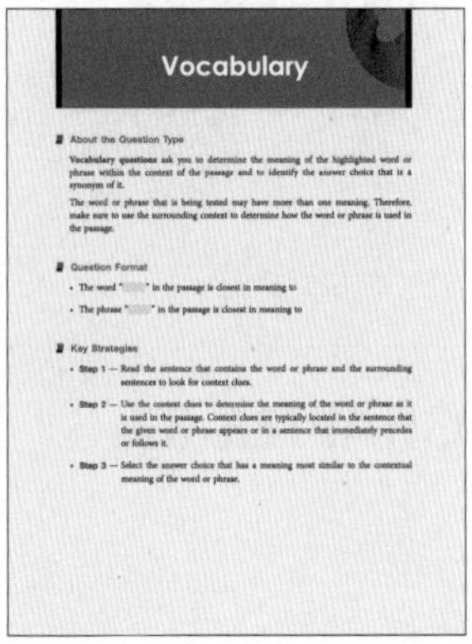
Vocabulary

2 Improve Your Skills with Reading Practice Exercises

Each chapter includes three Reading Practice exercises. These will help you become more familiar with the featured question type, as well as other question types.

Reading Practice 1

The Rococo Movement

3 Take the iBT Reading Tests

Each chapter includes two iBT Reading Tests. Each consists of a longer passage and 10 questions that are similar to those that appear on the TOEFL iBT. Taking these tests will enable you to improve your reading comprehension skills and prepare for the TOEFL iBT.

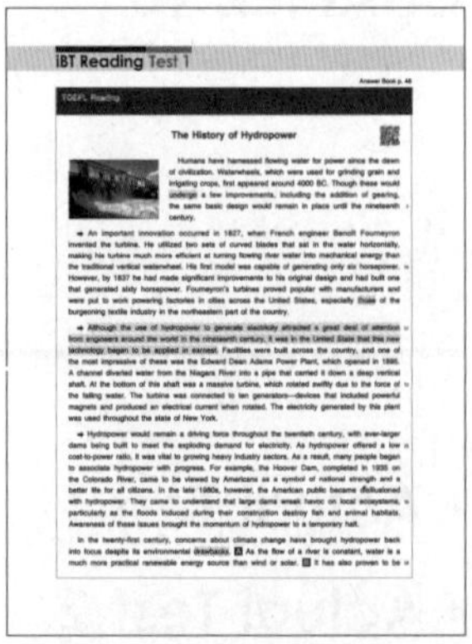
iBT Reading Test 1

The History of Hydropower

4 Review Essential Vocabulary

At the end of each chapter is a Vocabulary Review, which includes questions on essential vocabulary from the chapter. You will be able to easily memorize the vocabulary words by seeing them in sentences with various contexts.

5 Evaluate Your Progress with Actual Tests

The book includes two Actual Tests, which are full-length reading tests that include passages and questions that closely match what appears on the TOEFL iBT. They provide an excellent opportunity to apply the skills you have learned and evaluate your progress.

6 Check the Answer Book

The Answer Book specifies the correct answer choice for all questions and provides Korean translations of all passages and questions. It also includes a list of key vocabulary words from each passage with definitions.

About the TOEFL iBT

What Is the TOEFL iBT?

The TOEFL (Test of English as a Foreign Language) iBT (Internet-Based test) includes Reading, Listening, Speaking, and Writing sections to comprehensively assess English ability. Although most tasks require the application of only one of these skills, some require the use of two or more. The TOEFL iBT is designed to measure a student's capacity to use and understand English at a university level and is, therefore, much more difficult than many other English proficiency tests.

TOEFL iBT Structure

Section	No. of passages and questions	Time (min.)	Score	Notable Features
Reading	• 3-4 Passages • 10 Questions/Passage	54-72	30	• Each passage is approximately 700 words long.
Listening	• 2-3 Conversations • 5 Questions/Conversation • 3-4 Lectures • 6 Questions/Lecture	41-57	30	• Speakers have various accents, including American, British, Australian, etc.
10-minute break				
Speaking	• 1 Independent Task • 3 Integrated Tasks	17	30	• Independent Tasks ask you to state your opinion about a specific topic. • Integrated Tasks ask you to provide a response based on reading and listening content.
Writing	• 1 Integrated Task • 1 Independent Task	50	30	• Integrated Tasks ask you to provide a response based on reading and listening content. • Independent Tasks ask you to write about a specific topic.
Total Time: Approximately 3 hours 30 minutes / Total Score: 120				

TOEFL iBT Reading Section

The TOEFL iBT Reading Section evaluates a student's ability to read and comprehend English texts that are comparable to those encountered in a typical first- or second-year university class. Although the passages cover a wide variety of academic topics, there is no requirement to be familiar with the subject matter. The information in the passage is all that is needed to answer the questions.

TOEFL iBT Reading Question Types

Question Type	Description	Score	No. of Questions (per passage)
Vocabulary	Choose the answer choice that is closest in meaning to the given word or phrase.	1	1-2
Reference	Choose the answer choice that the given word or phrase refers to.	1	0-2
Sentence Simplification	Choose the answer choice that accurately and completely summarizes the key information in the given sentence.	1	0-1
Fact & Negative Fact	Choose the answer choice that restates (Fact) or contradicts (Negative Fact) the relevant information in the passage.	1	2-7
Inference	Choose the answer choice that can be inferred based on the relevant information in the passage.	1	1-2
Rhetorical Purpose	Choose the answer choice that best describes the function of a specific piece of information in relation to the immediate context or the passage as a whole.	1	1-2
Sentence Insertion	Choose the answer choice that corresponds to the correct location in the passage to insert the given sentence. Each possible location in the passage is marked by a square [■].	1	1
Summary	Choose three answer choices that best summarize the main points of the passage.	2	0-1
Category Chart	Choose the answer choices that match the given categories.	3	0-1

CHAPTER 01

Vocabulary

Vocabulary

About the Question Type

Vocabulary questions ask you to determine the meaning of the highlighted word or phrase within the context of the passage and to identify the answer choice that is a synonym of it.

The word or phrase that is being tested may have more than one meaning. Therefore, make sure to use the surrounding context to determine how the word or phrase is used in the passage.

Question Format

- The word "   " in the passage is closest in meaning to
- The phrase "   " in the passage is closest in meaning to

Key Strategies

- **Step 1** — Read the sentence that contains the word or phrase and the surrounding sentences to look for context clues.
- **Step 2** — Use the context clues to determine the meaning of the word or phrase as it is used in the passage. Context clues are typically located in the sentence that the given word or phrase appears or in a sentence that immediately precedes or follows it.
- **Step 3** — Select the answer choice that has a meaning most similar to the contextual meaning of the word or phrase.

Example

Answer Book p. 2

Blood Transfusion

When a blood transfusion is given, it is essential that the donor's blood matches the blood of the recipient. Blood is incompatible when certain factors in red blood cells and plasma differ between the donor and the recipient. In such a case, the antibodies in the recipient's blood will clump with the red blood cells of the donor's blood. The result is hemolysis, or the destruction of hemoglobin-bearing red blood cells and the consequent release of hemoglobin into the blood fluid. With hemoglobin in the circulatory system, kidney damage often results and can be lethal.

The factors that are most likely to cause a reaction in a recipient are substances in the ABO blood group system and the Rh factor system. In the former, persons with blood type AB are known as universal recipients because they can accept A, B, AB, or O blood. On the other hand, individuals with blood type O are sometimes called universal donors since their red cells are unlikely to trigger a response by the antibodies in any other type of blood. Generally, however, medical practitioners prefer to make an exact match so as to minimize adverse reactions. In the Rh factor system, the presence of a particular protein in the blood, the Rhesus factor, will determine if a person is Rh positive or Rh negative. If a Rh-negative patient receives Rh-positive blood, his or her body will produce antibodies to attack the protein, an undesirable effect.

1 The word "incompatible" in the passage is closest in meaning to

(A) visible
(B) divergent
(C) conflicting
(D) devastating

2 The word "adverse" in the passage is closest in meaning to

(A) detrimental
(B) advantageous
(C) neutral
(D) various

3 The word "undesirable" in the passage is closest in meaning to

(A) expansive
(B) unpredictable
(C) immediate
(D) unwelcome

Reading Practice 1

Answer Book p. 2

Computer-Aided Weather Forecasting

Meteorology is the study of weather, and one of a meteorologist's most important functions is to predict the weather ahead of time. People have tried to forecast the behavior of the atmosphere for thousands of years, dating back to the ancient Babylonians' observations of cloud formations in 650 BC. Over the centuries, closer and closer observation allowed people to make some simple predictions using weather maps. Weather maps were initially hand-drawn charts that contained meteorological data from an extended area. The first of these, created in 1816, was based on data collected from various locations using mail or the telegraph. Still, meteorologists had limited confidence until computer modeling became a reality in the mid-to-late twentieth century.

Computer models draw from a wide variety of information sources about the atmosphere, and the more data a meteorologist can input into a computer model, the more accurate the results will be. These days, some of the information that comprises a weatherperson's forecast comes from space in the form of satellite imagery. But weather scientists still use radar to gather information, a technology that was first utilized for weather forecasting during World War II to probe storms. Additional input for computer models comes from weather balloons, which are released into the sky from about 900 different locations around the world two times daily to measure pressure, temperature, and humidity.

Once the computer has compiled data from these sources, it divides a territory into sections. Bigger sections are short on local detail, but they provide a wide-range picture of weather systems as they move around the globe. Smaller sections have higher resolution, and they are used to predict local weather events. By exploiting each section type, a meteorologist can alter input to prioritize a certain variable over others. For instance, a forecaster might increase the emphasis a model places on wind speed and decrease its focus on humidity. For this reason, meteorologists who know local conditions can play an important role in weather forecasting even though much of the work is performed by a machine.

Contemporary weather forecasts are more accurate than at any point in history, but creating an accurate long-range prediction remains difficult. Although a five-day forecast is 90 percent accurate, a seven-day forecast comes true only about 80 percent of the time. If you are trying to find out whether it will rain on an important event ten days from now, the weather forecast will only be right 50 percent of the time. This uncertainty arises because there are so many variables to consider when making a prediction. Thus, practical long-range forecasting tends to focus on trends and anomalies at the seasonal level. Though they cannot be as precise as short-term forecasts, these are still helpful as they can suggest whether temperatures or precipitation amounts in the coming winter or spring, for instance, will be greater or smaller than normal.

1 According to paragraph 1, which of the following is true of the ancient Babylonians?

(A) They were the first people that tried to predict the weather.
(B) They used simple weather maps to forecast atmospheric behavior.
(C) They were able to accurately predict short-term weather trends.
(D) They collected data from a variety of different locations.

2 The word "probe" in the passage is closest in meaning to

(A) halt
(B) examine
(C) resolve
(D) impede

3 The word "its" in the passage refers to

(A) variable
(B) emphasis
(C) model
(D) speed

4 According to paragraph 3, which of the following is NOT true of the territorial sections?

(A) Smaller ones have higher resolution.
(B) Larger ones offer wide-range images of weather systems.
(C) Larger ones produce more detailed pictures.
(D) Smaller ones are used for local weather prediction.

5 The word "anomalies" in the passage is closest in meaning to

(A) averages
(B) setbacks
(C) proximities
(D) deviations

6 According to paragraph 4, which of the following is true of current weather forecasts?

(A) Their accuracy has dropped slightly due to the increasing number of variables.
(B) They are correct approximately half of the time for a ten-day period.
(C) They can make precise seven-day predictions 90 percent of the time.
(D) Their correctness reliability is 80 percent within a five-day period.

Reading Practice 2

Answer Book p. 3

The Rosetta Stone

The Rosetta Stone is a piece of granite with a multilingual statement of political support for an ancient Egyptian king carved into it. But after it was rediscovered centuries later by an invading French soldier in the employ of Napoleon, the Rosetta Stone helped to unlock the secrets of a long-dead civilization and became one of the most famous historical artifacts of all time.

[A] Carved in 196 BC, the Rosetta Stone was one of many stone slabs etched with the same message, and every temple in Egypt contained one like it. [B] The stones advertised the coronation of King Ptolemy V Epiphanes in flattering language that praised the ruler for lowering taxes, putting down rebellions, and granting benefits to his soldiers. [C] After Ptolemy's death, the Egyptians used the surviving stone as a structural element of an old fort near the port city of Rosetta. [D]

There it stayed until 1799, when a group of French soldiers attempted unsuccessfully to dislodge the heavy stone from its resting place. Napoleon had come to Egypt partly to drive the English out of the eastern Mediterranean and partly to explore Egypt, a famous and ancient land that had always fascinated him. Many of Napoleon's soldiers were trained scholars, including the officer who recognized the four-foot rock as an artifact of potential interest. Its message was written in three different scripts. One of these was Ancient Greek and the two others were both Ancient Egyptian, namely hieroglyphics and a more colloquial writing form known as Demotic script.

Before the Rosetta Stone was rediscovered, the meaning of the hieroglyphics had been lost to history. This form of writing was discarded entirely after the Roman Empire converted to Christianity and prohibited ancient religions like those practiced in Egypt at the time. Yet, the Rosetta Stone provided a key for deciphering the hieroglyphics since they were translated into Greek on the stone. In the early nineteenth century, a French scholar tackled the project. Egyptologist Jean-François Champollion realized that the individual hieroglyphs were sometimes pictorial (using a picture to depict the thing the character meant to describe), sometimes phonetic (sounding out characters in Egyptian), and sometimes ideographic (using symbols to express ideas). This made the translation difficult, but eventually Champollion managed to complete it.

Today, the Rosetta Stone is the most popular exhibit at the British Museum. Although the Egyptian government has declared that it would like the stone returned to its ancient home, British officials have made it clear that no such transfer will take place. The slab that taught the modern world how to read ancient Egyptian writing, thus opening the door to unprecedented historical understanding of a powerful civilization, will remain on display in a foreign land.

Glossary

· coronation: a ceremony at which a person is made king or queen

1 Look at the four squares [■] that indicate where the following sentence could be added to the passage.

However, this initial utilization was short lived, and before long, the stone served a more modest and purely practical purpose.

Where would the sentence best fit?

2 In paragraph 2, the author's description of the Rosetta Stone mentions which of the following?

(A) It was carved after the death of King Ptolemy V.
(B) It was intended to attract more people to temples.
(C) It praised the accomplishments of a political leader.
(D) It outlined the people's requests for the king.

3 Which of the following is NOT mentioned about Napoleon and his army?

(A) He invaded Egypt to expel another European force from the land.
(B) His army included people who were knowledgeable about cultural artifacts.
(C) He had held a strong interest in Egypt for a while.
(D) His soldiers managed to transport the Rosetta Stone to their homeland.

4 The word "discarded" in the passage is closest in meaning to

(A) abandoned
(B) restored
(C) promoted
(D) integrated

5 The word "deciphering" in the passage is closest in meaning to

(A) discrediting
(B) provoking
(C) improvising
(D) decoding

6 According to paragraph 4, which of the following is true of Jean-François Champollion?

(A) He found out that hieroglyphs served several different linguistic functions.
(B) He successfully translated the Rosetta Stone into French and English.
(C) He was a linguist who specialized in ancient African languages.
(D) He ultimately failed to correctly interpret the Rosetta Stone's inscriptions.

Reading Practice 3

Answer Book p. 4

Ansel Adams

Simply hearing the name Ansel Adams conjures up immaculate grayscale images of majestic mountains towering over winding streams or rocky fields. Adams is the best-known American photographer, and he was an undeniable master of landscape composition. His unfailing eye for the stately wildernesses of the American West secured him a lofty place among the photographers and other visual artists of the twentieth century.

As documented in his written works like *Making a Photograph*, Adams considered each photo to be the result of a careful technical process. Rather than merely snapping shots of beautiful things, he believed in meticulously visualizing landscape images. This meant not just choosing what to photograph and how it should be framed but also exactly how it would be lit. This deliberate thinking was codified in what Adams referred to as the "zone system." It dictated that a photographer should consider the desired intensity of the light in every element of the natural scene using a 0 to 10 rating scale before so much as touching a camera.

But it was Adams's eye for natural details and his vivid imagination for how to dramatically portray his subjects that truly set his work apart. Consider the first photograph that won him major acclaim, *Monolith, the Face of Half Dome*, from 1927. To convey the brooding majesty of Half Dome, Yosemite Park's iconic granite cliff, he imagined an image divided into three zones. There would be a shadowed cliff face and an even darker sky against a contrastingly bright white snowy landscape of the forest below. So, he hiked up to a remote spot and waited. While he was there, he determined that the only way to get his image was to use a red filter on his lens and an extended five-second-long exposure time. This technique resulted in a black-and-white image that is not a true depiction of the conditions that afternoon—especially since the clear sky is rendered dark—but its composition captures fine details of the shadowed cliff face and the feeling of having Half Dome looming over you.

With the appearance of stunning photos like *Monolith* alongside his best-selling instructional guides, Adams became a household name. Yet, the critical establishment was slow to recognize the seriousness of his accomplishments. Some art critics who did consider photography to be a powerful medium for expression minimized his contributions, dismissing his impeccable composition as emotionally cold and arguing that his work lacked the political topicality of other famous photographers of his day. But, in truth, Adams's work always had a political consciousness, and his effort in documenting the natural beauty of the American West had a tangible impact on conservationist causes. Adams's environmental activism was ahead of his time, and even they eventually accepted the social importance of his conservationist aesthetic. Late in life, he had acquired almost universal acclaim. Four years before he passed away, Adams won the Presidential Medal of Freedom for his work in helping to preserve the nation's parks.

1 The word "lofty" in the passage is closest in meaning to

(A) memorable
(B) elevated
(C) underrated
(D) appropriate

2 The word "visualizing" in the passage is closest in meaning to

(A) recording
(B) analyzing
(C) envisioning
(D) researching

3 According to paragraph 2, Ansel Adams's zone system required that a photographer

(A) make an appropriate choice regarding what to include in a picture
(B) use framing techniques effectively to create an image that is beautiful
(C) determine the preferred brightness for each aspect of the subject matter
(D) identify a suitable camera type for the outdoor lighting conditions

4 The word "its" in the passage refers to

(A) technique
(B) image
(C) depiction
(D) afternoon

5 All of the following are true of *Monolith, the Face of Half Dome* EXCEPT:

(A) It was Adams's first major success as a photographer.
(B) It resulted from Adams's attempt to depict the cliff in shadows.
(C) It was captured in dark and gloomy weather conditions.
(D) It required a relatively long exposure time.

6 According to paragraph 4, some critics disapproved of Adams because

(A) he failed to deal with prominent social issues of his day
(B) his framing of landscapes was considered too sentimental
(C) they failed to appreciate photography as an art form
(D) his book failed to make a positive impression on readers

Answer Book p. 5

TOEFL Reading

The Bantu Peoples

➡ The term *Bantu* has a complicated history. **A** Though at times it is used to refer to a specific ethnic group or even to Africans as a whole, it does not correctly convey either one. **B** Strictly speaking, *Bantu* is a linguistic term coined by Wilhelm Bleek, a nineteenth-century German specialist in African languages. **C** Bleek derived the term from the Zulu word *abantu*, meaning "people," and used it to refer generally to some 600 distinct but closely related indigenous languages spoken in regions of Africa that range from the northwest to the southeast. **D** The term *Bantu peoples* is also used as an umbrella term to refer to the speakers of the various Bantu languages, but the people it describes are not homogenous in ethnicity or culture.

The Bantu languages share a common origin, having evolved from a single Proto-Bantu language. This tongue emerged on the western African coast in 4000 BC, in present-day Cameroon. The Bantu—that is, the people who spoke Proto-Bantu—developed a civilization that was centered on agriculture, foraging, and fishing and formed into groups organized around family units. The spread of the culture and language across the continent occurred between 1000 BC and AD 1000, but anthropologists debate whether this was due to a physical migration or a dispersal of cultural traditions.

➡ From the first millennium until the establishment of European colonial governments in the 1800s, Bantu-speaking civilizations dominated central and southern Africa. Aiding in their rise was a cattle-herding practice known as pastoralism in which cattle were driven from pasture to pasture. Because the regional diet depended heavily on beef, pastoralists gained political power by loaning their cattle to neighboring peoples for breeding. As they gained influence, numerous powerful Bantu civilizations developed throughout the continent. These included the occupants of the Swahili coast, who interacted with Muslim cultures, bringing Arabic influences to their Bantu-descended tongue. Another Bantu power center emerged in present-day Zimbabwe, fueled by trade in precious materials like gold and ivory. Bantu-speaking people in the land occupied by Zimbabwe and Botswana also built elaborate stone fortresses between the eleventh and fourteenth centuries.

Despite the accomplishments of the people who spoke Bantu languages, the word *Bantu* fell out of favor with many Africans during the latter half of the twentieth century. The term had temporarily gained popularity to convey a shared ethnic identity among the black African population in the 1920s when South Africa was a British colony. However, this sentiment changed after the apartheid regime in that country officially replaced references to "Native" with the word *Bantu* in the 1960s. The adoption of the term by the discriminative colonial government prompted black South Africans to avoid using it as the word became associated with oppression. Recent scholarship has called into question the idea that Bantu-speaking communities share significant common ethnic history, although the languages likely did come from a common source. For that

Volume Review Help Back Next

reason, *Bantu* remains in use in its linguistic sense but is not used as an ethnic label.

Glossary

apartheid: an official policy of segregation or discrimination based on race

1 The word "homogenous" in the passage is closest in meaning to

(A) uniform
(B) systematic
(C) controversial
(D) diverse

2 According to paragraph 1, which of the following is true of the word *Bantu*?

(A) It describes the common ancestry of the Zulu tribe.
(B) It was coined by an African linguist.
(C) It is used to group related languages.
(D) It refers to an ethnic group from Western Africa.

Paragraph 1 is marked with an arrow [➡].

3 The word "this" in the passage refers to

(A) spread
(B) culture
(C) language
(D) continent

4 The word "dispersal" in the passage is closest in meaning to

(A) infusion
(B) estimation
(C) importance
(D) scattering

5 Why does the author discuss the cattle herding of the Bantu civilizations in paragraph 3?

(A) To show that they had a primitive way of life
(B) To identify what helped them acquire political strength
(C) To highlight the excellent quality of their beef
(D) To explain the method that they used for clearing pasture

Paragraph 3 is marked with an arrow [➡].

6 According to paragraph 3, which of the following is NOT true of the Bantu-speaking people before the 1800s?

(A) They constructed sophisticated defense facilities.
(B) Their influence was not restricted to one region.
(C) They could communicate in Arabic languages.
(D) Their commercial activities included the trade of valuable goods.

Paragraph 3 is marked with an arrow [➡].

7 Which of the sentences below best expresses the essential information in the highlighted sentence in the passage? *Incorrect* choices change the meaning of the sentence in important ways or leave out essential information.

(A) Scholars question whether the Bantu peoples have anything in common.
(B) Researchers think the Bantu share a source language but not a common ethnicity.
(C) Academics believe the Bantu languages descended from a single tongue.
(D) Research indicates that the Bantu do not have the same ancestors.

8 What can be inferred about the black South African population who lived under British rule?

(A) They were forced to use English rather than Bantu languages.
(B) They did not commonly refer to themselves as Bantu people prior to the 1920s.
(C) They were offended by the British reference to them as "Native."
(D) They were content with being part of a British colony before the 1960s.

Volume Review Help Back Next

9 Look at the four squares [■] that indicate where the following sentence could be added to the passage.

On the contrary, *Bantu* describes hundreds of different distinct tribes with over 85 million speakers of related languages.

Where would the sentence best fit?

Click on a square [■] to add the sentence to the passage.

10 Directions: An introductory sentence for a brief summary of the passage is provided below. Complete the summary by selecting the THREE answer choices that express the most important ideas in the passage. Some sentences do not belong in the summary because they express ideas that are not presented in the passage or are minor ideas in the passage. **This question is worth 2 points.**

Drag your answer choices to the spaces where they belong.
To remove an answer choice, click on it. To review the passage, click on **View Text**.

Bantu was originally conceived as a linguistic concept.

-
-
-

Answer Choices

Ⓐ The Bantu languages descended from the Proto-Bantu language, which was spoken by groups of people in western Africa.

Ⓑ Interactions between Bantu-speaking peoples and Muslims led to the development of a vast international trade network.

Ⓒ European scholars often characterized Bantu peoples as savages, prompting outrage among Bantu tribes.

Ⓓ From approximately 100 BC to AD 1000, Proto-Bantu speakers were divided into family units.

Ⓔ The term *Bantu* took on negative connotations in South Africa because of how it was used during British rule.

Ⓕ Bantu civilization was a major force across a wide part of Africa for a thousand years prior to European colonization.

Answer Book p. 5

Answer Book p. 6

TOEFL Reading

Plastic Pollution

➡ In 1869, the American engineer John Hyatt produced the first commercially viable plastic, which was named celluloid. This material actually received widespread approval from environmentalists because it was created to serve as a substitute for ivory, which was used to make billiard balls and other common items despite the fact that the only source of this substance was critically endangered elephants. The ensuing century was a golden age for plastics, as industrial corporations found that they could convert waste material from fossil fuel production into shopping bags, refrigerator dishes, and even prosthetic body parts. Not until the second half of the twentieth century did humans begin to realize that the ubiquity of plastics is choking the natural world.

As virtually indestructible plastics pile up in the world's landfills as well as the environment, they are poisoning the living creatures that populate planet Earth. Factories have produced 8.3 billion metric tons of plastic since the 1950s, and it does not disintegrate rapidly. ■A By design, plastic products are made up of lengthy molecules secured by durable carbon-to-carbon bonds. ■B As a result, birds, cows, and other animals consume the undigestible plastic garbage from our take-out meals and end up with intestinal blockages. ■C The chemicals that make up some plastics also leach into human bloodstreams, doing lasting damage to our hormonal systems. ■D

➡ Nowhere is the predicament of discarded plastic more serious than in the world's rivers and oceans. Some bodies of water are thoroughly inundated by plastic. Off the coast of Italy, the Tyrrhenian Sea now holds 186,000 pieces of microplastic in every square foot. Millions of tons of plastic debris washes into the water annually, and although some of it ends up on the ocean floor, some remains adrift at or near the surface where it is readily encountered by marine life. Over time, the seawater and sunlight begin to dissolve the larger objects into microplastics, leaving animals from the top to the bottom of the food chain, from whales to zooplankton, vulnerable to the accumulation of microplastics in their bodies. To make matters worse, microplastics contain toxic chemicals that are absorbed into the fatty tissue of an organism and remain there for an extended period of time.

➡ The good news is that awareness of the problem is increasing, leading to numerous attempts to reduce the impact of plastic pollution. Biodegradable plastics have become more common, plastic manufacturers are increasingly being compelled to collect and recycle their products, and some of the more dangerous plastics have been banned. Many municipalities have implemented shopping bag fees to promote the use of reusable cloth shopping bags. While it is unfeasible to eliminate all of the plastic that has already been deposited in places where it should not be, humanity is making strides toward minimizing additional contamination.

Volume Review Help Back Next

Glossary

prosthetic: relating to an artificial device to replace a body part

1 The word "ensuing" in the passage is closest in meaning to

(A) preceding
(B) entire
(C) unfortunate
(D) following

2 According to paragraph 1, which of the following is true of celluloid?

(A) It was invented by a group of engineers.
(B) It was not accepted by environmental activists.
(C) It was intended to replace the use of ivory.
(D) It was not thought to have any commercial uses.

Paragraph 1 is marked with an arrow [➡].

3 The word "disintegrate" in the passage is closest in meaning to

(A) amass
(B) decompose
(C) vanish
(D) regenerate

4 The word "inundated" in the passage is closest in meaning to

(A) overwhelmed
(B) examined
(C) associated
(D) isolated

5 The author mentions whales and zooplankton in paragraph 3 in order to

Ⓐ identify some of the marine wildlife that are immune to microplastic toxicity
Ⓑ emphasize the wide range of organisms threatened by microplastics
Ⓒ highlight the complexity of the food chain in the world's oceans
Ⓓ provide examples of creatures that inhabit the Tyrrhenian Sea

Paragraph 3 is marked with an arrow [➡].

6 Which of the following can be inferred from paragraph 3 about microplastics?

Ⓐ They are fatal to marine animals even in small quantities.
Ⓑ They are not readily expelled through an organism's bodily waste.
Ⓒ They do not disappear even after being exposed to water for six months.
Ⓓ They are dissolved in seawater only if exposed to sunlight.

Paragraph 3 is marked with an arrow [➡].

7 Which of the sentences below best expresses the essential information in the highlighted sentence in the passage? *Incorrect* choices change the meaning of the sentence in important ways or leave out essential information.

Ⓐ Even though entirely removing the existing plastic is not possible, humans are taking steps to reduce further pollution.
Ⓑ All of the plastic that has already been wrongly deposited should be eliminated before additional plastic is added.
Ⓒ Despite the fact that humans are trying to minimize plastic pollution, getting rid of plastic packaging is not feasible.
Ⓓ Because so much plastic has been irresponsibly discarded, it is necessary for humans to do something about the existing pollution.

8 According to paragraph 4, all of the following are strategies for reducing plastic pollution EXCEPT

Ⓐ encouraging the use of reusable shopping bags
Ⓑ making more biodegradable plastics
Ⓒ fining companies that improperly dispose of plastics
Ⓓ forcing plastic manufacturers to recycle

Paragraph 4 is marked with an arrow [➡].

Volume Review Help Back Next

9 Look at the four squares [■] that indicate where the following sentence could be added to the passage.

They do not decay naturally, and no organisms have evolved that can break them down.

Where would the sentence best fit?

Click on a square [■] to add the sentence to the passage.

10 **Directions:** An introductory sentence for a brief summary of the passage is provided below. Complete the summary by selecting the THREE answer choices that express the most important ideas in the passage. Some sentences do not belong in the summary because they express ideas that are not presented in the passage or are minor ideas in the passage. **This question is worth 2 points.**

Drag your answer choices to the spaces where they belong.
To remove an answer choice, click on it. To review the passage, click on **View Text**.

Although plastics are useful in a variety of industrial applications, they pose an ecological threat.

-
-
-

Answer Choices

(A) Fully synthetic plastics that are composed of manmade molecules are the type of plastics that pose the greatest risk to the environment.

(B) On a positive note, a substantial number of efforts are being made to decrease the effects of plastic pollution due to raised recognition of the issue.

(C) The problem of plastic pollution is most severe in the world's various bodies of water where it is a threat to marine organisms.

(D) The disposal and manufacture of large amounts of plastic creates a poisonous environment that leads to detrimental effects on animals and humans alike.

(E) Because the chemical bonds in manufactured plastics are so durable, they cause intestinal problems in animals that consume plastic.

(F) Research conducted in the world's oceans has discovered microplastics in every square foot of seawater that has been analyzed.

Answer Book p. 6

Vocabulary Review

Answer Book p. 7

A. Fill in the blanks with the appropriate words from the box.

consequent	confidence	tackle
practitioner	discriminative	undeniable

1 The movie director lost ______________ when he was heavily criticized by movie critics.

2 Due to the drug's side effects, patients must have prescriptions from a medical ______________ in order to purchase it.

3 It is a(n) ______________ fact that Earth completes its orbit around the Sun once every 365.25 days.

4 The civil rights movement was a reaction to the many ______________ policies against African-Americans.

5 Proponents of green energy hope to reduce greenhouse gas emissions and the ______________ warming of the planet.

6 He was determined to ______________ the project of removing the weeds in the garden.

B. Choose the closest meaning for each highlighted word or phrase.

7 The student's research paper was so full of colloquial expressions that he did not make a good impression on his professor.
(A) informal (B) exquisite (C) invented (D) precise

8 The lack of support for the tax increase has created a predicament for the government.
(A) rejection (B) dispute (C) controversy (D) dilemma

9 A nurse gave him emergency treatment to dislodge a piece of steak from his throat.
(A) abuse (B) reject (C) remove (D) catch

10 When I completed the form, I declined to specify whether my ethnicity was Asian or not.
(A) personality (B) ancestry (C) reckoning (D) inclination

11 Although I agree with him on many things, I couldn't understand his sentiment about recent political issues.
(A) nostalgia (B) opinion (C) concern (D) emphasis

12 You should not put open cans in the refrigerator because the aluminum can leach into the food.
(A) improve (B) seep (C) restrain (D) exhale

13 The president's speech was boastful about his accomplishments in the area of foreign policy.
(A) achievements (B) preferences (C) regulations (D) enemies

14 The impeccable performance of the vocalist ensured that she won the talent contest.
(A) memorable (B) original (C) perfect (D) popular

CHAPTER 02

Reference

Reference

About the Question Type

Reference questions ask you to identify what the highlighted word or phrase refers to in the passage.

The highlighted word or phrase is usually a pronoun (*it*, *they*, *this*, etc.). The correct answer choice will be the noun that the highlighted word or phrase refers to. The incorrect answer choices will be nouns that appear in the preceding sentences but are not referred to by the highlighted word or phrase.

Question Format

- The word "   " in the passage refers to
- The phrase "   " in the passage refers to

Key Strategies

- **Step 1** — Read the sentence that contains the highlighted word or phrase and the sentences that immediately precede it.
- **Step 2** — Find the noun that the highlighted word or phrase refers to. Determining whether the highlighted word or phrase is singular or plural can make it easier to identify its referent.
- **Step 3** — Substitute your answer choice for the highlighted word or phrase, and confirm that it makes sense.

Example

Answer Book p. 7

First Computers

In the late 1930s, a physics professor named John Atanasoff spent a long time pondering an automated method of solving equations that had many variables. Complex calculations are crucial in matters of physics, and they can be time-consuming to perform. Atanasoff was the first to dream up a digital solution to this challenge. He and a graduate student, Clifford Berry, constructed a 700-pound mechanism that used 280 vacuum tubes to perform algebraic calculations. The Atanasoff-Berry Computer, or ABC, was an important precursor to modern computers. The ABC was capable of solving twenty-nine-variable equations at a speed of one operation every fifteen seconds, which was fast in 1942 when the machine was completed but pales in comparison to the millions of operations per second performed by today's computers. Additionally, unlike the latter, Atanasoff's creation was not programmable as it could solve only linear equations.

The ABC became the subject of legal controversy in 1947. The inventors of another digital computer, the Electronic Numerical Integrator and Computer (ENIAC), filed a patent, something Atanasoff had never done for the ABC. However, when it was revealed that a member of the ENIAC design team had likely imitated Atanasoff's original design, a judge rejected the new machine's patent application, concluding that the concept of the computer could not be patented. The ruling set a precedent for the manufacture and design of digital computers as it held that anyone could make one without violating the protections of a patent.

1 The word "they" in the passage refers to

(A) equations (B) variables (C) calculations (D) matters

2 The phrase "the latter" in the passage refers to

(A) twenty-nine-variable equations
(B) one operation
(C) the machine
(D) today's computers

3 The word "it" in the passage refers to

(A) ruling (B) precedent (C) manufacture (D) design

Reading Practice 1

Answer Book p. 8

The World's First City

Today, the barren desert that surrounds Uruk, some 150 miles south of Iraq's capital city of Baghdad, is not a major urban center and holds little appeal for human habitation. But 5,500 years ago, this place was a fertile marshland with convenient access to the Euphrates River in the west and the Tigris River in the east. The soggy soil produced so much wheat and barley that residents found they did not need to devote all of their time to farming. The rivers teemed with fish and attracted waterfowl. Cattle, sheep, and goats thrived there, and the land bore fruit, including dates, figs, and apples. By 3100 BC, this corner of Mesopotamia was home to around 90,000 people, making Uruk the world's first major city.

With so many people in Uruk, writing became a necessity for the first time in human history. Using reeds to inscribe clay tablets, the people of Uruk were able to keep track of the amount of grain stored in their warehouses as well as the number of sheep and goats in their herds. It took 400 years for the primitive writing to progress from pictorial characters that represented the counted goods to abstract numerical symbols. After developing a script known as cuneiform, the people of Uruk also documented the professional roles performed by the city's residents, from kings and priests to weavers and jewelers.

The need for government quickly emerged as the population grew. At first, administrative duties were performed by priests. However, over time, neighboring cities emerged and engaged in warfare over the control of land and resources, and warriors consequently began to hold a larger share of power in Uruk. Eventually, they were succeeded by a single authoritarian king. The most famous king of Uruk was Gilgamesh, who ruled Uruk sometime between 3000 and 2500 BC and constructed the city's imposing outer walls. He was immortalized in an epic cuneiform poem portraying him as two-thirds divine. *The Epic of Gilgamesh* is considered to be one of the oldest works of literature in the history of humankind.

The fact that other Mesopotamian cities such as Babylon and Nineveh are better known to westerners than Uruk can be explained in part by the city's scant presence in the Bible, which mentions Uruk only in passing. Nevertheless, the world's first city left an indelible mark on archaeological history through the material culture that it left behind. Archaeologists have unearthed Uruk-era bowls that were mass produced and traded as far away as modern-day Iran and Turkey. Other notable artifacts include the Mask of Warka, a female head carved from marble that is one of the earliest depictions of a human face, and the Lion Hunt Stela, a narrative sculpture showing two men hunting lions with spears and arrows. Ancient Uruk is also the site of the remains of monumental wall-enclosed buildings with decorative columns featuring mosaic designs.

Glossary

· marshland: an area of soft and wet land

1 The phrase "this place" in the passage refers to

(A) barren desert
(B) Uruk
(C) Baghdad
(D) urban center

2 According to paragraph 1, which of the following is NOT true of the corner of Mesopotamia known as Uruk?

(A) Its soil supported abundant production of certain grains.
(B) It had rivers that were rich in wildlife.
(C) Its residents devoted all of their time to farming.
(D) It contained the earliest major city that is known.

3 According to paragraph 2, what did the people of Uruk begin to do after the development of cuneiform?

(A) Keep track of stored grain levels
(B) Monitor the number of animals in herds
(C) Record various professional duties
(D) Count the number of goods traded

4 The word "they" in the passage refers to

(A) priests
(B) cities
(C) resources
(D) warriors

5 According to paragraph 3, priests began to lose political power in Uruk because

(A) religion became less important to Mesopotamian culture
(B) their authority was usurped by authoritarian kings
(C) the city was conquered by neighboring invaders
(D) territorial conflicts increased the power of warriors

6 According to paragraph 4, which of the following is NOT part of the archaeological legacy of Uruk?

(A) Bowls imported from Iran and Turkey
(B) A carving portraying a human face
(C) A sculpture with a hunting scene
(D) Columns decorated with patterns

Answer Book p. 9

Islamic Calligraphy

The written word plays such a fundamental role in Islam that the religion's founder, the prophet Muhammad, is reported to have said, "The first thing God created was the pen." In that spirit, the spread of Islam in the seventh century brought the Arabic form of writing to territories across the Middle East and South Asia, providing a common means of communication in ethnically and culturally diverse regions. A critical form of Islamic writing is calligraphy, the art of writing characters in beautiful handwritten script.

The beauty of Islamic calligraphy comes largely from the dynamic character of Arabic. The written language is as old as the Islamic religion itself, having been derived from Nabataean, a sixth-century dialect of Aramaic that was a precursor of the Arabic alphabet. It is written right to left, with seventeen basic letters; however, short vowels are not counted in that number and are instead formed by the placement of a sign or signs above or below consonants and long vowels. Different characters have different rules for attachment to adjacent characters. Some are connected on both sides, while others are connected only to the preceding characters or, alternatively, those that follow. This distinctive connectivity gives written Arabic a flow that lends itself easily to decorative scripts.

There were two main scripts that were used by calligraphers early in Islamic history. The cursive script was used in informal contexts such as letter writing and was not subject to strict rules. On the other hand, the Kufic script, named for an Islamic city in Mesopotamia, was used for religious writings, such as the earliest copies of the Qur'an. This script was far more formal than cursive, conveying a certain majesty. The characters were large, resulting in writing that occupied no more than three lines per page. Kufic was largely replaced later, in the eleventh century, by Naskh, which remains the most popular form of Arabic writing. To some degree, it may be considered a merged form of the initial free-for-all of cursive and the more formal Kufic, featuring qualities of both.

Calligraphy is used to powerful effect in some of the most prominent examples of Islamic art throughout history. For example, India's Taj Mahal, a masterpiece of Islamic architecture, features verses of the Qur'an written in jasper and inlaid into the building's white marble surfaces. Calligraphy in architecture typically served several purposes, the first of which was to identify the name of the building, the patron, and the date of construction. It also served to demonstrate power, evoking reverence both for the wealth of the patron and the glory of God. On a less monumental scale, calligraphy commonly adorned ceramics or bronze mirrors that were inscribed with messages of goodwill. In any case, although calligraphic art typically did contain linguistic concepts, inscriptions were sometimes more like geometric patterns or abstract designs, so even some literate Muslims could not read them.

Glossary

·jasper: a colorful stone that in powdered form is useful for making paints

1 The word "It" in the passage refers to

(A) Islamic calligraphy
(B) written language
(C) Nabataean
(D) dialect of Aramaic

2 According to paragraph 2, which of the following is true of the Arabic language?

(A) It is older than the Islamic religion.
(B) It uses signs to make some vowels.
(C) Its characters have uniform rules.
(D) Its linguistic origin is still unknown.

3 The word "majesty" in the passage is closest in meaning to

(A) priority
(B) casualness
(C) dignity
(D) courtesy

4 According to paragraph 3, which of the following is true of the script that replaced Kufic?

(A) Its large size allowed for only three lines per page.
(B) It combined formal and informal styles.
(C) It remained in use until the eleventh century.
(D) Its name was shared by a city in Mesopotamia.

5 The word "them" in the passage refers to

(A) concepts
(B) inscriptions
(C) patterns
(D) designs

6 In paragraph 4, all of the following are mentioned as purposes that calligraphy served in Islamic architecture EXCEPT

(A) pinpointing when a building was constructed
(B) recognizing a building's name
(C) inspiring respect for God
(D) extending messages of well wishes

Reading Practice 3

Answer Book p. 10

Baby Bird Begging Behavior

Nestling birds are completely dependent on their parents for survival, so nature has favored those who are extremely vocal and demonstrative in signaling that food is required. When they are hungry, most baby birds turn their heads to the sky and open their beaks wide, sending an unmistakable message: "Feed me." In response, parent birds drop food into the gaping jaws of their offspring, whether that food is a regurgitated earlier meal or a fresh-picked insect. Sometimes there is enough food to satisfy the entire brood, but if there isn't, feeding adults are forced to make difficult choices.

Parental responses to begging behavior vary depending on the species. Tree swallows, for instance, follow the old adage "the squeaky wheel gets the grease," feeding the most vigorous beggars more than their quiet siblings. In contrast, hoopoe mothers pay no attention to the begging and simply provide more food for the bigger chicks. In some species, avian fathers share feeding duties with their female partners, and the provisioning strategies can differ based on the sex of the parent. Zebra finch fathers are inclined to distribute supplies on a first come, first served basis, while the mothers tend to select the chicks they wish to feed and stick to that choice regardless of which chicks are first in line. On the other hand, in families of sociable weavers (a southern African species), parental gender has little or no impact on a parent's response to begging.

One study of begging behavior revealed that parental feeding choices are dependent on the family's environmental context. A team from the University of Oxford compiled the results of 306 studies spanning 143 different bird species. They found that in optimal conditions—when a stable supply of food is available—parents favor loud beggars, presumably taking begging as a sign of greater need. But in lean times, adult birds will provide nourishment to the larger chicks. This decision is apparently strategic, based on the assumption that more mature babies have a better chance of survival whereas louder, smaller chicks may not make it anyway.

Tending to hungry young birds places a heavy burden on the parents, demanding energy that is equivalent to that expended by a human in a major bicycle race. For that reason, some bird species forgo the taxing process of caring for their own young altogether. For instance, brood parasites like indigobirds and whydahs place their young in the nests of rival species, effectively outsourcing their parental duties. **A** The parasitic babies mimic the begging behavior and even the mouth markings of the species that owns the nest. **B** The host parents are fooled and raise the little intruders as if they were their own. **C** Brood parasites typically grow faster and push the other young birds out of the nest. **D**

Glossary

· regurgitate: to bring back swallowed food into the mouth

1 According to paragraph 1, which of the following is true of nestling birds?

(A) They indicate hunger using verbal and nonverbal signals.
(B) They show a clear preference for regurgitated meals.
(C) They often steal food that is intended for other offspring.
(D) They quickly learn how to hunt prey such as insects.

2 The word "vigorous" in the passage is closest in meaning to

(A) forceful
(B) adjacent
(C) exaggerated
(D) irritating

3 In paragraph 2, the author's description of zebra finch feeding strategies mentions

(A) their tendency to feed premature chicks more
(B) differences in approach based on gender
(C) fathers carrying out most of the feeding
(D) mother birds favoring vocal babies first

4 The phrase "This decision" in the passage refers to

(A) compiling past studies
(B) offering a stable supply of food
(C) favoring needy chicks
(D) feeding larger babies

5 The word "their" in the passage refers to

(A) brood parasites
(B) young
(C) nests
(D) rival species

6 Look at the four squares [■] that indicate where the following sentence could be added to the passage.

However, by doing this, they are actually putting their offspring in significant jeopardy.

Where would the sentence best fit?

Answer Book p. 11

TOEFL Reading

Earth's Magnetic Field

About 1,800 feet below sea level, molten metal churns and swirls at a temperature as hot as the surface of the Sun. The motion creates an electrical current that flows for hundreds of miles at speeds of thousands of miles per hour. The currents generate a massive magnetic field that emanates from Earth's dense core, extends throughout its interior and radiates out into space, effectively turning the planet into a giant bar magnet. This feature, which Earth's closest neighbors (Mercury, Venus, and Mars) lack, has been crucial for the living organisms that occupy this planet.

➡ Scientists believe that many wildlife species find their way using Earth's magnetic field, which has both a northern and southern pole. For example, European robins have magnetic sensors in their upper beaks that work with the nervous system to help the birds navigate along the planet's magnetic field. **A** It is important to note that the magnetic poles differ slightly from the geographic poles, which are determined by the planet's axis of rotation. **B** The magnetic poles can even reverse entirely, with the north pole becoming the south pole and vice versa, as they have done ten times in the last 2.6 million years. **C** This can be disruptive to the species of wildlife that depend upon the magnetic field for migration. **D**

➡ Space is full of hazards for living creatures, and Earth's magnetic field provides protection from many of them. The upper atmosphere of the Sun constantly spits out charged particles, collectively known as the solar wind, including electrons, protons, and alpha particles. The magnetic field only deflects charged particles, allowing innocuous solar neutrinos, which bear no charge, to penetrate the atmosphere. Scientists believe the solar wind is responsible for degrading the atmosphere of Mars to a point where life has been unable to survive or take hold. The Sun also expels dangerous clouds of plasma and magnetism called coronal mass ejections. Worse, cancer-causing cosmic rays from beyond this solar system are continually bombarding Earth. Fortunately, the magnetosphere created by Earth's magnetic field provides a defense from these onslaughts, trapping them harmlessly in a pair of donut-shaped zones called Van Allen Belts.

➡ Without the protection of the magnetic field, higher organisms might never have developed. When Earth was formed four billion years ago, the metals in its core had not yet begun to solidify, so the magnetic field was not as strong as it is now. Life emerged while the magnetic field was still weak, but it remained stubbornly single-celled for billions of years. That may be because a barrage of radiation from space prevented the evolution of complex life. It was not until around 500 million years ago that the hardening of the core made the flourishing of evolution possible, and life became better protected from harmful radiation because of Earth's robust magnetic field.

Volume Review Help Back Next

1 The word "radiates" in the passage is closest in meaning to

Ⓐ splits
Ⓑ crawls
Ⓒ flows
Ⓓ disperses

2 The phrase "This feature" in the passage refers to

Ⓐ molten metal
Ⓑ electrical current
Ⓒ massive magnetic field
Ⓓ dense core

3 According to paragraph 2, which of the following is NOT true of the magnetic poles?

Ⓐ Their directions are detectable by sensors in some species.
Ⓑ They are the points around which Earth revolves.
Ⓒ They are not exactly the same as the geographic poles.
Ⓓ Their reversal can impede animal migration.

Paragraph 2 is marked with an arrow [➡].

4 The word "innocuous" in the passage is closest in meaning to

Ⓐ chronic
Ⓑ harmless
Ⓒ ephemeral
Ⓓ paramount

5 Why does the author mention "the magnetosphere" in the passage?

- (A) To illustrate how coronal mass ejections originate
- (B) To explain what renders cosmic rays harmless on Earth
- (C) To highlight that some ejections from the Sun can cause cancer
- (D) To give an example of a region in space with a neutral charge

6 Which of the following can be inferred from paragraph 3 about charged particles?

- (A) They are converted into neutrinos before reaching Earth.
- (B) They apparently are absent in the atmosphere of Mars.
- (C) They are transferred between the north and south pole.
- (D) They presumably are detrimental to the survival of life.

Paragraph 3 is marked with an arrow [➡].

7 The word "That" in the passage refers to the

- (A) development of higher organisms
- (B) formation of Earth
- (C) weakness of the magnetic field
- (D) long duration of simple life forms

8 According to paragraph 4, complex organisms evolved because

- (A) single-celled organisms died out
- (B) the magnetic field facilitated cell growth
- (C) the magnetic field reduced space radiation
- (D) harmful metals on Earth's surface receded

Paragraph 4 is marked with an arrow [➡].

Volume Review Help Back Next

9 Look at the four squares [■] that indicate where the following sentence could be added to the passage.

Scientists have determined that the strength of the magnetic field weakened by as much as 90 percent during these reversals.

Where would the sentence best fit?

Click on a square [■] to add the sentence to the passage.

10 **Directions:** An introductory sentence for a brief summary of the passage is provided below. Complete the summary by selecting the THREE answer choices that express the most important ideas in the passage. Some sentences do not belong in the summary because they express ideas that are not presented in the passage or are minor ideas in the passage. **This question is worth 2 points.**

Drag your answer choices to the spaces where they belong.
To remove an answer choice, click on it. To review the passage, click on **View Text**.

Earth's magnetic field is beneficial to living organisms.

-
-
-

Answer Choices

Ⓐ It is possible that complex life would never have come into existence if the magnetic field were absent.

Ⓑ Earth's inhabitants may be at serious risk if the reversal of the magnetic poles occurs again in the future.

Ⓒ According to the opinions of scientists, a wide range of organisms use the magnetic field for navigation.

Ⓓ Because of the magnetic field, the solar wind and all of its charged particles are deflected away from Earth's surface.

Ⓔ The magnetic field helps many living things by shielding them from harmful particles that exist in space.

Ⓕ Even though Earth had no magnetic field when it originally formed, life still somehow found a way to develop.

Answer Book p. 11

Answer Book p. 12

TOEFL Reading

Insomnia

➡ Sleep is characterized by reduced reactions to external stimuli and slowed involuntary bodily functions, such as breathing and heartbeat. Most medical professionals believe that when humans do not get the hours of rest that their bodies require to complete necessary cellular processes, they are unable to achieve full functionality during waking hours. It has been suggested that adults must sleep a minimum of seven hours each night in order to maintain health and well-being, and without it, the body accumulates "sleep debt." Some, if not all, of this debt may be paid back by catching up on rest during the weekend, for example, or taking an extended vacation.

People who are unable to get back to a normal condition, however, constantly live in a state of sleep deprivation. **A** A major cause of continual sleep loss is insomnia, which is the inability to sleep or achieve uninterrupted sleep for a minimum period of four hours per day. **B** Insomnia may be transient, lasting for only two or three days, or it can persist for weeks or months at a time. **C** Chronic sufferers experience a range of related physical and mental health problems, such as depression or addiction to drugs prescribed to induce sleep. **D**

Doctors have documented common factors that contribute to insomnia, which tend to fall into predictable categories. Physiological causes may be related to the consumption of stimulants, like caffeine and nicotine; these alter the level of certain chemicals in the nervous system, making it difficult for the brain to shut down and enter a proper sleep cycle. The disruption of the circadian rhythm, the natural timing of human sleeping and waking, can also contribute to insomnia. Disruption of the circadian rhythm can occur when, for instance, a person must adjust to a new environment after traveling across several time zones on an airplane, referred to colloquially as "jet lag," or when employment requires shift work that takes place in irregular patterns.

➡ Psychological factors, however, have been shown to be the more likely cause for extended periods of insomnia as opposed to physiological determinants. Feelings of stress and anxiety are the best documented causes, arising from a number of sources. Young adults, for example, may experience severe pressure to balance academic responsibilities, after-school activities, and personal relationships. This can make it challenging to calm down before bedtime and successfully fall asleep.

➡ Insomnia can also be related to more serious psychological ailments, such as post-traumatic stress disorder. In this case, the inability to sleep is related to the insomniac being regularly troubled by memories of past trauma, which resurface in the form of nightmares and flashbacks. The sufferer will either attempt to avert such negative reactions by avoiding sleep altogether or be constantly interrupted while trying to rest. He or she may also develop an excessive startle response that prevents continuous sleep for the extended period of time necessary to rejuvenate the body.

Volume Review Help Back Next

1 The word "they" in the passage refers to

(A) professionals
(B) humans
(C) hours
(D) processes

2 According to paragraph 1, a person who does not achieve a full night of sleep

(A) cannot regain lost hours of sleep
(B) will accrue a deficit of rest time
(C) generates unhealthy cellular processes
(D) is unable to function while awake

Paragraph 1 is marked with an arrow [➡].

3 The word "transient" in the passage is closest in meaning to

(A) inappropriate
(B) costly
(C) tenacious
(D) fleeting

4 Why does the author mention "caffeine and nicotine" in the passage?

(A) To illustrate substances that are taken into the body by ingestion
(B) To make evident the primary conditions leading to insomnia
(C) To demonstrate chemicals that are beneficial to the nervous system
(D) To give an example of the type of substances that affect sleep patterns

5 Which of the sentences below best expresses the essential information in the highlighted sentence in the passage? *Incorrect* choices change the meaning in important ways or leave out essential information.

Ⓐ Unpredictable work hours and travel can harm the circadian rhythm, but these are avoidable.
Ⓑ Overcoming jet lag after airline travel is necessary to reset the body's circadian rhythm.
Ⓒ The primary cause of circadian rhythm disruption is employment schedules that are irregular.
Ⓓ Traveling across time zones or working nonstandard hours can interfere with the circadian rhythm.

6 According to paragraph 4, young adults

Ⓐ must learn to overcome social pressure
Ⓑ should limit after-school activities
Ⓒ might have difficulty calming down before sleep
Ⓓ may struggle to maintain healthy relationships

Paragraph 4 is marked with an arrow [➡].

7 The word "rejuvenate" in the passage is closest in meaning to

Ⓐ examine
Ⓑ protect
Ⓒ stimulate
Ⓓ refresh

8 In paragraph 5, all of the following are mentioned in relation to post-traumatic stress disorder EXCEPT

Ⓐ unending dreams during sleep
Ⓑ the total avoidance of sleep
Ⓒ haunting memories of the past
Ⓓ the continual interruption of rest

Paragraph 5 is marked with an arrow [➡].

Volume Review Help Back Next

9 Look at the four squares [■] that indicate where the following sentence could be added to the passage.

Therefore, these severe cases may require medical or psychiatric assistance in order for sufferers to get relief.

Where would the sentence best fit?

Click on a square [■] to add the sentence to the passage.

10 Directions: An introductory sentence for a brief summary of the passage is provided below. Complete the summary by selecting the THREE answer choices that express the most important ideas in the passage. Some sentences do not belong in the summary because they express ideas that are not presented in the passage or are minor ideas in the passage. **This question is worth 2 points.**

Drag your answer choices to the spaces where they belong.
To remove an answer choice, click on it. To review the passage, click on **View Text**.

Insomnia leads to perpetual sleep deprivation in some people.

-
-
-

Answer Choices

(A) Psychological factors are probably mostly to blame for long-term issues with insomnia.

(B) Medical practitioners acknowledge that insomnia can last for long periods of time.

(C) Insomnia is a condition that is among the primary culprits of sleep deprivation.

(D) Chronic sufferers of insomnia resort to medical treatment to help them sleep.

(E) Among the common documented causes of insomnia are physiological conditions that can disrupt the circadian rhythm.

(F) People can overcome sleep debt by using a weekend or long vacation to catch up on rest.

Answer Book p. 12

Vocabulary Review

Answer Book p. 13

A. Fill in the blanks with the appropriate words from the box.

precursor	outsource	literate
patented	abstract	scant

1 There was ____________ food available in the region during the extended drought.

2 The inventor ____________ his new technology so that nobody else could use it.

3 Many companies ____________ human resources services rather than providing them.

4 The strong wind was a(n) ____________ to the storm that was moving into the area.

5 Her essay was short on concrete examples but full of ____________ philosophical concepts.

6 Some letters include numerous spelling and grammar errors as they were written by soldiers who were barely ____________.

B. Choose the closest meaning for each highlighted word or phrase.

7 The representative of the company negotiated with the factory workers in order to avert a strike.
(A) prohibit (B) prevent (C) authorize (D) ignore

8 The lawyer pondered the proposed changes to the contract before finally accepting them.
(A) revised (B) negotiated (C) supported (D) considered

9 After the concrete has been poured, it will take approximately twenty-four hours to solidify.
(A) collapse (B) harden (C) spread (D) disperse

10 The accused criminal decided to forgo his right to a trial and plead guilty.
(A) take over (B) account for (C) give up (D) insist on

11 The Capitol Building was soon invaded by intruders determined to stop the counting of votes.
(A) guests (B) officers (C) invaders (D) exhibitors

12 Charities like Doctors Without Borders have been provisioning food supplies to refugees from the war.
(A) supplying (B) pacifying (C) greeting (D) exposing

13 The children figured out what I was baking when the unmistakable smell of homemade pie began to fill the house.
(A) smelly (B) placid (C) immaculate (D) distinct

14 I don't know much about the topic of the meeting because my boss only mentioned a few problems in passing.
(A) briefly (B) vehemently (C) merely (D) specifically

CHAPTER 03

Sentence Simplification

Sentence Simplification

About the Question Type

Sentence Simplification questions ask you to choose the sentence that best summarizes the highlighted sentence in the passage.

Incorrect choices often change the original meaning of the highlighted sentence or leave out essential information. Therefore, make sure that your answer choice paraphrases the key information of the sentence.

Question Format

Which of the sentences below best expresses the essential information in the highlighted sentence in the passage? *Incorrect* choices change the meaning in important ways or leave out essential information.

Key Strategies

- **Step 1** — Read the highlighted sentence in the passage and identify its essential information.
- **Step 2** — Select the answer choice that most accurately paraphrases the essential information of the sentence. Keep in mind that an answer choice that does not fully restate the essential information cannot be the correct one.

Example

Answer Book p. 13

Aquifers

An aquifer is a layer of rock or sediment that is saturated with groundwater. [1]Sometimes the aquifer is accessible directly through permeable soil, in which case it is referred to as an unconfined aquifer, but at other times the water is confined by a thick layer of rock or clay that cannot be penetrated. This is a key distinction because aquifers are common sources of water for drinking, or for agricultural or industrial purposes. A confined aquifer can be expensive to drill into, whereas water in an unconfined aquifer can be more easily and cheaply obtained.

Confined aquifers are often consolidated, which means that the rock containing water is porous but cemented together. Common materials in consolidated aquifers include sandstone, shale, granite, and basalt. Unconfined aquifers tend to be unconsolidated, consisting of loose sediment like sand, clay, and silt. [2]The downside to drilling into unconfined aquifers is that they are easily contaminated by lawn chemicals, overloaded septic tanks, or industrial pollution, and harmful substances then seep into the water supply. A certain amount of natural filtration occurs as water passes through the sediment or rock, but some contaminants may not necessarily be filtered out. Another factor to consider when dealing with aquifers is that they are often filled by precipitation, which can be a slow and unstable process. Thus, aquifers are fairly easily depleted if the water is used faster than it can be replenished naturally.

1 Which of the sentences below best expresses the essential information in the highlighted sentence in the passage?

(A) In the event that an aquifer can be accessed through soil that is permeable, it is considered unconfined.
(B) If the aquifer is confined by a thick layer of rock or clay, directly accessing it can be impossible.
(C) An aquifer is either accessible through permeable soil or enclosed by an impenetrable layer.
(D) Both types of aquifers are potentially accessible, though unconfined ones are harder to penetrate.

2 Which of the sentences below best expresses the essential information in the highlighted sentence in the passage?

(A) Industrial pollution has contaminated so many unconfined aquifers that using them for a water supply is harmful.
(B) Drilling into unconfined aquifers is problematic because it can result in contamination of the water supply.
(C) Dangerous chemicals can easily enter unconfined aquifers, so drilling into them is strictly prohibited.
(D) Unconfined aquifers contain the greatest water supply, but drilling onto them also has a downside.

Reading Practice 1

Answer Book p. 14

The Rococo Movement

Rococo is an artistic movement that dominated French painting, architecture, design, and literature from roughly 1715 to 1770 and spread through much of Europe. [1]The style reflected the light-hearted, pleasure-driven culture of the French aristocracy, an elite segment of the population who deployed its control of 90 percent of the country's wealth in unnecessary and decadent pursuits. Rococo art, a mocking designation applied to the movement by those who disdained its insincerity, was defined by its rejection of the seriousness and grandeur of the Baroque tradition that flourished in European art during the early eighteenth century in favor of playfulness, vanity, and conspicuous displays of wealth and luxury.

Rococo painting was preoccupied with cheerfully romantic and pastoral themes. [2]In place of Baroque art's dramatic Biblical treatments, Rococo artists offered depictions of elaborately dressed aristocrats dining, dancing, and flirting in lush outdoor settings. For instance, in Jean-Honoré Fragonard's *The Swing* (1767), a winking cherub in a flowery wooded scene looks on as a woman on a swing entices her reclining lover. The attire of the man and the woman, as well as the fact that they are free to spend their day engaging in such an indolent leisure activity, marks them as members of the social elite. Furthermore, their uninhibited romantic interest in each other would have seemed somewhat scandalous to contemporary viewers as it violated many rules of social etiquette.

In Rococo interior design, decoration was valued more highly than utility. The center of the home was the salon, a room where men and women could socialize in intricately ornamented surroundings. The colors in Rococo salons tended to be light and glamorous, with pastels, whites, and golds on prominent display. The furniture was covered in patterns of flora and fauna, and set away from the walls as if to encourage mingling. The ceilings featured elaborate, winding moldings and showy chandeliers. In a nod to the vanity of the aristocracy, mirrors were liberally utilized. Fun and festivity were emphasized in every minute design choice.

The French Revolution of 1789 challenged the political and economic dominance of the nobility and brought an end to the Rococo era in France. Its festive style seemed trivial in the wake of such solemn events. One nineteenth-century architect described Rococo as a "ridiculous jumble of shells, dragons, reeds, palm trees, and other plants." But the aesthetic had already made its mark on European design, gaining popularity in countries like Italy, Bavaria, and Prussia. It has even been resurrected in the twenty-first century, becoming fashionable in certain environments, such as luxury hotels. Although the elaborate decorations of the modern movement are sometimes crafted with ironic intent, the fun-loving merriment of the seventeenth-century French aristocracy still has appeal among today's wealthy and powerful elites.

Glossary

· cherub: an angelic child with wings

1 Which of the sentences below best expresses the essential information in the highlighted sentence in the passage?

(A) French artists who employed this style of art depended on the patronage of individuals with great wealth.
(B) The self-indulgent activities of the nation's wealthy upper class were presented in this artistic movement.
(C) French aristocrats were inspired to engage in immoral and silly acts by works of art created in this style.
(D) The majority of the population considered this art movement to be an imprudent pastime of aristocrats.

2 Which of the sentences below best expresses the essential information in the highlighted sentence in the passage?

(A) Baroque art appealed to many people because it rejected representations of social activities in favor of expressions of spirituality.
(B) The primary difference between Baroque and Rococo artists was the manner in which they presented the aristocracy's behavior.
(C) Baroque art fell out of favor with aristocrats because they preferred the more entertaining subject matter of Rococo works.
(D) Rococo art focused on wealthy, powerful people at their leisure rather than the serious religious themes of Baroque works.

3 According to paragraph 2, the element of *The Swing* that was viewed as controversial is

(A) the behavior of the cherub
(B) the clothing of the man and woman
(C) the natural setting of the scene
(D) the relationship of the subjects

4 The word "ornamented" in the passage is closest in meaning to

(A) situated (B) adorned (C) inundated (D) disrupted

5 The word "trivial" in the passage is closest in meaning to

(A) oblivious (B) enjoyable (C) absurd (D) unimportant

6 According to paragraph 4, the Rococo art movement fell out of favor due to

(A) a rise of a new art movement that viewed displays of luxury with a sense of irony
(B) an increase in competition between the elites of various European states
(C) an economic recession that forced the wealthy of France to reduce spending
(D) a period of social and political upheaval that threatened the role of the aristocracy

Reading Practice 2

Answer Book p. 15

Infantile Amnesia

In psychology, infantile amnesia refers to the relative absence among adults of any autobiographical memories from their first few years of life. Exactly when the first enduring memory is formed varies from person to person, but that it happens after infancy is universal. Not until around the age of three do people have a recollection of events that happened to them or in which they participated. Psychologists have been investigating this phenomenon for over 100 years, yet the answers remain elusive.

The earliest studies of childhood memory date back to the late nineteenth century, but progress has been relatively slow. In 1910, Sigmund Freud contributed the terminology that is still used by contemporary psychologists. [2]Although his suggestion that adults forget childhood episodes in order to repress early embarrassments about unmentionable desires is no longer accepted by most psychologists, they still use the term he coined: *infantile amnesia*. Amnesia is a term that refers to memory loss, but for most of the twentieth century, psychologists debated whether young children actually forget infant memories or whether babies' developing brains are simply incapable of embedding long-term memories in the first place. The latter view was predominant until the 1980s and 1990s, when studies revealed that babies could retain certain memories for months at a time. Today, most researchers agree that infants establish memories but forget them faster than adults.

It seems that memories of events that occur prior to the age of two fade rapidly in early childhood. [4]Whereas most adults have no recollection of events that occurred prior to their third or fourth year, children from five to nine years old retain events earlier than that threshold. One study documented the rapid dwindling of memories from age three, finding that six-year-old children recalled about 70 percent of the events that interviewers asked about but forgot about half of them by the time they were nine. In contrast, memory is quite stable between the ages of 20 and 70, and the earliest adult memories tend to be consistently of events that occurred around the age of four.

There is little consensus as to the causes of infantile amnesia. Some scientists believe that the capacity to form lasting memories coincides with the development of a sense of a cognitive self or with the acquisition of language, both of which provide a means of organizing past experiences. Others focus on neurological factors such as the production of neurons in the hippocampus, the part of the brain responsible for forming, organizing, and storing autobiographical memories. Research shows that neurons continue to form into early childhood, tapering off in adulthood. This suggests that competition between new and old neurons may result in less memory retention. Psychologists and neurologists continue to study the subject of infantile amnesia, attempting to find answers to one of the most significant mysteries of the human mind.

Glossary

· autobiographical: of memory of personally experienced events in the past

1 The word "phenomenon" in the passage is closest in meaning to

(A) realization (B) complication (C) drawback (D) occurrence

2 Which of the sentences below best expresses the essential information in the highlighted sentence in the passage?

(A) *Infantile amnesia* is Freud's explanation of the tendency of adults to block memories of socially unacceptable desires.
(B) Unspeakable desires are repressed by adults, but children remember those desires in a process known as *infantile amnesia.*
(C) Freud's theory that people repress early embarrassing memories has not lasted as long as the term he used to describe it.
(D) Adults forget embarrassing events from childhood, and Freud developed a term for that embarrassment.

3 According to paragraph 2, all of the following have been considered as explanations for infantile amnesia EXCEPT:

(A) Young children forget infant memories.
(B) Infants lack the ability to form memories.
(C) Young children replace infant memories with new ones.
(D) Infants form memories but forget them fairly quickly.

4 Which of the sentences below best expresses the essential information in the highlighted sentence in the passage?

(A) The majority of adults do not recall things that happened at three years of age, but five-to-nine-year-old children do.
(B) Recalling events from several years ago is common in all age groups, but memories that lasted longer than nine years are reserved for adults.
(C) Although many children have memories that last longer than four years, adults forget most things within a few years.
(D) Kids of five to nine are able to remember what happened to them at the age of three, just as adults do.

5 The word "them" in the passage refers to

(A) memories (B) children (C) events (D) interviewers

6 According to paragraph 4, the ability to communicate using language may

(A) serve as a method to structure what has been experienced
(B) lead to the development of a person's sense of self
(C) stimulate increased neurological activity in the hippocampus
(D) allow memories of past events to be significantly altered

Reading Practice 3

Answer Book p. 16

The End-Permian Extinction Event

Scientists have identified five mass extinction events that occurred over the course of Earth's history, with the best-known being the Cretaceous-Paleogene extinction that wiped out the dinosaurs 66 million years ago. Before the dinosaurs emerged, though, an even more devastating extinction event wiped out 95 percent of marine species and 70 percent of terrestrial vertebrates. The end-Permian extinction event, unofficially known as the Great Dying, occurred about 250 million years ago. [1]The damage may have spanned only 100,000 years, a mere blink of the eye in geological time, particularly considering that it took 10 million years for the planet to recover what it lost in biodiversity. However, while the disappearance of millions of species is clearly documented in the fossil record, the causes of the die-off between the Permian and Triassic periods are not well understood.

Some scientists believe that the cause of the two mass extinction events mentioned above was the same: massive asteroids colliding with Earth. In 2004, a 75-mile crater was discovered buried off the shore of Australia that dates back to the late Permian period. [2]This Bedout crater is similar in size to the Chicxulub crater in the Gulf of Mexico that is considered prime evidence that the dinosaur extinction was caused by an asteroid. An asteroid impact as large as this could have produced an enormous cloud of particles that would have blocked the Sun for months, causing temperatures to fall. Acid rain would have followed, and the combination of total darkness, sudden cold, and this would have destroyed most of the plant life that herbivores required for survival. In turn, the death of the herbivores would have led to the death of the carnivores that ate them. However, other experts contest the asteroid hypothesis, contending that the Bedout structure is not an impact crater after all.

A less dramatic explanation is based on signs of oxygen depletion in rocks formed underwater during the Permian period. [A] This hypothesis suggests that the mass death of marine life was due to low oxygen levels in shallow waters brought on by the absence of polar ice caps. [B] There might have been a buildup of carbon dioxide in the Permian oceans, which would have gradually poisoned sea life. [C] However, proponents of the oxygen deprivation hypothesis are unsure of the catalyst for these changes. [D]

One potential catalyst is widespread volcanic activity in present-day Siberia. Numerous erupting Siberian volcanoes could have covered the planet in hot lava, filling the atmosphere with volcanic gases and producing acid rain, just as in the asteroid scenario. The resulting fires and decay would have filled the air with greenhouse gases and have heated the world beyond a hospitable level for the world's animals. The volcano theory remains the most popular explanation for the Great Dying.

Glossary

· vertebrate: an animal that has a back bone

1 Which of the sentences below best expresses the essential information in the highlighted sentence in the passage?

(A) It took the planet several million years to return to its previous level of biodiversity.
(B) Because of the damage to geological structures, the effects of the event lasted for millions of years.
(C) The planet recovered surprisingly quickly when the extent of the devastation is taken into account.
(D) Given the length of the biodiversity recovery period, the time period of the destruction was remarkably short.

2 Which of the sentences below best expresses the essential information in the highlighted sentence in the passage?

(A) The dimensions of the Bedout crater are comparable to those of an asteroid impact site associated with dinosaur extinction.
(B) Both the Bedout and Chicxulub craters are confirmed to have been produced by the impact of an asteroid.
(C) The Chicxulub crater was the result of an asteroid, so it is likely that the Bedout crater has the same origin.
(D) Studies of the Chicxulub crater have provided insight into the most probable cause of the Bedout crater.

3 The word "this" in the passage refers to

(A) the Sun
(B) Acid rain
(C) total darkness
(D) sudden cold

4 According to paragraph 2, the asteroid hypothesis is disputed because some scientists

(A) doubt that acid rain could kill so many animals
(B) claim the Bedout crater was not caused by an asteroid
(C) think the extinction was caused by a warm climate
(D) believe the dinosaurs could have survived an asteroid

5 Look at the four squares [■] that indicate where the following sentence could be added to the passage.

These play an important role in the convection currents that cycle water throughout the world's oceans.

Where would the sentence best fit?

6 The word "hospitable" in the passage is closest in meaning to

(A) survivable
(B) certain
(C) refreshing
(D) distressing

Answer Book p. 17

TOEFL Reading

Brain-Computer Interface

Brain-computer interface (BCI) includes a range of technologies designed to create direct communication channels between a human brain and a computer. The primary goal of BCI is to develop ways for humans to control devices or tools using brain signals only, capabilities that not only would help scientists better understand the human brain but also would offer opportunities for people who have severe physical disabilities but normal cognitive functions. For example, someone who has been paralyzed in an automobile accident might be able to operate a wheelchair even though the person cannot move his or her arms and hands.

➡ Currently, there are two main categories of brain-computer interface systems, noninvasive and invasive. A common noninvasive technique entails the use of an electroencephalogram (EEG), which is a test that detects changes in brain waves. In this method, small metal discs called electrodes are pasted onto the scalp, and electrical signals from the brain are measured and recorded. Conversely, an invasive BCI procedure implants tiny electrodes directly into the brain during neurosurgery, which is costlier and riskier for the patient. However, the benefit is that invasive electrodes produce a much higher graphic resolution and are more specific as each electrode can target a single neuron.

➡ In either case, the electrodes are wired to an external computer for processing, which typically requires several steps in which the brain's electrical signals are interpreted, classified, and translated using mathematical formulas. **A** This processing is necessary in order to discover what kind of mental task the subject is performing so that the data can be converted into a digital command. **B** Once a digital command is generated, it is transmitted to an external device in an attempt to achieve a corresponding action, such as the movement of a cursor or a robotic arm. **C** The success or failure of an intended action is determined by the feedback returned to the user from the device. **D**

➡ Although the notion of harnessing the brain's neuron activity dates to the 1960s, practical scientific applications of BCI technology are still in their infancy. One reason is that the brain's electrical signals are different across individuals, so the creation of universal digital output commands is not feasible. Moreover, in BCI, the process is not merely a one-way stream of information from the brain to the external environment. In fact, the brain's neurons are malleable and must adapt in response to the BCI environment. Each subject, often through trial and error, still must learn how to think in a particular way so that the electrical signals and digital commands successfully achieve the intended task. Thus, a one-size-fits-all approach to BCI may never come to fruition, and third-party mediation between subjects and computers remains important. In this sense, even though BCI is a high-tech undertaking, the process is similar to that of an injured athlete undergoing rehabilitation with the aid and guidance of a licensed physical therapist.

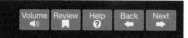

Volume Review Help Back Next

1 Which of the sentences below best expresses the essential information in the highlighted sentence in the passage? *Incorrect* choices change the meaning in important ways or leave out essential information.

Ⓐ If people could control machines solely with their minds, scientists could learn more about the brain and certain people with physical disabilities could also benefit.

Ⓑ BCI's main goal is to offer scientists the opportunity to use computers to help people overcome cognitive and physical disabilities so that they can live more normal lives.

Ⓒ Scientists have gained much knowledge about human cognition through the use of BCI, but its practical applications have been limited to people with mental disabilities.

Ⓓ For scientists to learn more about how the human brain functions, subjects must combine their physical and cognitive abilities to control remote devices and tools.

2 The word "entails" in the passage is closest in meaning to

Ⓐ precludes

Ⓑ involves

Ⓒ delineates

Ⓓ fosters

3 Which of the following can be inferred from paragraph 2 about using an electroencephalogram in a BCI?

Ⓐ It is costlier and riskier to use than alternative BCI methods.

Ⓑ It is the least commonly implemented BCI procedure in current science.

Ⓒ It provides more comprehensive data than direct electrode implants.

Ⓓ It offers a less detailed image of brain activity than invasive techniques.

Paragraph 2 is marked with an arrow [➡].

4 Which of the following is NOT mentioned in paragraph 3 as part of the processing of the electrodes and the brain's electrical signals?

Ⓐ Converting data into a digital command

Ⓑ Translating data into a graphical chart

Ⓒ Providing feedback from the device to the user

Ⓓ Sending a digital command to an external machine

Paragraph 3 is marked with an arrow [➡].

5 The word "fruition" in the passage is closest in meaning to

Ⓐ controversy
Ⓑ inception
Ⓒ completion
Ⓓ acceptance

6 According to paragraph 4, what must users of BCI devices develop the ability to do?

Ⓐ Adjust to a rapidly changing technology
Ⓑ Recognize various forms of electronic messages
Ⓒ Form thoughts that lead to suitable signals and commands
Ⓓ Interpret commands from digital devices

Paragraph 4 is marked with an arrow [➡].

7 According to paragraph 4, what is the reason that creating universal digital output commands is not feasible?

Ⓐ Information streams only travel in one direction.
Ⓑ The electrical signals of different brains vary.
Ⓒ The cost of producing them is prohibitive.
Ⓓ Neurons in the brain are slow to adapt to them.

Paragraph 4 is marked with an arrow [➡].

8 In paragraph 4, why does the author mention the physical rehabilitation of an injured athlete?

Ⓐ To emphasize that BCI uses cutting-edge technology
Ⓑ To provide an analogy for the way BCI is conducted
Ⓒ To highlight the role of trial and error in therapy
Ⓓ To give an example of a potential future application of BCI

Paragraph 4 is marked with an arrow [➡].

Volume Review Help Back Next

9 Look at the four squares [■] that indicate where the following sentence could be added to the passage.

The conversion is made by using a specific algorithm to translate brain waves into programmed instruction that a computer can understand.

Where would the sentence best fit?

Click on a square [■] to add the sentence to the passage.

10 **Directions:** An introductory sentence for a brief summary of the passage is provided below. Complete the summary by selecting the THREE answer choices that express the most important ideas in the passage. Some sentences do not belong in the summary because they express ideas that are not presented in the passage or are minor ideas in the passage. **This question is worth 2 points.**

Drag your answer choices to the spaces where they belong.
To remove an answer choice, click on it. To review the passage, click on **View Text**.

Scientists are pursuing brain-computer interface (BCI) technologies that would allow direct communication between the human brain and a computer.

-
-
-

Answer Choices

(A) Useful applications of brain-computer interface technology are still quite undeveloped despite the idea of exploiting brain signals not being new.

(B) BCI is a process that allows a computer to understand neuron signals through a one-way communication stream from the brain to the environment.

(C) An important application of BCI is offering people who have been paralyzed the possibility of hands-free machine operation.

(D) Noninvasive and invasive procedures are the two primary classifications of BCIs that are currently in use.

(E) Scientists have made some progress in BCI technology, but they have been unable to return feedback from the device to the user.

(F) During any BCI procedure, wired electrodes are connected to an external computer and the brain's electrical messages are processed.

Answer Book p. 17

Answer Book p. 18

TOEFL Reading

The US Interstate Highway System

➡ In the 1920s, Ford Motor Company introduced an affordable vehicle for the working class, so more people could own automobiles. This made driving popular, so there was an increased demand for the expansion of the highway system. However, government funding for highways was limited, and private companies helped fulfill the demand. The Pennsylvania Turnpike, a private toll road opened in 1940, was the first example of a modern highway in America. It proved to be a highly profitable route, demonstrating the economic value of highways to politicians. With automobiles becoming the norm and a growing public interest in interstate travel, the federal government began to consider a large-scale interstate highways project.

➡ A planned interstate highway system gained official support after Dwight D. Eisenhower became president in the 1950s. During the Second World War, Eisenhower had encountered enormous German autobahns, multi-lane highways that stretched across the country. Witnessing these made him believe that highways were essential for expediting military transportation. Therefore, in 1956, he commenced with building the Interstate Highway System by approving the Federal-Aid Highway Act. Through this legislation, Congress secured federal funding for 90 percent of the project costs, and it was funded by a tax on gasoline.

➡ What made the new system of interstate highways different from earlier ones were methodical planning and scale. All of the interstates were designed in a similar manner. They had two lanes going in either direction, and these were separated by a wide median. They also had a large right-of-way on each side, so no buildings could be built beside them. Access to the interstates was highly controlled as entrance and exit ramps were the only access points. This type of controlled-access highway is known as a freeway or expressway. The nearly 75,000 kilometers of freeway construction was the largest and most expensive public works project in history.

➡ The new Interstate Highway System had a significant economic impact on America. **A** For each dollar spent, the roads generated a further six dollars for the economy. **B** Construction alone added an annual 31 percent to American productivity for an entire decade. **C** On top of these benefits, transportation costs decreased as freight could be quickly transported across the country. **D**

Despite the benefits the highways created, however, they also caused social problems. Nearly 800,000 properties were bulldozed, and the families, many of whom were African American, were not suitably compensated for the destruction of their homes. Furthermore, African-American families were less likely to own a car. This meant that they were heavily reliant on public transportation and suffered when public transportation funds were diverted to road building.

Volume Review Help Back Next

In addition, the publication of the popular novel *Silent Spring* in 1962 encouraged greater environmental awareness. It pointed out the damage that highway construction was doing to the environment. The public was outraged by the apparent disregard for the environment in the development of the highways, as they were planned with construction costs and travel time as priorities, rather than nature.

1 Why does the author mention "The Pennsylvania Turnpike" in the passage?

Ⓐ To list contemporary construction methods
Ⓑ To show its popularity among federal employees
Ⓒ To explain the purpose of highways
Ⓓ To offer an example of a private project

2 The word "norm" in the passage is closest in meaning to

Ⓐ successor
Ⓑ border
Ⓒ condition
Ⓓ standard

3 According to paragraph 1, what factor made driving popular in the 1920s?

Ⓐ Ford offered free gasoline with every purchase.
Ⓑ Cars became inexpensive for the majority.
Ⓒ Driving was made convenient with highways.
Ⓓ Low taxes reduced the cost of long-distance travel.

Paragraph 1 is marked with an arrow [➡].

4 According to paragraph 2, which of the following is true of the Federal-Aid Highway Act?

Ⓐ It provided federal money to cover all interstate project costs.
Ⓑ It required a special highway lane for military transportation.
Ⓒ It was initially rejected by Congress before being approved.
Ⓓ It primarily used a gas tax to finance the interstate system.

Paragraph 2 is marked with an arrow [➡].

5 What can be inferred from paragraph 2 about President Dwight D. Eisenhower?

Ⓐ He was the first politician to consider an interstate project.
Ⓑ He developed a disdain for Germany because of the war.
Ⓒ He was impressed by the practical utility of the German highways.
Ⓓ He believed that taxpayers would be skeptical of a highway's worth.

Paragraph 2 is marked with an arrow [➡].

6 According to paragraph 3, which of the following is NOT true of how the interstates were designed?

Ⓐ A spacious median separated each set of lanes.
Ⓑ A right-of-way prevented adjacent building construction.
Ⓒ Access was strictly limited to on and off ramps.
Ⓓ Each set of lanes allowed two-way traffic.

Paragraph 3 is marked with an arrow [➡].

7 According to paragraph 4, what impact did the Interstate Highway System have on freight?

Ⓐ Transportation fees were reduced.
Ⓑ It abolished delivery expenses.
Ⓒ Truck taxes were removed.
Ⓓ It lowered toll charges.

Paragraph 4 is marked with an arrow [➡].

8 Which of the sentences below best expresses the essential information in the highlighted sentence in the passage? *Incorrect* choices change the meaning in important ways or leave out essential information.

Ⓐ Highway construction focused on width and length rather than environmental concerns.
Ⓑ The prioritization of costs over nature during construction raised public anger.
Ⓒ Road construction was not influenced by environmental pressures.
Ⓓ Environmental impact was as important as convenience in highway construction.

Volume | Review | Help | Back | Next

9 Look at the four squares [■] that indicate where the following sentence could be added to the passage.

This reduced the prices of most consumer goods.

Where would the sentence best fit?

Click on a square [■] to add the sentence to the passage.

10 **Directions:** An introductory sentence for a brief summary of the passage is provided below. Complete the summary by selecting the THREE answer choices that express the most important ideas in the passage. Some sentences do not belong in the summary because they express ideas that are not presented in the passage or are minor ideas in the passage. **This question is worth 2 points.**

Drag your answer choices to the spaces where they belong.
To remove an answer choice, click on it. To review the passage, click on **View Text**.

As more people owned and traveled in cars, the federal government began to invest in interstate highways.

-
-
-

Answer Choices

Ⓐ The interstate highways were different from previous ones because of their organization and extent.

Ⓑ The Interstate Highway System resolved the congestion problems faced by the US military.

Ⓒ It was under the Eisenhower administration that the system of interstate highways became a reality.

Ⓓ The construction of the highways involved the displacement of hundreds of thousands of people.

Ⓔ African-American families were the minority group least likely to utilize the Interstate Highway System.

Ⓕ Although the interstate highways generated significant benefits, they also caused social and environmental issues.

Answer Book p. 18

Vocabulary Review

Answer Book p. 20

A. Fill in the blanks with the appropriate words from the box.

predominant	terrestrial	methodical
replenished	indolent	malleable

1 My energy is ______________ after a good meal and a nap.

2 The ancestors of modern whales were ______________ creatures that walked the earth upon legs.

3 In the early twentieth century, newspapers and radio were the ______________ forms of media.

4 The teacher was concerned about her ______________ student who never studied.

5 The tailor was ______________ in his attention to every crease and wrinkle in his jackets.

6 The ______________ plastic could be stretched and bent into almost any shape.

B. Choose the closest meaning for each highlighted word or phrase.

7 The resort's advertisements try to entice customers with photos of beautiful beaches and sunsets.
(A) deter (B) promote (C) assure (D) tempt

8 Many residents of the city were outraged by the scandal and demanded that the mayor resign.
(A) infuriated (B) gratified (C) professed (D) defeated

9 The movie was about a wizard who was able to resurrect the dead.
(A) supply (B) revive (C) control (D) develop

10 Insects are distinguished by bodies with three distinct segments.
(A) parts (B) antennae (C) defenses (D) reputations

11 According to the weather forecast, the rain will taper off before the end of the day.
(A) resume (B) intensify (C) disappear (D) decline

12 My grandfather enjoys sharing his recollections of his childhood with me.
(A) preparations (B) stories (C) memories (D) demands

13 The lawyers debated the merits of the case, with the prosecutor contending that the crime was committed intentionally.
(A) demanding (B) receding (C) arguing (D) competing

14 Exposure to air pollution and excessive noise is one of the downsides of living in a big city.
(A) disadvantages (B) factors (C) experiences (D) barriers

CHAPTER 04

Fact

Fact

About the Question Type

Fact questions ask you to identify specific information that is explicitly stated in the passage.

The correct answer choice restates specific information in the passage that directly answers the question. Incorrect answer choices include information that is contradicted by the passage, irrelevant to the question, or not mentioned in the passage.

Question Format

- According to paragraph #, which of the following is true of X?
- According to paragraph #, what/how/why . . . ?
- The author's description/discussion of X mentions which of the following?

Key Strategies

- **Step 1** — Read the question and identify the keywords. If the question indicates a specific paragraph, you can ignore the rest of the passage.
- **Step 2** — Scan the passage for the keywords, and locate the relevant information.
- **Step 3** — Select the answer choice that correctly paraphrases the relevant information in the passage.

Example

Answer Book p. 20

The Clovis-First Theory

Most scientists agree that modern humans first appeared in Africa approximately 300,000 years ago before migrating to other parts of the planet. As North and South America had already separated from the other continents at this point, they were settled last. So, when did people arrive in the New World?

For decades, the leading explanation was the Clovis-First hypothesis, which suggests that the first humans walked there across the Bering Land Bridge connecting Alaska and Siberia during the Late Pleistocene and then progressed through a narrow ice-free corridor in the middle of the territory that is now Canada. Clovis-First theorists believed the first settlers were the same hunter-gatherers who expertly crafted a collection of hunting tools that were found in Clovis, New Mexico in the 1930s. Those tools were radiocarbon dated to around 11,000 years ago, which made them the earliest archaeological evidence of humans in the Americas.

More recent evidence, however, has cast doubt upon the Clovis-First explanation. An excavation of the Bluefish Caves along the Bluefish River in Yukon, Alaska yielded tools that may be up to 18,000 years old. In addition, a large mammoth bone was discovered in 1985 with flakes removed from it for tools. The mammoth bone was dated at 24,500 years old, making the Bluefish Cave the oldest site of human occupation in North America. Other studies have amassed radiocarbon, DNA, and macrofossil data to conclude that the ice-free corridor was impassable until well after the Clovis tools were formed.

1 According to paragraph 2, the Clovis-First hypothesis states that the first humans in the Americas

(A) migrated there from Africa about 300,000 years ago
(B) sailed from Alaska to Siberia during the Late Pleistocene
(C) walked through an area without ice in modern-day Canada
(D) arrived in the region long before the continents separated

2 According to the passage, which of the following is true about the Bluefish Caves?

(A) They were untouched by humans until after the Clovis tools were formed.
(B) They were excavated in 1985, revealing human bones from 24,500 years ago.
(C) They contained tools that were more recently made than the Clovis ones.
(D) Their excavation turned up an animal bone that had been altered by humans.

Answer Book p. 20

Uniformitarianism and Neptunism

In the late eighteenth century, Scottish geologist James Hutton presented a new theory that summarized twenty-five years of diligent observations. Later known as uniformitarianism, it asserted that all geological changes were the result of uniform processes over an infinite period. His theory was highly controversial as it contrasted with the popular contemporary theory of Neptunism. This stated that all geological formations were the result of water from flooding. Despite the opposition, Hutton's theory gradually gained acceptance in scientific circles, and he is considered the founder of modern geology.

Neptunism theorists, notably German geologist Abraham Gottlob Werner, claimed that the earth was initially covered in water. ■A According to him, the watery planet was created approximately six thousand years ago by God. ■B Moreover, fossils were explained as the remnants of animals that had perished in the Biblical flood. ■C Neptunism stated that all geological formations and fossils were therefore the result of flooding and erosion. ■D It argued that the recession of water into oceans created the present continents and islands, although it did not explain why such a recession would occur.

Hutton's observations contradicted Neptunism. He claimed that sedimentary rocks and fish fossils on cliffs were the result of lifting land rather than receding water. For evidence, Hutton visited numerous sites across Scotland. He studied exposed rock faces for unconformities, surfaces where two opposite forms of geological activity are visible. At Siccar Point, Hutton noticed that the lower, Silurian rocks pointed vertically, while the red sandstone rocks above were deposited horizontally. This structure occurred through the uplifting and reorienting of the Silurian rocks prior to the deposition of the red sandstone rocks, an action that developed over an extensive period of time. This effect could not have been achieved through flooding. It required immense pressure emanating from the earth itself. Consequently, he believed that landforms, rocks, and minerals were formed through an infinite process of erosion and uplift from internal pressure. He argued that this process took an extraordinarily long time, and he postulated that the age of the earth was much greater than six thousand years.

However, Hutton was mistaken in his belief that geological changes were uniform and unchanging over time. The rate of geological change can be altered depending on a convection process in the earth's core. Therefore, modern geologists contend that the earth was formed through a combination of three different processes. Water is responsible for the creation of sedimentary rocks; however, heat and uplift form igneous rocks. Geologists have made claims that sudden catastrophic events, such as floods or volcanic eruptions, have their own role in shaping the earth. But these have a limited effect and are not responsible for the earth's geological structure overall, as Neptunism suggested. Instead, the uniformitarianism theory posited by Hutton and expanded by later scientists explains the majority of geological formations around the world.

1 According to paragraph 1, uniformitarianism was controversial because

(A) it was based on minimal observations
(B) it argued that geological processes were fleeting
(C) it made unsupported claims about the impact of flooding
(D) it conflicted with the prevailing theory of the day

2 Look at the four squares [■] that indicate where the following sentence could be added to the passage.

The time frame satisfied the fervent Christian beliefs that were widely accepted during this era.

Where would the sentence best fit?

3 The word "perished" in the passage is closest in meaning to

(A) submerged
(B) expired
(C) thrived
(D) developed

4 According to paragraph 3, which of the following is true of the red sandstone rocks?

(A) They were formed by gradually declining water levels.
(B) They pointed vertically in some locations and horizontally in others.
(C) They were elevated above the Silurian rocks in the sites Hutton studied.
(D) They were deposited at an earlier point than the Silurian rocks.

5 The word "these" in the passage refer to

(A) claims
(B) events
(C) floods
(D) eruptions

6 According to paragraph 4, the primary flaw in Hutton's theory was related to

(A) the force with which devastating natural phenomena occur
(B) the overall structure of the inner core of the planet
(C) the consistency with which geological processes occurred
(D) the time required for the creation of different types of rock

Reading Practice 2

Answer Book p. 21

The Nefertiti Controversy

In a 1912 excavation of a workshop belonging to the Egyptian pharaoh Akhenaten's official court sculptor, German archaeologist Ludwig Borchardt set off a controversy that would last more than a century. He discovered a bust of Akhenaten's royal wife, Queen Nefertiti, that was over 3,000 years old. The sculpted head is made of limestone and stucco with beeswax used to affix the original quartz eyes, and it is nineteen inches tall and weighs forty-four pounds. Mysteriously, one of the eyes has since gone missing. Borchardt took the bust home with him to Germany, where it resides today—much to the dissatisfaction of the Egyptian government.

The German side of the story is that Borchardt was legally granted ownership of Nefertiti by an Egyptian official, but the Egyptians maintain that Borchardt downplayed the value of the bust. Documents show that Borchardt met with an Egyptian official in 1913 to divide the artifacts from the dig between them. The official was shown an unflattering photograph rather than the statue itself, and Borchardt described it as a gypsum bust of a princess, concealing that it depicted the famous queen. Since 1924, the Egyptians have described the German acquisition as looting.

Although the bust is currently the most popular museum exhibit in Berlin, the Egyptian authorities have refused to accept this situation and have made numerous attempts to repatriate the artwork. The closest this ever came to occurring was in 1933, when the German government promised to return the sculpture to celebrate the anniversary of the Egyptian king's ascension to the throne. Unfortunately, Adolph Hitler intervened and declared that Germany would never relinquish the bust. Since the end of World War II, the German government has refused all requests from Egypt, and the object remains on display in the Neues Museum to this day.

In 2016, two German artists staged a dramatic repudiation of the German government's policy. They secretly created a data map of Queen Nefertiti's head with a mobile 3D scanning device designed for use with a gaming system. The scan was made amid crowds of visitors by circling the bust whenever the museum guards looked the other way. They subsequently created two copies of the sculpture with a 3D printer. The first copy was buried in Egyptian desert sand while the second was donated to a museum in Cairo. The artists issued a statement declaring, "Archaeological artifacts as a cultural memory originate for the most part from the Global South; however, a vast number of important objects can be found in Western museums and private collections. We should face the fact that colonial structures continue to exist today." It is still possible to download the artists' 3D data and make copies of the queen's head for free. The stunt brought renewed attention to the controversy over the ownership of the Nefertiti bust.

1 The word "it" in the passage refers to

(A) head
(B) limestone
(C) stucco
(D) beeswax

2 According to paragraph 1, the bust of Queen Nefertiti was

(A) adorned with numerous precious stones
(B) displayed in an ancient ruler's private residence
(C) located in the workplace of an Egyptian artist
(D) sold before being shipped to Germany

3 According to paragraph 2, the Egyptians are unhappy with the fact that Borchardt

(A) covered a statue with a substance to change its appearance
(B) refused to meet with a representative of the government
(C) misrepresented an object to make it seem less valuable
(D) removed an item from a historical site without permission

4 Which of the sentences below best expresses the essential information in the highlighted sentence in the passage?

(A) The Egyptian government rejects the German museum's claim to the statue and has taken action to retrieve it.
(B) The Berlin museum is in negotiations with representatives of Egypt regarding that country's claim to the artifact.
(C) The popularity of the sculpture in Berlin has prompted Egyptian officials to demand that it be returned as soon as possible.
(D) The Egyptian government's refusal to accept German ownership of the object has led to conflict between the two countries.

5 The word "relinquish" in the passage is closest in meaning to

(A) acknowledge
(B) demonstrate
(C) understand
(D) surrender

6 According to paragraph 4, the German artists made copies of the bust because they wished to

(A) support Egypt's right to reclaim the statue
(B) sell blueprints for making copies of the bust
(C) display the copies in a museum in Germany
(D) donate both copies to the Egyptian government

Reading Practice 3

Answer Book p. 22

The History of Cattle Domestication

Cattle have provided numerous benefits for humans, including meat, milk, leather, and transport, since ancient humans domesticated them centuries ago. They have also played an important role in religious rituals, most commonly as sacrifices to honor gods or ancestors. Bovine animals are inextricably intertwined with the history of the human species. But the precise timeline of the domestication of cattle remains a subject of debate. Traditionally, researchers learned about the history of bovine species by examining fossils and archaeological evidence. More recently, scholars have been able to expand their understanding in this area by analyzing mitochondrial DNA, which is more durable and plentiful in organic cells than nuclear DNA.

Modern cattle evolved from a species of wild oxen known as aurochs. These now-extinct grazers were almost as tall as elephants, much larger than their present-day descendants, and they featured enormous horns that could be as long as 31 inches. They likely first emerged in Asia some 11.7 million years ago and endured until 1627, when the last ones died in Poland of natural causes. Extinction came about as a result of the destruction of the forests of Central Europe in which they lived and overhunting in both Asia and Africa. But long before the species began its decline, people discovered the utility of these animals.

Aurochs were first domesticated about 10,500 years ago in the Fertile Crescent, a region that spanned the territory occupied today by Iraq, Syria, Lebanon, Palestine, Israel, Jordan, as well as northern Egypt and Kuwait. Fossil and gene studies have shown that aurochs gradually became smaller, as usually happens when humans find a use for a species. In an effort to document this change, one study found that beef and dairy cattle have significantly smaller brains than their bullfighting counterparts. These animals have brains in sizes comparable to those of ancient aurochs. Small-bodied cattle begin to show up in the fossil record in Mesopotamia (between the Tigris and Euphrates rivers) around 6000 BC. By the Middle Ages, the smaller bulls and cows of today were firmly established.

The taming of aurochs in the Fertile Crescent is not the only instance of domestication in the historical record. A second bovine domestication event took place in the Indus Valley region of modern-day Pakistan about 7,000 years ago. Mitochondrial DNA from a species of humped cattle known as zebu shows that those animals are directly related to the contemporary grazing cows that number 1.4 billion across the world. Another event in southern parts of Egypt could have occurred around 6500 BC, but DNA evidence that the earliest domesticated cattle in these regions actually originated in the Fertile Crescent casts doubt on that hypothesis. Continued research is necessary to pin down the precise evolution of the modern cow, an animal that rivals the horse as the most useful ever to cross paths with human beings.

1 The word "intertwined" in the passage is closest in meaning to

(A) tangled
(B) superseded
(C) expanded
(D) observed

2 In paragraph 1, all of the following are mentioned as being studied by researchers to learn about cattle domestication EXCEPT

(A) animal remains
(B) human artifacts
(C) written records
(D) genetic materials

3 According to paragraph 2, which of the following is true of aurochs?

(A) They competed with early elephants for resources.
(B) They were comparable in size to their modern descendants.
(C) They died off as a result of habitat loss and overhunting.
(D) They were considered unsuitable for use by humans.

4 The word "those" in the passage refers to

(A) cattle
(B) counterparts
(C) brains
(D) sizes

5 According to paragraph 3, the process of domestication results in

(A) a rise in overall intelligence
(B) a decline in body mass
(C) an improvement in health
(D) an increase in genetic diversity

6 According to the passage, domestication in southern parts of Egypt is considered controversial because

(A) other domesticated species such as horses were not common to the region
(B) studies of the genetic origins of bovine species do not support that conclusion
(C) modern cows do not share many features with earlier zebu species
(D) research has shown that cattle were raised in the Indus Valley earlier

Answer Book p. 23

TOEFL Reading

Savanna Grassland Biome

Savanna grasslands are one of Earth's eight major land biomes, which are large areas that are classified by their vegetation, climate, wildlife, and soil. A savanna shares features with both a forest and a desert, as it is characterized by grass, shrubs, and widely scattered trees. Most commonly located near the equator, savannas are found on every continent apart from Antarctica, amounting to about 20 percent of the land on the planet. On some continents, like North America and Asia, the savannas are quite small. The largest concentration of savanna grassland is in Africa, where this distinctive biome covers five million square miles, around half of the continent.

The climate in a savanna is exceptionally dry; in fact, there are only two seasons. The rainy season, also known as the monsoon season due to the intensity of the rainfall, lasts about six months and usually features about twenty to fifty inches of rainfall. The dry season that extends throughout the rest of the year is essentially rainless. Temperatures remain fairly constant throughout both seasons, ranging from sixty to one hundred degrees Fahrenheit.

➡ Plant life in the savanna must be capable of surviving without much water for about half of the year. The grass grows to be quite thick and tall during the rainy season, sometimes reaching heights of ten feet, but then turns brown when there is a scarcity of water. Even though lightning often causes fire in the dry season, the grass survives because it stores water in its roots, ensuring that these remain unharmed even if the stems and leaves are destroyed by the flames. The grass roots actually supply water to the porous red soil rather than the other way around. Few trees can survive these conditions, but the baobab tree has adapted by growing leaves only when the rain falls and storing water in its thick trunk. The acacia tree grows roots so deep that they get past the soil, finding groundwater underneath. Acacia trees have also evolved to defend their leaves from animals. The leaves of these trees have sharp thorns, are often covered by stinging ants, and contain a poisonous chemical that discourages giraffes from munching on them.

➡ Wildlife, too, must cope with the extreme climate. Many species accomplish this by migrating throughout the savanna in search of territory that is not experiencing drought. Fortunately for the birds, insects, and mammals that thrive there, droughts are often localized. Some small animals burrow into the ground and remain inactive during the dry season. **A** In Africa, elephants utilize their long trunks and brute strength to break open baobab trees and suck water from the trees' trunks. **B** Other animals that make their homes in the African savanna include zebras, rhinoceroses, ostriches, cheetahs, hyenas, and leopards. **C** These creatures must contend with fire as well as drought. **D** The fork-tailed drongo bird, however, benefits from wildfires as it deliberately flies into the flames in order to dine on roasting insects. The savanna illustrates the remarkable ability of living organisms to adapt to harsh conditions.

Volume Review Help Back Next

1 Why does the author mention "a forest and a desert" in the passage?

Ⓐ To provide a description of landmasses near the equator
Ⓑ To explain why savannas are mostly found in Africa
Ⓒ To indicate the most common biomes on the planet
Ⓓ To introduce the physical features of a type of ecosystem

2 The word "intensity" in the passage is closest in meaning to

Ⓐ depth
Ⓑ distribution
Ⓒ length
Ⓓ power

3 Which of the sentences below best expresses the essential information in the highlighted sentence in the passage? *Incorrect* choices change the meaning in important ways or leave out essential information.

Ⓐ Only a small number of baobab trees have developed the ability to collect and store water.
Ⓑ The physical adaptations of the baobab tree enable it to stay alive where many others cannot.
Ⓒ Trees that can endure the harsh conditions typically only produce leaves when moisture is available.
Ⓓ The thickness of a tree's trunk determines whether it will be able to maintain an adequate water supply.

4 The word "them" in the passage refers to

Ⓐ leaves
Ⓑ trees
Ⓒ thorns
Ⓓ giraffes

5 According to paragraph 3, which of the following is NOT true of acacia trees?

Ⓐ They are full of stinging insects.
Ⓑ They have long and deep roots.
Ⓒ Their leaves are toxic.
Ⓓ They store water in their trunks.

Paragraph 3 is marked with an arrow [➡].

6 According to paragraph 3, why is grass in the savannah able to survive fires?

Ⓐ It grows quickly in the rainy season in order to store moisture.
Ⓑ It becomes thick and tall to protect the interior of its stem from flames.
Ⓒ It retains moisture in its roots so that part of it is not destroyed.
Ⓓ It absorbs water from the soil to make its leaves less flammable.

Paragraph 3 is marked with an arrow [➡].

7 The word "deliberately" in the passage is closest in meaning to

Ⓐ directly
Ⓑ obviously
Ⓒ immediately
Ⓓ intentionally

8 According to paragraph 4, migration is a viable strategy for some animals in a savanna because

Ⓐ rainfall is more common in the regions bordering a savanna
Ⓑ droughts occur in certain places with greater regularity
Ⓒ rain results in the creation of temporary bodies of water
Ⓓ water shortages are limited to specific parts of a savanna

Paragraph 4 is marked with an arrow [➡].

Volume Review Help Back Next

9 Look at the four squares [■] that indicate where the following sentence could be added to the passage.

For example, burrowing animals dig deeper into the ground to avoid the heat and flames.

Where would the sentence best fit?

Click on a square [■] to add the sentence to the passage.

10 **Directions:** An introductory sentence for a brief summary of the passage is provided below. Complete the summary by selecting the THREE answer choices that express the most important ideas in the passage. Some sentences do not belong in the summary because they express ideas that are not presented in the passage or are minor ideas in the passage. **This question is worth 2 points.**

Drag your answer choices to the spaces where they belong.
To remove an answer choice, click on it. To review the passage, click on **View Text**.

The savanna biome presents significant challenges for the organisms that inhabit it.

•
•
•

Answer Choices

Ⓐ Animals have acquired a number of physical and behavioral traits to survive the extreme climatic conditions.

Ⓑ Both baobab and acacia trees have developed a unique method to access water when it is available.

Ⓒ The existence of distinct wet and dry seasons means that rainfall does not occur throughout much of the year.

Ⓓ Savannas are most common in Africa, where they cover a significant portion of the landmass.

Ⓔ This type of ecosystem includes plants that are less likely to die during periods of extended drought.

Ⓕ The threat of fires caused by lightning strikes is higher in the dry season than in the rainy season.

Answer Book p. 23

Answer Book p. 24

TOEFL Reading

Factors in Jellyfish Population Growth

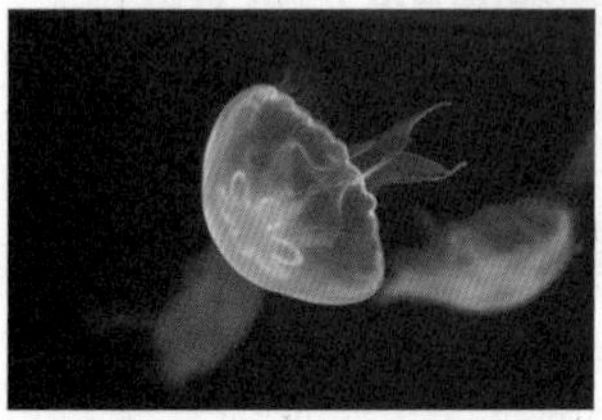

Jellyfish are a broad group of sea creatures that includes over 2,000 species of gelatinous zooplankton. These unusual creatures lack most of the vital organs that are considered important for animal survival. Yet, their simple physiology allows them to adapt to a wide variety of conditions. This adaptability has enabled their numbers to rise despite factors like pollution and climate change.

➡ Scientists posit that carbon dioxide (CO_2) pollution plays a considerable role in the population growth of jellyfish. CO_2 emissions have steadily altered temperatures through global warming. This process restricts the escape of heat from the atmosphere, warming the air and water. Researchers have discovered that warmer water results in an increase in the population size of many types of jellyfish because it enables them to reproduce for longer periods of the year and to generate more offspring. Moreover, global warming results in the increased acidification of the oceans, as atmospheric CO_2 dissolves in water to form carbonic acid. Acid lowers the pH of the water to a level that can be fatal to many organisms. For example, it diminishes the survival rate of fish larvae by removing their ability to smell, making them vulnerable to predators. However, for jellyfish, high acidity seems to have little impact, and, with less biological diversity due to the die-offs of other creatures, jellyfish can become dominant in the ecosystem.

➡ The excessive fertilization of agricultural crops can also positively affect the jellyfish population through eutrophication, wherein fertilizer runoff eventually ends up in a water source. In this process, the overly nutritious water generates dense plant growth by providing a fresh source of nitrogen. **A** This can provoke an algae bloom on the water's surface, creating a problem when a large population of algae reproduces and dies, sinking to the sea floor. **B** The abnormal volume of algae decomposition then depletes the oxygen supply, thereby suffocating the oxygen-dependent species and forming dead zones. **C** Jellyfish, however, have a high tolerance to low-oxygen conditions, meaning that they can survive in areas where eutrophication has taken place. **D**

➡ In addition, overfishing reduces the innate predation and competition that keep jellyfish populations in check and prevent their spread to new territory. Commercial fishing continues to remove great numbers of the large fish that are the primary predators of jellyfish. It also harvests small fish like anchovies, which are major competitors of jellyfish as they depend upon the same food resources. The removal of these species encourages the proliferation of jellyfish. For example, industrial fishing in the Black Sea in the 1980s led to an irreversible decline in mackerel and bluefish, the fish that feed on jellyfish in the region. This resulted in a massive explosion in the number of jellyfish; in fact, it is now common for many coastal areas of the Black Sea to be inundated with millions of jellyfish at certain times of year.

Volume Review Help Back Next

1 Which of the sentences below best expresses the essential information in the highlighted sentence in the passage? *Incorrect* choices change the meaning in important ways or leave out essential information.

(A) The rising acidity of water encourages jellyfish reproduction at the expense of other marine species.
(B) Jellyfish can prevail in a habitat because unlike other organisms they are barely affected by the increase in acidity.
(C) The environmental effects of water acidification have been identified as a key factor in the decline of biological diversity.
(D) Creatures that are unable to cope with high acidity typically leave an ecosystem, allowing jellyfish to thrive.

2 According to paragraph 2, which of the following is true of carbon dioxide?

(A) It can limit ocean circulation.
(B) It can poison jellyfish.
(C) It can trap heat.
(D) It can increase the pH level of water.

Paragraph 2 is marked with an arrow [➡].

3 According to paragraph 2, highly acidic water affects fish populations by

(A) relocating critical resources
(B) changing the water temperature
(C) introducing new biological matter
(D) eliminating an important sense

Paragraph 2 is marked with an arrow [➡].

4 The word "provoke" in the passage is closest in meaning to

(A) demonstrate
(B) hinder
(C) persuade
(D) incite

5 Which of the following can be inferred from paragraph 3 about algae?

Ⓐ They absorb large quantities of oxygen as they decay.
Ⓑ They rise to the water's surface once they have died.
Ⓒ They serve as a food source for some jellyfish species.
Ⓓ They reproduce more rapidly in water with little oxygen.

Paragraph 3 is marked with an arrow [➡].

6 The word "irreversible" in the passage is closest in meaning to

Ⓐ deliberate
Ⓑ gradual
Ⓒ significant
Ⓓ permanent

7 The author discusses the Black Sea in paragraph 4 in order to

Ⓐ explain how native species can be protected from overfishing
Ⓑ show how certain jellyfish species have spread around the globe
Ⓒ demonstrate how a practice contributes to an increase in jellyfish
Ⓓ identify a potential candidate for the commercial fishing industry

Paragraph 4 is marked with an arrow [➡].

8 According to paragraph 4, why are anchovies a factor in managing jellyfish population size?

Ⓐ They rely on the same sources of nutrition as jellyfish.
Ⓑ They consume significant quantities of jellyfish.
Ⓒ They occupy habitats that are preferred by jellyfish.
Ⓓ They attract predatory species that hunt jellyfish.

Paragraph 4 is marked with an arrow [➡].

Volume Review Help Back Next

9 Look at the four squares [■] that indicate where the following sentence could be added to the passage.

These areas typically form where large rivers enter the sea and can create large marine deserts that are incapable of supporting much life.

Where would the sentence best fit?

Click on a square [■] to add the sentence to the passage.

10 **Directions:** An introductory sentence for a brief summary of the passage is provided below. Complete the summary by selecting the THREE answer choices that express the most important ideas in the passage. Some sentences do not belong in the summary because they express ideas that are not presented in the passage or are minor ideas in the passage. **This question is worth 2 points.**

Drag your answer choices to the spaces where they belong.
To remove an answer choice, click on it. To review the passage, click on **View Text**.

Scientists around the world are attempting to understand the factors behind the recent jellyfish population boom.

-
-
-

Answer Choices

(A) Jellyfish are able to circumvent the dangers of predation by eating fish larvae.

(B) Researchers discovered that jellyfish are able to regenerate within highly acidic waters.

(C) The pollution of water by overly nutritious runoff has contributed to the jellyfish problem.

(D) Many natural predators and rivals of jellyfish are commercially profitable.

(E) The rise in global temperatures has contributed to an increase in jellyfish reproduction.

(F) Overfishing diminishes the natural hazards and restrictions of the jellyfish population.

Answer Book p. 24

Vocabulary Review

Answer Book p. 25

A. Fill in the blanks with the appropriate words from the box.

downplayed	expertly	adaptability
porous	inactive	vulnerable

1 I have spider plants in my office because of their ______________ to a variety of temperatures.

2 In the past, most goods were ______________ made, but today, products are made to fall apart within a few years.

3 Though the volcano was very dangerous, it has been ______________ for thousands of years.

4 As elderly people are ______________ to many diseases, they need to take care of their health.

5 Margaret walked with a limp, but she ______________ the injury, insisting she didn't need help.

6 Athletes typically wear ______________ apparel that allows sweat and air to pass through.

B. Choose the closest meaning for each highlighted word or phrase.

7 The article published by the prominent writer was a repudiation of the current administration's immigration policies.
(A) deployment (B) rejection (C) examination (D) installation

8 Although the flood occurred very quickly, the recession of the water took weeks.
(A) saturation (B) inspection (C) transport (D) withdrawal

9 As we did not have a key for the abandoned building's door, we used brute force to open it.
(A) combined (B) superficial (C) external (D) physical

10 Some scholars believe William Shakespeare wrote the plays attributed to him, but others posit that they were written by a different author.
(A) endure (B) signify (C) assert (D) write

11 Coyotes have moved into urban neighborhoods, and many residents fear their tendency toward predation of local pets.
(A) restoration (B) hunting (C) accompaniment (D) detestation

12 Many Japanese families attempted the taming of raccoons, but these animals make terrible pets due to their aggressiveness.
(A) desolation (B) recognition (C) communication (D) domestication

13 The president insisted that all prisoners being held by the foreign government be repatriated to the United States at once.
(A) returned (B) exiled (C) reported (D) followed

14 There was a crime in the neighborhood, and the police must pin down who is responsible.
(A) deny (B) memorize (C) specify (D) analyze

CHAPTER 05

Negative Fact

Negative Fact

About the Question Type

Negative Fact questions ask you to identify specific information that is NOT true according to the passage or NOT mentioned in the passage.

These questions usually contain the words *NOT* or *EXCEPT*. Be careful to select the answer choice that includes information that is contradicted by the passage or not mentioned in the passage.

Question Format

- According to paragraph #, which of the following is NOT true of X?
- According to paragraph #, all of the following are true of X EXCEPT
- The author mentions all of the following EXCEPT

Key Strategies

- **Step 1** — Read the question and identify the keywords. If the question indicates a specific paragraph, you can ignore the rest of the passage.
- **Step 2** — Scan the passage for the keywords, and locate the relevant information.
- **Step 3** — Verify each answer choice. Select the answer choice that includes information that is contradicted by the passage or not mentioned in the passage.

Example

Answer Book p. 26

Agrarian Reform after the American Civil War

Agrarian reform is the redistribution of a country's agricultural resources, and it is typically initiated by that country's government. The United States government made an attempt at agrarian reform after the American Civil War. In January 1865, the war had not yet ended, but the outcome had become clear, and the government began to prepare for victory. Chief among the issues to be resolved was the fate of thousands of African-American slaves who were to be freed. Union General William Sherman met with a group of African-American ministers in the Confederate state of Georgia. The consensus among the group was that African Americans wanted freedom, education, and land. Four days later, Sherman issued an order setting aside 400,000 acres of land that had been confiscated from Confederate landholders for 40,000 African-American families. Because Sherman's order specified that each family was eligible to receive up to 40 acres of land and some families were also given leftover Army mules, the plan became known as "40 acres and a mule."

This attempt at agrarian reform did not succeed, however. Sherman's directive was reversed in the autumn of 1865 by President Andrew Johnson, who insisted that the land be returned to its Confederate owners. Other land distribution programs approved by Congress, such as the Homestead Act of 1862 and the Southern Homestead Act of 1866, might have provided opportunities for freed slaves to procure land, but prices were set too high for people with virtually no access to money. Instead, most of the land offered by those programs went to whites.

1 According to paragraph 1, which of the following is NOT true of the "40 acres and a mule" plan?

(A) It offered land to the families of former slaves.
(B) It proposed that each black family receive a mule.
(C) It was ordered by Union General William Sherman.
(D) It was inspired by a meeting with African-American ministers.

2 According to paragraph 2, all of the following prevented freed slaves from acquiring land EXCEPT

(A) the will of the President of the United States
(B) the high price of land distributed by the government
(C) their lack of access to funds to buy land
(D) discriminatory laws passed by Congress

Answer Book p. 26

The Geology of the Appalachian Mountains

Among the world's oldest mountains, the Appalachians stretch across the eastern seaboard of North America for 2,000 miles, all the way from Alabama to Newfoundland in Canada. The mountain range features a variety of rocks that reflect different eras and causes of formation. These include outcroppings of truly ancient rocks, and, most famously, rich coal beds, which powered much of the region's economy in the industrial era. Studying the Appalachians' long and tumultuous geological history provides a window into how the earth's landmasses have formed and transformed over the ages.

In broad terms, the Appalachians can be divided into two distinct subcategories. In the northeast, the Old Appalachians are composed of crystalline rocks that formed between 1.1 billion and 541 million years ago. In that Precambrian era of violent upheavals in the earth's crust, intense volcanic activity formed rocks that were immediately transformed under extremes of pressure and heat. This created quartz and marble, as well as hard granite, outcroppings of which can still be found in the US and Canada today. These rocks predate the appearance of plant or animal life on the planet and were formed under harsh enough conditions that they bear no trace of microorganisms either.

Further south sit the New Appalachians, which mostly consist of sedimentary rocks that date back 252 to 541 million years to the Paleozoic age. This region's rocks formed with a gentler and slower process and had plentiful contact with plants and animals, making them rich in fossils. These softer sedimentary rocks like sandstone, shale, and limestone are accumulations of other rocks and organic material that came together on the ocean floor or at the edge of a shallow sea that divided the emerging North American continent from Gondwanaland—a continent that included present-day Florida, along with South America and Africa. In some places, which were deep underwater, rich veins of metal, particularly copper, fused into rock. In the second half of this time frame, as the sea receded, much of the new Appalachian region was covered in swamp forests. These accumulated huge amounts of organic material, which would go on to form the rich coal beds found in present-day West Virginia and Pennsylvania.

But regardless of whether their rocks formed in volcanoes, swamps, or on sea floors, both ends of the Appalachian range rose up from the surrounding land due to the same cause: continental collision. First, around 400 million years ago, the Old Appalachians rose as proto-North America crashed into proto-Europe. Then, the New Appalachians soared as they slammed into Gondwanaland around 250 million years ago. These collisions would fuse together the supercontinent of Pangea, with mountains pushed up via the process of subduction—the same force that formed the mighty Himalayas; in fact, 200 million years ago, the Appalachians would have been of comparable height. The Appalachians are thus not only an example of the power of erosion but also a testament to the enduring nature of their history.

1 According to paragraph 1, the Appalachian Mountains benefit people living in the region because they

(A) extend for a great distance along the coast
(B) include large quantities of coal
(C) attract tourists from all over the world
(D) feature rock formations that do not appear elsewhere

2 The word "predate" in the passage is closest in meaning to

(A) facilitate
(B) accommodate
(C) antedate
(D) instigate

3 According to paragraph 2, all of the following are features of the crystalline rocks in the Old Appalachians EXCEPT:

(A) They are hundreds of millions of years old.
(B) They are found in multiple countries.
(C) They were formed by volcanic eruptions.
(D) They were created after life developed.

4 According to paragraph 3, which of the following did NOT play a role in the formation of the New Appalachians?

(A) The buildup of substances in marine environments
(B) The incorporation of metal into rock formations
(C) The growth of vegetation after sea levels dropped
(D) The absorption of large coal deposits in certain areas

5 Which of the sentences below best expresses the essential information in the highlighted sentence in the passage?

(A) The presence of rocks formed in different conditions determined the characteristics of each part of the Appalachians.
(B) No matter the source of the rocks, the collision of landmasses caused the rise of the Appalachians.
(C) Because of continental collision, the Appalachians are composed of a wide range of rocks at various heights.
(D) The movement of the continents combined with other forces to lift the Appalachian rocks high above their surroundings.

6 According to paragraph 4, which of the following do the Himalayas and the Appalachians have in common?

(A) They were shaped through subduction.
(B) They were formed at the same time.
(C) They were fused when Pangea appeared.
(D) They were originally part of Gondwanaland.

Reading Practice 2

Answer Book p. 27

Fauvism

The early twentieth-century art movement known as Fauvism was a brightly colored declaration of independence from Impressionism, which itself represented a significant break from long-standing Western art traditions. In the 1870s, the Impressionists' subjective rendering of everyday things had liberated painting from its bondage to realistic forms in historical, religious, or mythological contexts. The 1880s found Post-Impressionist artists like Vincent Van Gogh and Paul Cezanne extending the bounds of Impressionism from merely recording subjective visual perceptions to experimenting with expressing the emotional impact of what they viewed. However, by 1905, Henri Matisse and André Derain, both of whom had previously been adherents of the Post-Impressionist approach, were ready for an even bolder experiment based on the idea that unmixed colors straight from the tube could express emotion without regard to the colors that appeared in nature.

The two young painters spent a summer working together in a small fishing port on the Mediterranean coast, impulsively splashing outlandish colors on traditional images. When these paintings were presented at the Salon d'Automne in Paris, the usually progressive jury found them offensive. Matisse, the elder and more accomplished of the duo, was urged to withdraw *Woman with a Hat*, a portrait of his wife rendered in splotches of unnatural green, purple, and pink. After a friend ensured that the painting would be hung next to Derain's turquoise-faced portrait of Matisse, *Woman with a Hat* was purchased by the celebrated American writer Gertrude Stein, whose brother Leo described it as "the nastiest smear of paint I had ever seen." A dismayed critic defined the movement by referring to the painters and their works as *fauves*, a disparaging French term meaning "wild beasts," and this was quickly adopted as the name of the new movement.

Fauvist paintings are characterized by their bold palette of bright colors. **A** In essence, the Fauvist painters were interested in utilizing the potential of colors to convey intense feelings rather than in accurately portraying how objects appeared in real life. **B** Their goal was to free color from the subject matter and to instead use it to stimulate an emotional response from a viewer. **C** In order to achieve this, Fauvist artists would often intentionally juxtapose clashing colors. **D**

The intensity of the Fauvist movement was matched by its brevity. By 1908, many of the artists who had played an important role in the development of this artistic style had moved on to other endeavors. For example, the artist Georges Braque, whose Fauvist paintings include repeating geometric shapes, pioneered Cubism along with the Spanish artist Pablo Picasso. However, Fauvism would have an enduring influence, as many modern art movements, in particular Expressionism, incorporated the Fauvist permissive approach to color and applied it to other elements of a painting, such as the composition, lines, and shapes.

Glossary

· juxtapose: to put contrasting things next to each other

1 According to paragraph 1, how did Van Gogh and Cezanne push the boundaries of Impressionism?

(A) They included subjects that had a mythological origin.
(B) They tried to express interpretations of visual stimuli.
(C) They attempted to convey the feelings a scene invoked.
(D) They placed commonplace objects in an artistic context.

2 The word "outlandish" in the passage is closest in meaning to

(A) external
(B) bizarre
(C) incoherent
(D) mandatory

3 According to paragraph 2, which of the following is NOT true of Matisse's painting *Woman with a Hat*?

(A) It generated controversy when it was introduced.
(B) It depicts a person with whom Matisse had a relationship.
(C) It was first displayed next to a self-portrait by Matisse.
(D) It was purchased by an acclaimed author from the US.

4 Look at the four squares [■] that indicate where the following sentence could be added to the passage.

In some cases, they went further than this by selecting just a few hues from opposite ends of the color spectrum to serve as the palette for a painting.

Where would the sentence best fit?

5 The word "stimulate" in the passage is closest in meaning to

(A) administer
(B) dismiss
(C) arouse
(D) detach

6 All of the following are mentioned about Fauvism EXCEPT:

(A) Its developers had been followers of the Post-Impressionist movement.
(B) Its name was derived from a derogatory comment by a critic.
(C) Its works included atypical colors to more accurately reflect reality.
(D) Its premise was adopted and expanded by subsequent art styles.

Reading Practice 3

Answer Book p. 28

The Empire of Alexander the Great

Almost from the moment he became the king of Macedonia in 336 BC, Alexander the Great began his military conquests. The twenty-year-old ruler inherited a collection of Greek city-states that had already been united by his father, Philip II, and he aspired to add to that kingdom. Influenced by his childhood teacher, the great Greek philosopher Aristotle, Alexander was determined to spread Greek culture throughout the world. To do that, however, he knew that he would have to respect the cultures of the states he conquered. By balancing these two seemingly conflicting goals, Alexander was able to build the most expansive empire the world had ever seen.

After Philip II was assassinated by a royal bodyguard, Alexander's first aim was to fulfill his father's dream of defeating the Persian Empire. The Persians controlled a vast territory from the Balkans to Pakistan and had attempted to take over the Greek states. In 334 BC, Alexander invaded cities in the western portion of modern-day Turkey, cutting off the Persians from their naval bases. The next year, he defeated Darius III of Persia in a battle near modern Syria despite being badly outnumbered. From the beginning, Alexander showed great respect for Persian culture by wearing Persian clothes, adopting many of Persian customs, and acknowledging the right of defeated leaders to continue to run day-to-day affairs. He was so zealous in his acceptance of his enemy's ways that some of his companions began to resent him for it.

Alexander then marched into northern Africa and conquered Egypt, once a leading world power. He asked to be crowned pharaoh, which won him the favor of the Egyptian public as well as the priests. Using this political capital to propagate his own culture, he founded the Greek-style city of Alexandria, which featured a Greek theater, a Greek gymnasium, and became famous for its vast Greek library. With this done, Alexander moved his army into the Punjab region of India. In 326 BC, he met King Porus of Paurava in battle. It was the first time the Macedonian emperor had ever encountered an army flanked by elephants. He ordered that the massive animals be attacked with javelins, but that only created a chaotic scene in which both armies were trampled. In the end, however, Porus's inexperienced soldiers were no match for Alexander's professional warriors. Alexander agreed to treat Porus like a king, once again gaining political advantage by adopting a respectful attitude toward his enemies.

The great warrior-king died at the age of 32, perhaps the victim of malaria, assassination by a rival who wanted to take over his empire, or overconsumption of wine, but the Greek influence that Alexander the Great brought to the far reaches of the world known to him lasted for centuries. He had accomplished both of his primary goals, spreading Greek ideas while allowing the territories he conquered with his armies to retain their essential characteristics.

1 According to paragraph 1, which of the following is true of the empire of Alexander the Great?

(A) Most of it was inherited from his father.
(B) It was the largest in world history at the time.
(C) All of it was gained through military conquests.
(D) It suppressed the cultures of conquered states.

2 According to paragraph 2, all of the following were true of the Persians EXCEPT:

(A) Their rulers remained in power after Alexander's victory.
(B) They operated military facilities in an area now part of Turkey.
(C) Their armies were always smaller than Alexander's forces.
(D) They had tried to conquer territories controlled by the Greeks.

3 The word "propagate" in the passage is closest in meaning to

(A) investigate
(B) neglect
(C) eradicate
(D) spread

4 Which of the following can be inferred from paragraph 3 about King Porus?

(A) He conquered the Punjab using tactics learned from the Macedonians.
(B) His strategy of using elephants in battle proved to be ineffective.
(C) His army was involved in many conflicts before fighting the Macedonians.
(D) He was executed after being defeated by Alexander in battle.

5 The word "their" in the passage refers to

(A) goals
(B) ideas
(C) territories
(D) armies

6 Which of the following is NOT mentioned in paragraph 4 as a potential explanation of Alexander's death?

(A) He was injured in battle.
(B) He became stricken with illness.
(C) He drank too much alcohol.
(D) He was killed by a political enemy.

Answer Book p. 29

TOEFL Reading

The Environmental Cost of Organic Farming

➡ In the minds of many environmentally conscious consumers concerned about the excesses of conventional farming, organic products are a "green" alternative. This perception is rooted in fact: organic farms do not use synthetic pesticides or fertilizers, which can damage soil, reduce biodiversity in local ecosystems, contaminate water supplies, and compromise the health of farmers. Consequently, despite prices that are considerably higher than those of conventional products, revenues from sales of organic goods are expected to increase from $52.3 billion in 2020 to $96 billion by 2028 in the United States. The South Asian nation of Bhutan even aims to convert to 100 percent organic by 2035. However, most consumers are unaware of the environmental costs of organic farming.

➡ Organic farms actually increase the burden of carbon in our atmosphere more than conventional farms, thereby increasing the dangers of climate change. The problem is that chemical pesticides, while potentially harmful to many organisms (including humans), are actually effective at increasing crop yields. Organic farms lose crops to insects and other pests, so they require more land to grow the same amount of produce as conventional farms. More land for food leaves less land for forests, and the resulting decline in the amount of carbon being stored is a direct contributor to global warming because greater quantities of greenhouse gases accumulate in the atmosphere.

➡ Also of concern are the environmental costs of some of the natural pesticides and fertilizers used by organic farmers. Many organic farms use sulfur to deter crop-consuming creatures because it is believed to be less toxic than pesticides made with synthetic chemicals. **A** While this substance is relatively less harmful, there are still serious issues associated with its use. **B** For example, farmers handling sulfur must wear eye and skin protection to avoid irritation during field work, and it is also known to cause harmful acid rain. **C** Additionally, while manure is a natural fertilizer, less than 50 percent of the nitrogen produced by manure is absorbed by crops. **D** Just because a substance is naturally produced does not necessarily mean it is not harmful to the environment.

➡ A variety of solutions are required to address the environmental concerns raised by the organic approach to agriculture. Because they are less efficient at producing large crop yields, organic farms may not be capable of meeting the global 59 percent increase in demand for food expected over the next three decades without creating dangerous increases in greenhouse gas emissions. Therefore, the world's agriculture industries must strike a balance between organic and conventional farming. With regard to the problem of environmentally harmful pesticides and fertilizers, organic farmers in industrialized nations could learn from organic farmers in developing countries like India. There, organic farms use biodiversity as a strategy for sustainability by growing plants that naturally inhibit pests and using <u>legumes</u> as an organic source of nitrogen

Volume Review Help Back Next

instead of manure or synthetic fertilizers.

Glossary
legume: A plant that has seeds in a pod, like beans and peas

1 The word "conscious" in the passage is closest in meaning to

(A) mainstream
(B) deliberate
(C) aware
(D) compliant

2 Why does the author mention the nation of Bhutan in paragraph 1?

(A) To stress the extent to which organic farming is expected to increase
(B) To suggest that organic farming methods originated outside the US
(C) To explain why organic farm products have risen in cost significantly
(D) To compare the value of organic goods in countries around the world

Paragraph 1 is marked with an arrow [➡].

3 The word "they" in the passage refers to

(A) farms
(B) crops
(C) insects
(D) pests

4 According to paragraph 2, which of the following is true of organic farms?

(A) They have lower crop yields than conventional farms.
(B) They use less land than conventional farms.
(C) They capture more carbon emissions than conventional farms.
(D) They are preferable to conventional farms from an environmental perspective.

Paragraph 2 is marked with an arrow [➡].

5 According to paragraph 3, why is the use of sulfur a popular form of pest control among organic farmers?

(A) It does not result in health problems among farm laborers.
(B) It neutralizes the effects of acidic precipitation on plants.
(C) It does not cause as much harm as artificial products.
(D) It costs significantly less than other types of pesticides.

Paragraph 3 is marked with an arrow [➡].

6 Which of the sentences below best expresses the essential information in the highlighted sentence in the passage? *Incorrect* choices change the meaning of the sentence in important ways or leave out essential information.

(A) Relying on organic farms, which have smaller yields, to feed a growing population will result in increased greenhouse gas emissions.
(B) Population growth may prevent organic farms from producing adequate yields, since greenhouse gases have increased.
(C) Organic farms do not have enough land to produce the food required by a growing population.
(D) Greenhouse gases will increase if the demand for food rises over the next three decades.

7 The word "inhibit" in the passage is closest in meaning to

(A) imply
(B) discourage
(C) extricate
(D) manage

8 Which of the following is NOT mentioned in paragraph 4 as a potential solution?

(A) Using both organic and conventional farming techniques
(B) Growing legumes to release nitrogen into the atmosphere
(C) Selecting crops that do not require pesticides
(D) Avoiding the use of certain types of fertilizers

Paragraph 4 is marked with an arrow [➡].

Volume Review Help Back Next

9 Look at the four squares [■] that indicate where the following sentence could be added to the passage.

The rest can contaminate groundwater and end up in the atmosphere as a greenhouse gas.

Where would the sentence best fit?

Click on a square [■] to add the sentence to the passage.

10 **Directions:** An introductory sentence for a brief summary of the passage is provided below. Complete the summary by selecting the THREE answer choices that express the most important ideas in the passage. Some sentences do not belong in the summary because they express ideas that are not presented in the passage or are minor ideas in the passage. **This question is worth 2 points.**

Drag your answer choices to the spaces where they belong.
To remove an answer choice, click on it. To review the passage, click on **View Text**.

Despite the perceived benefits of organic farming, this practice is known to cause harm to the environment.

-
-
-

Answer Choices

Ⓐ A reduction in crop yields has led many organic farmers to begin using more toxic forms of pesticides.

Ⓑ Reduced crop production necessitates the utilization of more land, leaving fewer potential trees to lessen atmospheric carbon.

Ⓒ Combining organic and conventional farming methods and adopting less harmful organic agriculture practices are likely solutions.

Ⓓ The overall value of organic farm goods has increased significantly, and this trend is likely to continue in the near future.

Ⓔ Farmers in developing countries must adopt more advanced organic farming techniques to address environmental issues.

Ⓕ Organic methods of pest control and soil fertilization contribute to both air and water pollution.

Answer Book p. 29

Answer Book p. 30

TOEFL Reading

The History of the Adding Machine

➡ Blaise Pascal, a gifted mathematician and inventor, was the son of a tax collector in a small town in southern France. To assist his father in his work, he devised a simple adding machine consisting of ten numbered wheels linked by gears. Called the Pascaline, this first mechanical calculator could add and subtract numbers up to eight digits long. Although offering a substantial improvement over manual calculations, the machine was considered expensive and unreliable, and only Pascal himself had the knowledge to make the necessary repairs if it malfunctioned. In addition, accountants discouraged the use of the machine for fear of losing their jobs. Despite these issues, Pascal's innovative device laid the groundwork for future devices and was the precursor to the modern computer.

➡ The Burroughs adding machine, named after its inventor William Seward Burroughs, was built and patented in 1885. This adding machine required users to pull a handle in order to execute a calculation. Novice users would get wildly differing sums depending on the amount of force they applied to it. The design flaws and prohibitive cost of the original machines led to commercial failure, and the first 50 were recalled. Burroughs, however, continued working on an improved calculating machine, which incorporated the use of a hydraulic governor. **A** The component enabled the machine to operate properly regardless of the manner in which the handle was pulled. **B** The machine caught on with businesses, and sales had climbed dramatically by the turn of the century. **C** Later models would include electronic motors to replace the hand-driven cranks. **D** Depressible keys were also added to this second-generation model, and it had the ability to print its calculations on paper.

➡ In 1887, a young mechanic named Dorr Felt developed the first practical calculator to use a keyboard, named the Comptometer. His design was based on a carry mechanism that was fast enough to allow the keys to return to their original state after being depressed and a lever to clear calculations. Though exceedingly fast and reliable, these machines had to be used by an expert who was specially trained in their operation. The machine was produced for over 40 years because of its unique capabilities, and a number of improvements were made to it during this time.

➡ Fail-safe keys locked the machine, which prevented a partial press from generating errors as it would have in earlier models. An unlimited number of keys could also be pressed, allowing for faster calculations. Another feature, called a duplex design, held a running total in a second set of dial wheels while the primary wheels continued to add, and subtotal amounts that could be transferred at any time to the running total.

Glossary

governor: an attachment to a machine for automatic control or limitation of speed

Volume Review Help Back Next

1 Why does the author mention "the modern computer" in the passage?

(A) To suggest that Pascal's adding machine had a wide variety of useful functions
(B) To stress the influence of an invention on the development of later technologies
(C) To demonstrate that Pascal's calculator was more advanced than others at the time
(D) To make a comparison between different types of devices utilized to make calculations

2 In paragraph 1, the author mentions all of the following about Blaise Pascal EXCEPT:

(A) His father was a government official.
(B) He was knowledgeable about arithmetic.
(C) His adding machine included many flaws.
(D) He took a position as an accountant.

Paragraph 1 is marked with an arrow [➡].

3 The word "execute" in the passage is closest in meaning to

(A) modify
(B) display
(C) confirm
(D) perform

4 The word "it" in the passage refers to

(A) machine
(B) handle
(C) calculation
(D) force

5 According to paragraph 2, which of the following is true of the original Burroughs adding machines?

Ⓐ They were closely modeled on the design of the Pascaline.
Ⓑ They did not attract many buyers.
Ⓒ They were affordable to the majority of people.
Ⓓ They did not succeed in receiving a patent.

Paragraph 2 is marked with an arrow [➡].

6 Which of the sentences below best expresses the essential information in the highlighted sentence in the passage? *Incorrect* answer choices change the meaning in important ways or leave out essential information.

Ⓐ The device was upgraded during its period of production, which was substantial due to its special functions.
Ⓑ The extensive length of time that the device was manufactured was the result of several enhancements to its design.
Ⓒ Although the device was utilized for over four decades, there were many changes to its features.
Ⓓ Because of its unusual abilities, the adding machine remained in use for much longer than expected.

7 According to paragraph 3, the original Comptometer included a component that

Ⓐ allowed multiple keyboards to be attached
Ⓑ enabled keys to go back to their initial position
Ⓒ prevented operators from inputting inaccurate data
Ⓓ eliminated the need to remove calculations with a lever

Paragraph 3 is marked with an arrow [➡].

8 According to paragraph 4, which of the following was NOT an improvement made to the Comptometer?

Ⓐ A feature to speed up calculations
Ⓑ A mechanism to delete errors
Ⓒ Fail-safe keys
Ⓓ Two sets of dial wheels

Paragraph 4 is marked with an arrow [➡].

Volume Review Help Back Next

9 Look at the four squares [■] that indicate where the following sentence could be added to the passage.

In fact, the machine was so successful that the company Burroughs founded would become the largest manufacturer of adding machines in the United States.

Where would the sentence best fit?

Click on a square [■] to add the sentence to the passage.

10 Directions: An introductory sentence for a brief summary of the passage is provided below. Complete the summary by selecting the THREE answer choices that express the most important ideas in the passage. Some sentences do not belong in the summary because they express ideas that are not presented in the passage or are minor ideas in the passage. **This question is worth 2 points.**

Drag your answer choices to the spaces where they belong.
To remove an answer choice, click on it. To review the passage, click on **View Text**.

The adding machine or calculator was developed by several people over a period of hundreds of years.

-
-
-

Answer Choices

Ⓐ Dorr Felt was the inventor of the first useful device with a keyboard to input the information necessary to do calculations.

Ⓑ Blaise Pascal learned how to make adding machines by watching his father calculate large sums while performing his work duties.

Ⓒ Although the adding machine invented by Blaise Pascal had significant problems, his work laid the foundation for subsequent, more effective devices.

Ⓓ Once William Burroughs had addressed the initial problems with the design of the calculator he invented, it became popular with consumers.

Ⓔ Although Dorr Felt's device enabled operators to perform calculations more quickly than could be done with other machines, it was very unreliable.

Ⓕ After working with Pascal as an accountant for several years, Burroughs began to design and build his own style of adding machines.

Answer Book p. 30

Vocabulary Review

Answer Book p. 31

A. Fill in the blanks with the appropriate words from the box.

deter	testament	tumultuous
confiscated	upheavals	adherents

1 ______________ of Confucius tried to live up to his commitment to education and ethics.

2 The award Ellen received serves as a(n) ______________ to her commitment to our community.

3 French history is full of political ______________, but none was more violent and disruptive than the French Revolution.

4 After inspecting the suitcase, the customs officer ______________ several items from the traveler.

5 The 1960s are remembered for ______________ events such as the Vietnam War and the civil rights movement.

6 The municipality put up DO NOT ENTER signs intended to ______________ trespassers.

B. Choose the closest meaning for each highlighted word or phrase.

7 Judges should not let their subjective opinions influence their decisions in legal matters.
(A) personal (B) repugnant (C) political (D) merited

8 In *The Seagull*, a young playwright's mother makes disparaging comments about his play, prompting him to run away.
(A) belittling (B) laudatory (C) thoughtful (D) academic

9 Collin resented his colleague's promotion as he felt he was better suited for the position.
(A) protested (B) prevented (C) disliked (D) rejected

10 The ski resort had to close early because there was virtually no snow on the mountain.
(A) immediately (B) partly (C) nearly (D) already

11 In order to be eligible to win a cruise in the Bahamas, you have to make a donation to charity.
(A) inspired (B) qualified (C) destined (D) willing

12 Lincoln's speech about the end of slavery is remembered as much for its brevity as its content.
(A) briefness (B) complacency (C) importance (D) kindness

13 After World War II ended, soldiers in the streets of New York impulsively kissed women who were strangers.
(A) spontaneously (B) unfortunately (C) sedately (D) gently

14 After the votes were counted, the candidate acknowledged his opponent's victory in the election.
(A) insisted (B) denied (C) forgave (D) recognized

CHAPTER 06

Inference

Inference

About the Question Type

Inference questions ask you to identify information that is implied but not explicitly stated in the passage.

These questions require you to draw a logical conclusion based on the information in the passage. Be careful to use only the information presented in the passage to select the correct answer choice. Do not draw any conclusions based on what you know about the topic from other sources.

Question Format

- Which of the following can be inferred from paragraph # about X?
- In paragraph #, what does the author imply about X?
- It can be inferred from paragraph # that

Key Strategies

- **Step 1** — Read the question and identify the keywords.
- **Step 2** — Scan the passage for the keywords, and locate the relevant information.
- **Step 3** — Select the answer choice that is a logical conclusion based on the information in the passage.

Example

Answer Book p. 32

Bird Feathers

Although the shape and size of feathers vary according to the type of bird, the formation process is the same in all cases. Feathers are outgrowths of tissue that receive nourishment from blood vessels in the skin. When the feather is fully grown, the blood supply is halted and the central shaft becomes hollow. Should the feather fall off in a process known as molting or be pulled out, a secretion from the bird's thyroid gland will stimulate the follicle to develop a new feather.

Feathers serve multiple purposes. For a bird to use its feathers in flight, the feathers need to be very strong but also light and flexible. Birds with heavy feathers cannot become airborne. The feathers are arranged in an ordered fashion over the body. They overlap each other, usually covering most of a bird's skin. This overlapping in a curved and streamlined shape is perfect for flight. Feathers are also useful to birds for various forms of display and camouflage. For example, the colorful, spiraling feathers of the male king bird-of-paradise help it find a mate, while the bright green feathers of the parrot help it blend in with its surroundings in the rainforest. In some climates, birds need feathers to provide insulation from cold and rain. Loons, for instance, spend most of their time in the water, making their feather's waterproof qualities essential.

Glossary

- thyroid gland: a cluster of cells that produce and regulate certain hormones in the body
- follicle: a small cavity in which material is contained or from which a structure grows

1 Which of the following can be inferred from paragraph 1 about feathers?

(A) Feathers contain blood before they are fully grown.
(B) Older birds cannot generate new feathers after molting.
(C) The bird's blood vessels stimulate the follicles to grow new feathers.
(D) Once a feather falls out, new follicles grow in the skin.

2 In paragraph 2, what does the author imply about the king bird-of-paradise?

(A) Flight is impossible due to the shape and texture of the feathers.
(B) The display methods used by females increase their chance of mating.
(C) Visual appearance plays a role in the reproductive success of males.
(D) The qualities of the feathers make camouflage an effective survival method.

Answer Book p. 32

Human Activity and Erosion

Erosion often involves the transportation of soil by water or wind. In the case of the former, water from torrential rains or overflowing rivers moves over the ground's surface, displacing the soil. Wind erosion occurs when strong air currents pick up soil particles and carry them great distances. Regardless of the mechanism, the end result is the same: a large quantity of soil is dispersed over a vast area. Although erosion is a natural process, it is exacerbated by human activities such as farming and logging.

Soil can become susceptible to erosion due to agricultural practices, particularly mechanical tilling. This process involves the use of tractors to loosen the surface soil so that seeds can be planted. Unfortunately, the heavy machines compact the underlying soil, meaning that water cannot penetrate easily. The soil then dries out and becomes highly vulnerable to the wind. A notable example of this is the North American Dust Bowl of the 1930s, when the central United States was battered by dust storms carrying millions of tons of topsoil through the air. These storms made many areas unsuitable for growing crops and forced masses of agricultural workers to migrate. The event was triggered in part by the rapid mechanization of the agriculture industry in the US: farmers tilled vast tracts of land with their new motorized equipment, leaving the soil precariously exposed to erosion.

Another human activity that contributes to erosion is overgrazing. When livestock is permitted to continuously consume the wild grasses and shrubs in an area for an extended period of time, the plants are unable to recover and the land soon lacks vegetation. With the topsoil uncovered, water and wind erosion become a significant risk. Perhaps nowhere are the effects of overgrazing more apparent than in the Sahel. This region of Africa, which extends from the Atlantic Ocean to the Red Sea, forms the boundary between the Sahara Desert and the more fertile savanna farther south. Although it has always been prone to drought, the Sahel has long supported farmers and nomadic herders. However, the rise in the human population during the early twentieth century resulted in an increasing number of cattle and sheep being let loose on the land to graze. Within a remarkably short period of time, many parts of this region became devoid of vegetation and subject to erosion.

Logging operations are another significant factor with regard to erosion, as deforestation directly contributes to soil mobility. Tree roots hold soil in place, and the threat of erosion significantly increases when these are removed. This is illustrated by the case of Costa Rica, which lost approximately 50 percent of its rainforest from 1940 to 1963. Ironically, much of the land was cleared to make it suitable for farming, but the process caused the loss of over 860 million tons of topsoil on an annual basis. The eroded soil washed into rivers and creeks and was carried downstream into the ocean, leaving the land much less fertile than it was before.

Glossary

· logging: the activity of cutting down trees in order to use their wood

1 According to paragraph 1, which of the following is true of human activities like farming and logging?

(A) They make the process of erosion worse.
(B) They are dependent on abundant soil.
(C) They cause soil to accumulate in certain areas.
(D) They cause more damage than natural erosion.

2 The word "precariously" in the passage is closest in meaning to

(A) exasperatingly
(B) perilously
(C) cumulatively
(D) tentatively

3 Which of the following can be inferred from the discussion of agriculture in paragraph 2?

(A) The use of mechanized farm equipment is an ineffective way to plant seeds.
(B) Compacted soil will only dry out during periods of limited rainfall.
(C) Seeds placed in the lower soil levels have a greater chance of producing crops.
(D) Past tilling methods were less likely to compress the soil than the modern approach.

4 Which of the sentences below best expresses the essential information in the highlighted sentence in the passage?

(A) Animals became an important food source as the human population exploded.
(B) Raising livestock became increasingly difficult as food became harder to locate.
(C) People devoted more time to caring for farm animals in the early 1900s.
(D) More livestock were allowed to graze as the number of people increased.

5 In paragraph 3, the author implies that the negative effects of grazing livestock can be avoided by

(A) keeping livestock in regions that include a wide variety of vegetation
(B) preventing herders from bringing their animals too close to farming communities
(C) allowing a mixture of different species to graze together in the same area
(D) ensuring that animals are regularly unable to access areas for set periods

6 According to paragraph 4, deforestation in Costa Rica occurred in part due to

(A) the need to augment falling revenues in the agricultural sector
(B) the interest of foreign logging companies in the rainforest
(C) the desire to acquire land to grow crops
(D) the urge to reclaim farms that had been lost to flooding

Answer Book p. 33

The End of the Silent Film Era

Audio and video reproduction both became possible in the same burst of invention that took place in the late nineteenth century. However, despite the efforts of Thomas Edison and others, it soon became conventional wisdom that sound and film were incompatible. And the film industry did not seem to need sound. In the early 1900s, Hollywood managed to become the cultural and commercial hub it is today thanks to silent films with soundtracks provided by local theater musicians.

Without the benefit of human voices, silent movies had developed into an art form characterized by broad, crowd-pleasing spectacle. Although silent films often included title cards with dialogue or exposition, these took up the entire screen and slowed down the action. To keep the public entertained, silent movies were mostly wordless and full of simple situations that could be taken in at a glance. Words were not essential to understanding the death-defying stunts of action-adventure pictures, nor were they necessary to interpret the exaggerated facial expressions and slapstick physicality of comedies.

Even as audio technology improved, major studios were reluctant to alter their winning formula. So it makes sense that the first one to match human voices to the action on screen was the relatively obscure Warner Brothers Studios in 1926. But even Warner Brothers mainly conceived of this as a way of adding music and comedy. At first, Vitaphone, the amplified sound system they licensed from Western Electric, was used to show brief vaudeville stage performances in which entertainers sang songs and told jokes directly to the camera, but these were shown only during interludes between silent movies. Only after 1927's *The Jazz Singer*, a full-length movie including some recorded music and a few pieces of dialogue, proved to be a surprise success at the box office did studios consider synchronizing speech throughout entire motion pictures.

Despite a steady stream of production in the late 1920s and early 1930s, movies with sound—or *talkies* as they came to be called—did not dominate the market quickly. [A] Purists insisted that this new form of cinema was an inferior product and a cheap gimmick. [B] Primitive microphones required actors to remain stationary onscreen. [C] This made for listless scenes with little action, and the problem was worsened by the fact that the loud whir of cameras meant camera operators had to remain inside a box to baffle the sound. [D] It also proved to be a major career obstacle for some popular actors whose voices did not match their looks. Moreover, the now-overworked projectionists struggled to keep the audio synchronized, as they had to drop a needle onto a record player when changing reels—and the audience erupted in boos whenever their timing was off. It would take years of improvements to camera systems, microphones, and projectors before talkies replaced silent films at the cinema.

1 It can be inferred from paragraph 2 that title cards were

(A) included in a film only when it was necessary
(B) employed to slow down the pace of a narrative
(C) used to cover a screen before a new scene began
(D) shown to present long dialogues between actors

2 The word "these" in the passage refers to

(A) performances
(B) entertainers
(C) songs
(D) jokes

3 According to paragraph 3, which of the following is true about the 1927 film *The Jazz Singer*?

(A) It was the first film with audio released by Warner Brothers.
(B) It featured a number of well-known musical performers.
(C) It was notably longer than other movies of the period.
(D) It exceeded expectations in terms of overall ticket sales.

4 Look at the four squares [■] that indicate where the following sentence could be added to the passage.

And there were a number of critical issues related to the new technology that made this criticism valid.

Where would the sentence best fit?

5 The word "listless" in the passage is closest in meaning to

(A) inaudible
(B) breathtaking
(C) unenergetic
(D) emboldened

6 Which of the following can be inferred from paragraph 4 about early projectionists?

(A) They improvised a variety of methods to add sound while a film was playing.
(B) They campaigned to prevent talkies from being shown in some theaters.
(C) They used cues from audience members to synchronize audio and video recordings.
(D) They resented the introduction of the technologies that made talkies possible.

Reading Practice 3

Answer Book p. 34

Fungi

Because fungi are typically immobile and grow on surfaces or from the soil, they were once viewed as plant relatives. However, scientists now recognize that fungi represent their own kingdom. A distinguishing characteristic of fungi is the way they absorb carbon externally rather than making it internally like photosynthetic plants. However, they are unlike animals in that they digest food before ingesting it. All fungi species are believed to have evolved from a single-celled organism with a flagellum, which is a whip-like tail used for locomotion. Collectively, fungi consist of an extremely variable group of approximately 150,000 species that occupy virtually every habitat on the planet.

Many fungi species depend on decaying organic matter, such as fallen trees, and aid in the process of decomposition by converting the cellulose and lignin in dead matter into sugars. They acquire nutrients by emitting enzymes that help to break down organic molecules, and then the complex cells of the fungi absorb nutrients left over from those. As a result of their activity, fungi recycle nutrients such as nitrogen and phosphorus, returning them to the earth so they can fortify soils and make it possible for new plants to flourish. Fungi that are decomposers can be classified as primary, secondary, or tertiary. Primary decomposers can survive on living or dying organisms and may be parasitic, but they mostly feed on dead matter and turn it into compost. Secondary decomposers rely on this compost for survival, whereas tertiary ones persist in the soil layer itself where organic matter is already highly decomposed.

Fungal reproduction is very diverse and can be either asexual or sexual. A simple type of asexual reproduction occurs in the root-like structure called the mycelium. The mycelium consists of thin white filaments that branch out in many directions. These filaments are called hyphae, and, if they are fragmented, the fragments each produce a new organism in the way that a severed root of some plants can produce a new shoot. Asexual reproduction can also occur through budding, whereby a bulge on the side of a cell forms and ultimately detaches with part of the original nucleus and creates a new cell. Another form of asexual reproduction is when a single parent releases spores. All of these methods result in the production of clones. In contrast, sexual reproduction requires two different parents and thus combines DNA from separate organisms. The process typically involves the fusing of two cells from separate fungi to create a zygote that contains a complete set of DNA from each of the original cells. The zygote then splits apart into four new cells with a different combination of this DNA. These are then dispersed by spores to form new fungi. The advantage of sexual reproduction is that it increases the overall diversity of the species.

Glossary

· zygote: a cell formed by the merger of two cells

1 The word "ingesting" in the passage is closest in meaning to

(A) completing
(B) acquiring
(C) identifying
(D) consuming

2 According to paragraph 1, fungi are different from plants because they

(A) are not dependent on the soil for nutrition
(B) acquire carbon from external sources
(C) are capable of fully digesting food
(D) evolved from single-celled organisms

3 The word "those" in the passage refers to

(A) enzymes
(B) organic molecules
(C) complex cells
(D) nutrients

4 What can be inferred from paragraph 2 about secondary decomposers?

(A) A small percentage of them are parasitic.
(B) They are the most common type of decomposer.
(C) They could not survive without primary decomposers.
(D) The majority of them reside within the soil layer.

5 Which of the following is NOT mentioned in paragraph 3 about asexual reproduction?

(A) It involves the fusing of two different cells.
(B) It can entail a portion of the nucleus detaching.
(C) It can occur when a single parent produces spores.
(D) It results in the generation of clones.

6 Which of the following can be inferred from paragraph 3 about the cells that result from the division of the zygote?

(A) They create offspring identical to the parents.
(B) They are genetically distinct from each other.
(C) They exchange DNA before their dispersal.
(D) They split into several cells with unique features.

iBT Reading Test 1

Answer Book p. 35

TOEFL Reading

The White House

➡ The construction of the White House resulted from a 1790 act of Congress declaring that the federal government would be situated in a district on the Potomac River, which led to the relocation of the presidential residence from New York to Washington D.C. in 1800. A city planner together with President George Washington chose the site for the residence. Nine proposals for the architectural design were submitted, with the one by Irish-born architect James Hoban being selected. His design was influenced by Leinster House, the parliamentary building in Dublin, which in turn was influenced by the Renaissance architecture of Andrea Palladio. Although George Washington oversaw the construction of the White House, he never lived in it. Its first residents were John Adams, the second president of the United States, and his wife Abigail.

➡ President Thomas Jefferson created a museum in the entrance hall and was also the first president to open the White House to public tours. It has remained open ever since, except during wartime. Jefferson also opened the doors on special days such as the Fourth of July and Inauguration Day. When "man of the people" Andrew Jackson was inaugurated in 1829, the White House was inundated with more than 20,000 ordinary citizens, who arrived to celebrate their candidate's victory. The party grew so large and disorderly that Jackson was forced to flee to the safety of a hotel. After that, the practice changed, and a grandstand was built in front of the White House for a presidential review of the troops. This procession evolved into the official inauguration parade of today.

➡ The White House has undergone substantial repairs and alterations over the centuries. During the War of 1812, British troops set the house on fire. Afterward, only a few external walls were still standing, and most of these needed to be replaced; however, new President James Monroe was able to move back in a year later. Further renovations occurred in 1881, when Chester Arthur installed Victorian decorations including a stained-glass window, and 1902, when Theodore Roosevelt restored the building's original classical look. The latter moved the president's offices from the second floor of the residence to the building's newly furnished West Wing. The next chief executive, William Howard Taft, had the famous Oval Office constructed in 1909. [A] By 1948, the aging White House was in danger of collapse due to poor maintenance, leading many people to promote tearing it down entirely. [B] However, First Lady Elizabeth Truman advocated restoring it to preserve its historical importance. [C] This intervention solidified the role of the first lady in White House affairs, and many subsequent ones, such as Jackie Kennedy and Hillary Clinton, have made major contributions to refurbishing the White House without sacrificing its legacy. [D]

Volume Review Help Back Next

1 Which of the sentences best expresses the essential information in the highlighted sentence in the passage? *Incorrect* choices change the meaning in important ways or leave out essential information.

Ⓐ It was in 1800 that the Congress approved a district on the Potomac River as the nation's capital.
Ⓑ A legislative act calling for the relocation of the president's home led to the creation of the White House.
Ⓒ After the passing of an act of Congress, the residence of the president was moved to New York.
Ⓓ In 1790, the Congress officially relocated the residence of the president to Washington D.C.

2 The word "oversaw" in the passage is closest in meaning to

Ⓐ mandated
Ⓑ supervised
Ⓒ approved
Ⓓ engineered

3 According to paragraph 1, which of the following is true of the location of the White House?

Ⓐ It was determined by an act of Congress in 1790.
Ⓑ It was jointly selected by the president and a city planner.
Ⓒ It was inspired by the layout of the city of Dublin.
Ⓓ It was originally intended to be New York City.

Paragraph 1 is marked with an arrow [➡].

4 The word "disorderly" in the passage is closest in meaning to

Ⓐ unruly
Ⓑ admiring
Ⓒ violent
Ⓓ dignified

5 According to paragraph 2, which of the following is true of Thomas Jefferson?

(A) He allowed citizens to view the White house museum for a small charge.
(B) He was the first United States president to live in the White House.
(C) He demanded that the White House stay open during wartime.
(D) He initiated the practice of offering public tours of the White House.

Paragraph 2 is marked with an arrow [➡].

6 Which of the following can be inferred from paragraph 2 about the grandstand in front of the White House?

(A) It was constructed to celebrate the inauguration of Andrew Jackson.
(B) It was temporarily closed after a president fled in fear for his personal security.
(C) An official inauguration parade had never been held when it was constructed.
(D) Troops continue to march by it today for the purpose of presidential review.

Paragraph 2 is marked with an arrow [➡].

7 According to paragraph 3, all of the following were renovations made to the White House EXCEPT

(A) the expansion of the West Wing
(B) the replacement of the outside walls
(C) the addition of a stained-glass window
(D) the construction of the Oval Office

Paragraph 3 is marked with an arrow [➡].

8 Why does the author mention the War of 1812 in paragraph 3?

(A) To highlight an event that led to significant renovation of the White House
(B) To provide the reason that the White House had to be torn down and rebuilt
(C) To explain why political tensions between America and Britain were so severe
(D) To emphasize the importance of the White House as a patriotic symbol

Paragraph 3 is marked with an arrow [➡].

Volume Review Help Back Next

9 Look at the four squares [■] that indicate where the following sentence could be added to the passage.

In particular, she wanted to save the walls that had survived damage by the British as she viewed them as crucial symbols of American independence.

Where would the sentence best fit?

Click on a square [■] to add the sentence to the passage.

10 **Directions:** An introductory sentence for a brief summary of the passage is provided below. Complete the summary by selecting the THREE answer choices that express the most important ideas in the passage. Some sentences do not belong in the summary because they express ideas that are not presented in the passage or are minor ideas in the passage. **This question is worth 2 points.**

Drag your answer choices to the spaces where they belong.
To remove an answer choice, click on it. To review the passage, click on **View Text**.

Since the late eighteenth century, the White House has been an enduring symbol of the American president and the country itself.

-
-
-

Answer Choices

(A) Throughout its history, the White House has experienced many changes, but its historical legacy remains intact.

(B) Although the presidents have received most of the attention, first ladies have also contributed to the White House's development.

(C) Early on, the White House was open to the public, but public access was eliminated after Andrew Jackson's election.

(D) Congress allowed architects of all backgrounds to submit proposals, and ultimately a design from a foreign-born architect was selected.

(E) The White House was conceived and planned during the presidency of George Washington, though he never lived in it himself.

(F) Each presidency, especially those of Jefferson and Jackson, has shaped the public's access to the White House.

Answer Book p. 35

Answer Book p. 36

TOEFL Reading

Zebra Mussel

The zebra mussel is a freshwater species that derives its name from the distinctive black-and-white striped pattern of its shell. The introduction of this species to foreign water sources has caused severe environmental disruptions in many regions. Originating from the drainage basins of Eastern Europe, zebra mussel populations quickly spread from these to major ports with the expansion of maritime commerce. By 1824, its presence had been detected as far as London. Over a century and a half later, the species was identified in Lake St. Clair in the American Great Lakes area.

➡ The zebra mussels were transported through the ballast tanks of cargo ships. Ballast tanks take on water filled with aquatic organisms, which are discharged upon arrival in a foreign port, abruptly depositing the exotic species into a new ecosystem. If dumped into saline seawater, the zebra mussels quickly die as they find saltwater intolerable. However, the freshwater lakes of North America match the original habitat of these organisms, thereby facilitating their survival. In addition, these lakes lack the common aquatic predators of Eastern Europe, including the silver bream and common carp.

➡ The rapid spread of this species has caused numerous ecological problems. For example, zebra mussels are water filterers, with each one capable of cleaning one liter per day. An established colony can substantially increase the water clarity by ingesting pollutants and particulates. While this might seem beneficial, the sudden change in transparency increases the penetration of sunlight, which leads to an algae bloom. When these microorganisms die, the amount of oxygen in the water declines. Zebra mussels can also have a direct impact on native animals. With their ability to stick to hard surfaces, zebra mussels frequently become attached to the shell of native mollusks in the Great Lakes. In this way, they occupy a prime position to steal nourishment from them. The growing zebra mussel will crush the shell top and make it too heavy to open, and the other organism subsequently dies of starvation.

➡ The presence of zebra mussels also poses economic issues in afflicted human communities. The larvae are able to enter and travel up water pipes unimpeded. Over time, the mature shells can obstruct the pipes completely. In addition, decaying mussels emit a foul smell that discourages visitors. For this reason, shoreside enterprises, such as restaurants and water sports companies, experience a decrease in profits.

National and local organizations have issued a number of informative pamphlets to educate the public on how to stop the transportation of larvae and adults. **A** The main recommendation is to carefully clean and dry all boating and fishing equipment before entering a new body of water. **B** Additionally, laws regulating the chemical treatment of ballast water in all non-recreational vessels are enforced by the US Coast Guard. **C** Furthermore, power companies have invested in forms

Volume Review Help Back Next

of liquid fertilizer and biopesticides in an attempt to flush the shellfish out from their pipelines. D

1 The word "these" in the passage refers to

Ⓐ foreign water sources
Ⓑ many regions
Ⓒ drainage basins of Eastern Europe
Ⓓ zebra mussel populations

2 Which of the sentences below best expresses the essential information in the highlighted sentence in the passage? *Incorrect* choices change the meaning in important ways or leave out essential information.

Ⓐ The ballast tank is a piece of equipment designed to carry aquatic species.
Ⓑ Aquatic creatures are incidentally transported between ecosystems through ballast tanks.
Ⓒ Ballast tank water is used to rinse aquatic creatures off the outside of vessels.
Ⓓ Aquatic organisms intentionally enter ballast tanks as a method of transportation.

3 The word "intolerable" in the passage is closest in meaning to

Ⓐ acceptable
Ⓑ fascinating
Ⓒ distasteful
Ⓓ unbearable

4 According to paragraph 2, why are North American lakes favorable to the growth of zebra mussels?

Ⓐ They do not have the low salinity that is fatal to reproduction.
Ⓑ They do not contain creatures that hunt the mussels.
Ⓒ They do not feature toxins that are harmful to the larvae.
Ⓓ They do not experience the icy weather that freezes the mussels.

Paragraph 2 is marked with an arrow [➡].

5 The word "penetration" in the passage is closest in meaning to

Ⓐ collection
Ⓑ blockage
Ⓒ entrance
Ⓓ dispersal

6 Which of the following can be inferred from paragraph 3 about clear water?

Ⓐ It does not usually contain any chemical pollutants.
Ⓑ It is preferred by the majority of freshwater species.
Ⓒ It is rare in places that are inhabited by mussels.
Ⓓ It does not necessarily benefit all aquatic species.

Paragraph 3 is marked with an arrow [➡].

7 According to paragraph 3, what method is used by zebra mussels to defeat rival shellfish?

Ⓐ They break open the shells of the shellfish.
Ⓑ They deprive the shellfish of water.
Ⓒ They limit the shellfish's supply of oxygen.
Ⓓ They remove the shellfish's ability to catch food.

Paragraph 3 is marked with an arrow [➡].

8 Why does the author discuss decaying mussels in paragraph 4?

Ⓐ To illustrate the harm that they cause to water pipes
Ⓑ To explain how they negatively impact certain businesses
Ⓒ To emphasize that they can be harmful to human health
Ⓓ To give an example of an economical use of them

Paragraph 4 is marked with an arrow [➡].

Volume Review Help Back Next

9 Look at the four squares [■] that indicate where the following sentence could be added to the passage.

However, these options can cause further harm to the ecosystem by introducing new chemicals to water sources.

Where would the sentence best fit?

Click on a square [■] to add the sentence to the passage.

10 **Directions:** An introductory sentence for a brief summary of the passage is provided below. Complete the summary by selecting the THREE answer choices that express the most important ideas in the passage. Some sentences do not belong in the summary because they express ideas that are not presented in the passage or are minor ideas in the passage. **This question is worth 2 points.**

Drag your answer choices to the spaces where they belong.
To remove an answer choice, click on it. To review the passage, click on **View Text**.

Zebra mussels have wrought considerable damage since their arrival in North American waterways.

-
-
-

Answer Choices

Ⓐ Zebra mussels were carried by trading ships to new areas, where their populations rapidly increased.

Ⓑ Zebra mussels are sometimes used to improve water quality where visibility is poor.

Ⓒ The proliferation of zebra mussels has had adverse effects on native species in ecosystems.

Ⓓ Government regulation of how ballast water is used has recently solved the problem of zebra mussels.

Ⓔ The existence of zebra mussels creates economic costs for affected communities.

Ⓕ Because zebra mussels require very specific water conditions, they rarely infringe on the territory of native mussels.

Answer Book p. 36

Vocabulary Review

Answer Book p. 37

A. Fill in the blanks with the appropriate words from the box.

inaugurated	airborne	insulation
locomotion	tertiary	torrential

1 Scientists have studied the ______________ of spiders to learn how their narrow legs can transport such relatively heavy bodies.

2 The ______________ rainfall flooded many homes and even sent cars floating down the street.

3 At the science fair, the students tested numerous paper airplanes to see which could remain ______________ the longest.

4 In the early twentieth century, many buildings used newspapers as ______________ against the cold.

5 Ethics is of ______________ importance in many religions, behind kindness and forgiveness.

6 The new governor was ______________ just two days after winning the election.

B. Choose the closest meaning for each highlighted word or phrase.

7 The surgeon worked very quickly to reconnect the accident victim's severed thumb.
(A) damaged (B) detached (C) injured (D) infected

8 Trucks use shipping containers to baffle oil and other liquids during shipment.
(A) block (B) confuse (C) guzzle (D) leak

9 The members of the choir raised their voices collectively and sang the song beautifully.
(A) jointly (B) passionately (C) beautifully (D) morosely

10 In the north, the Nile discharges its waters into the Mediterranean Sea.
(A) features (B) releases (C) contaminates (D) alleviates

11 At the Christmas Eve service, a long procession of people marched out of the church holding candles.
(A) presence (B) smattering (C) community (D) parade

12 In the film, the alien shot the astronaut with a laser that left him immobile.
(A) ready (B) reluctant (C) motionless (D) bold

13 The store was called Best Value, but, ironically, its prices were rather high.
(A) emphatically (B) originally (C) intentionally (D) paradoxically

14 The amplified radio signal could be detected over 1,000 kilometers from the broadcasting station.
(A) concealed (B) boosted (C) initiated (D) weakened

CHAPTER 07

Rhetorical Purpose

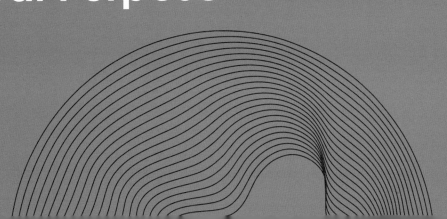

Rhetorical Purpose

About the Question Type

Rhetorical Purpose questions ask you to identify the function of a particular piece of information presented in the paragraph or the passage. Possible functions include explaining a concept, suggesting an option, illustrating a point, making a comparison, and providing an example.

Rhetoric refers to the writing techniques that an author uses to make his or her point effectively. Make sure to understand why the specified piece of information was presented by the author.

Question Format

- Why does the author mention "   " in the passage?
- In paragraph #, the author mentions/discusses/includes "   " in order to
- What is the author's primary purpose in paragraph #?

Key Strategies

- **Step 1** — Read the question and locate the specified piece of information in the passage.
- **Step 2** — Use the surrounding context to determine its purpose.
- **Step 3** — Select the answer choice that best describes the rhetorical function of the piece of information.

Example

Answer Book p. 37

The Origins of Rice

The origins of rice have been debated for some time. Evidence from the middle and lower Yangtze River Valley in China indicates that humans used rice in the region as early as 12,000 BC. Some archaeological sites dated to 8,000 BC contained substantial quantities of rice, suggesting that it had become an integral part of people's lives in the area. However, it is unknown whether the rice discovered at these locations was wild or domesticated. Carbon dating of rice grains unearthed in an archaeological site in Kunshan from the oldest-confirmed rice paddy field put rice cultivation several thousand years later. Chinese rice-cultivation techniques reached Korea and Japan, neither of which had native wild rice species, by around 4,000 years ago and also spread to Southeast Asia. Prior to this, rice cultivation occurred independently in India and, subsequently, in Africa as well.

A prerequisite to the successful domestication of rice was the ability to control or reduce seed shattering so that rice could be harvested before the seeds fell. Shattering is the process by which mature seeds are released by mother plants for dispersal. Genetic analysis has identified mutant genes that decrease or eliminate seed shattering. Thus, early rice cultivation likely involved selecting rice plants that had these traits and incorporating them into agriculture in a very slow, gradual process. With more detailed genetic sequencing and improved technology, experts hope to learn more about this process in the near future.

1 Why does the author mention "Kunshan" in the passage?

(A) To illustrate the earliest methods used to grow rice
(B) To identify the earliest confirmed case of rice cultivation
(C) To highlight the source of rice exports to Korea and Japan
(D) To emphasize the place where people first consumed rice

2 What is the author's primary purpose in paragraph 2?

(A) To explain how early farmers overcame a problem
(B) To describe the process by which a plant reproduces
(C) To point out a weakness of an agricultural product
(D) To identify a requirement for the cultivation of a crop

Reading Practice 1

Answer Book p. 38

Wormhole Theory

Before Albert Einstein, scientists like Sir Isaac Newton erroneously assumed that the universe was flat. However, in his theory of general relativity, Einstein proposed that the universe was in fact dynamic and could be bent, stretched, and curved like rubber or plastic. In this view of the universe, the combination of space, time, and gravity determines where matter exists and how it moves relative to other objects. Later, modern astronomers took Einstein's theory further and surmised that it might be possible for matter to traverse great distances in space much more quickly than would normally be expected. The mechanism by which this could be achieved is known as a wormhole, which is defined as a hypothetical shortcut between two points that are otherwise far more remote from one another in time and space.

According to contemporary science, the formation of a wormhole depends on a relationship between a black hole and a white hole, the former of which is an extremely dense area of space that emits no light and from which nothing can escape. The lesser-known white hole is exactly the opposite, meaning that it is extremely bright and that matter rushes out of it in a constant stream. In theory, a wormhole could form between these two entities, connecting them and creating a portal through which an object could move. This would generate a pathway between two points in space, and it would allow for the possibility of them being much closer to each other than they are in normal space and time outside the wormhole. To visualize this, imagine a long piece of paper that is bent so that the two ends are parallel, one above the other. Near each end, there is a hole in the paper, and these openings are connected by a short tube. The distance between the two holes is shorter when measured through the tube than it is along the surface of the bent piece of paper. In this scenario, the paper represents space, the openings a black hole and white hole, and the tube a wormhole.

Although the wormhole theory is fascinating and has attracted the attention of numerous astronomers and enthusiasts, it is not without some serious problems. ■A Ignoring the fact that the observation of black and white holes is still fraught with difficulty, current analytics in physics suggest that if a wormhole were possible, it would vanish very quickly after formation. ■B In fact, it would dissipate so rapidly that there would most likely be insufficient time for anything to pass through. ■C Even so, some researchers have theorized that it may be possible at some point in the future to stabilize wormholes for utilization in space travel. ■D

1 Why does the author mention "rubber or plastic" in the passage?

(A) To illustrate an element of a scientist's hypothesis
(B) To point out an underlying problem with a theory
(C) To compare the research of Einstein and modern astronomers
(D) To provide support for Newton's belief about the universe

2 The word "surmised" in the passage is closest in meaning to

(A) precluded
(B) speculated
(C) declared
(D) acknowledged

3 The author discusses a long piece of paper that is bent in paragraph 2 in order to

(A) compare the shapes of perfectly opposing objects
(B) emphasize the vast distance between two points in space
(C) explain how entities can become mirror images of each other
(D) show that the distance between two locations can vary

4 According to paragraph 2, which of the following is true of a white hole?

(A) It is significantly denser than a black hole.
(B) All objects that approach it are rejected.
(C) Matter flows out of it continually.
(D) It is one of the rarest objects in space.

5 Look at the four squares [■] that indicate where the following sentence could be added to the passage.

Exactly how this might be achieved, however, is not known, leading critics of this proposal to dismiss it as science fiction.

Where would the sentence best fit?

6 According to paragraph 3, why is the passage of matter through a wormhole problematic?

(A) A wormhole would destroy any matter that entered it.
(B) Wormholes would disappear almost immediately.
(C) The size of the wormhole would be extremely small.
(D) The formation of two wormholes would never be simultaneous.

Reading Practice 2

Answer Book p. 39

Zoroastrianism

As a contemporary religion, Zoroastrianism is practiced by an estimated 100,000 to 200,000 believers. Compare that to the approximately 3.8 billion followers of the world's two largest religions, Christianity and Islam, and the 4,000-year-old faith founded by the prophet Zoroaster might seem to have little influence in the modern world. However, many ideas that apparently originated with Zoroastrianism are now important tenets of the so-called Abrahamic religions (Judaism, Christianity, and Islam) that are so visible around the globe today. By this measure, this seemingly obscure religion ranks among the most influential in history regardless of its present-day following.

Some historians consider Zoroastrianism the world's first monotheistic religion. Scholars debate the exact dates that the prophet Zoroaster, who is also known as Zarathustra, walked the earth, but there is considerable archaeological evidence to suggest that he lived in an area near the border of modern-day Iran and Afghanistan sometime around 1500 and 1200 BC. He was likely a part of a polytheistic tribe. The Zoroastrians believe that Zoroaster was involved in a pagan ritual at the age of thirty when he encountered the divine presence of Ahura Mazda, who Zoroaster came to accept as the one true god. His faith eventually became the state religion of the Persian Empire and then spread across Asia along the famous Silk Road that connected China, the Middle East, and Europe.

But monotheism is not the only similarity between Zoroastrianism and the Abrahamic faiths. Zoroaster's message also featured the concepts of heaven and hell, Satan, and a final judgment day. The beliefs of the Zoroastrians may have made their way to the Babylonians and been reinforced by the Persians led by the emperor Cyrus the Great, who liberated the Jews from Babylonian captivity in 538 BC, allowing them to return to their homeland in the kingdom of Judea. Meanwhile, Zoroastrianism remained the dominant religion in Persia until the Muslims conquered it in the seventh century AD. Most Iranian Zoroastrians subsequently accepted the Islamic faith, having been coerced by targeted taxes and other pro-Islamic policies, and many of those that continued to practice the older faith escaped to India and founded the Parsi religion, which retains its Zoroastrian characteristics today.

While relatively few Zoroastrian believers remained by the time of the Enlightenment, Zoroastrianism had a significant impact on some of Europe's most important thinkers during that period (1685-1815). French author Voltaire wrote *Zadig*, a philosophical novella about a Persian Zoroastrian, in 1747. Not much later, the German poet Johann Wolfgang von Goethe wrote about Zoroastrianism in *West-Eastern Divan*. Even the Austrian composer Wolfgang Amadeus Mozart worked Zoroastrian themes into his opera *The Magic Flute*. Those works and others have lived to the present day, bringing echoes of a relatively unknown faith to the Western world.

Glossary

- monotheistic: believing there is only one God
- polytheistic: believing there is more than one God

1 Why does the author mention "Christianity and Islam" in the passage?

(A) To demonstrate the relative longevity of a particular faith
(B) To suggest that a belief system has gradually lost influence
(C) To compare the tenets of two different religious movements
(D) To show that a religion has a small number of adherents

2 According to paragraph 2, which of the following was NOT true of Zoroaster?

(A) He grew up in a polytheistic tribe.
(B) He lived in present-day Iran or Afghanistan.
(C) He traveled the Silk Road to China.
(D) His beliefs became the state religion of an empire.

3 The word "coerced" in the passage is closest in meaning to

(A) compelled
(B) designated
(C) compensated
(D) prepared

4 According to paragraph 3, which of the following was true of Cyrus the Great?

(A) He freed the Jews from their captors.
(B) He tried to convert the Jews to Zoroastrianism.
(C) He imposed a tax on those who did not believe in Zoroastrianism.
(D) He was defeated by Islamic warriors in the seventh century.

5 Why does the author mention "*Zadig*" in the passage?

(A) To suggest that Voltaire was a believer in the Zoroastrian religion
(B) To provide an example of the influence of Zoroastrianism
(C) To argue that *Zadig* was a superior work to *West-Eastern Divan*
(D) To contrast Zoroastrianism with the ideas of the Enlightenment

6 Which of the following can be inferred from paragraph 4 about the Enlightenment's impact on Zoroastrianism?

(A) It led to fewer people practicing the faith.
(B) It made more Europeans aware of the religion.
(C) It inspired many people to convert to Zoroastrianism.
(D) It introduced translations of Zoroastrian literature.

Answer Book p. 40

The Enigma Machine

During World War II, the Allied and Axis powers both attempted to develop effective ways to communicate without the enemy gaining knowledge of the content of their messages. When successful, this strategy allowed them to securely send memos about the details of military operations. Some security measures included coded messages, and the most famous of these was implemented by Nazi Germany with an encryption device called an Enigma machine. Before it was eventually decoded, the Enigma machine was considered to be a completely secure method of communication.

Although the Enigma machine had more than one design, a typical one might be described as a typewriter with some additional features. Viewed from above, at the bottom of the device's surface was a keyboard, with each key representing a letter of the alphabet. Above the keyboard was a set of lights. These corresponded to a letter, and the letters were in the same layout. Above the lights, there were three thumb-movable wheels called rotors, which, from right to left, were designated fast, medium, and slow. Each rotor contained twenty-six electrical contacts on one side, and these were wired to twenty-six letters on the other side, and each rotor could be manually set to any letter at any time. When an operator pressed a key, the right rotor advanced with every typed character, while the middle rotor advanced once per twenty-six characters, and the left rotor moved forward only once per 676 characters. Moving any of the three rotors resulted in a continual reordering of the letters of the alphabet, so this arrangement created a seemingly boundless combination of possible outputs.

As electrical signals moved through the three rotors, they encountered an electronic reflector, which redirected the current back through the rotors in the opposite direction. However, the wiring was set up so that the current went back through a separate route. For instance, if an operator pressed *A*, the signal might go through *A*, *P* and *Z*, then the reflector might redirect the current through the *Z*, *G* and *B* contacts on its way back through the rotors. In this example, *B* would be the *ciphertext*, or encrypted text, form of *A*, and the *B* light would illuminate. If *A* was pressed a second time, a completely different sequence would be produced for the following route.

An Enigma machine's electrical circuit was perfectly symmetrical. Consequently, when using two machines that were configured in an identical manner, a message could be encrypted on one machine and readily decrypted on the other. The symmetry was convenient for anyone who had the key to the configuration because the receiver could quickly decipher the message without further conversion or interpretation. However, it also made the Enigma machine more vulnerable, and this weakness was exploited by the Allied Polish and British cryptographers who ultimately broke its mysterious codes.

1 What can be inferred from paragraph 1 about the Enigma machine?

(A) The Germans used it to relay the most sensitive of information.
(B) The Allied powers hoped to copy it to create their own codes.
(C) Military personnel were initially uncertain about its utility.
(D) Enemy communications could be easily decoded with it.

2 The word "boundless" in the passage is closest in meaning to

(A) priceless
(B) abundant
(C) unlimited
(D) constrained

3 The author mentions a typewriter in paragraph 2 in order to

(A) specify the inspiration behind an invention
(B) illustrate the basic appearance of a device
(C) identify the first machine with a manual keyboard
(D) explain the methods used to operate an instrument

4 Which of the following is NOT mentioned in paragraph 2 in relation to the Enigma machine's rotors?

(A) The rotor on the right moved with every keystroke.
(B) Moving any rotor rearranged the alphabet.
(C) The rotor in the middle moved the slowest.
(D) Each rotor was wired to twenty-six letters.

5 According to paragraph 3, what happened if an Enigma machine operator pressed the same letter twice?

(A) The electrical signal would travel in the opposite direction.
(B) The light representing that letter would illuminate.
(C) The second route would have a totally different sequence.
(D) The encrypted text would end in the same letter.

6 What is the author's primary purpose in paragraph 4?

(A) To compare a German device with its Allied counterpart
(B) To present a feature that turned out to be a security flaw
(C) To explain why the produced codes were hard to decipher
(D) To suggest an improvement to a way of encoding a message

Answer Book p. 41

TOEFL Reading

Climate Change and Ocean Currents

➡ Although scientists continue to debate the extent and implications of global warming, they all agree that the phenomenon is real and will have a significant impact on the world's oceans. The most obvious concern is that the melting of the polar ice caps will cause sea levels to rise dramatically, creating a risk of flooding in coastal regions. However, a much more serious threat is the potential for the interruption of the system of currents that transports water throughout the planet's oceans.

Oceanic currents can be divided into two main types: surface and deep-water. Surface currents are primarily driven by the prevailing winds, such as the air masses that move constantly eastward in the tropical and polar regions, and the ones that travel westward in the middle latitudes. Deep-water currents are an outcome of what is known as thermohaline circulation—a term derived from the Greek words *thermo* and *haline*, meaning "heat" and "salinity" respectively. As the name suggests, thermohaline circulation is dependent on variations in the temperature and salt content of seawater, with the density of water increasing as it becomes colder and saltier. At a certain point, it will sink to the ocean floor, displacing the water below. These two types of currents working in unison cause vast quantities of seawater to travel immense distances in a fixed pattern, a process that has come to be known as the global ocean conveyor belt.

➡ When tracking this network of currents, scientists typically begin in the North Atlantic, where freezing temperatures lead to ice formation. Ice does not include salt, so the cold seawater that remains has a very high salinity and, as a result, is very dense. When it inevitably sinks, it pushes the water already present in the deep Atlantic south until it reaches Antarctica and begins to move eastward along the continental shelf. Eventually, this water flows north into the Indian and Pacific Oceans, where it mixes with warmer, less salty water and begins to rise to the surface. At this point, it comes under the influence of wind currents, such as the Gulf Stream, and is carried back up to the North Atlantic, where it starts the entire journey again.

➡ **A** The global ocean conveyor belt is critically important to the overall health of the planet, as the constant movement and mixing of warm and cold water regulates the global climate and transports nutrients that are vital for marine life. **B** Unfortunately, there is a significant chance that global warming may interrupt this network of currents. **C** The main issue is that the ongoing melting of the ice cap in the northern hemisphere is resulting in massive quantities of freshwater entering the North Atlantic. **D** In response, the seawater is becoming less salty and, therefore, less dense. If this continues to the point that the incoming seawater no longer descends to the ocean floor, the thermohaline current may cease to exist, causing the global ocean conveyor belt to break down completely.

Volume Review Help Back Next

1 The word "extent" in the passage is closest in meaning to

Ⓐ authenticity
Ⓑ consequence
Ⓒ application
Ⓓ magnitude

2 According to paragraph 1, all of the following are problems associated with global warming EXCEPT

Ⓐ the loss of ice in the northern and southern regions of the planet
Ⓑ an increase in the height of the surface levels of the world's oceans
Ⓒ the erosion of coastlines due to floodwaters moving to the sea
Ⓓ a disruption of the movement of seawater over great distances

Paragraph 1 is marked with an arrow [➡].

3 The word "ones" in the passage refers to

Ⓐ types
Ⓑ currents
Ⓒ masses
Ⓓ regions

4 Which of the sentences below best expresses the essential information in the highlighted sentence in the passage? *Incorrect* choices change the meaning in important ways or leave out essential information.

Ⓐ Thermohaline circulation can be triggered by either a decrease in the temperature of seawater or an increase in its salinity.
Ⓑ The increase in the density of water as its temperature falls and its salinity rises is the basis of thermohaline circulation.
Ⓒ Without thermohaline circulation, seawater will become increasingly colder and its salt content will continuously rise.
Ⓓ The degree of thermohaline circulation can be determined by measuring the temperature and saltiness of seawater.

5 The word "inevitably" in the passage is closest in meaning to

Ⓐ immediately
Ⓑ separately
Ⓒ continually
Ⓓ necessarily

6 Why does the author mention "the Gulf Stream" in the passage?

Ⓐ To explain why water from Antarctica becomes warmer
Ⓑ To provide an example of a current that moves surface water
Ⓒ To demonstrate that wind currents can reach the North Atlantic
Ⓓ To stress the number of factors that affect seawater movement

7 According to paragraph 3, what boosts the salinity of the seawater in the North Atlantic?

Ⓐ Ice formation causes salt deposits to coalesce.
Ⓑ Seawater becomes denser as its temperature drops.
Ⓒ Freshwater is removed from the ocean as it freezes.
Ⓓ Salt is pushed downward as the cold water descends.

Paragraph 3 is marked with an arrow [➡].

8 According to paragraph 4, the global ocean conveyor belt is important because it

Ⓐ facilitates the migration of marine animals in search of nutrition
Ⓑ ensures the correct balance between saltwater and freshwater
Ⓒ circulates food resources required by ocean organisms
Ⓓ slows the rate at which sea ice is melting in some regions

Paragraph 4 is marked with an arrow [➡].

Volume Review Help Back Next

9 Look at the four squares [■] that indicate where the following sentence could be added to the passage.

At the same time, new sea ice is forming at a slower rate due to rising temperatures.

Where would the sentence best fit?

Click on a square [■] to add the sentence to the passage.

10 Directions: An introductory sentence for a brief summary of the passage is provided below. Complete the summary by selecting the THREE answer choices that express the most important ideas in the passage. Some sentences do not belong in the summary because they express ideas that are not presented in the passage or are minor ideas in the passage. **This question is worth 2 points.**

Drag your answer choices to the spaces where they belong.
To remove an answer choice, click on it. To review the passage, click on **View Text**.

The global ocean conveyor belt is vital to the health of the planet's oceans but is threatened by global warming.

-
-
-

Answer Choices

Ⓐ Winds that blow constantly in one direction are responsible for the currents that move along the ocean's surface.

Ⓑ Surface wind currents and deep-water thermohaline currents combine to form the global ocean conveyor belt.

Ⓒ The water at the floor of the North Atlantic is much colder and saltier than the water in other parts of the ocean.

Ⓓ Seawater moves from the North Atlantic to Antarctica and then returns via the Indian and Pacific Oceans.

Ⓔ Rising temperatures have increased the amount of freshwater entering the world's oceans from melting ice.

Ⓕ Climate change is reducing the salinity of seawater, which may disrupt the deep-water ocean currents.

Answer Book p. 41

Answer Book p. 42

TOEFL Reading

Beak Evolution

➡ The hypothesis that the 10,000 living species of birds are directly descended from the dinosaurs is no longer a subject of controversy in scientific circles. The connection was debated for decades after biologist Thomas Henry Huxley proposed it in his 1870 book, *Further Evidence of the Affinity between the Dinosaurian Reptiles and Birds*, but every objection to his hypothesis was answered one by one by a new fossil discovery. There were flying dinosaurs, dinosaurs with wishbones, dinosaurs with three clawed toes, and dinosaurs with wrists that have an extensive range of movement. In 1996, a Chinese farmer effectively ended the debate when he discovered *Sinosauropteryx*, a feathered dinosaur. It is now believed that many dinosaurs, possibly even the massive Tyrannosaurus rex, had feathers. However, scientists remain puzzled by one distinction between dinosaurs and birds. **A** How did birds develop their toothless beaks? **B** These remarkably versatile structures are capable of grasping, prying, and tearing food, as well as fastidiously grooming parasites from feathers. **C** Explanations for the absence of teeth in birds tend to fall into two categories: ecological and developmental. **D**

➡ The most common ecological explanation for the development of beaks in birds posits that food acquisition was the driving factor. This explanation dates back to Charles Darwin's journey to the Galapagos Islands in the 1830s. He observed differences in the shapes of the beaks of the finches on the various islands and concluded that the beaks had evolved to accommodate the seeds available to the birds. Numerous contemporary studies have supported Darwin's hypothesis, but the evolution of individual species of birds is of dubious significance when tracing the development of beaks on a much broader scale. In 2016, Derek Larson documented the extinction of numerous toothed bird-like dinosaurs in the Cretaceous-Paleogene extinction event, speculating that toothless birds survived because they relied on seed banks that likely outlasted the meteor impact that doomed carnivorous bird-like dinosaurs. In other words, birds endured because of their beaks. However, some toothless Mesozoic birds perished in the extinction event, suggesting that ecological explanations have their limitations.

➡ The developmental model explains how beaks developed by combining genetic science and fossil evidence. In 2017, Chinese paleontologist Shuo Wang scanned the interiors of early bird fossils, which made it possible to observe the step-by-step progression of tooth loss. Some dinosaurs related to birds had teeth early in life that came out in adulthood. Others were toothless but retained tooth sockets in their jaws. Studies of modern birds have revealed that the genetic molecule known as BMP-4 regulates both beak growth and the suppression of teeth. It is likely that it also played a significant role in the gradual progression from toothed jaws to beaks in the dinosaur ancestors of contemporary bird species.

Volume Review Help Back Next

1 The word "fastidiously" in the passage is closest in meaning to

- (A) reluctantly
- (B) grotesquely
- (C) meticulously
- (D) immediately

2 According to paragraph 1, the biologist Thomas Henry Huxley

- (A) opposed the theory that dinosaurs are the ancestors of birds
- (B) suggested the relationship between two types of organisms
- (C) discovered fossils that resulted in a scientific controversy
- (D) made a proposal that has been rejected by modern scientists

Paragraph 1 is marked with an arrow [➡].

3 According to paragraph 1, all of the following characteristics of dinosaurs support the claim that these extinct animals are the ancestors of birds EXCEPT

- (A) the shape of feet
- (B) the flexibility of a joint
- (C) the growth of feathers
- (D) the density of a bone

Paragraph 1 is marked with an arrow [➡].

4 The word "dubious" in the passage is closest in meaning to

- (A) questionable
- (B) exaggerated
- (C) inaccurate
- (D) outdated

5 According to paragraph 2, the finches observed by Darwin on the Galapagos Islands

- (A) exhibited a variety of beak forms
- (B) consumed the same type of seed
- (C) lived in large groups on one island
- (D) migrated regularly in search of food

Paragraph 2 is marked with an arrow [➡].

6 Which of the following can be inferred from paragraph 2 about toothed bird-like dinosaurs during the Cretaceous-Paleogene extinction event?

- (A) They were unable to access sufficient food to survive.
- (B) They competed for the same resources as toothless birds.
- (C) They were largely unaffected by the effects of the meteor strike.
- (D) They underwent rapid physiological changes to survive

Paragraph 2 is marked with an arrow [➡].

7 Which of the sentences below best expresses the essential information in the highlighted sentence in the passage? *Incorrect* choices change the meaning in important ways or leave out essential information

- (A) Data pertaining to the gradual loss of teeth in birds was gathered by a Chinese scientist studying fossils.
- (B) The fossils examined by a Chinese researcher clearly showed that the earliest birds had jaws with teeth.
- (C) Tooth loss in birds may have occurred much earlier than originally thought according to a Chinese paleontologist.
- (D) Not all of the birds studied by the Chinese expert had teeth, as they had evolved over time to be toothless.

8 Why does the author discuss BMP-4 in paragraph 3?

- (A) To show that modern birds are similar to early dinosaurs
- (B) To explain why some organisms lose teeth due to aging
- (C) To identify a possible cause of a physiological transition
- (D) To suggest that many avian species are closely related

Paragraph 3 is marked with an arrow [➡].

Volume Review Help Back Next

9 Look at the four squares [■] that indicate where the following sentence could be added to the passage.

These functions could not be performed with the toothy, inflexible snouts that characterized most dinosaurs.

Where would the sentence best fit?

Click on a square [■] to add the sentence to the passage.

10 **Directions:** An introductory sentence for a brief summary of the passage is provided below. Complete the summary by selecting the THREE answer choices that express the most important ideas in the passage. Some sentences do not belong in the summary because they express ideas that are not presented in the passage or are minor ideas in the passage. **This question is worth 2 points.**

Drag your answer choices to the spaces where they belong.
To remove an answer choice, click on it. To review the passage, click on **View Text**.

Scientists have accepted the lineage of birds from dinosaurs but remain uncertain about the development of the beak.

-
-
-

Answer Choices

(A) Ecological explanations for the development of beaks focus on their use in acquiring food.

(B) The theories that Darwin developed during his trips to the Galapagos Islands are supported by more recent research.

(C) An occurrence that resulted in worldwide devastation may have made having a beak a significant advantage.

(D) Developmental explanations are derived from both genetic science and fossil studies.

(E) There were some flying dinosaurs that had tooth sockets in their jaws even though they lacked teeth.

(F) Birds began to evolve separately from dinosaurs when some bird species developed feathers.

Answer Book p. 42

Vocabulary Review

Answer Book p. 43

A. Fill in the blanks with the appropriate words from the box.

unearthed	monotheistic	visualize
doomed	pried	erroneously

1 You have explained your job to me before, but it is difficult to ______________ your daily duties without observing them.

2 The otter broke the shellfish open and ______________ out the meat using its claws.

3 The fossil was ______________ by a farmer in central China as he was plowing his field.

4 Although some animals survived the wildfire, those that did not escape were ______________.

5 Pharaoh Akhenaten wanted all Egyptians to practice his ______________ religion, but his son encouraged the worship of multiple gods.

6 The politician claimed ______________ that the president determines gas prices, but they are actually set by the oil industry.

B. Choose the closest meaning for each highlighted word or phrase.

7 The exact sequence of Shakespeare's plays is debated by scholars, but most believe that *Twelfth Night* was written before *Hamlet*.
(A) merit (B) revenue (C) topic (D) order

8 Unhappy with the stricter environmental rules, oil companies submitted objections to the government agency.
(A) challenges (B) references (C) praises (D) agreements

9 QWERTY keyboards are common in North America, and they are named for the configuration of the first six letters.
(A) extent (B) arrangement (C) totality (D) reversal

10 According to doctors, the new drug is helpful for the suppression of flu symptoms.
(A) constraint (B) discarding (C) isolation (D) monitoring

11 Stephanie's people skills and attention to detail have made her an integral member of our team.
(A) flawed (B) casual (C) plausible (D) indispensable

12 After the American Civil War, all slave owners were required to liberate their slaves.
(A) neglect (B) sponsor (C) free (D) oppress

13 The twins often answered questions in unison, as though they shared the same thoughts.
(A) time (B) motion (C) concord (D) wonder

14 An important tenet of the Islamic faith is that believers should not consume pork.
(A) goal (B) fact (C) question (D) principle

CHAPTER 08

Sentence Insertion

Sentence Insertion

About the Question Type

Sentence Insertion questions ask you to identify the best place within a paragraph to insert the given sentence.

Pay attention to words or phrases that indicate the logical relationships between the sentences before and after the squares. These include, among others, conjunctive adverbs such as *however*, *therefore*, *nevertheless*, *yet*, and *moreover*, as well as pronouns like *it*, *they*, *this*, and *that*.

Question Format

Look at the four squares [■] that indicate where the following sentence could be added to the passage.

[A given sentence]

Where would the sentence best fit?

Click on a square [■] to add the sentence to the passage.

Key Strategies

- **Step 1** — Read the given sentence and look for transitional words or phrases. Use these to determine the logical relationships between the given sentence and the rest of the paragraph.
- **Step 2** — Determine the location the sentence should be placed in the paragraph.
- **Step 3** — Confirm that the paragraph has a logical flow with the sentence inserted.

Example

Answer Book p. 43

The Bald Eagle

Americans have not always been the greatest caretakers of their national bird, the bald eagle, and the regal predator was on the endangered species list for forty years. [A] Its numbers were reduced by hunters, who took aim at the bird for years for sport and because they were concerned the eagle was eating too many fish. [B] Starting in the 1940s, however, a synthetic pesticide called DDT supplanted hunting as the greatest threat to the bald eagle. [C] The chemical substance permeated the fish that were the bird's primary source of food, and it had a devastating effect on eagle fertility. [D] By 1970, only 400 breeding pairs of eagles remained in the lower forty-eight states, though they did remain plentiful in the wilder territory of Alaska.

The bald eagle population began to rebound in the early 1970s thanks to a concentrated effort on the part of the US government and conservationists. [A] The most significant factor in the bird's proliferation was a national DDT ban in 1972. [B] Extensive areas of bald eagle habitat were designated for preservation, reversing a trend of habitat reduction and degradation in the preceding decades. [C] Moreover, fewer eagles were electrocuted by power lines after design improvements were made, and captive eaglets were introduced into wild eagle nests. [D] By 2007, these efforts had paid off so substantially that the national bird was removed from the nation's endangered species list.

1 Look at the four squares [■] in paragraph 1 that indicate where the following sentence could be added to the passage.

It also resulted in thinner eggshells, so fewer bald eagles made it to adulthood.

Where would the sentence best fit?

2 Look at the four squares [■] in paragraph 2 that indicate where the following sentence could be added to the passage.

However, this was not the only factor that played a role in the resurgence.

Where would the sentence best fit?

Answer Book p. 44

Indigenous Astronomy in North America

In the time before colonization, astronomy played an important role in the lives of the indigenous peoples in North America. It was a source both of a practical wisdom and a key part of their culture. And while much of the indigenous knowledge about astronomy has been lost, efforts to preserve it reveal a wealth of alternative ways to see the stars.

For instance, although most Native American tribes lacked a written language, they kept track of astronomical events by other means. **A** Most of the recordings made were in the form of drawings. **B** Drawings on animal skins and stories that were passed down from generation to generation still exist, although their dates of origin are unknown. **C** An example of a historical event among the recordings of the Native Americans is the Leonid meteor shower, which occurred in 1833. **D** The Maricopa tribe kept calendar sticks that recorded the event. Each notch made to the stick represented a year that had passed since "the stars fell."

The explanations that Native Americans had for meteors and comets showed that certain tribes had a varying range of attitudes. Some showed little fear, but others had an enormous apprehension when astronomical events took place. Those tribes that did not show fear believed that meteors and comets were spirits of shamans traveling to the afterlife. For the Luiseño of California, for instance, these were merely stars on the move. Some tribes, though, did feel a sense of foreboding because they associated meteors and comets with events they believed would happen: the end of the earth or the destruction of almost all living things. Such tribes strongly believed the latter to be true because of the discovery of the fossilized bones of dinosaurs. A few tribes saw such events to be omens that required the explanation of a shaman.

Even today, each tribe's knowledge of the stars reflects knowledge of its own mythology. Just as Europeans named constellations after Greek legends, Native Americans drew from their own traditions when describing the stars. For instance, someone with a European background looks at three of the most luminous stars in the sky and thinks of the hunter Orion. The Ojibwe from North America's Great Lakes region look at the same bright stars and think of the Wintermaker, a sign that cold weather is coming soon. Similarly, the Skidi ascribed great meaning to a constellation known as the Corona Borealis. They referred to this collection of stars as the Council of Chiefs. This interpretation provided both a model for government by a committee of elders as well as a guide for agricultural planning. So important was this constellation that the Skidi lived in open-topped lodges with clear sightlines of their beloved council. Today, Native American astronomy is passed on by tribal leaders who advocate "two-eyed seeing:" the ability to simultaneously view astronomical phenomena through the lens of their ancient religions and the lens of scientific knowledge.

1 The word "it" in the passage refers to

(A) wisdom
(B) culture
(C) knowledge
(D) astronomy

2 Look at the four squares [■] that indicate where the following sentence could be added to the passage.

This occurrence made such an enormous impression that chronological accounts of the shower were made by the Sioux on animal skins.

Where would the sentence best fit?

3 According to paragraph 2, the Maricopa tribe put notches in calendar sticks in order to

(A) divide the year into different months
(B) keep up with the annual migration of animals
(C) calculate the exact number of days since 1833
(D) denote anniversaries of a meteor shower

4 According to paragraph 3, which of the following was NOT a Native American explanation for comets and meteors?

(A) They were the spirits of the dead in motion.
(B) They were signs of impending tragic events.
(C) They were the remains of giant creatures.
(D) They were stars traveling from place to place.

5 The word "ascribed" in the passage is closest in meaning to

(A) perpetuated
(B) experienced
(C) assigned
(D) intuited

6 According to paragraph 4, which of the following is true of the Skidi's view of the Corona Borealis?

(A) They considered it a model for designing their lodges.
(B) They saw it as a guide for government and agriculture.
(C) They interpreted it as a sign of oncoming winter.
(D) They regarded it as having deep religious significance.

Reading Practice 2

Answer Book p. 45

Pacific Ocean Ecosystems

The Pacific Ocean is one of the most important environmental systems on Earth due to its sheer size as well as its expanse across a wide variety of geographical regions. [A] Stretching from the Antarctic in the southern hemisphere to the Arctic in the northern hemisphere, the Pacific is the world's largest body of water. [B] It also contains a wide array of different ecosystems that are important not only biologically but also commercially. [C] Thus, the Pacific's role in maintaining both wild organisms and human populations is crucial. [D]

The Pacific has particularly tremendous biodiversity in areas adjacent to land. For instance, the offshore waters of western North America and western South America have some of the most prolific and profitable fisheries on Earth. One of the reasons for this is that the Pacific is extremely deep, and the connection between the land and sea often creates abrupt rather than gradual variations in depth. This underwater topography facilitates the mixing of cold and warm water in a process called upwelling, whereby deep, nutrient-rich water is brought to the surface. The recycling of nutrients supplies a continual source of sustenance to the microorganisms, such as plankton, that make up the base of the food chain. In turn, small fish feed on the plankton, and they provide food for larger predatory fish and marine mammals.

The volcanic activity in the Pacific Ring of Fire has also formed numerous unique habitats that are home to a substantial variety of life. Volcanoes created rocky coastlines that, unlike sandy shores, support ecosystems like tide pools. When seawater spills onto rocky shores at high tide, pools of water form, and these are extremely biodiverse for their small size. Similarly, just offshore, the cool water of the Pacific supports kelp forests, areas of dense vegetative growth that harbor perhaps the greatest diversity of plants and animals of any oceanic community. In more remote regions of the Pacific, volcanic activity has resulted in numerous islands. The Pacific is home to more than 25,000 islands, the most of any ocean. These and coral atolls, which form near undersea volcanoes, as well as coral reefs are vital habitats in areas of the Pacific that would otherwise be open sea with comparatively little life.

In addition, the deep sea of the Pacific is an ecosystem in itself. This environment is the vastest of all, though it contains significantly less biodiversity by volume than the others. Some deep-sea organisms, such as certain species of king crab, are well known due to their commercial value, but many are peculiar and most remain enigmatic. An extensive three-year study by the National Oceanic and Atmospheric Administration discovered approximately 350,000 individual deep-sea organisms across a range of nearly 600,000 square kilometers. Only 20 percent of these were identifiable at the species level, so scientists still have much to learn about the deep-sea environment of the Pacific.

1 Look at the four squares [■] that indicate where the following sentence could be added to the passage.

In fact, it is almost twice the size of the next biggest, the Atlantic Ocean.

Where would the sentence best fit?

2 According to paragraph 2, why are the fisheries in the waters west of the Americas abundant?

(A) The recycling of nutrients is gradual rather than sudden.
(B) The underwater terrain prevents cold water from surfacing.
(C) The shore frequently generates sharp changes in depth.
(D) The number of predatory mammals is lower than in other areas.

3 Which of the following can be inferred from paragraph 3 about tidal pools?

(A) They are common in all of the world's oceans.
(B) They are incapable of sustaining many species.
(C) They support fewer total species than kelp forests.
(D) They occur primarily in remote areas of the Pacific.

4 According to paragraph 3, all of the following are features of remote regions of the Pacific EXCEPT

(A) many volcanic islands
(B) various coral habitats
(C) subsurface volcanoes
(D) primarily lifeless environments

5 The word "peculiar" in the passage is closest in meaning to

(A) ordinary
(B) rare
(C) sparse
(D) strange

6 According to paragraph 4, which of the following is true of the three-year study by the National Oceanic and Atmospheric Administration?

(A) It focused on creatures with significant commercial value.
(B) It covered approximately 20 percent of the Pacific Ocean's area.
(C) It revealed how little is known about deep-sea organisms.
(D) It discovered several species that had been considered extinct.

Reading Practice 3

Answer Book p. 45

Weeds and Invasive Plants

Confusion often arises about the difference between weeds and invasive plant species. Both can be frustrating for farmers, landowners, and conservationists, but they are not the same thing. A weed can be invasive or non-invasive, and an invasive species is not necessarily considered a weed. *Weed* is not a scientific term; it is simply a farmer or gardener's word for an unwanted plant. The term *invasive*, on the other hand, has a very specific meaning for biologists. It refers to plants that are foreign to the ecosystem in which they are growing and that do harm to native species.

A key distinction between the two terms is that weeds are never grown intentionally while invasives often are introduced by humans for a specific purpose. Weeds such as crabgrass and dandelions freely sprout without human intervention in farms, lawns, and gardens. They are especially damaging in agriculture, where crops that are grown for food and sustenance have to compete with weeds for space, sunlight, moisture, and nutrients. In contrast, an invasive species is sometimes planted intentionally, whether because people in an area to which the plant is foreign find it attractive or because it is introduced to outcompete other undesirable species. For example, the banana poka, a plant from the Andes, was introduced to Hawaii early in the twentieth century for its edible fruit and pretty flowers.

Another difference between weeds and invasives is that weeds are not always harmful. Some weeds even assist in enriching the soil and preventing erosion. They are considered weeds because they grow unbidden, but they actually provide value to the ecosystem. Invasive plants, however, are detrimental by definition. It should be noted that a plant can be non-native without being invasive. One example is crested wheatgrass, which came to the United States from Siberia but is considered manageable and useful for soil stabilization in the American prairies. Thus, the utility of non-native plants must not be ignored, even though many native plant enthusiasts and some environmentalists view all foreign plant species as threats.

Once introduced, both kinds of plants have the potential to cause severe economic damage. For farmers, weeds reduce yields and contribute to maintenance costs, doing more collective harm around the world than insects, plant diseases, and grazing pests such as rodents and deer. **A** Invasive species are also a major cause of trouble. **B** In one case, a South American plant called the water hyacinth was brought to Uganda for its attractive blossoms and ended up closing ports and bankrupting fishermen because it grew so densely that boats could not get through the country's largest lake. **C** Because the potential for damage is so great, careful species management is required when dealing with both weeds and invasive species. **D**

1 The word "intervention" in the passage is closest in meaning to

(A) instruction
(B) interference
(C) judgement
(D) protection

2 According to paragraph 2, weeds are a problem in agriculture because they

(A) utilize resources that other plants require to grow
(B) destroy the vegetation that has been planted
(C) prevent farmers from easily harvesting their crops
(D) increase the amount of land that must be cultivated

3 Why does the author mention "crested wheatgrass" in the passage?

(A) To establish the economic dangers of invasive species
(B) To show that some invasive plants were intentionally introduced
(C) To provide evidence that non-native plants can be beneficial
(D) To demonstrate the reasons that invasive plants are introduced

4 Look at the four squares [■] that indicate where the following sentence could be added to the passage.

An important aspect of this is community education programs to teach relevant parties how best to prevent undesirable plants from taking over.

Where would the sentence best fit?

5 According to paragraph 4, the introduction of the water hyacinth into Uganda

(A) increased the overall aesthetic appeal of a large body of water
(B) caused hardship for people who depended on a lake for income
(C) resulted in significant damage to many privately owned boats
(D) encouraged coastal communities to improve their port facilities

6 According to the passage, which of the following is NOT true of weeds and invasive species?

(A) Invasive plants are sometimes intentionally grown, but weeds are not.
(B) Weeds are any unwanted plants in a general, non-scientific sense.
(C) Weeds are always as harmful as invasive species.
(D) Invasive species are not necessarily weeds.

TOEFL Reading

The History of Hydropower

Humans have harnessed flowing water for power since the dawn of civilization. Waterwheels, which were used for grinding grain and irrigating crops, first appeared around 4000 BC. Though these would undergo a few improvements, including the addition of gearing, the same basic design would remain in place until the nineteenth century.

➡ An important innovation occurred in 1827, when French engineer Benoît Fourneyron invented the turbine. He utilized two sets of curved blades that sat in the water horizontally, making his turbine much more efficient at turning flowing river water into mechanical energy than the traditional vertical waterwheel. His first model was capable of generating only six horsepower. However, by 1837 he had made significant improvements to his original design and had built one that generated sixty horsepower. Fourneyron's turbines proved popular with manufacturers and were put to work powering factories in cities across the United States, especially those of the burgeoning textile industry in the northeastern part of the country.

➡ Although the use of hydropower to generate electricity attracted a great deal of attention from engineers around the world in the nineteenth century, it was in the United States that this new technology began to be applied in earnest. Facilities were built across the country, and one of the most impressive of these was the Edward Dean Adams Power Plant, which opened in 1895. A channel diverted water from the Niagara River into a pipe that carried it down a deep vertical shaft. At the bottom of this shaft was a massive turbine, which rotated swiftly due to the force of the falling water. The turbine was connected to ten generators—devices that included powerful magnets and produced an electrical current when rotated. The electricity generated by this plant was used throughout the state of New York.

➡ Hydropower would remain a driving force throughout the twentieth century, with ever-larger dams being built to meet the exploding demand for electricity. As hydropower offered a low cost-to-power ratio, it was vital to growing heavy industry sectors. As a result, many people began to associate hydropower with progress. For example, the Hoover Dam, completed in 1935 on the Colorado River, came to be viewed by Americans as a symbol of national strength and a better life for all citizens. In the late 1980s, however, the American public became disillusioned with hydropower. They came to understand that large dams wreak havoc on local ecosystems, particularly as the floods induced during their construction destroy fish and animal habitats. Awareness of these issues brought the momentum of hydropower to a temporary halt.

In the twenty-first century, concerns about climate change have brought hydropower back into focus despite its environmental drawbacks. [A] As the flow of a river is constant, water is a much more practical renewable energy source than wind or solar. [B] It has also proven to be

Volume | Review | Help | Back | Next

more cost-effective. **C** As a result, there has been a significant increase in the amount of power generated by hydroelectric facilities worldwide. **D**

1 The word "undergo" in the passage is closest in meaning to

Ⓐ experience
Ⓑ transport
Ⓒ augment
Ⓓ demonstrate

2 The word "those" in the passage refers to

Ⓐ turbines
Ⓑ manufacturers
Ⓒ factories
Ⓓ cities

3 According to paragraph 2, a distinguishing feature of Fourneyron's turbine was

Ⓐ the amount of power needed to move it
Ⓑ its orientation relative to the water
Ⓒ the extent to which its blades were curved
Ⓓ its ability to withstand damage from a river

Paragraph 2 is marked with an arrow [➡].

4 Which of the sentences below best expresses the essential information in the highlighted sentence in the passage? *Incorrect* choices change the meaning in important ways or leave out essential information.

Ⓐ During the nineteenth century, American experts brought hydroelectric technologies from other countries to the United States.
Ⓑ The utilization of hydropower to produce electricity began in the United States and was transferred to other countries in the 1800s.
Ⓒ The production of hydroelectric power was initially centered on the United States in the 1800s, but there was global interest in this field.
Ⓓ That hydropower could be used to create an electrical current was first discovered by American engineers in the nineteenth century.

5 According to paragraph 3, the turbine used in the Edward Dean Adams Power Plant was

(A) located at the entrance to a deep hole in the ground
(B) attached to multiple components that generated electricity
(C) dependent on an electrical current produced by a generator
(D) installed in a facility at the center of the Niagara River

Paragraph 3 is marked with an arrow [➡].

6 Why does the author mention the Hoover Dam in paragraph 4?

(A) To stress the importance of heavy industry in the US
(B) To suggest that the demand for hydropower was increasing
(C) To demonstrate the economic benefits of a new power source
(D) To illustrate the cultural significance of a technology

Paragraph 4 is marked with an arrow [➡].

7 Which of the following can be inferred from paragraph 4 about the American people prior to 1980?

(A) They were willing to allow the destruction of river ecosystems to generate electricity.
(B) They lacked knowledge about the negative environmental impact of hydropower.
(C) They insisted that dams only be constructed in areas with small wildlife populations.
(D) They were frustrated that hydroelectric plants were being built in many places.

Paragraph 4 is marked with an arrow [➡].

8 The word "drawbacks" in the passage is closest in meaning to

(A) policies
(B) influences
(C) standards
(D) downsides

Volume Review Help Back Next

9 Look at the four squares [■] that indicate where the following sentence could be added to the passage.

In fact, electricity produced from wind and solar power is approximately 70 percent and 170 percent more expensive respectively.

Where would the sentence best fit?

Click on a square [■] to add the sentence to the passage.

10 Directions: An introductory sentence for a brief summary of the passage is provided below. Complete the summary by selecting the THREE answer choices that express the most important ideas in the passage. Some sentences do not belong in the summary because they express ideas that are not presented in the passage or are minor ideas in the passage. **This question is worth 2 points.**

Drag your answer choices to the spaces where they belong.
To remove an answer choice, click on it. To review the passage, click on **View Text**.

Technological developments from the nineteenth century onwards have significantly increased the utility of hydropower.

-
-
-

Answer Choices

Ⓐ Changes to the gear systems of waterwheels resulted in these machines being used for a wide variety of purposes.

Ⓑ The invention of the turbine in 1827 greatly improved the efficiency of converting water power into mechanical energy.

Ⓒ The discovery that hydropower could be used to produce electricity led to the construction of these types of power plants throughout the US.

Ⓓ The Edward Dean Adams Power Plant had a large enough capacity to supply electricity to communities across New York State.

Ⓔ Concerns about habitat destruction led many Americans to demand a halt to the construction of new hydropower facilities.

Ⓕ Despite environmental issues, the use of hydroelectric power continues to expand because it is currently the best form of renewable energy.

Answer Book p. 46

Answer Book p. 48

TOEFL Reading

The Nature of Art

For over two millennia, artists and art critics have discussed and debated the theory of art put forward in Aristotle's *Poetics*, in which the philosopher described art as "following the pattern of nature." Aristotle's interpretation of the Greek term *mimesis* (usually translated as "imitation") has been at the center of the discussion. A prevalent assumption among art critics has been that Aristotle used mimesis in a single literal sense to show that genuine art should replicate nature, but this view fails to capture the dual meaning of his theory as he also likened the make-believe of children to the creative intent of artists.

➡ Still, many Renaissance artists inherited the strict interpretation of Greek mimesis, as demonstrated by their love of the story of Zeuxis and Parrhasius, two ancient Greek artists. According to Roman philosopher Pliny the Elder, Zeuxis and Parrhasius held a competition to determine who the greater artist was between them. When Zeuxis unveiled his painting of grapes, birds descended from the sky and began trying to consume them. The birds were thus deceived by the realistic portrayal of the fruit. Proud of this result, Zeuxis promptly asked that the curtain be removed from Parrhasius's painting, but no sooner than he had made his request, he realized that the curtain was part of the painting.

➡ This story was popular in the Netherlands during the seventeenth century, and its direct influence is apparent in some Dutch paintings of the period. Adrian van der Spelt, for instance, used a similar motif in his *Flower Still Life with Curtain*, which realistically displayed a curtain pulled to the side of the canvas as if to reveal the painting behind it. Many other Dutch still lifes were equally lifelike, and a fashionable trend at the time was for artists to attempt to generate a perception of illusion. **A** To a casual viewer, most Dutch still lifes would seem purely imitative; but a closer observation reveals they included symbolic elements. **B** Though the subjects of paintings often included tangible items, the objects were not merely depictions of nature. **C** The presence of burning candles or hourglasses, for instance, was representative of the fleeting nature of wealth, riches, and life itself. **D**

➡ In modern history, numerous artists and art critics have rejected the notion that art should imitate nature. Some artists have viewed art as a means of personal expression or even as an abstract, impersonal essence. According to them, the natural appearance of an object should be a subordinate concern. For example, Vasily Kandinsky believed that abstraction was an eternal artistic force that was not related to the world of form but only to that of pure experience. Regardless of the definition of art's true nature, like all things learned, art is evaluated within the cultural context of artists, and all people engaged in artistic crafts share one thing in common: they operate within the bounds of the institutions, traditions, and expectations of a culture.

Volume Review Help Back Next

1 Which of the sentences below best expresses the essential information in the highlighted sentence in the passage? *Incorrect* choices change the meaning in important ways or leave out essential information.

(A) Despite the fact that Aristotle specifically emphasized his view that genuine art should closely imitate nature, many art critics ignored it.
(B) Aristotle did not intend for art critics to interpret his theory as only applying to artists who developed creative intentions.
(C) Aristotle thought that art involved both an accurate depiction and a creative interpretation of nature, but many experts ignore the latter part of his definition.
(D) An aspect of Aristotle's theory that is not well understood by critics is that he favored creative expression over replication of nature.

2 The word "unveiled" in the passage is closest in meaning to

(A) promoted
(B) revealed
(C) repudiated
(D) initiated

3 Which of the following can be inferred from paragraph 2 about the Greek artist Zeuxis?

(A) His art was more popular than that of Parrhasius.
(B) His story was fabricated by Pliny the Elder.
(C) He was ultimately victorious in the art competition.
(D) He was initially confused about Parrhasius's painting.

Paragraph 2 is marked with an arrow [➡].

4 The word "it" in the passage refers to

(A) motif
(B) curtain
(C) canvas
(D) painting

5 According to paragraph 3, which of the following was mentioned as a popular goal of Dutch artists in the 1600s?

Ⓐ They intended to invent a totally new art form.
Ⓑ They wanted to recreate classical paintings.
Ⓒ They tried to produce a sense of illusion.
Ⓓ They sought to portray unusual subjects.

Paragraph 3 is marked with an arrow [➡].

6 Why does the author mention burning candles and hourglasses in paragraph 3?

Ⓐ To indicate themes that Dutch artists borrowed from the Greeks
Ⓑ To emphasize how lifelike most Dutch paintings were
Ⓒ To illustrate that Dutch art included symbolic representations
Ⓓ To highlight the primary objects depicted in Dutch art

Paragraph 3 is marked with an arrow [➡].

7 The word "subordinate" in the passage is closest in meaning to

Ⓐ secondary
Ⓑ primary
Ⓒ sincere
Ⓓ frivolous

8 According to paragraph 4, an assessment of an artistic work must take into account

Ⓐ the degree to which the artist adheres to tradition
Ⓑ the environment of the person who created it
Ⓒ the accuracy with which the subject material is presented
Ⓓ the craftsmanship of its various components

Paragraph 4 is marked with an arrow [➡].

Volume Review Help Back Next

9 Look at the four squares [■] that indicate where the following sentence could be added to the passage.

Even flowers and fruit carried this meaning, as they were sometimes shown fading or rotting to convey the transitory nature of life's pleasures.

Where would the sentence best fit?

Click on a square [■] to add the sentence to the passage.

10 **Directions:** An introductory sentence for a brief summary of the passage is provided below. Complete the summary by selecting the THREE answer choices that express the most important ideas in the passage. Some sentences do not belong in the summary because they express ideas that are not presented in the passage or are minor ideas in the passage. **This question is worth 2 points.**

Drag your answer choices to the spaces where they belong.
To remove an answer choice, click on it. To review the passage, click on **View Text**.

What constitutes the true nature of art is a topic that has been deliberated for many years, starting with the art theory of Aristotle.

-
-
-

Answer Choices

(A) A tale that illustrates how realistic art could be was appreciated among Dutch artists, who combined very realistic subjects with symbolic elements in their art.

(B) In a refusal to accept the idea that art should mimic nature, many modern artists and critics have turned to more diverse forms of artistic expression.

(C) Despite having deep respect for Greek art, Renaissance artists gradually began to reject the theory of art that Aristotle promoted.

(D) The tendency toward abstraction in modern art ignores the most important element of Aristotle's view of the relationship between art and the natural world.

(E) Even though Aristotle's theory contained both imitative and creative aspects, many artists of the Renaissance continued to accept that art should closely follow nature.

(F) Adrian van der Spelt's *Flower Still Life with Curtain* is an excellent example of a Dutch still life, but its use of a preexisting motif is far from original.

Answer Book p. 48

Vocabulary Review

Answer Book p. 49

A. Fill in the blanks with the appropriate words from the box.

disillusioned	replicate	predatory
foreboding	diverted	astronomical

1 The teacher's announcement of a surprise test filled many of the students with ______________.

2 I voted for the candidate twice but later became ______________ with his misuse of campaign donations.

3 The street was closed for construction, so drivers were ______________ to the expressway.

4 Hawks are ______________ creatures, eating rodents and other small animals.

5 The solar wind is a(n) ______________ event that has a direct impact on the lives of people on Earth.

6 There are a number of software applications available to ______________ human speech.

B. Choose the closest meaning for each highlighted word or phrase.

7 The construction of the pyramids in ancient Egypt was a tremendous engineering achievement.
(A) immense (B) meager (C) natural (D) pitiable

8 Manure became a much less significant pollution problem after cars supplanted horses.
(A) enveloped (B) outpaced (C) recharged (D) replaced

9 During the 1990s, many new tech companies entered the burgeoning Internet market.
(A) stagnating (B) demanding (C) expanding (D) commanding

10 Reassurances from my teachers did nothing to reduce my apprehension about final exams.
(A) confidence (B) anxiety (C) misery (D) appreciation

11 During World War II, the family harbored Jews in their home to save them from the Nazis.
(A) sheltered (B) cheered (C) evaded (D) mixed

12 The detective struggled to understand the enigmatic clues at the scene of the crime.
(A) complex (B) bountiful (C) mysterious (D) obvious

13 The team was in last place several months ago, but they were able to rebound and win the World Series.
(A) repress (B) recover (C) reexamine (D) resolve

14 During the Great Depression, Franklin D. Roosevelt tried in earnest to create jobs and stimulate the economy.
(A) ingeniously (B) temporarily (C) intently (D) rebelliously

CHAPTER 09

Summary

Summary

About the Question Type

Summary questions ask you to complete a summary of the passage by selecting three out of six sentences that best express the major ideas in the passage.

Correct answer choices are restatements of the main idea of one or more paragraphs in the passage. Incorrect answer choices often express inaccurate information, minor points (examples, supporting ideas, etc.), or details that are not mentioned in the passage.

Question Format

Directions: An introductory sentence for a brief summary of the passage is provided below. Complete the summary by selecting the THREE answer choices that express the most important ideas in the passage. Some sentences do not belong in the summary because they express ideas that are not presented in the passage or are minor ideas in the passage. **This question is worth 2 points.**

Drag your answer choices to the spaces where they belong.
To remove an answer choice, click on it. To review the passage, click on **View Text**.

[An introductory sentence]
-
-
-

Answer Choices

Key Strategies

- **Step 1** — Read the introductory sentence that represents the main idea of the passage.
- **Step 2** — Scan the passage to see if each answer choice is supported by the passage.
- **Step 3** — Select the three answer choices that express the major ideas in the passage.

Example

Answer Book p. 49

The Stock Market Crash of 1929

The New York Stock Exchange experienced an unprecedented collapse in the final days of October 1929, losing a third of its value in the space of a week. The Dow Jones, an index designed to reflect the US stock market's performance, fell by 11 percent on Black Thursday (October 24), recovered slightly on Friday due to a concerted effort by bankers to purchase shares, but then plummeted by 13.47 percent when the stock market reopened on Black Monday. On Black Tuesday, panicked investors unloaded a record sixteen million shares.

The crash was a result of an unsustainable boom over the course of the 1920s, which saw the prices of many stocks quadruple. Millions of people believed this trend would continue and borrowed money to invest, incurring debts that they would not be able to repay if the market collapsed. When stock prices began to decline in 1929, these people immediately began selling their shares in order to avoid ruin. At the same time, concerns about the stability of the nation's financial intuitions caused masses of people to withdraw their funds from their banks, making the situation worse.

In the ensuing months and years, the Great Depression enveloped the country, and economic hardship spread around the globe. The mass sell-off of stocks resulted in billions of dollars of losses and cost many Americans their life savings or businesses. By 1933, unemployment reached 30 percent, and almost half of the nation's banks had closed their doors.

1 **Directions:** An introductory sentence for a brief summary of the passage is provided below. Complete the summary by selecting the THREE answer choices that express the most important ideas in the passage.

Over the course of a week in October 1929, the stock market suddenly lost a large percentage of its value.

(A) The stock market experienced a massive decline in 1929, with investors selling millions of shares in a single day.

(B) A deliberate attempt to sustain the stock market succeeded, as the market recovered briefly on Friday.

(C) The crash was preceded by a decade of economic growth in which many people took on debt to buy stocks.

(D) Many banks were forced to limit the amount of money that their customers could withdraw from their accounts.

(E) Although the Great Depression ruined the US economy, its worldwide impact was much more limited.

(F) The stock market crash of 1929 resulted in devastating losses and led to the Great Depression.

Reading Practice 1

Answer Book p. 50

Early Mechanical Clocks in Europe

The first fully mechanical clocks in Europe were developed in the thirteenth century, and the earliest of these were known as *verge-and-foliot* clocks. The verge was a vertical rod, and the foliot was a horizontal bar that was affixed to the top of the verge. On each end of the foliot, adjustable weights could be placed to keep the bar in balance and alter the distance that it moved. The other major parts of this early design were toothed wheels (gearwheels), which turned as the foliot moved back and forth like a horizontal seesaw.

Normally, suspended weights accelerate with each movement. However, the verge-and-foliot system prevented this natural acceleration so that the foliot would move at a slow, uniform speed. This allowed the teeth of the wheels to move at regular intervals, with each release or "escape" of the gearwheel representing the equivalent of one tick of the clock. A device that transfers energy to intermittently impede and release a counting mechanism like a gearwheel is known as an *escapement.* Although the verge-and-foliot escapement was a significant improvement over prior timekeeping technologies like sundials, it was only precise enough to mark the hours. Improvements had to be made for clocks to be accurate at the level of minutes and seconds.

The first major step in this direction was the invention of the pendulum. A pendulum consists of a vertical rod, which is attached to a pivot, and a suspended weight attached to the bottom of the rod. When set in motion, a pendulum continues to swing back and forth on its own. The time a pendulum takes to make one complete cycle is its *period*, and the period depends solely on the length of the rod rather than the mass of the weight. In many pendulum clocks, an anchor escapement was used. It was named for its shape as it looked like a marine anchor. The top of an anchor escapement was typically shaped like an upside-down *V* with a sharp inward-directed point on each end of the "legs." Attached to the center was a pendulum, and as the pendulum swung, the two points alternately caught and released the teeth of a rotating gearwheel.

Over time, clockmakers learned to modify pendulum clocks in order to continually increase their precision. Through experiments, they discovered that a pendulum must be 0.994 meters in length to create a period of exactly two seconds so that each swing lasted precisely one second. Another innovation occurred after the realization that pendulum clocks ran slower in summer and faster in winter due to the expansion and contraction of the metal rod, causing the loss of up to one second per week during the warm season. To compensate for this, metal rods were replaced with wooden ones. Eventually, these and other improvements led to the development of pendulum clocks that fluctuated by as little as one second per year, so they rarely needed adjustment.

Glossary

· sundial: a device measuring the time of the day by the position of the Sun

1 The word "impede" in the passage is closest in meaning to

(A) duplicate
(B) inhibit
(C) compel
(D) revise

2 Which of the following is NOT mentioned as a characteristic of verge-and-foliot clocks?

(A) They were less precise than sundials at marking hours.
(B) They used a horizontal bar to control the motion of gearwheels.
(C) They were not accurate enough to indicate minutes and seconds.
(D) They prevented suspended weights from speeding up.

3 According to paragraph 3, which of the following determines the time a pendulum takes to complete a cycle?

(A) The speed of the rotating gearwheel
(B) The shape of the escapement
(C) The length of the rod
(D) The mass of the weight

4 According to paragraph 4, why were metal pendulum rods replaced with wooden ones?

(A) Metal rods produced seasonal fluctuations.
(B) The weight of the metal interrupted movement.
(C) The wood allowed for two-second periods.
(D) Wooden rods were more efficient to produce.

5 **Directions:** An introductory sentence for a brief summary of the passage is provided below. Complete the summary by selecting the THREE answer choices that express the most important ideas in the passage.

Europeans began producing fully mechanical clocks in the thirteenth century, and their development evolved over time.

(A) Makers of pendulum clocks gradually increased their accuracy through advances like mastering the length of the pendulum and altering the material used to make the rod.
(B) A major upgrade over the verge-and-foliot escapement, the anchor escapement allowed clockmakers to replace the gearwheel with a weighted rod that swung back and forth.
(C) Verge-and-foliot clocks were the first fully mechanical clocks, and they used several interworking parts to control a gearwheel to keep time.
(D) The invention of the pendulum led to the development of clocks that employed a rod and a suspended weight to generate periodic movements.
(E) Because refined pendulum clocks produced fluctuations of approximately one second in each annual cycle, it was rarely necessary to adjust them.
(F) Clockmakers eventually realized that after a pendulum was set in motion, a series of gearwheels were needed to recycle energy in order to keep it swinging.

Reading Practice 2

Answer Book p. 51

Romanticism

The late eighteenth century was known as the Age of Revolutions as social and political upheavals, such as the American and French Revolutions, dramatically changed the way Western people viewed their societies and the world. After centuries in which monarchs ruled, the people turned to more democratic forms of government. The development of a revolutionary spirit also occurred in literature and the arts when a generation of intellectuals and artists began to challenge the literary and artistic trends of the previous centuries. From the end of the eighteenth century and well into the nineteenth century, this generation inspired the ideas behind the movement known as Romanticism.

Advocates of Romanticism strongly prioritized the role of imagination over reason and logic. They believed that imagination was the principal creative force of humans and that it was the most essential element for understanding ourselves and the world around us. In the words of the English Romantic poet William Wordsworth, humans not only discern the world but also help to form it. In this sense, the human ability to imagine things is similar to a god's or deity's capacity to create the universe. Imagination is how human beings interpret their experiences, and then it is up to the Romantic artist or writer to create works based on this.

Another central feature of Romanticism was the focus on subjective individualism and freedom. A This emphasis was clearly in line with the revolutionary spirit of the times, in which liberalism was gaining substantial momentum. B With regard to the arts, this meant that the artist or writer should be free of the restraints of convention. C Therefore, Romanticism represented a strong objection to the obsession with standardized beauty in Neoclassicism and the insistence on reason in the Enlightenment as it highlighted subjectivity, disdain for conformity to rules, and the supremacy of bold individualism. D

To pursue the ideal of individualism, many Romantics experimented with a solitary life away from society in order to gain greater self-awareness and a stronger connection to nature. The practice of meditating, writing, and painting outdoors became a major trend of the period. Indeed, the Romantics venerated nature in a way that previous generations had not. Rather than passively accepting man's control over the environment as was the tendency during the Industrial Revolution, Romantic intellectuals sought to elevate the natural world to a higher status, even equal with or above that of mankind. This aspect of Romanticism inspired similar movements, such as Transcendentalism, that added an even deeper spiritual and moral character to Romanticism. Transcendentalists like Henry David Thoreau and Ralph Waldo Emerson believed that God could be found in nature and that the human soul's striving to become one with God and nature was the highest form of spiritual attainment.

1 According to paragraph 2, what did Romantic poet William Wordsworth say about humans?

(A) They always interpret their experiences in a subjective way.
(B) They can never truly understand the world around them.
(C) They are made in the form of gods and deities.
(D) They both perceive the world and aid in its creation.

2 Look at the four squares [■] that indicate where the following sentence could be added to the passage.

A social and political movement, liberalism was centered on ideas such as equality and an individual's right to pursue happiness and live a life of his or her choosing.

Where would the sentence best fit?

3 The word "disdain" is closest in meaning to

(A) passivity
(B) contempt
(C) logic
(D) flexibility

4 Which of the following can be inferred from paragraph 4 about Romantics and Transcendentalists?

(A) They believed that society should enforce strict moral rules.
(B) They were opposed to some aspects of the Industrial Revolution.
(C) They denied that the human soul could become one with God.
(D) They were inspired by Neoclassical and Enlightenment thought.

5 **Directions:** An introductory sentence for a brief summary of the passage is provided below. Complete the summary by selecting the THREE answer choices that express the most important ideas in the passage.

A generation of thinkers and artists began to challenge conventional views and encourage new ways of expression during the Romanticism movement.

(A) Although Romanticism flourished during the eighteenth century, it was superseded by Transcendentalism at the beginning of the nineteenth century.
(B) Individualistic intellectuals sought refuge from society in order to concentrate on getting in touch with nature and themselves.
(C) Romantic artists objected strongly to the formality of the Neoclassicism, but they shared its appreciation of beauty.
(D) Among the ideals of promoters of Romanticism was the subordination of logic and reason to creativity.
(E) Like Romantics, Transcendentalists believed that the superior form of spiritual experience was to communicate directly with God.
(F) Parallel with the revolutionary spirit of the times, Romantic thinkers championed the values of individualism, freedom, and equality.

Reading Practice 3

Answer Book p. 51

Free Radicals

Aerobic cellular respiration is the process by which humans and other organisms convert oxygen obtained from the atmosphere into energy. Most of the oxygen absorbed by the body, primarily through the lungs and skin, is transformed into water and carbon dioxide. But about 5 percent of the oxygen produces waste products known as reactive oxygen species (ROS). These toxic compounds often form or become free radicals, which are atoms or molecules distinguished by the fact they include unpaired electrons. Electrons usually travel in twos; when one or more electrons are separated from their mates, the atoms and molecules that contain them become unstable. When a free radical is generated in an organic cell, a chain reaction is triggered in which the free radical attempts to stabilize itself by obtaining its missing electron from a neighboring molecule, transforming it into a free radical. As the number of free radicals increases, cell damage occurs.

Free radicals play a role in the development of a wide range of human diseases and may even be responsible for the degenerative processes associated with aging. These problems arise when the proportion of free radicals among a cell's estimated 100 trillion atoms becomes too great, creating a condition known as oxidative stress. The body's cells, proteins, lipids, and DNA are compromised by oxidative stress. Damaged molecules sometimes mutate and become tumors. Lipids can change shape and become trapped in arteries, causing cardiovascular problems. As the body ages, its share of free radicals increases, contributing to age-related complications such as wrinkled skin, muscle and joint pain, and memory loss.

Although free radicals are produced naturally by the body during aerobic respiration, they can also be generated as a result of exposure to external factors. These outside causes of free radicals include air pollutants, ozone, cigarette smoke, X-rays, fried foods, and industrial chemicals. Free radicals are also produced during physical exercise. However, the net effect of a workout on the body's cells is still positive because exercise also generates antioxidants, which are molecules that can contribute their own electrons to a free radical, resolving the unstable molecule's need for a pair of electrons without becoming destabilized by the contribution.

Despite the considerable destructive potential of free radicals, scientists have come to realize that they play a salutary role in multiple biological processes. Most importantly, a number of studies have shown that the human body's immune system makes active use of free radicals to destroy pathogens. When a bacterium or virus is detected, a large number of free radicals will be generated and directed toward the pathogen to neutralize it. Furthermore, their potential for causing cellular damage can be harnessed to treat cancer in radiation therapy, which generates free radicals in strategically targeted locations in the body. Free radicals are also useful for regulating the growth and death of cells.

Glossary

· lipid: a fatty organic compound that is insoluble in water

1 According to paragraph 1, which of the following is true of reactive oxygen species?

(A) They are transformed into water and carbon dioxide by aerobic respiration.
(B) They are harmful byproducts of a biological process that produces energy.
(C) They never contain electrons that are paired with others.
(D) They try to stabilize themselves by releasing electrons to other molecules.

2 According to paragraph 2, oxidative stress results from

(A) the mutation of molecules damaged by free radicals
(B) a person's DNA altered by a degenerative disorder
(C) an excessive number of atoms in the body's cells
(D) a surplus of free radicals in an individual cell

3 Why does the author mention "antioxidants" in the passage?

(A) To explain why an activity does not pose a health risk
(B) To refute a common belief that exercise is entirely beneficial
(C) To demonstrate that free radicals can have a positive impact
(D) To show that a physical response does not remove electrons

4 The word "harnessed" in the passage is closest in meaning to

(A) developed
(B) adapted
(C) utilized
(D) examined

5 **Directions:** An introductory sentence for a brief summary of the passage is provided below. Complete the summary by selecting the THREE answer choices that express the most important ideas in the passage.

Free radicals are unstable atoms or molecules containing unpaired electrons.

(A) Cell damage can result from the accumulation of too many free radicals in the body.
(B) A variety of age-related problems are known to result from the presence of free radicals.
(C) Smoking and other unhealthy activities can increase the number of free radicals in the body's cells.
(D) Both internal and external factors contribute to the generation of free radicals in the human body.
(E) Free radicals are a treatment for cancer rather than a cause of the formation of cancerous cells.
(F) Cardiovascular problems result from the influence of free radicals on the lipids in the arteries.

Answer Book p. 52

TOEFL Reading

Forest Fire Ecology of the Blue Mountains

Australia's Blue Mountain National Park spans over 267,000 hectares of land and includes thousands of rare species of trees, plants, and wildlife. Forest fires have made a number of contributions to the development of the diverse ecological features of the Blue Mountains. These have also led to adaptations by numerous plant species, such as trees in the genus *Eucalyptus*. Eucalyptus trees produce highly combustible fragrant oil in their leaves, and this attribute ensures that the forest floor beneath them becomes covered with highly flammable leaves, which provide a potent fuel for forest fires.

➡ The majority of fires occur during summer, when lightning strikes in the forest are more prevalent. The lower mountain regions have a greater risk of ignition because the air there is drier due to less rainfall. As the lower regions experience a greater frequency of fires, resulting in little time for flammable leaves from the eucalyptus trees to pile up on the forest floor, fire intensity is relatively low in those regions.

➡ The intensity of a forest fire is a significant factor in rejuvenating the diverse plant life of the region. Approximately 250 separate plant species within the national park require fire for seed germination to transpire. In many of these species, the seeds remain dormant in the soil until a fire develops. The storage of seeds in the ground is referred to as the soil seedbank. Some of these seeds just require the release of smoke or charcoal for activation, which can be achieved even at a low temperature, while others can only sprout after intense heat.

➡ To avoid competition, plant species without soil seedbanks have evolved different strategies for surviving forest fires. Evergreen shrubs in the genus *Petrophile* keep their seeds in hard wooden cones on their branches, and the seeds are released when a fire causes the cones to pop open. **A** In some herbaceous species, mature plants have evolved to quickly regrow if they are not completely burned to ashes. **B** Meanwhile, adult eucalyptus trees feature a unique adaptation to fire as their thick protective bark can spare the trunk from damage. **C** After being burnt, the trunk can sprout new limbs. **D** This protection offers eucalyptus trees a competitive advantage over other fire-damaged plants.

➡ Besides facilitating plant propagation, forest fires can provide several other benefits. A four-decade long experiment performed by the Tall Timbers Research Station in Florida demonstrated that fires are essential aspects of the forest ecosystem by revealing that a forest protected from fires experienced a 90 percent drop in plant diversity. One way that fires help is through the eradication of a competitive species. By burning dominant plants, the biodiversity of an area can surge, as less dominant species have an opportunity to bloom in the sudden ecological vacancy. At the same time, burning can turn decaying plant matter into ashes rich with nutrients. These nutrients, including carbon and nitrogen, are returned to the soil and encourage healthy seedling growth. Finally, a fire destroys many of the insects that are harmful to trees and

Volume Review Help Back Next

other forms of vegetation, keeping the forests healthy.

1 The word "These" in the passage refers to

Ⓐ Forest fires
Ⓑ contributions
Ⓒ features
Ⓓ Blue Mountains

2 The word "attribute" in the passage is closest in meaning to

Ⓐ fluctuation
Ⓑ property
Ⓒ synopsis
Ⓓ quantity

3 Which of the following can be inferred from paragraph 2 about the relationship between elevation and forest fires?

Ⓐ Lower locations undergo intense fires.
Ⓑ Slow-forming fires occur in higher areas.
Ⓒ Higher regions experience fewer fires.
Ⓓ Larger fires develop on smaller mountains.

Paragraph 2 is marked with an arrow [➡].

4 According to paragraph 3, which of the following is true about the soil seedbank?

Ⓐ It conserves seeds after they sprout.
Ⓑ It protects seeds until a season changes.
Ⓒ It retains seeds until conditions prompt germination.
Ⓓ It stores seeds for preservation during bad weather.

Paragraph 3 is marked with an arrow [➡].

5 Why does the author mention Evergreen shrubs in paragraph 4?

Ⓐ To demonstrate that a variation of the seedbank is used by many species
Ⓑ To provide an example of fire-survival adaptation by a species without a seedbank
Ⓒ To suggest that some reproductive methods are more effective than seedbanks
Ⓓ To compare two different types of plants with seedbanks in fire-prone ecosystems

Paragraph 4 is marked with an arrow [➡].

6 According to paragraph 4, what do Eucalyptus trees do to recover from a fire?

Ⓐ They release new seeds onto the soil via cones.
Ⓑ They begin to sprout as juveniles on the ground.
Ⓒ They start to grow new branches from the trunk.
Ⓓ They use heat to initiate a reproduction strategy.

Paragraph 4 is marked with an arrow [➡].

7 Which of the sentences below best expresses the essential information in the highlighted sentence in the passage? *Incorrect* choices change the meaning in important ways or leave out essential information.

Ⓐ An experiment in Florida has shown that biological growth can be diminished by forest fires.
Ⓑ Research in Florida revealed how the negative effects of forest fires can be prevented through conservation.
Ⓒ A study indicates that protected forests are unable to maintain a high volume of plants.
Ⓓ An extended study of a protected area determined that eliminating fires results in a decline in forest biodiversity.

8 According to paragraph 5, forests enjoy all of the following benefits from fires EXCEPT:

Ⓐ Highly successful species are removed, allowing others to thrive.
Ⓑ Pests are destroyed, improving the overall health of many plants.
Ⓒ Chemicals necessary for plant growth are released into the atmosphere.
Ⓓ The nutrient-rich burnt remains of vegetation are added to the soil.

Paragraph 5 is marked with an arrow [➡].

Volume Review Help Back Next

9 Look at the four squares [■] that indicate where the following sentence could be added to the passage.

In particular, grasses and orchids recover rapidly and become reproductively mature almost immediately.

Where would the sentence best fit?

Click on a square [■] to add the sentence to the passage.

10 **Directions:** An introductory sentence for a brief summary of the passage is provided below. Complete the summary by selecting the THREE answer choices that express the most important ideas in the passage. Some sentences do not belong in the summary because they express ideas that are not presented in the passage or are minor ideas in the passage. **This question is worth 2 points.**

Drag your answer choices to the spaces where they belong.
To remove an answer choice, click on it. To review the passage, click on **View Text**.

The ecology of the Australian Blue Mountains is influenced by frequent forest fires.

-
-
-

Answer Choices

Ⓐ A number of species in the region are specifically adapted to survive a forest fire.

Ⓑ Research has shown that fires are often necessary to ensure that a forest includes a wide variety of plant species.

Ⓒ Forest fires provide an opportunity to clear the forest floor of decaying biological litter.

Ⓓ The lack of rainfall in the upper regions of the mountains results in more frequent forest fires.

Ⓔ Fire intensity is an important aspect in determining the seed germination of tree in the Blue Mountains.

Ⓕ The location of the Blue Mountains contributes to the increased likelihood of forest fires in the region.

Answer Book p. 52

Answer Book p. 54

TOEFL Reading

Hagia Sophia

The Hagia Sophia (Greek for "Holy Wisdom") is a domed structure in Istanbul, Turkey that is regarded as one of the world's great monuments. It is remarkable not only as a sample of Byzantine architecture dating back to the sixth century AD but also for its highly varied history, reflecting the profound political and religious shifts that have rocked the region over the centuries. It served first as a Christian cathedral, then as an Islamic mosque, then as a museum and popular tourist attraction, and has once again become a place of worship for Muslims.

➡ When the Hagia Sophia was erected in 532, Constantinople—as present-day Istanbul was called then—was the capital of the Byzantine Empire, and it was a large metropolis. Although the Western Roman Empire had fallen about a half century earlier, the eastern part thrived as the Byzantine Empire under Justinian the Great. A church in Constantinople was burned in 532 during a riot by individuals angry about high taxes and government corruption. Justinian decided to take the opportunity to assert his authority by building an elaborate new church on the site of the old one. This was the Hagia Sophia, and it was constructed at an astounding pace, reaching completion within six years.

➡ The Hagia Sophia is the finest surviving example of Byzantine architecture, and it is made in the style of a Christian basilica. **A** The central feature of the church is its 107-foot, brick-and-mortar dome. **B** Just below the dome are 40 windows, which drench the marble floor in sunlight. **C** At the request of Justinian, the building materials came from all over the vast empire, including bricks from North Africa and 104 columns from Ephesus and Egypt. **D**

➡ When Constantinople fell into the hands of the Ottoman Empire in 1453, the city was renamed Istanbul. Mehmet the Conqueror ordered that Islam become the official religion, and consequently the Hagia Sophia became a mosque. To achieve consistency with the Islamic architectural style, four 200-foot minarets were added at the corners of the structure. The Christian mosaics, including an image of Jesus Christ on the interior of the dome, were replaced with Islamic calligraphy.

In 1935, Kemal Atatürk, the Republic of Turkey's first president, decided that the Hagia Sophia should serve as a museum. Significant renovations were performed to restore the decorations on the floors and mosaics on the walls that had been covered while the building functioned as a mosque. Furthermore, international organizations, such as the World Monuments Fund (WMF), provided grants that allowed the large domed roof to be repaired and further improvements to be made to the interior. These projects proved to be an overwhelming success, and, by 2014, the Hagia Sophia was attracting approximately 3.2 million tourists annually. However, the Hagia Sophia was converted back to a mosque in 2020, leading to concerns about the conservation of

Volume Review Help Back Next

this treasured site.

1 The word "profound" in the passage is closest in meaning to

Ⓐ accidental
Ⓑ impulsive
Ⓒ significant
Ⓓ deliberate

2 The word "it" in the passage refers to

Ⓐ Hagia Sophia
Ⓑ Constantinople
Ⓒ Istanbul
Ⓓ Byzantine Empire

3 The word "riot" in the passage is closest in meaning to

Ⓐ failure
Ⓑ disaster
Ⓒ invasion
Ⓓ protest

4 It can be inferred from paragraph 2 that the construction of the Hagia Sophia

Ⓐ required high taxes to be imposed on all regions of the Byzantium Empire
Ⓑ took significantly less time than was normal for a project of this scale
Ⓒ angered religious authorities because it caused the destruction of a church
Ⓓ encouraged Emperor Justinian to take a greater interest in Constantinople

Paragraph 2 is marked with an arrow [➡].

5 According to paragraph 3, which of the following is NOT true of the Hagia Sophia?

(A) It was modeled after other Christian houses of worship.
(B) It contains materials acquired all over the world.
(C) It has a lot of natural light during the daytime.
(D) It is covered by a dome made from bricks.

Paragraph 3 is marked with an arrow [➡].

6 According to paragraph 4, how did the Hagia Sophia change in 1453?

(A) It received a new Arabic name.
(B) Artworks in the dome were removed.
(C) Minarets replaced the columns.
(D) It was torn down and rebuilt in the Islamic style.

Paragraph 4 is marked with an arrow [➡].

7 Which of the sentences below best expresses the essential information in the highlighted sentence in the passage? *Incorrect* choices change the meaning of the sentence in important ways or leave out essential information.

(A) The renovated mosque included a smaller number of artworks on its walls than it had previously.
(B) Many new images were added to the floors and walls once the space stopped being used as a mosque.
(C) To make the structure suitable for religious ceremonies, many decorations were removed during remodeling.
(D) Ornamental features that had been hidden when the building was a place of worship were made visible again.

8 Why does the author mention "the World Monuments Fund" in the passage?

(A) To identify a financial incentive for changing the purpose of facility
(B) To provide an example of an organization that made use of a structure
(C) To explain why it was possible to perform some work on a building
(D) To suggest that a remodeling project was more extensive than planned

Volume Review Help Back Next

9 Look at the four squares [■] that indicate where the following sentence could be added to the passage.

This is elevated 180 feet above the church's main nave, or worship area.

Where would the sentence best fit?

Click on a square [■] to add the sentence to the passage.

10 **Directions:** An introductory sentence for a brief summary of the passage is provided below. Complete the summary by selecting the THREE answer choices that express the most important ideas in the passage. Some sentences do not belong in the summary because they express ideas that are not presented in the passage or are minor ideas in the passage. **This question is worth 2 points.**

Drag your answer choices to the spaces where they belong.
To remove an answer choice, click on it. To review the passage, click on **View Text**.

The Hagia Sophia has changed over the centuries in ways that reflect the history of the region.

•
•
•

Answer Choices

(A) The original church was constructed upon the site of an earlier one in the capital of the Byzantine Empire.

(B) Architects from various parts of the Byzantine Empire worked together to design the new religious facility.

(C) Much damage was done to the Hagia Sophia when the city of Constantinople was conquered by Ottoman forces.

(D) In the fifteenth century, the Hagia Sophia became a mosque and underwent significant changes because of its new function.

(E) The building was restored and converted into a museum in modern times, although it is now a mosque again.

(F) The number of tourists visiting the Hagia Sophia increased significantly following the completion of a renovation project.

Answer Book p. 54

Vocabulary Review

Answer Book p. 55

A. Fill in the blanks with the appropriate words from the box.

prioritized	adjustable	quadrupled
interval	alternately	unsustainable

1 I prefer ________________ baseball caps to the fitted kind because I can easily change the size for better comfort.

2 I ________________ rehearsal over homework because I was a devoted member of the school's theater community.

3 The soldier was ________________ confident and fearful as he witnessed the battle around him.

4 During his six-month ________________ between jobs, Mr. Braxton took several business courses at the local community college.

5 The number of foreign students at the university has ________________ over the past five years.

6 Experts think the current use of fossil fuels is ________________ as the supply will eventually run out.

B. Choose the closest meaning for each highlighted word or phrase.

7 When my father hugged me, I felt enveloped in love.
(A) encompassed (B) aggrieved (C) enthused (D) decimated

8 Although mother tigers and their young spend a lot of time together, adult male tigers are mostly solitary creatures.
(A) quiet (B) disorderly (C) amused (D) isolated

9 Michael entered the house, saw the mess, and wondered what had transpired.
(A) surpassed (B) accumulated (C) changed (D) happened

10 An economic contraction followed a period of immense growth, resulting in a recession.
(A) agreement (B) constriction (C) fallacy (D) destruction

11 Diabetes can be a complication of COVID-19, developing after an infection.
(A) demonstration (B) treatment (C) diagnosis (D) ailment

12 The band's first single debuted at number one but soon plummeted to the bottom of the charts.
(A) dropped (B) climbed (C) ascended (D) pivoted

13 The construction of the Hoover Dam presented overwhelming challenges, but the project was a major success.
(A) staggering (B) unprecedented (C) irrational (D) disappointing

14 Most scientists promote the eradication of invasive species that are harmful to local ecosystems.
(A) invitation (B) elimination (C) exclamation (D) participation

CHAPTER 10

Category Chart

Category Chart

About the Question Type

Category Chart questions ask you to complete a table by placing the relevant information in the appropriate categories.

When reading the passage, try to identify what is being compared or contrasted, and recognize the important information for each category.

Question Format

Directions: Select the appropriate phrases from the answer choices and match them to the type to which they relate. **This question is worth 3 points.**

Drag your answer choices to the spaces where they belong.
To remove an answer choice, click on it. To review the passage, click on **View Text**.

Answer Choices	Category 1
	• • •
	Category 2
	• •

Key Strategies

- **Step 1** — Check the categories in the table.
- **Step 2** — Scan the passage and identify the important information for each category.
- **Step 3** — Select the answer choices that best paraphrase the important information in the passage for each category. Answer choices that include information from the passage that is unrelated to the categories or inaccurate information can be eliminated.

Example

Answer Book p. 55

Alkaline and Lithium-Ion Batteries

Batteries power more and more aspects of people's lives in the twenty-first century. There are two main types of batteries on the market today: alkaline and lithium-ion. Both types of batteries store chemical energy and then convert that energy into electrical energy by sending electrons and ions from a negative terminal, or anode, to a positive terminal, or cathode. The electrons move through the battery's circuit, and the ions move through a chemical divider called an electrolyte, which is positioned between the terminals.

Most alkaline batteries transfer ions through the electrolyte in only one direction. The more ions move to the anode, the less voltage is available to the battery, meaning that the amount of electricity it generates declines. When all of the ions have been transferred, a standard alkaline battery is dead and cannot be recharged. The anode for standard alkaline batteries is made with zinc, while manganese dioxide serves as the cathode. By contrast, lithium-ion batteries move their ions back and forth from one side of the battery to the other, making them reusable. Users simply connect the battery to a power source in order to move used lithium ions from the metal oxide cathode to the porous carbon anode in a process known as recharging. Unlike alkaline batteries, the electrical output of a lithium-ion battery is constant.

1 **Directions:** Select the appropriate statements from the answer choices and match them to the battery to which they relate.

Answer Choices	Alkaline
(A) Standard versions are not rechargeable.	•
(B) Ions travel in both directions.	•
(C) Ions are sent through the battery's circuit.	•
(D) The electrical output is constant.	Lithium-Ion
(E) The voltage decreases as it is used.	
(F) Manganese dioxide is used for the cathode.	•
(G) The battery has three terminals.	•

Reading Practice 1

Answer Book p. 56

Sunni and Shia Muslims

Islam is one of the world's largest religions, with over two billion followers worldwide. However, Muslims, as Islamic people are commonly called, are not unified. In fact, Islam is divided into two main sects, Sunni and Shia. The members of these groups have lived in close contact with each other for hundreds of years, coexisting peacefully for much of their shared history.

One reason for this is that the theological differences between the two groups are minor. Both hold that the Quran—the holy book of Islam—is a divine communication from God to the prophet Muhammad through the angel Gabriel. In addition, the followers of each sect take the same steps to adhere to the basic tenets of Islam: fasting during the religious holiday Ramadan, making a pilgrimage to the holy site of Mecca, saying five prayers each day, giving to the poor, and publically professing an acceptance of the central beliefs of the faith. There are minor variations with regard to these tenets—for example Shia Muslims say the five prayers in three sessions while Sunni Muslims have five separate sessions—but both groups maintain the same basic religious practices overall.

The primary difference is how the followers of each sect perceive religious leadership. **A** Shia Muslims regard their clerics—known as imams—as God's representatives on Earth and believe that they have the potential to become saints, putting them at the same level as the prophets in the Quran. **B** In contrast, Sunni Muslims view their imams simply as learned individuals who have become both mosque and community leaders. **C** Sunnis have a great deal of respect for their imams because of their knowledge and devotion to Islam, but they do not consider them to be chosen by God. **D**

This divergent view of spiritual authority can be traced back to AD 632, when the prophet Muhammad, who established the Islamic faith, passed away. Shia Muslims believe that Muhammad appointed his cousin Ali, who was also married to his daughter, to take over the leadership of Islam. As a result, they argue that an individual can only hold religious authority if he is from this family line, and they only accept imams with a claim to this heritage. The value that Shia Muslims place on this requirement is reflected in the original name of the sect, *Shia't-Ali*, which means "follower of Ali." Sunni Muslims, however, maintain that Muhammad never chose a successor and, therefore, an imam should simply be a learned man who is elected to his position by the members of a community. This approach seems to hold greater appeal than the more rigid one of Shia; approximately 85 percent of Muslims are Sunni, while only 15 percent of Shia.

Glossary

· prophet: a person who is believed to speak on behalf of God

1 The word "divine" in the passage is closest in meaning to

(A) private
(B) effective
(C) nonverbal
(D) sacred

2 According to paragraph 2, the Shia and Sunni Muslims disagree about

(A) the need to fast during religious holidays
(B) the value of visiting the holy city of Mecca
(C) the requirement to support the less fortunate
(D) the number of prayer sessions to be held daily

3 Look at the four squares [■] that indicate where the following sentence could be added to the passage.

This is because an imam possesses authority that has been received directly from God.

Where would the sentence best fit?

4 Why does the author mention "*Shia't-Ali*" in the passage?

(A) To identify a key figure in a movement
(B) To call into question a longstanding tradition
(C) To explain the origin of a religious conflict
(D) To stress the importance of bloodline to a sect

5 **Directions:** Select the appropriate phrases from the answer choices and match them to the sect to which they relate.

<table>
<tr><th>Answer Choices</th><th>Sunni Muslims</th></tr>
<tr><td rowspan="3">(A) Maintain that imams can become saints
(B) Hold that the prophets in the Quran were elected
(C) Argue that Muhammad's daughter held religious authority
(D) Believe Muhammad was succeeded by a relative
(E) Claim that imams must have a connection to Islam's founder
(F) Assert that Muhammad did not appoint an heir
(G) Make up the majority of the Muslim population</td><td>•
•</td></tr>
<tr><th>Shia Muslims</th></tr>
<tr><td>•
•
•</td></tr>
</table>

Reading Practice 2

Answer Book p. 57

William the Conqueror

The year 1066 marks the end of the Anglo-Saxon era of English rule and the beginning of the current lineage of English royalty. After William the Conqueror of Normandy defeated the Anglo-Saxon King Harold II at the Battle of Hastings, the language, architecture, and social organization of the British Isles changed dramatically. Historians have long debated whether William's consequential conquest of England was based purely on military superiority or whether he had a legitimate claim to the throne. Given the role that this pivotal event played in the eventual establishment of the modern British state, there is a great deal of interest in establishing the validity of William's assertion that he was the rightful English monarch.

William's right to the English throne was based on his claim that his predecessor had made a verbal promise to make him king of England. In 1051, William is said to have met with the Anglo-Saxon King Edward the Confessor, a deeply religious ruler who lacked a male heir. William was the powerful Duke of Normandy, which was a territory on the European mainland that belonged to the Kingdom of France, and he was loyal to the French king. He was also a distant cousin to Edward the Confessor. At their meeting, William volunteered his services as king. According to tradition, Edward agreed to name William his successor.

There was, however, another contender for the crown. Harold Godwinson already enjoyed control of southern England in his capacity as Earl of Wessex. Although he was not a blood relative of the king, Harold's sister married Edward, which gave him substantial political power. According to Norman historians of the day, Harold was such a close friend to William that he had pledged to renounce his own claim to England's throne. Despite both alleged promises to William, it was Harold and not William who was present at Edward's deathbed in January 1066. Harold was able to convert this proximity to Edward into a recommendation from the dying king to his council that they select Harold as his successor.

There is no way to verify whether these verbal oaths were ever actually uttered. What historians do know is that William arrived on the southeast coast of England nine months later with thousands of soldiers in tow. The Battle of Hastings ensued. The new Anglo-Saxon King Harold II was killed in the battle. As a result, William was crowned on Christmas Day, and his line has controlled England ever since. While William's military conquest remains subject to interpretation—some historians argue that it was an act of unprovoked aggression against a sovereign nation that amounted to the colonization of England by the French, while others see it simply as a powerful ruler taking what was rightfully his—there can be no debate about the long-lasting effects of his actions on British history.

1 The word "legitimate" in the passage is closest in meaning to

(A) formal
(B) notorious
(C) accurate
(D) valid

2 In paragraph 2, all of the following are mentioned about William the Conqueror EXCEPT:

(A) He did not have a son to inherit his lands.
(B) He ruled lands that were not located in England.
(C) He gave his allegiance to a non-English monarch.
(D) He was a relative of the ruler he replaced.

3 According to paragraph 3, Norman scholars maintained that Harold Godwinson

(A) was not actually related to the English king
(B) had acquired position of earl by illegal means
(C) had offered to give up his rights to kingdom
(D) was not present when Edward passed away

4 According to paragraph 4, the Battle of Hastings

(A) resulted from the English invasion of France
(B) involved fewer combatants than originally planned
(C) led to the death of an English monarch
(D) caused a serious injury to William the Conqueror

5 **Directions:** Select the appropriate phrases from the answer choices and match them to the person to which they relate.

Answer Choices	William the Conqueror
(A) Met with King Edward in 1051 (B) Was King Edward's brother-in-law (C) Showed a high level of religious conviction	• •
(D) Controlled much of northern England before 1066	**Harold II of England**
(E) Remained with a monarch as he died (F) Invaded England with a large army (G) Served as a monarch for less than a year	• • •

Answer Book p. 57

Greek and Roman Theaters

Theater was an important means of cultural expression in the ancient world. The Greeks invented the art form in the sixth century BC as an offshoot of a religious ritual, and, while they did perform comedies, tragedy was considered the highest form of theater. The Romans were far less serious about theater, and their greatest contributions to the art form were in the genre of comedy. Nevertheless, the Romans owed an incalculable debt to the Greeks in most cultural areas that could never be repaid. Theatrical architecture was no exception. Both built performance spaces with the same three distinct components.

Watching plays was a popular activity in both civilizations, so theaters needed ample seating. Although a standard classical Greek *theatron*, or seating area, could accommodate between 15,000 and 17,000 spectators, people were still turned away. By the fifth century BC, the Greeks began charging entrance fees to control the overwhelming demand to attend religious festivals. The Romans, who considered theater to be a form of mass entertainment, included even more seats in their theaters. The average *cavea* (the Roman version of the theatron) held 25,000 onlookers. In both Greek and Roman theaters, patrons sat in bleachers—rows of benches that were arranged in a large semicircle facing the performance area. In Greek theaters, the bleachers were placed on the slope of a hill so that each row of bleachers was slightly higher than the one in front of it, ensuring that all attendees could see the performance. In Roman theaters, the bleachers ascended massive structures made of concrete to achieve the same effect.

Designers in both countries placed an *orchestra* in front of the audience. In Greek theaters, the orchestra was a circular stage where the actors performed, with an altar at its center that was probably used for offerings and as a sort of prop in the action of the play. The Roman orchestra was in the shape of a semicircle, and it served a different purpose. The actors appeared on a rectangular stage that was up to 300 feet wide and elevated several feet above the ground. Instead of providing a place for performances to be given, the orchestra was used for seating political leaders.

The backdrop behind both the Greek and Roman theaters was a scene building called a *skene* in Greek and a *scaena* in Latin. The Greek version was used to house props and costumes. The skene was originally made out of wood and eventually made out of stone. Additionally, it served as a set, probably designed to look like a Greek palace. The Roman version was more elaborate and was usually two or three stories high. Its front was ornately designed with columns and doorways. For comedies, it represented a Roman street, but it could double as a palace if a tragedy was performed. Sometimes a painted backdrop was placed in front of the scaena.

1 The word "incalculable" in the passage is closest in meaning to

(A) immeasurable
(B) remaining
(C) increasing
(D) perpetual

2 It can be inferred from paragraph 1 that tragedies were

(A) never performed in Roman theaters
(B) less popular with the Romans than the Greeks
(C) disapproved of by Greek religious authorities
(D) thought to be unsophisticated in both civilizations

3 According to paragraph 2, which of the following is true of the bleachers in an ancient Greek theater?

(A) They were positioned next to a large hill.
(B) They were set up on a natural landform.
(C) They were arranged into straight rows.
(D) They were attached to concrete structures.

4 According to paragraph 3, the purpose of the Greek orchestra was to

(A) provide the actors with a performance space
(B) allow set pieces to be changed quickly
(C) offer special seating for important people
(D) house musicians and their instruments

5 **Directions:** Select the appropriate statements from the answer choices and match them to the theater to which they relate.

Answer Choices	Greek
(A) Theaters were used for religious festivals. (B) Actors performed on a circular stage. (C) Bleachers were fashioned from clay. (D) Actors performed on a rectangular platform.	• • •
(E) Tragedies featured offerings at the altar.	Roman
(F) Backdrops were sometimes painted for the play. (G) The skene was used to store costumes.	• •

iBT Reading Test 1

Answer Book p. 58

TOEFL Reading

Butterflies and Moths

Most moths and butterflies are easy to distinguish based solely on appearance. However, these insects have a lot in common, and their differences are not as stark as they may seem. Both belong to the order Lepidoptera, which is Greek for "scale wings," an acknowledgment of the dense layers of scales on their wings, legs, and bodies. According to scientists, the remarkably diverse order of insects (there are 160,000 species of moths and 11,000 species of butterflies) descended from a common ancestor that emerged 300 million years ago, even before the evolution of the flowering plants that both moths and butterflies feed on today. This shared ancestry explains their numerous similarities, including the fact that they both have three-part segmented bodies, three pairs of legs, one pair of antennae, and an exoskeleton. In addition, the life cycle of both types of insects is almost identical, as butterflies and moths transform from caterpillar to pupa to winged insect.

➡ Lepidoptera diverged into two distinct lines some 100 million years ago, with day-flying butterflies evolving from the larger group of nocturnal moths. [A] Like many other colorful animals, butterflies developed brilliant pigmentation in order to convince daytime predators that they contain foul-tasting chemicals. [B] The colorful wings also help to camouflage butterflies when they are flying among colorful flowers. [C] In contrast, moths tend to feature duller hues, like beige, brown, or gray, so that they blend in with the tree bark they rest upon during the day. [D] Some moths evade bats, their most dangerous nocturnal predator, by using a technique known as acoustic camouflage, whereby the scales on their wings actually absorb sound energy. This prevents bats from finding them using echolocation, a hunting technique that utilizes reflected sound waves.

➡ In addition to their coloring, there are other notable physical differences between moths and butterflies. Moths have feathery antennae, while butterflies have thin, club-tipped antennae with a bulb at the end. The front and back wings of a moth are held together during flight by a bristly structure called a frenulum, a feature that butterflies do not exhibit. There are important physical differences between moths and butterflies even before they reach their adult stage. For example, moth pupae are protected by a silk cocoon, while butterfly pupae—called chrysalis—form a hard, smooth shell.

➡ Moths and butterflies are so closely related that even these differences are not without exceptions. For example, there are some butterflies that do not feature the spectacular coloring that usually distinguishes their wings from those of moths. The Schaus swallowtail, an endangered butterfly species from Florida, has dull, brown wings. Neither can you count on moths to be consistently dull in coloration. The comet moth has bright yellow wings with red spots. It is even diurnal, meaning that it is active during the day. In recent years, some researchers have argued that butterflies should be considered a subgroup of moths rather than a separate group, and they are slowly gathering support among the scientific community for this reclassification.

Volume Review Help Back Next

1 The word "stark" in the passage is closest in meaning to

Ⓐ frivolous
Ⓑ unambiguous
Ⓒ prevalent
Ⓓ debilitated

2 Which of the sentences below best expresses the essential information in the highlighted sentence in the passage? *Incorrect* choices change the meaning in important ways or leave out essential information.

Ⓐ Thousands of species of moths and butterflies evolved from a single species even before their current means of subsistence evolved.
Ⓑ Moths are more numerous than butterflies, but they both eat the same kinds of plants because they evolved from the same species.
Ⓒ There are too many species of butterflies and moths for them to have evolved from a common ancestor, even if they both feed on flowers.
Ⓓ Flowering plants evolved just prior to the emergence of the insect species that spawned both moths and butterflies.

3 Why does the author mention "foul-tasting chemicals" in the passage?

Ⓐ To explain why butterflies are rarely hunted in the wild
Ⓑ To describe a substance that butterflies secrete
Ⓒ To explain how butterflies avoid predators
Ⓓ To provide an example of the butterfly's diet

4 According to paragraph 2, certain species of moths evade bats by

Ⓐ preventing sound from reflecting off their wings
Ⓑ avoiding making noises that can be detected
Ⓒ matching the color of the exterior of a tree
Ⓓ having scales that are hard to see at night

Paragraph 2 is marked with an arrow [➡].

5 According to paragraph 3, which of the following is true of moths?

Ⓐ Their antennae are thinner than butterfly antennae.
Ⓑ They form a hard cocoon that does not contain silk.
Ⓒ Their wings are bound together when they fly.
Ⓓ They have a bulb at the end of their antennae.

Paragraph 3 is marked with an arrow [➡].

6 The word "they" in the passage refers to

Ⓐ years
Ⓑ researchers
Ⓒ butterflies
Ⓓ moths

7 According to paragraph 4, the Schaus swallowtail is notable for its

Ⓐ abundance in Florida ecosystems
Ⓑ tendency to be active at night
Ⓒ classification as both butterfly and moth
Ⓓ unusually muted coloration

Paragraph 4 is marked with an arrow [➡].

8 What can be inferred from paragraph 4 about the comet moth?

Ⓐ The colors of its wings are a disadvantage when avoiding predators.
Ⓑ A close inspection is required to distinguish it from a butterfly.
Ⓒ A debate is underway about whether it is misclassified as a moth.
Ⓓ The ability to be active during the night increases its access to food.

Paragraph 4 is marked with an arrow [➡].

Volume Review Help Back Next

9 Look at the four squares [■] that indicate where the following sentence could be added to the passage.

Many of the differences between moths and butterflies are a result of their respective waking and sleeping hours.

Where would the sentence best fit?

Click on a square [■] to add the sentence to the passage.

10 Directions: Select the appropriate phrases from the answer choices and match them to the insect to which they typically relate. **This question is worth 3 points.**

Drag your answer choices to the spaces where they belong.
To remove an answer choice, click on it. To review the passage, click on **View Text**.

Answer Choices	Butterflies
Ⓐ Are active during the daytime Ⓑ Are difficult to spot among flowering plants Ⓒ Hide on trees throughout the day Ⓓ Use echolocation to avoid nighttime predators Ⓔ Have thin antennae that widen at the end Ⓕ Enter a chrysalis after developing wings Ⓖ Produce a silk cocoon before their final life cycle stage	• • • **Moths** • •

Answer Book p. 58

Answer Book p. 60

TOEFL Reading

Natural and Chemical Fertilizers

➡ Natural fertilizers are derived through composting, which is the combination of food waste and animal byproducts, including manure and bone meal. In this process, microorganisms and macroorganisms utilize decaying organic matter as a vital energy source. Simultaneously, these organisms excrete valuable byproducts, such as ammonia, into the soil. Earthworms, for instance, discard nutritionally rich casings each day, which are a source of nitrogen, calcium, and phosphorus for plants. They also increase soil aeration by crawling through the decomposing plant matter, thereby improving water drainage. Furthermore, organisms offer plants protection against harmful pathogens by reducing contaminants in the soil and water. As a result, soil richness and crop productivity are enhanced through the efforts of biological organisms.

➡ However, natural fertilizers are cost prohibitive on an industrial scale, as the decomposition of the waste used to generate them is a time-consuming process. Furthermore, the restoration of nutrients by organisms is highly variable, making the composition of natural fertilizers irregular. Therefore, some natural fertilizers may not replace deficiencies within the soil. Due to this unpredictable variation, natural fertilizers are considered by farmers to be undependable for boosting crop yields.

➡ In contrast, chemical fertilizers are manufactured through a series of reliable chemical reactions. These fertilizers consist primarily of phosphorus, potassium, and nitrogen. Phosphorus acid is acquired through a wet process, which involves mixing sulfuric acid, water, and phosphate rocks in a reactor. [A] The resulting acid form encourages plants to create the enzymes and proteins required for growth. [B] Similarly, concentrated potassium is combined with chlorine to create potassium chloride, which regulates water intake and promotes plant protein formation. [C] The final compound, nitrogen, is obtained through the Haber process, wherein atmospheric nitrogen is exposed to hydrogen and metal catalysts. [D]

Chemical fertilizers have an undeniably negative environmental impact. Excessively fertilized soil can result in fertilizer burn, killing the plant with an oversaturation of toxic salts. The chemicals also do not contribute to macro and microorganisms in the soil, and, in many cases, exterminate the beneficial organisms. In addition, chemical fertilizers can release chemicals too rapidly, enriching the leafy portion of the plant but leading to weak roots, increasing the potential risk of infectious diseases and lower fruit production. Finally, the runoff of these dangerous chemicals into water sources, including rivers and ponds, has caused severe ecological harm.

➡ While there are risks associated with the use of chemical fertilizers, they are the most effective method to optimize crop growth. They are increasingly vital, as the expanding global population necessitates ever-greater volumes of food. It is currently estimated that the world crop production will need to double by 2050 in order to feed the population. Unfortunately, these gains cannot be achieved without the utilization of chemical fertilizers to augment agricultural efficiency,

Volume Review Help Back Next

which will cause further injury to the environment. Therefore, greater efforts must be expended to reduce the negative effects of chemical fertilizers on the earth.

Glossary
macroorganism: an organism large enough to be seen with the naked eye

1 The word "excrete" in the passage is closest in meaning to

(A) sustain (B) discharge (C) replace (D) assimilate

2 According to paragraph 1, soil-based organisms perform all of the following actions EXCEPT

(A) increasing soil drainage
(B) removing contaminants
(C) isolating decayed matter
(D) supplying nutrients

Paragraph 1 is marked with an arrow [➡].

3 According to paragraph 2, farmers prefer not to use natural fertilizers because

(A) they require a great deal of effort to produce
(B) they are expensive to make because of the raw materials
(C) they contain an inconsistent amount of nutrients
(D) they are detrimental to certain types of crops

Paragraph 2 is marked with an arrow [➡].

4 According to paragraph 3, what function does phosphorus serve in soil?

(A) It initiates the Haber process to produce nitrogen.
(B) It prompts the generation of plant-growing cells.
(C) It stimulates the plant to encourage water intake.
(D) It absorbs an acidic compound that harms plants

Paragraph 3 is marked with an arrow [➡].

5 The word "exterminate" in the passage is closest in meaning to

Ⓐ destroy
Ⓑ entice
Ⓒ impart
Ⓓ mutate

6 Which of the sentences below best expresses the essential information in the highlighted sentence in the passage? *Incorrect* choices change the meaning in important ways or leave out essential information.

Ⓐ Frequently used chemicals develop plant growth, consistently increasing the length of the plant's roots.
Ⓑ Quickly utilized nutrients cause growth imbalances, resulting in degradation of the health of the plant.
Ⓒ Swiftly absorbed chemicals cause extensive plant growth, raising the quality of the resulting fruit.
Ⓓ Hastily released nutrients stunt growth potential, causing the fruit of the plant to develop diseases.

7 Why does the author mention the doubling of the world crop production in paragraph 5?

Ⓐ To explain how crop production has expanded
Ⓑ To demonstrate the importance of natural fertilizers
Ⓒ To provide an example of how fertilizers are used
Ⓓ To show the necessity of chemical fertilizers

Paragraph 5 is marked with an arrow [➡].

8 Which of the following can be inferred from paragraph 5 about chemical fertilizers?

Ⓐ They have declined in importance because technology has enhanced natural fertilizers.
Ⓑ The yield associated with them is insufficient to meet the needs of coming generations.
Ⓒ Efforts to mitigate their harmful environmental effects have been largely successful.
Ⓓ Their efficacy in increasing crop output outweighs their environmental drawbacks.

Paragraph 5 is marked with an arrow [➡].

Volume | Review | Help | Back | Next

9 Look at the four squares [■] that indicate where the following sentence could be added to the passage.

This creates liquid anhydrous ammonia, a substance with a high nitrogen content that can easily be applied to soil.

Where would the sentence best fit?

Click on a square [■] to add the sentence to the passage.

10 Directions: Select the appropriate phrases from the answer choices and match them to the type of fertilizer with which they are associated. **This question is worth 3 points.**

Drag your answer choices to the spaces where they belong.
To remove an answer choice, click on it. To review the passage, click on **View Text**.

Answer Choices	Natural Fertilizers
(A) Made from food waste and animal byproducts	•
(B) Favored for environmental benefits and reliable yield increase	•
(C) Create deficiencies in the soil that reduce yields	•
(D) Produced through dependable chemical reactions	**Chemical Fertilizers**
(E) Take more time to produce than is practical for some farmers	•
(F) Require interaction with organisms living in the soil	•
(G) Known to poison nearby water sources	

Answer Book p. 60

Vocabulary Review

Answer Book p. 61

A. Fill in the blanks with the appropriate words from the box.

consequential	optimize	lineage
theological	divergent	diurnal

1 Immediate actions should be taken to prevent the ______________ environmental damage from the oil spill.

2 A(n) ______________ dispute led to the Protestant Revolution in the sixteenth century.

3 People hold ______________ opinions on controversial social issues such as gun control and the death penalty.

4 Unlike owls, eagles are ______________ predators that are active throughout the day.

5 After extensive research, Greg was able to trace his ______________ back to a famous general.

6 The company decided to hire a consultant to help ______________ its employees' productivity.

B. Choose the closest meaning for each highlighted word or phrase.

7 The immigration official checked the validity of the passport before stamping it.
(A) legitimacy (B) suitability (C) accuracy (D) durability

8 On December 11, 1936, Edward VIII renounced his title of King of the United Kingdom.
(A) inherited (B) announced (C) discovered (D) relinquished

9 The building manager pledged to have the elevator repaired by Tuesday at the latest.
(A) arranged (B) promised (C) attempted (D) accepted

10 He uttered his words quietly so as not to offend anyone, as they did not express the kindest thoughts.
(A) articulated (B) conceived (C) contested (D) pondered

11 During the press conference, the politician professed his intention to run for president.
(A) assumed (B) questioned (C) confirmed (D) declared

12 Historians consider rock and roll to be an offshoot of earlier musical styles such as the blues.
(A) influence (B) derivative (C) duplicate (D) simulation

13 Before taking office, the president must make an oath to uphold the constitution.
(A) vow (B) choice (C) accord (D) reprieve

14 Benjamin Franklin was appointed the US ambassador to France in December of 1776.
(A) designated (B) terminated (C) elected (D) permitted

Actual Test

Answer Book p. 61

TOEFL Reading

Passage 1

Solar Luminosity and Greenhouse Gases

➡ The amount of light given off by an object is measured as luminosity. For a star, peak luminosity occurs towards the end of its life, after billions of years. The Sun has existed for 4.6 billion years and will continue to brighten by 10 percent every billion years until it is depleted. When Earth first formed 4.5 billion years ago, the luminosity of the Sun was approximately 30 percent lower than its present strength. Solar radiation, or sunlight, was inadequate to heat early Earth above freezing temperatures. Therefore, certain gases in the planet's atmosphere were requisite to maintain positive temperatures. In particular, primitive microbes discharged a huge quantity of methane, which has a large capacity for trapping solar radiation. As a result, the heat from the Sun was stored on Earth, keeping temperatures warm enough to retain liquid oceans.

The methane warming mechanism continued until 2.5 billion years ago, when cyanobacteria developed the ability to photosynthesize. Oxygen is a byproduct of photosynthesis. [A] However, the small molecules of oxygen can only capture small amounts of solar radiation, whereas methane absorbs larger amounts. [B] As oxygen was toxic to the bacteria that produced methane, the increase in oxygen led to a sharp decline in the amount of methane in the atmosphere. [C] Without methane for retention, heat from the Sun was scattered back into space. [D] Fortunately, carbon dioxide in the atmosphere began to be generated through the evolution of carbon-producing organisms. After several hundred million years, atmospheric carbon dioxide reached the amount required to trap heat from solar radiation, allowing Earth to unfreeze and become suitable for the evolution of larger creatures.

➡ The increasing luminosity of the Sun will leave Earth inhospitable within one billion years. Prior to that point, Earth will be subject to fluctuations in solar luminescence throughout the eleven-year solar cycle discovered in 1843 by German astronomer Samuel Schwabe. This affects the amount of solar radiation emitted by the Sun. Scientists have determined that sunspots, areas of intense magnetic activity, are directly correlated to higher radiation levels. Sunspots appear close to the edge of the Sun and migrate to the center over the eleven-year period. Variations in the solar cycle of sunspots and the subsequent changes in luminosity can impact temperatures on Earth.

➡ Experts fear that increased solar luminosity, combined with the abnormally high amounts of carbon dioxide and methane entering the atmosphere as a result of human activity, will eventually cause what is known as a runaway greenhouse effect. This phenomenon will occur when the volume of heat-trapping gases in the planet's atmosphere increases to the point that the heat from the Sun is fully restricted from exiting. This will cause both the atmosphere and the surface of the planet to heat up dramatically in a relatively short period of time. As the temperature rises from the trapped heat, organisms capable of producing oxygen and nitrogen will begin to die off. In contrast, microbes that release carbon dioxide and methane will be able to survive under these extreme conditions, so their numbers will be unaffected by the changing climate. They will steadily produce these two gases while the evaporating oceans add even more carbon dioxide to the atmosphere. Eventually, Earth will resemble the planet Venus, which is surrounded by a thick atmosphere that is over 96 percent carbon dioxide, resulting in temperatures of approximately 462 degrees Celsius. Humans can delay and even prevent this outcome by significantly reducing the amount of greenhouse gas emissions.

1 The word "requisite" in the passage is closest in meaning to

(A) replaced (B) required (C) retained (D) recovered

2 According to paragraph 1, when is a star at its brightest?

(A) At the start of its existence
(B) Near to its extinction
(C) After four billion years
(D) Halfway through its life

Paragraph 1 is marked with an arrow [➡].

3 Why does the author mention "cyanobacteria" in the passage?

(A) To explain how solar radiation began to appear in the atmosphere
(B) To describe the multiple phases of photosynthesis
(C) To identify the organisms behind early oxygen production
(D) To differentiate between various types of microbes

4 Which of the sentences below best expresses the essential information in the highlighted sentence in the passage? *Incorrect* choices change the meaning in important ways or leave out essential information.

(A) As carbon dioxide became abundant enough to trap solar heat, more substantial creatures could evolve on Earth.
(B) Evolution on Earth was made possible largely due to the formation of carbon dioxide.
(C) Solar radiation allowed larger creatures on Earth to evolve although some of the heat was lost to carbon dioxide.
(D) Melted water resulted in an increased amount of carbon dioxide, which enabled larger creatures to appear on Earth.

5 The word "This" in the passage refers to

Ⓐ Sun
Ⓑ Earth
Ⓒ luminescence
Ⓓ cycle

6 The phrase "correlated to" in the passage is closest in meaning to

Ⓐ associated with
Ⓑ distinguished by
Ⓒ composed of
Ⓓ attached to

7 According to paragraph 3, sunspots shape weather conditions on Earth by

Ⓐ changing the speed of solar radiation
Ⓑ impacting the direction of magnetic activity
Ⓒ changing the composition of solar radiation
Ⓓ affecting the luminosity of the sun

Paragraph 3 is marked with an arrow [➡].

8 According to paragraph 4, which of the following would NOT happen as a result of a runaway greenhouse effect?

Ⓐ Methane-secreting microbes would perish.
Ⓑ Some organisms would die off.
Ⓒ Oceans would evaporate.
Ⓓ Temperatures would become elevated.

Paragraph 4 is marked with an arrow [➡].

Volume Review Help Back Next

9 Look at the four squares [■] that indicate where the following sentence could be added to the passage.

The loss of heat would have caused glaciation, freezing the planet-wide oceans.

Where would the sentence best fit?

Click on a square [■] to add the sentence to the passage.

10 **Directions:** An introductory sentence for a brief summary of the passage is provided below. Complete the summary by selecting the THREE answer choices that express the most important ideas in the passage. Some sentences do not belong in the summary because they express ideas that are not presented in the passage or are minor ideas in the passage. **This question is worth 2 points.**

Drag your answer choices to the spaces where they belong.
To remove an answer choice, click on it. To review the passage, click on **View Text**.

Earth's climate was influenced by weak solar luminescence and methane gas for two billion years.

-
-
-

Answer Choices

(A) The lower luminosity of the Sun initially prevented temperatures on Earth from rising above the freezing point.

(B) Once sufficient carbon dioxide was produced on Earth, heat from the Sun began to be trapped in the atmosphere.

(C) Regularly occurring variations in solar luminescence due to sunspots have a significant effect on global temperatures.

(D) The eleven-year cycle that dictates the formation of sunspots was discovered by a German astronomer in 1843.

(E) A rise in solar luminosity and the amount of greenhouse gases emitted may cause Earth to become uninhabitable for many life forms.

(F) As the atmosphere of Venus is composed primarily of carbon dioxide, the planet has average temperatures much higher than Earth's.

Answer Book p. 61

TOEFL Reading

Passage 2

English Feudalism

The feudal system was a method of economic and legal governance that developed in Europe following the decline of the Roman Empire. This system emphasized a highly stratified society, headed by the king. While there is a great deal of scholarly debate as to the precise beginnings of feudalism in England, historians generally agree that feudal contracts were not fully incorporated into English society until after the kingdom was conquered by William I in 1066.

➡ Prior to his invasion of England, the Norman ruler William I promised noblemen land grants, known as *fiefs*, in exchange for their support of his claim to the English throne. These fiefs were attached with certain conditions, upheld by a feudal contract. A feudal contract was an agreement between a monarch and a subject, or between any noble of higher rank and one of lower rank, through which the latter gave an oath of loyalty to the former in exchange for land rights. After obtaining the throne, William I retained about 20 percent of English land for himself, gave a further 25 percent to the church, and divided the rest of it among the 170 nobles who had contributed support for the conquest. The noblemen who received land directly from the king were known as barons.

A feudal contract at the highest level was between the king and his direct vassals, the barons. The contract stated the responsibilities of each party. The barons promised to supply knights and soldiers at the king's request; this on-demand army was beneficial to the king because it reduced the need for a full-time military force, which was very expensive. In turn, a feudal contract was highly profitable for the barons as they could also use it to become lords of the people beneath them in social standing. In fact, the resources that the barons supplied to the king, although costly, were minimal expenses compared to those owed to the barons from the lower ranks in the feudal system. Therefore, the barons could generate wealth without effort by parceling their estates off to lower-ranking nobles, who became vassals of the barons through a feudal contract. Often, the vassals used the land for agriculture, and they pledged knights, a portion of the crop yield, and cash payments to the baron in exchange for use of the land.

➡ The lower-ranking vassals in turn divided some of their land into small strips and leased them to serfs and freemen through feudal contracts and, by doing so, became lords themselves. Serfs were effectively servants who were required to farm their lord's land for five days a week and received a small portion of farmland and housing for themselves. The freemen, approximately 10 percent of the lower class, merely rented farmland. However, both groups were required to pay numerous taxes, in the form of food, to their lord.

➡ After several hundred years of this system, feudal contracts became severely degraded. The barons became immensely powerful in their own right. Additionally, the king was wealthy enough to afford his own armies and was not dependent on the military service of the barons. This imbalance led to wars in the thirteenth century as the barons sought greater power and freedom

Volume Review Help Back Next

Questions 11-14 of 30

from the king. [A] Furthermore, a series of deadly plagues collectively known as the Black Death spread through England. [B] An immediate consequence was an agricultural labor shortage. [C] Numerous villages disappeared entirely as serfs and freemen alike relocated to areas with better opportunities. [D] Vassals were no longer reliant upon or loyal to their superiors, resulting in instability at every level of feudalism.

11 The word "stratified" in the passage is closest in meaning to

Ⓐ violent
Ⓑ refined
Ⓒ hierarchical
Ⓓ antiquated

12 According to paragraph 2, an English feudal contract always involved

Ⓐ a promise of allegiance in return for the use of property
Ⓑ a guarantee of promotion to the upper levels of the nobility
Ⓒ an offer of exemption from some duties of a royal subject
Ⓓ a declaration of loyalty between individuals of equal rank

Paragraph 2 is marked with an arrow [➡].

13 What can be inferred from paragraph 2 about William I?

Ⓐ He retained most of the English land he obtained for himself.
Ⓑ He hoped to receive the support of a religious institution.
Ⓒ He rejected many requests for fiefs from his followers.
Ⓓ He refused to give church officials the same rights as nobles.

Paragraph 2 is marked with an arrow [➡].

14 Why does author mention an "on-demand army" in the passage?

Ⓐ To stress an advantage enjoyed by the barons
Ⓑ To emphasize that kings needed much money
Ⓒ To explain why a monarch wanted to have vassals
Ⓓ To present an innovation of the English military system

15 Which of the sentences below best expresses the essential information in the highlighted sentence in the passage? *Incorrect* choices change the meaning of the sentence in important ways or leave out essential information.

Ⓐ Those below the barons in social status paid less than those above the barons.
Ⓑ The king required the barons to compensate him amply with monetary payments.
Ⓒ The barons received more wealth from their vassals than was owed to the king.
Ⓓ The poor were expected to pay the barons large sums on a regular basis.

16 According to paragraph 4, which of the following is true about serfs?

Ⓐ They paid their taxes by trading food in a market.
Ⓑ They worked their lord's farmland every day.
Ⓒ They were granted a plot of land by their lord.
Ⓓ They constituted a minority of the lower class.

Paragraph 4 is marked with an arrow [➡].

17 The word "degraded" in the passage is closest in meaning to

Ⓐ augmented
Ⓑ ingrained
Ⓒ deformed
Ⓓ weakened

18 According to paragraph 5, which of the following was NOT a reason that the feudal system declined?

Ⓐ The relationship between the barons and the king deteriorated.
Ⓑ The wealthy were disinterested in maintaining links with the poor.
Ⓒ The services of the barons became less important to the king.
Ⓓ The spread of disease led to increased mobility in the lower classes.

Paragraph 5 is marked with an arrow [➡].

19 Look at the four squares [■] that indicate where the following sentence could be added to the passage.

This disease was transmitted by fleas that were found on rodents such as rats.

Where would the sentence best fit?

Click on a square [■] to add the sentence to the passage.

20 **Directions:** An introductory sentence for a brief summary of the passage is provided below. Complete the summary by selecting the THREE answer choices that express the most important ideas in the passage. Some sentences do not belong in the summary because they express ideas that are not presented in the passage or are minor ideas in the passage. **This question is worth 2 points.**

Drag your answer choices to the spaces where they belong.
To remove an answer choice, click on it. To review the passage, click on **View Text**.

The feudal contract was used to uphold a system of governance in England after the Norman Conquest.

-
-
-

Answer Choices

(A) A well-established form of feudalism existed in England prior to the Norman invasion in AD 1066.

(B) Fiefs were provided by William I because he was unable to otherwise compensate his military leaders.

(C) William I distributed much of England to a group of nobles who entered into feudal contracts.

(D) The recipients of land through feudal agreements had specific duties to perform for their lords.

(E) The plots provided to serfs and freemen was usually unsuitable for any form of agriculture activity.

(F) A number of factors resulted in the collapse of the English feudal system in the thirteenth century.

Answer Book p. 63

Answer Book p. 64

TOEFL Reading

Passage 3

Volcanoes and Climate Change

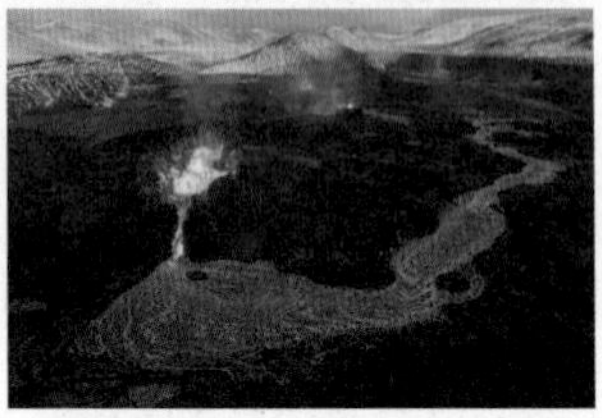

➡ Major volcanic eruptions can impact climate patterns for years. The first clear connection between volcanism and climate change was made by American diplomat Benjamin Franklin in 1784 while he was stationed in Paris. He recorded a number of observations about what he believed were anomalous weather conditions. These included a cool summer followed by a frigid winter in which a persistent fog hovered over much of North America and Europe. His contention that these phenomena may have been linked to a series of volcanic eruptions in Iceland was correct. For eight months, huge eruptions in Iceland's Laki fissure system spewed lava, ash, and gases into the environment. **A** Locally, the massive quantities of sulfur dioxide, hydrogen chloride, and other toxic gases led to acid rain that killed livestock and crops and created tremendous famine. **B** Approximately 25 percent of Iceland's human population was lost as a result of the eruptions. **C** Moreover, the circulation of volcanic clouds caused lower temperatures that threatened crops and the survival of people throughout the northern hemisphere. **D**

➡ What makes volcanoes significant factors in Earth's climate is their potential to eject materials high above the surface. The lowest part of the atmosphere is the troposphere, which extends from the ground to approximately ten kilometers above the surface. In this range, the ejected gases and solids create air pollution but generally fall back to the surface through their own weight or when combined with rain. However, the long-term effects result from massive eruptions that eject particles and chemicals beyond the troposphere and into the stratosphere. Sulfuric acids are common in volcanic plumes, and high in the atmosphere they convert to sulfate aerosols, which are tiny droplets mostly made up of sulfuric acid. These small particles create aerosol clouds that can remain in the stratosphere and circulate around the planet for several years following eruptions.

➡ The aerosol clouds have a two-fold effect on the climate, as they influence the terrestrial radiation leaving the surface and the incoming radiation from the Sun. Scientists refer to this alteration of the radiation balance as *radiative forcing*. The degree of radiative forcing seems to be related to the size of the aerosol particles; if they are bigger than two microns, they tend to prevent terrestrial radiation from escaping while allowing sunlight in, which promotes global warming. If they are smaller, then the opposite pattern tends to occur.

➡ In modern times, scientists have had the opportunity to closely study several massive eruptions. The most notable of these was the Mount Pinatubo eruption in the Philippines in 1991. Pinatubo ejected approximately twenty million tons of debris and gas thirty-five kilometers into the atmosphere. Satellite images revealed a sulfur dioxide cloud that was the biggest in recorded history, and it led to a general cooling of the earth's surface for the next three years.

However, radiative forcing created complex patterns depending on where scientists looked in the atmosphere or the planet's surface. To better understand the patterns, researchers entered data into a computer simulation in which they compared two models: one with the presence of the Pinatubo-generated aerosols and one without them. The findings corroborated that the stratosphere warmed up while the troposphere cooled down, but there were seasonal variations in the troposphere that impacted temperatures at the surface. In particular, the researchers discovered that despite global cooling overall, there was a clear warming of surface air during the winter months in the northern hemisphere.

21 The word "anomalous" in the passage is closest in meaning to

Ⓐ normal Ⓑ unpleasant Ⓒ unusual Ⓓ difficult

22 Which of the following is NOT mentioned about Benjamin Franklin?

Ⓐ He was an American official in Paris.
Ⓑ He observed a cold summer and winter.
Ⓒ He noted the existence of a lingering fog.
Ⓓ He was in Iceland during the eruptions.

23 According to paragraph 1, what endangered crops and human life throughout the northern hemisphere after the Laki eruptions?

Ⓐ temperature change
Ⓑ acid rain
Ⓒ toxic gases
Ⓓ lava and ash

Paragraph 1 is marked with an arrow [➡].

24 According to paragraph 2, what determines whether a volcanic eruption will have a long-term impact on the climate?

Ⓐ The altitude to which the ejected substances ascend
Ⓑ The dimensions of the particles in the sulfate clouds
Ⓒ The ratio of gases to solids in the volcanic material
Ⓓ The amount of rain that immediately follows the eruption

Paragraph 2 is marked with an arrow [➡].

25 What can be inferred from paragraph 3 about aerosol particles?

Ⓐ Most are significantly larger than two microns.
Ⓑ Ones that are small cause temperatures to fall.
Ⓒ All prevent radiation from escaping the atmosphere.
Ⓓ Some have no influence on incoming or outgoing energy.

Paragraph 3 is marked with an arrow [➡].

26 The word "corroborated" in the passage is closest in meaning to

Ⓐ disputed
Ⓑ suggested
Ⓒ confirmed
Ⓓ realized

27 Which of the sentences below best expresses the essential information in the highlighted sentence in the passage? *Incorrect* choices change the meaning in important ways or leave out essential information.

Ⓐ A seasonal aberration to a worldwide climate trend in a specific region was observed by scientists.
Ⓑ The decline in global temperatures was more pronounced in the northern hemisphere than other areas.
Ⓒ Scientists noticed that the cooling process was accelerated in some parts of the world in winter.
Ⓓ Although temperatures in the northern hemisphere fell in winter, they rose at other times of the year.

28 The author discusses the eruption in the Philippines in paragraph 4 in order to

Ⓐ provide an example of recent findings regarding volcanism and climate change
Ⓑ document the impact of human activity on volcanic global warming
Ⓒ show that the relationship between volcanoes and climate is considered controversial
Ⓓ demonstrate that troposphere responds differently to volcanism than the stratosphere

Paragraph 4 is marked with an arrow [➡].

29 Look at the four squares [■] that indicate where the following sentence could be added to the passage.

Even as far away as Japan, the impact was felt as the rice harvest failed, resulting in the worst famine in the nation's history.

Where would the sentence best fit?

Click on a square [■] to add the sentence to the passage.

30 **Directions:** An introductory sentence for a brief summary of the passage is provided below. Complete the summary by selecting the THREE answer choices that express the most important ideas in the passage. Some sentences do not belong in the summary because they express ideas that are not presented in the passage or are minor ideas in the passage. **This question is worth 2 points.**

Drag your answer choices to the spaces where they belong.
To remove an answer choice, click on it. To review the passage, click on **View Text**.

Very large volcanic eruptions have significant local effects and can also impact the global climate for years.

-
-
-

Answer Choices

Ⓐ The eruption of Mount Pinatubo gave scientists an opportunity to measure how large eruptions affect climate, and they used computer simulations to generate useful data.

Ⓑ A volcanic eruption in the late eighteenth century provided an early clue to the impact of volcanic activity on global climate patterns, showing that local damage was just part of the devastating impact.

Ⓒ Although large amounts of radiation from the Sun enters the planet's atmosphere, energy from the surface of Earth is emitted back into space.

Ⓓ Volcanoes' influence on the climate stems from their ability to eject material high into the atmosphere, where it affects the radiation from the ground and the Sun.

Ⓔ Due to the infrequency of gigantic volcanic events, scientists have had few opportunities to study in detail how volcanic clouds affect the atmosphere.

Ⓕ Because there was no warning system in place to notify the population about the Mount Pinatubo eruption, virtually all of the people in the vicinity lost their lives.

Answer Book p. 64

Answer Book p. 65

TOEFL Reading

Passage 1

The Book of Kells

Created in the eighth or ninth century AD, the Book of Kells is an illuminated manuscript—a handwritten work with illustrations—that includes passages from the Bible along with indexes of names and other supplementary materials. While the textual content of the book is comparable to what is found in many others produced by representatives of the Catholic Church during this period, its visual elements set it apart. Currently on display in Trinity College in Dublin, the book is one of the most important works of European art from the medieval period.

➡ Although it is not known with certainty where the Book of Kells was made, most historians subscribe to one of two theories. The first is that the book was produced in the Abbey of Kells, located in the northeastern part of Ireland. This is because the first mention of the Book of Kells is in the Annals of Ulster. This document records that the book was stolen from the Abbey of Kells in AD 1007 during a Viking raid but was eventually recovered. However, some experts point out that this monastery received an influx of monks from the Iona Abbey in Scotland in the early ninth century. As the Scottish monastery had a long tradition of bookmaking, it is argued that the Book of Kells was transported from there to the Abbey of Kells when the monks relocated.

➡ Whoever made the Book of Kells incorporated a number of features that result in it standing out as a work of art. One of these is the superiority of the calligraphy. An analysis of the Book of Kells has determined that three scribes copied out the biblical passages and other texts. Each employed a distinctive form of calligraphy known as the insular script that is both visually appealing and easy to read. Another key attribute is the elaborate illustrations. Every page of the Book of Kells contains highly detailed decorative elements that blend Catholic symbolism with the Celtic artistic style of complex, interlocking geometric shapes. The Book of Kells also includes thirty-three full-page images depicting religious figures and scenes from the Bible. All of these are noteworthy artworks in their own right. **A** The use of vivid and varied colors in the illustrations is another significant characteristic of the Book of Kells. **B** The artists employed a wide range of natural substances to create colored inks in many different hues. **C** For example, a purple pigment was extracted from a type of shellfish, and blue inks were produced using lapis lazuli, a semiprecious stone imported from the Middle East. **D**

➡ Given the obvious effort that was put into the visual aspects of the Book of Kells, most historians agree that the work was intended to function as a showpiece rather than as a resource to study the Bible. In all likelihood, the book was displayed prominently in the church and then read from only during ceremonial occasions. This assertion is supported by the layout of the text in the Book of Kells. The chapter headings necessary to quickly find specific sections of the Gospels are omitted to allow more room for decoration. In addition, words and even whole sentences are sometimes repeated to create uniform blocks of text on the page. This suggests that when a church official "read" from the Book of Kells, he was probably reciting from memory while the book was held up for display to the people in attendance.

1 The word "supplementary" in the passage is closest in meaning to

(A) irrelevant
(B) obligatory
(C) peripheral
(D) voluntary

2 Which of the sentences below best expresses the essential information in the highlighted sentence in the passage? *Incorrect* choices change the meaning in important ways or leave out essential information.

(A) Limits placed by the Church prevented the content of the book from being different than that of other publications.
(B) The combination of the images and text differentiates this book from those typically produced by Church officials.
(C) As the book includes written materials copied from religious sources, the illustrations are its only interesting feature.
(D) The artwork is what distinguishes the book because its written content is similar to that of other religious texts.

3 The phrase "subscribe to" in the passage is closest in meaning to

(A) agree with
(B) figure out
(C) decide on
(D) prepare for

4 Why does the author mention the "Annals of Ulster" in the passage?

(A) To compare two historical records from the same period
(B) To show that an institution had a long history of creating books
(C) To provide evidence for a claim about the origin of a work
(D) To suggest that an art piece was created later than first thought

5 According to paragraph 2, monks of the Iona Abbey

(A) exported books to many other kingdoms
(B) constructed a new facility in Scotland
(C) taught bookmaking skills to Irish monks
(D) moved to a monastery in another region

Paragraph 2 is marked with an arrow [➡].

6 The word "these" in the passage refers to

(A) shapes
(B) images
(C) figures
(D) scenes

7 According to paragraph 3, all of the following are distinctive features of the Book of Kells EXCEPT

(A) the style and quality of the lettering
(B) the intricate images on each of the pages
(C) the accurate portrayals of religious leaders
(D) the diverse assortment of bright colors

Paragraph 3 is marked with an arrow [➡].

8 According to paragraph 4, it was difficult to locate information in the Book of Kells because

(A) the order of the Gospels was changed
(B) the titles of the parts were left out
(C) the names of the chapters were repeated
(D) the layout of the text was inconsistent

Paragraph 4 is marked with an arrow [➡].

Volume Review Help Back Next

9 Look at the four squares [■] that indicate where the following sentence could be added to the passage.

Both of these ingredients were difficult to acquire and incredibly expensive at the time.

Where would the sentence best fit?

Click on a square [■] to add the sentence to the passage.

10 **Directions:** An introductory sentence for a brief summary of the passage is provided below. Complete the summary by selecting the THREE answer choices that express the most important ideas in the passage. Some sentences do not belong in the summary because they express ideas that are not presented in the passage or are minor ideas in the passage. **This question is worth 2 points.**

Drag your answer choices to the spaces where they belong.
To remove an answer choice, click on it. To review the passage, click on **View Text**.

The Book of Kells is an illuminated manuscript that is considered a significant piece of medieval art.

-
-
-

Answer Choices

(A) Most researchers agree that the book was either made in the Abbey of Kells in Ireland or the Iona Abbey in Scotland.

(B) The first written reference to the book is in a description of a Viking attack on a monastery in the eleventh century.

(C) The Book of Kells has several notable characteristics that greatly increase its overall value as a work of visual art.

(D) The colored inks used to create the illustrations in the Book of Kells include pigments from a variety of sources.

(E) The book was most likely produced to be displayed prominently as it was not suitable for studying the Bible.

(F) The text of the book includes many layout errors, which makes it doubtful that it was ever used in church ceremonies.

Answer Book p. 65

Answer Book p. 67

TOEFL Reading

Passage 2

Concern about Extinctions

Ecosystems are composed of species that compete with one another for a limited quantity of resources, and this competition necessitates species adaptation, which is a key driving force behind evolution. **A** Species that are successful survive and reproduce, but those unable to adapt to changing conditions or to the competition of others die out. **B** Extinctions can also result from cataclysmic events, such as earthquakes, volcanic eruptions, and floods. **C** According to evolutionary theory, extinctions are both natural and inevitable. **D** In fact, they have been happening for millions of years. But if extinction is simply a natural aspect of life on Earth, why are people concerned about it?

➡ Although extinctions are a natural phenomenon, they have been occurring recently at an increased rate. The natural, or background, extinction rate is estimated by studying the fossil record and calculating averages over millions of years. Considering both terrestrial and marine fossil groups, scientists estimate that the average life span for a single species is approximately one to ten million years, but it varies depending on the type of organism. Mammalian species, for example, have an average life span of one million years, and their background extinction rate is one species per two hundred years. But during the past four hundred years, eighty-nine mammals have been formally listed as extinct; therefore, mammals have been disappearing at more than forty times their natural rate. This number is particularly alarming because there are currently only around 5,400 living mammal species. During the same period, 128 bird species disappeared among the approximately 10,000 known avian species, and an estimated 10 percent of birds are listed as critically endangered.

➡ The main cause for the recent acceleration in extinctions is human activity. By exerting increasing pressure on organisms, humans have inadvertently caused the extinction of numerous species. Two notable examples are the dodo and the cassowary, birds which were historically harvested in unsustainable numbers as a source of meat. Similarly, Caribbean monk seals were hunted to extinction in the mid-twentieth century, and the last confirmed sighting of the marine mammal was in 1952. Among the greatest threats to today's organisms is the unprecedented deforestation that is happening in rain forests across the globe. The Amazon River Basin, home to more than a third of the planet's species, is a prime example of a rain forest ecosystem that is being rapidly degraded by logging and farming. It is estimated that as many as 130 species (35 of which are animals) are being driven to extinction every day in the world's rain forests.

Still, the question remains: Why bother to preserve biodiversity? It is well known that a significant portion of the world's pharmaceuticals contain extracts from plants, but only a tiny fraction of Earth's flora has been screened for medicinal substances. Consequently, every untested species of plant lost to habitat destruction potentially represents a missed opportunity to discover chemicals with curative properties. There is also the risk of losing existing plants with known medicinal qualities. But beyond the direct value of biodiversity, people should act as responsible stewards of the earth. This moral imperative—to preserve as much of Earth's richness for posterity as possible—has been stressed by great thinkers in every civil society. Even the political philosopher John Locke, famed for his writings on individual liberty and the pursuit of happiness, said that humans should leave as much for successive generations as they take for themselves. In other words, liberty must be balanced with responsibility.

11 Which of the sentences below best expresses the essential information in the highlighted sentence in the passage? *Incorrect* choices change the meaning in important ways or leave out essential information.

(A) Evolution provides the impetus for the competition for resources among the various groups of organisms that inhabit the same habitat.

(B) Competition for resources among the organisms that make up ecosystems compels adaptation among species, which is a major determinant of evolution.

(C) The adaptations of individual organisms promote increased competition among species for various resources.

(D) Species compete with one another for scarce resources, and this competition plays a key role in their evolution.

12 What can be inferred from paragraph 2 about mammals?

(A) They become extinct faster than many other types of animals.

(B) They are less likely to go extinct if they live in a marine environment.

(C) They have longer life spans now than they did in the distant past.

(D) They are difficult to identify when examining the fossil record.

Paragraph 2 is marked with an arrow [➡].

13 According to paragraph 2, approximately 10 percent of bird species

(A) have gone extinct over the past two centuries

(B) face an imminent threat of dying off completely

(C) have not yet been identified by the scientific community

(D) are not facing any significant risks to their survival

Paragraph 2 is marked with an arrow [➡].

14 The word "exerting" in the passage is closest in meaning to

Ⓐ applying
Ⓑ alleviating
Ⓒ managing
Ⓓ ignoring

15 In paragraph 3, all of the following are mentioned as specific examples of human activities that cause extinctions EXCEPT

Ⓐ killing animals for food
Ⓑ blocking waterways with dams
Ⓒ harvesting trees to get wood
Ⓓ clearing areas of land for agriculture

Paragraph 3 is marked with an arrow [➡].

16 The word "curative" in the passage is closest in meaning to

Ⓐ healing
Ⓑ stimulating
Ⓒ outstanding
Ⓓ defining

17 Why does the author discuss "the political philosopher John Locke" in the passage?

Ⓐ To show the relationship between personal liberty and environmentalism
Ⓑ To emphasize the long history of the environmental movement
Ⓒ To provide support for claim about an obligation to protect nature
Ⓓ To suggest that self-interest is a barrier to caring for the natural world

18 The author claims that many species of plants

Ⓐ include substances with health benefits for humans
Ⓑ absorb potentially dangerous chemicals on a regular basis
Ⓒ develop new properties when their habitats change
Ⓓ exhibit characteristics that reduce the threat of extinction

19 Look at the four squares [■] that indicate where the following sentence could be added to the passage.

Such extinctions usually occur when a species has a limited geographic range.

Where would the sentence best fit?

Click on a square [■] to add the sentence to the passage.

20 **Directions:** An introductory sentence for a brief summary of the passage is provided below. Complete the summary by selecting the THREE answer choices that express the most important ideas in the passage. Some sentences do not belong in the summary because they express ideas that are not presented in the passage or are minor ideas in the passage. **This question is worth 2 points.**

Drag your answer choices to the spaces where they belong.
To remove an answer choice, click on it. To review the passage, click on **View Text**.

Recent changes in extinction rates can largely be attributed to the actions of humans.

-
-
-

Answer Choices

Ⓐ The number of terrestrial and marine organisms lost to extinction during recent times has been higher than at any time in the historical record.

Ⓑ Extinction rates during the past four hundred years have far exceeded natural extinction rates.

Ⓒ The medicinal value of plants is well known, but a large number of the world's plant species have yet to be tested.

Ⓓ Although overhunting directly led to several notable extinctions, it is no longer the widespread problem that it once was.

Ⓔ Habitat destruction is a threat to a significant portion of the world's organisms.

Ⓕ Whether for their beauty or role in creating a rich life experience for humans, organisms should be protected.

Answer Book p. 67

TOEFL Reading

Passage 3

Civil and Common Law

Written legal systems have become much more sophisticated and diverse since their inception nearly four thousand years ago, but they typically still fall into two broad categories: civil and common.

➡ Civil law can be traced back to the Roman emperor Justinian around the beginning of the seventh century, and it represents the most prevalent legal system in the world. It refers to law that is highly codified, meaning that it has comprehensive legal codes that are continually updated. Civil law is primarily reliant on statutes, which are acts established by a legislature. Statutes allow judges to rapidly review the facts of a case and then precisely apply the relevant provisions of the statute. Once a judge determines whether an accused person is in violation of the law, the statutes make his or her interpretation of procedures and punishments fairly straightforward. Before and during a case in civil law courts, attorneys are allowed to represent clients, advise them about details of the law, and help them prepare legal documents. However, their role during court proceedings is extremely limited. The judge functions like a head investigator and takes the lead in establishing facts and examining witnesses.

➡ Common law is generally associated with the United Kingdom and countries that are strongly influenced by British legal traditions. In these countries, case law is of primary importance even though codified statutes also exist. [A] Case law consists of the published opinions of certain judges who have ruled on notable cases and therefore established legal precedents, which are judicial decisions that can be applied to similar cases. [B] These precedents have much authority and strongly influence future judicial rulings. [C] Criminal court proceedings under common law highlight the role of the attorney in representing a client. [D] Lawyers stand in front of judges, and sometimes a jury, and try to persuade them on points of law as well as the guilt or innocence of the accuser or the accused. Judges are mainly just moderators. Because of this dynamic, criminal proceedings in case law are similar to sports events, in which the attorneys and clients represent the teams and the judges are the referees. In the case of a jury trial, ordinary citizens called jurors vote to determine the guilt or innocence of a defendant, and the judge accepts their decision in the vast majority of cases. However, in the event of a guilty verdict by the jury, the punishment is the sole decision of the judge.

➡ In practice, many legal systems operate in a manner in which aspects of both civil and common law are used. The United States is a perfect example of this in that it has comprehensive codified laws at both the federal and state levels. The US Code is the formal set of statutes for the entire country. It applies to all US citizens and thus practically functions as a universal form of civil law. In addition, each state has its own set of statutes that apply only to residents of, or visitors to, that state. What makes the US a common law country is the central role of judges in shaping the law. For instance, federal and state supreme courts have a tremendous amount of power as their judges can uphold or reject laws made by federal or state legislatures. Thus, the common law is ultimately superior to the civil law if ever the two are in conflict, and in supreme court cases, judges may determine whether laws made by legislative bodies are accordant with their interpretations of the US Constitution.

21 The word "inception" in the passage is closest in meaning to

Ⓐ innovation
Ⓑ discovery
Ⓒ emergence
Ⓓ detection

22 According to paragraph 2, which of the following is true of civil law?

Ⓐ It tends to have strict punishments.
Ⓑ It is the most common legal system.
Ⓒ It is used in only a few countries.
Ⓓ It relies on ancient legal precedents.

Paragraph 2 is marked with an arrow [➡].

23 According to paragraph 2, statutes help judges to do all of the following EXCEPT

Ⓐ review case details quickly
Ⓑ explain legal concepts clearly
Ⓒ apply relevant provisions accurately
Ⓓ interpret procedures and punishments simply

Paragraph 2 is marked with an arrow [➡].

24 Why does the author mention sports events in paragraph 3?

Ⓐ To describe how attorneys interact with their clients in court
Ⓑ To emphasize the importance of attorneys in criminal cases
Ⓒ To explain the method that judges use to determine innocence and guilt
Ⓓ To provide an analogy for how certain court processes work

Paragraph 3 is marked with an arrow [➡].

25 Which of the following can be inferred from paragraph 3 about a decision of a jury?

(A) It determines the punishment for a crime.
(B) It requires agreement among all jurors.
(C) It must be approved by the attorneys on the case.
(D) It is occasionally overturned by the judge.

Paragraph 3 is marked with an arrow [➡].

26 The word "accordant" in the passage is closest in meaning to

(A) apparent
(B) consistent
(C) standard
(D) natural

27 According to paragraph 4, the United States is considered a common law country despite having codified laws because

(A) federal statutes apply to all states
(B) judges play a key part in forming the law
(C) each state has its own set of laws
(D) legislatures continually update statutes

Paragraph 4 is marked with an arrow [➡].

28 According to paragraph 4, which of the following is true of federal and state supreme courts?

(A) They can approve or dismiss statutes.
(B) They have the power to make laws.
(C) They can appoint their own judges.
(D) They are less powerful than legislatures.

Paragraph 4 is marked with an arrow [➡].

29 Look at the four squares [■] that indicate where the following sentence could be added to the passage.

For example, judges of the US Supreme Court are often very reluctant to overturn prior Supreme Court decisions.

Where would the sentence best fit?

Click on a square [■] to add the sentence to the passage.

30 **Directions:** Select the appropriate statements from the answer choices and match them to the type of legal system to which they relate. **This question is worth 3 points.**

Drag your answer choices to the spaces where they belong.
To remove an answer choice, click on it. To review the passage, click on **View Text**.

Answer Choices	Civil Law
(A) The role of attorneys in the courtroom is very restricted.	•
(B) Emphasis is placed on previously published views of judges.	•
(C) Judges function as chief examiners during criminal proceedings.	**Common Law**
(D) The lawyers submit evidence to judges prior to court cases.	
(E) The role of the judge is that of a moderator in criminal cases.	•
(F) Criminal cases are always argued in front of a jury.	•
(G) Attorneys attempt to persuade judges on their clients' behalf.	•

Answer Book p. 68

MEMO

|H|A|C|K|E|R|S|

APEX READING for the TOEFL iBT® Advanced

September 28, 2022

Hackers Language Research Institute
23, Gangnam-daero 61-gil, Seocho-gu, Seoul, Korea
Inquiries publishing@hackers.com

ISBN 978-89-6542-510-6 (53740)

Printed in South Korea

2 3 4 5 6 7 8 9 10 28 27 26 25 24

HACKERS

APEX READING for the TOEFL iBT®

Advanced

HACKERS

APEX READING for the TOEFL iBT®

Advanced

Answer Book

HACKERS

CHAPTER 01
Vocabulary

Example

본문 p.13

1 (C) 2 (A) 3 (D)

수혈

수혈이 제공될 때, 공혈자의 혈액이 수혈자의 혈액과 일치하는 것은 중요하다. 공혈자와 수혈자 간에 적혈구와 혈장 안의 특정 요소들이 다를 때 혈액은 맞지 않는다. 그러한 경우, 수혈자의 혈액에 있는 항체는 공혈자 혈액의 적혈구와 응집할 것이다. 그 결과는 용혈, 즉 헤모글로빈을 함유한 적혈구의 파괴와 그 결과로서 일어나는 헤모글로빈의 혈액 내 방출이다. 순환계에 헤모글로빈이 있게 되면, 종종 신장 손상이 일어나며 치명적일 수 있다.

수혈자에게서 반작용을 일으킬 가능성이 가장 높은 요인들은 ABO식 혈액형 및 Rh식 혈액형 내 물질들이다. 전자에서, AB형인 사람들은 A, B, AB, O형 혈액을 받아들일 수 있기 때문에 만능 수혈자라고 알려져 있다. 반면에, O형인 사람들은 그들의 적혈구가 다른 어떤 혈액형의 항체에 의한 반응도 촉발시킬 가능성이 적기 때문에 때때로 만능 공혈자라고 불린다. 그러나, 일반적으로, 의료 종사자들은 부정적인 반작용을 최소화하기 위해 정확히 일치시키는 것을 선호한다. Rh식 혈액형에서는, 혈액 내의 특정 단백질인 리서스 인자의 존재가 사람이 Rh 양성인지 Rh 음성인지를 결정하게 된다. Rh 음성인 사람이 Rh 양성 혈액을 받을 경우, 그 사람의 신체는 그 단백질을 공격하기 위해 항체를 생성하게 되고, 이는 바람직하지 않은 효과이다.

blood transfusion 수혈 recipient 명 수혈자, 받는 사람
incompatible 형 (혈액형이) 맞지 않는 red blood cell 적혈구
plasma 명 혈장 antibody 명 항체 clump 동 응집하다
hemolysis 명 용혈 consequent 형 결과로서 일어나는
circulatory system 순환계 lethal 형 치명적인
substance 명 물질 practitioner 명 (전문직) 종사자
adverse 형 부정적인 undesirable 형 바람직하지 않은

1 지문의 단어 "incompatible"과 의미가 가장 비슷한 것은?
(A) 보이는
(B) 나뉘는
(C) 일치하지 않는
(D) 파괴적인

2 지문의 단어 "adverse"와 의미가 가장 비슷한 것은?
(A) 해로운
(B) 이로운
(C) 중립적인
(D) 다양한

3 지문의 단어 "undesirable"과 의미가 가장 비슷한 것은?
(A) 포괄적인
(B) 예측할 수 없는
(C) 즉각적인
(D) 반갑지 않은

Reading Practice 1

본문 p.14

1 (A) 2 (B) 3 (C) 4 (C) 5 (D) 6 (B)

컴퓨터의 도움을 받은 날씨 예측

기상학은 날씨를 연구하는 학문이며, 기상학자의 가장 중요한 기능들 중 하나는 날씨를 사전에 예측하는 것이다. [1]사람들은 수천 년 동안 대기의 움직임을 예측하려고 노력해 왔으며, 이는 기원전 650년 고대 바빌로니아인들의 구름 형성에 대한 관찰로 거슬러 올라간다. 수 세기에 걸쳐, 점점 더 면밀한 관찰이 사람들로 하여금 기상도를 이용한 몇몇 간단한 예측을 할 수 있게 해주었다. 처음에 기상도는 넓은 지역으로부터의 기상 데이터를 포함했던 손으로 그린 차트였다. 이것들 중 최초의 것은 1816년에 만들어졌으며, 우편이나 전보를 이용하여 다양한 장소에서 수집된 데이터를 기반으로 했다. 그럼에도, 기상학자들은 20세기 중후반에 컴퓨터 모델링이 현실화되기 전까지는 제한된 확신을 가지고 있었다.

컴퓨터 모델은 매우 다양한 정보원으로부터 대기에 관한 정보를 얻으며, 기상학자가 컴퓨터 모델에 더 많은 데이터를 입력할 수 있을 수록 그 결과는 더 정확해질 것이다. 오늘날, 일기 예보자의 예측을 구성하는 정보의 일부는 인공위성 사진의 형태로 우주에서 온다. 그러나 기상 과학자들은 정보를 모으기 위해 여전히 레이더를 사용하는데, 그것은 제2차 세계대전 중에 날씨 예측을 위해 폭풍우를 조사하는 데 처음 사용된 기술이다. 컴퓨터 모델을 위한 추가적인 데이터는 기상 관측 풍선에서 오는데, 이것들은 압력, 기온, 습도를 측정하기 위해 전 세계 약 900곳의 서로 다른 장소에서 하루에 두 번씩 하늘로 날려 보내진다.

일단 컴퓨터가 이러한 원천들에서 나온 데이터를 수집하면, 그것은 지역을 구획들로 나눈다. [4B]더 큰 구획들은 지역적 세부 사항이 부족하지만, 지구를 돌아다니며 기상 시스템의 광범위한 사진을 제공한다. [4A/4D]더 작은 구획들은 더 높은 해상도를 가지고 있으며, 그것들은 지역적 날씨 현상을 예측하는 데 사용된다. 각각의 구획 유형을 이용하여, 기상학자는 다른 것들보다 특정한 변수를 우선시하기 위해 데이터를 변경할 수 있다. 예를 들어, 기상 요원은 모델이 풍속에 두는 중점을 키우고 습도에 대한 그것의 초점을 줄일 수 있다. 이러한 이유로, 많은 작업이 기계에 의해 수행됨에도 불구하고, 지역의 상황을 아는 기상학자들은 날씨를 예측하는 데 있어 중요한 역할을 수행할 수 있다.

현대의 날씨 예측은 역사상의 어느 시점보다 더 정확하지만, 정확한 장기적 예측을 하는 것은 여전히 어렵다. 5일 예측이 90퍼센트 정확함에도 불구하고, 7일 예측은 대략 80퍼센트 정도만 들어맞는다. [6]만약 당신이 지금으로부터 10일 후에 있을 중요한 행사 날에 비가 올지 알아보려고 한다면, 날씨 예측은 50퍼센트의 경우에만 정확할 것이다. 이러한 불확실성은 예측을 할 때 고려할 변수가 너무 많기 때문에 발생한다. 따라서, 실용적인 장기적 예측은 계절적 수준에서의 추세와 이례적인 것들에 초점을 맞추는 경향이 있다. 그것들이 단기적인 예측만큼 정확할 수 없음에도 불구하고, 이것들은 여전히 도움이 되는데, 이는 그것들이 예를 들어 다가오는 겨울이나 봄의 기온이나 강수량이 평소보다 많을지, 혹은 적을지를 시사할 수 있기 때문이다.

meteorology 명 기상학 ahead of time 사전에
telegraph 명 전보 confidence 명 확신 probe 동 조사하다
humidity 명 습도 compile 동 수집하다 be short on ~이 부족하다
resolution 명 해상도 exploit 동 이용하다 alter 동 변경하다
prioritize 동 우선시하다 variable 명 변수
place an emphasis on ~에 중점을 두다 contemporary 형 현대의
come true 들어맞다 uncertainty 명 불확실성
anomaly 명 이례적인 것 precipitation 명 강수

1 1단락에 따르면, 다음 중 고대 바빌로니아인들에 관해 사실인 것은?
(A) 날씨를 예측하려고 시도한 최초의 사람들이었다.
(B) 대기의 움직임을 예측하기 위해 간단한 기상도를 사용했다.
(C) 단기적 날씨 추세를 정확하게 예측할 수 있었다.
(D) 서로 다른 다양한 장소로부터 데이터를 수집했다.

2 지문의 단어 "probe"와 의미가 가장 비슷한 것은?
(A) 정지시키다
(B) 조사하다
(C) 해결하다
(D) 방해하다

3 지문의 단어 "its"가 가리키는 것은?
(A) 변수
(B) 중점
(C) 모델
(D) 속도

4 3단락에 따르면, 다음 중 지역적 구획에 관해 사실이 아닌 것은?
(A) 더 작은 것들은 더 높은 해상도를 가지고 있다.
(B) 더 큰 것들은 기상 시스템의 광범위한 이미지를 제공한다.
(C) 더 큰 것들은 더 자세한 사진을 제공한다.
(D) 더 작은 것들은 지역적 날씨 예측을 위해 사용된다.

5 지문의 단어 "anomalies"와 의미가 가장 비슷한 것은?
(A) 평균
(B) 방해
(C) 근접
(D) 일탈

6 4단락에 따르면, 다음 중 현재의 날씨 예측에 관해 사실인 것은?
(A) 증가하는 수의 변수들 때문에 정확성이 약간 떨어졌다.
(B) 10일 예측에서 대략 절반 정도 정확하다.
(C) 90퍼센트 정확한 7일 예측을 할 수 있다.
(D) 5일 이내의 정확성 신뢰도는 80퍼센트이다.

Reading Practice 2

본문 p.16

1 (C) 2 (C) 3 (D) 4 (A) 5 (D) 6 (A)

로제타석

로제타석은 한 고대 이집트 왕에 대한 여러 언어로 된 정치적 지지 성명이 새겨진 화강암 조각이다. 그러나 그것이 수 세기 후에 나폴레옹에게 고용된 침략한 프랑스 군인에 의해 재발견된 후, 로제타석은 오래전에 쇠망한 문명의 비밀을 푸는 것을 도왔고, 지금껏 가장 유명한 역사적 유물들 중 하나가 되었다.

기원전 196년에 조각된 로제타석은 동일한 메시지가 식각된 많은 석판들 중 하나였으며, 이집트의 모든 신전은 그와 같은 것을 하나씩 가지고 있었다. [2]그 돌들은 세금을 낮추고, 반란을 진압하고, 그의 군인들에게 혜택을 준 것에 대해 통치자를 칭찬하는 듣기 좋은 말로 프톨레마이오스 5세 에피파네스의 대관식을 선전했다. **그러나, 이러한 초기의 활용은 오래가지 못했으며, 얼마 지나지 않아 그 돌들은 더 소박하며 순전히 실용적인 목적으로 쓰였다.** 프톨레마이오스의 사망 이후, 이집트인들은 남아 있는 돌을 항구 도시 로제타 근처에 있는 오래된 요새의 구조적인 요소로 사용했다.

그것은 1799년까지 그곳에 있었는데, 이때 한 무리의 프랑스 군인들은 그 무거운 돌을 그것이 놓여 있던 장소에서 제거하려 했으나 실패했다. [3A/3C]나폴레옹은 부분적으로는 지중해 동부에서 영국을 몰아내기 위해, 그리고 부분적으로는 언제나 그를 매료시켰던, 유명한 고대의 땅인 이집트를 탐험하기 위해 이집트에 왔다. [3B]나폴레옹의 군인들 중 다수는 훈련된 학자들이었는데, 그중에는 그 4피트 높이의 바위를 관심을 끌 만한 잠재력이 있는 유물로 알아본 장교도 있었다. 그것의 메시지는 세 개의 서로 다른 문자로 쓰여 있었다. 이것들 중 하나는 고대 그리스어였고 다른 두 개는 모두 고대 이집트어로, 즉 상형문자와, 민중문자로 알려진 보다 일상적 대화체의 글자 형태였다.

로제타석이 재발견되기 전에, 상형문자의 의미는 역사 속으로 사라져 있었다. 이 글자 형태는 로마 제국이 기독교로 개종하고 당시 이집트에서 행해졌던 것과 같은 고대 종교들을 금지한 후에 완전히 폐기되었다. 그러나, 상형문자들이 돌 위에 그리스어로 번역되어 있었기 때문에 로제타석은 그것들을 해독하는 것에 대한 열쇠를 제공했다. 19세기 초에 한 프랑스 학자가 이 프로젝트에 착수했다. [6]이집트학자 장 프랑수아 샹폴리옹은 각각의 상형문자가 때로는 (글자가 설명하도록 의도된 것을 묘사하는 그림을 사용하여) 그림을 이용하고, 때로는 (이집트어로 글자들의 소리를 내어) 표음식이며, 때로는 (생각을 표현하기 위해 기호를 사용하여) 표의적이라는 것을 깨달았다. 이것이 번역을 어렵게 만들었지만, 샹폴리옹은 결국 그것을 완수해냈다.

오늘날, 로제타석은 대영박물관에서 가장 인기 있는 전시품이다. 이집트 정부가 그 돌이 고대의 고향으로 반환되기를 원한다고 선언했음에도 불구하고, 영국 관리들은 그러한 이전이 일어나지 않을 것임을 분명히 했다. 현대 세계에 고대 이집트 글자를 읽는 법을 가르쳐준, 그래서 강력한 문명에 대한 전례 없는 역사적 이해의 문을 열어준 그 판은 계속해서 외국 땅에서 전시될 것이다.

granite 명 화강암　multilingual 형 여러 언어의
in the employ of ~에게 고용된　artifact 명 유물　slab 명 판
etch 동 식각하다, 뚜렷이 새기다　coronation 명 대관식
flattering 형 듣기 좋은　grant 동 주다　dislodge 동 제거하다
fascinate 동 매료시키다　script 명 문자
hieroglyphics 명 상형문자　colloquial 형 일상적 대화체의
discard 동 폐기하다, 버리다　convert 동 개종하다
prohibit 동 금지하다　decipher 동 해독하다　tackle 동 착수하다
pictorial 형 그림을 이용하는　phonetic 형 표음식의
ideographic 형 표의적인　exhibit 명 전시품
unprecedented 형 전례 없는

1 네 개의 네모[■]는 다음 문장이 삽입될 수 있는 곳을 나타내고 있다.
그러나, 이러한 초기의 활용은 오래가지 못했으며, 얼마 지나지 않아 그 돌들은 더 소박하며 순전히 실용적인 목적으로 쓰였다.
이 문장은 어디에 들어가는 것이 가장 적절한가?

2 다음 중 2단락에서 글쓴이가 로제타석에 관해 묘사하는 것은?
(A) 프톨레마이오스 5세의 사망 이후에 조각되었다.
(B) 더 많은 사람들을 신전으로 끌어들이려고 했다.
(C) 정치 지도자의 업적을 칭찬했다.
(D) 왕에 대한 사람들의 요청을 기술했다.

3 다음 중 나폴레옹과 그의 군대에 관해 언급되지 않은 것은?

(A) 그는 그 땅에서 또 다른 유럽의 세력을 쫓아내기 위해 이집트를 침략했다.
(B) 그의 군대는 문화적 유물에 관해 많이 아는 사람들을 포함했다.
(C) 그는 얼마 동안 이집트에 대한 강한 관심이 있었다.
(D) 그의 군인들은 로제타석을 그들의 고국으로 운송해냈다.

4 지문의 단어 "discarded"와 의미가 가장 비슷한 것은?

(A) 버려진
(B) 복원된
(C) 촉진된
(D) 통합된

5 지문의 단어 "deciphering"과 의미가 가장 비슷한 것은?

(A) 의심하는
(B) 불러일으키는
(C) 즉석에서 하는
(D) 해독하는

6 4단락에 따르면, 다음 중 장 프랑수아 샹폴리옹에 관해 사실인 것은?

(A) 상형문자가 다양한 언어적 기능을 한다는 것을 알아냈다.
(B) 성공적으로 로제타석을 영어와 프랑스어로 번역했다.
(C) 고대 아프리카 언어를 전공한 언어학자였다.
(D) 로제타석에 새겨진 글을 정확하게 해석하는 데 결국 실패했다.

Reading Practice 3

본문 p.18

1 (B) 2 (C) 3 (C) 4 (B) 5 (C) 6 (A)

앤설 애덤스

단지 앤설 애덤스의 이름을 듣는 것만으로도 굽어진 개울이나 바위투성이 들판 위로 높이 솟은 장엄한 산들의 완벽한 회색톤 이미지가 떠오른다. 애덤스는 가장 잘 알려진 미국인 사진작가이며, 그는 부인할 수 없는 경관 구성의 대가였다. 위엄 있는 미국 서부 황야에 대한 그의 한결같은 안목은 그가 20세기의 사진작가들과 다른 시각 예술가들 사이에서 높은 지위를 확보하게 해주었다.

'사진 만들기' 같은 그의 저서에 기록되어 있듯이, 애덤스는 각각의 사진이 세심한 기술적 과정의 결과라고 생각했다. 단지 아름다운 것들의 사진을 찍는 것 대신에, 그는 풍경 이미지를 꼼꼼하게 시각화하는 것이 좋다고 생각했다. 이것은 단지 무엇의 사진을 찍을지와 그것이 어떻게 구성되어야 하는지를 선택하는 것뿐만 아니라 정확히 어떻게 그것에 빛이 비추어지는지를 의미하기도 했다. 이 신중한 사고는 애덤스가 "존 시스템"이라고 지칭한 것으로 체계화되었다. [3]그것은 사진작가가 카메라를 만지기도 전에 0에서 10까지의 평가 척도를 이용하여 자연 풍경의 모든 요소에 요구되는 빛의 강도를 숙고해야 한다고 지시했다.

그러나 진정으로 그의 작품을 차별화한 것은 자연적 세부 사항에 대한 애덤스의 안목과 그의 피사체를 극적으로 묘사하는 방법에 대한 그의 생생한 상상력이었다. [5A]그에게 큰 찬사를 안겨준 첫 번째 사진인 1927년의 '암석, 하프 돔의 얼굴'을 생각해 보자. 요세미티 공원의 상징적인 화강암 절벽인 하프 돔의 음울한 장엄함을 전달하기 위해, 그는 세 구역으로 나누어진 이미지를 상상했다. [5B]아래에 있는 숲의 대조적으로 밝은 하얀 눈 덮인 풍경에 반대되는 그늘진 절벽 면과 훨씬 더 어두운 하늘이 있을 것이었다. 그래서, 그는 멀리 떨어진 곳으로 올라가 기다렸다. [5D]그가 거기에 있는 동안, 그는 그의 이미지를 얻는 유일한 방법이 그의 렌즈에 빨간색 필터를 사용하는 것과 5초간의 긴 노출 시간을 사용하는 것이라는 걸 알아냈다. 이 기술은, 특히 깨끗한 하늘이 어둡게 표현되었기 때문에 그날 오후 상황의 진실된 묘사가 아닌 흑백 이미지를 낳았지만, 그것의 구성은 그늘진 절벽 면의 미세한 세부 사항과 하프 돔이 당신 위로 드리우는 기분을 포착한다.

그의 베스트셀러가 된 교육용 지침서들과 함께 '암석' 같은 놀라운 사진들이 등장하면서 애덤스는 누구나 아는 이름이 되었다. 하지만, 비판적인 기득권층은 그의 업적의 중대함을 느리게 인지했다. [6]사진을 표현의 강력한 매체로 생각했던 일부 예술 비평가들은 그의 완벽한 구성을 감정적으로 냉담한 것으로 일축하고 그의 작품에는 당대의 다른 유명한 사진가들의 정치적 화제성이 결여되어 있다고 주장하면서 그의 기여를 과소평가했다. 하지만, 사실 애덤스의 작품은 언제나 정치적 의식을 가지고 있었고, 미국 서부의 자연적 아름다움을 기록하려는 그의 노력은 자연 보호론자들의 명분에 실체적인 영향을 끼쳤다. 애덤스의 환경적 행동주의는 그의 시대를 앞서 있었고, 심지어 그들조차도 결국에는 그의 자연보호 주의 미학의 사회적 중요성을 받아들였다. 말년에, 그는 거의 전 세계적인 찬사를 얻었다. 그가 세상을 떠나기 4년 전에, 애덤스는 국가의 공원을 보존하는 데 도움을 준 그의 공로로 대통령 자유 훈장을 받았다.

conjure up 떠오르게 하다 immaculate 형 완벽한, 흠 없는 majestic 형 장엄한 undeniable 형 부인할 수 없는 composition 명 구성 unfailing 형 한결같은 stately 형 위엄 있는 lofty 형 높은 meticulously 부 꼼꼼하게 visualize 동 시각화하다 deliberate 형 신중한 codify 동 체계화하다 intensity 명 강도 dramatically 부 극적으로 acclaim 명 찬사 brooding 형 음울한 iconic 형 상징적인 contrastingly 부 대조적으로 replicate 동 재현하다 fine 형 미세한 loom 동 드리우다 stunning 형 놀라운 household name 누구나 아는 이름 establishment 명 기득권층 accomplishment 명 업적 contribution 명 기여 impeccable 형 완벽한 topicality 명 화제성 tangible 형 실체적인 cause 명 명분 aesthetic 명 미학

1 지문의 단어 "lofty"와 의미가 가장 비슷한 것은?

(A) 기억할 만한
(B) 높은
(C) 과소평가된
(D) 적절한

2 지문의 단어 "visualizing"과 의미가 가장 비슷한 것은?

(A) 기록하는
(B) 분석하는
(C) 상상하는
(D) 연구하는

3 2단락에 따르면, 앤설 애덤스의 존 시스템은 사진가가

(A) 사진에 무엇을 포함할지에 대해 적절한 선택을 할 것을 요구했다
(B) 아름다운 이미지를 만들어 내기 위해 구성 기법을 효과적으로 사용할 것을 요구했다
(C) 피사체의 각 면에 선호되는 밝기를 결정할 것을 요구했다
(D) 야외 조명 조건에 적합한 카메라 종류를 확인할 것을 요구했다

4 지문의 단어 "its"가 가리키는 것은?

(A) 기술
(B) 이미지
(C) 묘사
(D) 오후

5 다음 중 '암석, 하프 돔의 얼굴'에 관해 사실이 아닌 것은?

(A) 애덤스의 사진가로서의 첫 번째 큰 성공이었다.
(B) 그늘 속의 절벽을 묘사하려는 애덤스의 시도에서 비롯되었다.
(C) 어둡고 음울한 날씨 조건에서 포착되었다.
(D) 상대적으로 긴 노출 시간을 필요로 했다.

6 4단락에 따르면, 일부 비평가들이 애덤스를 못마땅해한 것은

(A) 그가 당대의 주요한 사회적 문제를 다루지 못했기 때문이다
(B) 그의 풍경 구성이 너무 감상적인 것으로 여겨졌기 때문이다
(C) 그들이 사진을 예술의 형태로서 감상하지 못했기 때문이다
(D) 그의 책이 독자들에게 긍정적인 인상을 주지 못했기 때문이다

iBT Reading Test 1

본문 p.20

1 (A) 2 (C) 3 (A) 4 (D)
5 (B) 6 (C) 7 (B) 8 (B)
9 (B) 10 (A), (E), (F)

반투족들

'반투'라는 용어는 복잡한 역사를 가지고 있다. 그것은 때로 특정 민족 집단이나 심지어는 아프리카인들 전체를 지칭하는 데 사용되지만, 그것은 둘 중 어느 하나도 정확하게 의미하지 않는다. **이와는 반대로, '반투'는 관련된 언어를 사용하는 8천 5백만 명 이상의 수백 개의 서로 다른 부족들을 지칭한다.** 엄밀히 말하면, '반투'는 아프리카어 전문가인 19세기의 독일인 빌헬름 블릭에 의해 만들어진 언어학 용어이다. [2]블릭은 "사람들"을 의미하는 줄루어 '아반투'에서 그 용어를 가져왔고, 북서쪽에서 남동쪽에 이르는 아프리카의 지역들에서 사용되는 600여 개의 서로 다르지만 밀접한 관계가 있는 토착어들을 통칭하기 위해 그것을 사용했다. '반투족들'이라는 용어는 또한 다양한 반투어를 사용하는 사람들을 지칭하는 포괄적 용어로 사용되지만, 그것이 묘사하는 사람들은 민족성이나 문화에서 동질적이지 않다.

반투어들은 하나의 원형 반투어에서 발달했기 때문에 공통된 기원을 공유한다. 이 언어는 기원전 4000년에 오늘날의 카메룬이 있는 서아프리카 해안 지방에서 생겨났다. 반투족, 즉 원형 반투어를 사용했던 사람들은 농업, 수렵, 어업이 중심이 된 문명을 발달시켰고 가족 단위 중심으로 조직된 집단으로 형성되었다. 그 대륙을 가로지르는 그 문화와 언어의 전파는 기원전 1000년에서 서기 1000년 사이에 일어났지만, 인류학자들은 이것이 물리적 이주 때문인지 문화적 전통의 확산 때문인지에 대해 논쟁하고 있다.

첫 천 년부터 1800년대에 유럽 식민지 정부가 수립될 때까지, 반투어를 사용하는 문명들은 중부 및 남부 아프리카를 지배했다. 그들의 발흥을 도운 것은 한 목초지에서 다른 목초지로 소를 모는 유목이라고 알려진 소몰이 관습이었다. 그 지역의 식습관이 소고기에 크게 의존했기 때문에, 유목민들은 그들의 소를 번식을 위해 이웃의 민족들에게 빌려줌으로써 정치적 힘을 얻었다. [6B]그들이 영향력을 얻으면서, 많은 강력한 반투 문명들이 그 대륙 전체에 걸쳐 발전했다. 이들 중에는 이슬람교 문화들과 교류한 스와힐리 해안의 거주자들도 포함되어 있었는데, 이들은 반투어에서 유래한 그들의 언어에 아랍어의 영향을 가져왔다. [6D]금과 상아와 같은 귀중한 재료들의 무역에서 동력을 공급받은 또 다른 반투 세력 중심지가 오늘날의 짐바브웨에서 생겨났다. [6A]짐바브웨와 보츠와나에 의해 점령된 지역에 있던 반투어를 사용하는 사람들은 또한 11세기와 14세기 사이에 정교한 석조 요새들을 건설했다.

반투어를 사용했던 사람들의 업적에도 불구하고, '반투'라는 단어는 20세기 후반에 많은 아프리카인들에게 인기를 잃었다. [8]그 용어는 남아프리카 공화국이 영국의 식민지였던 1920년대에 일시적으로 인기를 얻어 흑인 아프리카인들 사이에 공유된 민족적 정체성을 의미하게 되었다. 그러나, 이러한 정서는 1960년대에 그 나라의 아파르트헤이트 정권이 공식적으로 "토착민"을 지칭하는 용어를 '반투'라는 단어로 대체한 이후에 바뀌었다. 그 단어가 억압과 연관 지어졌기 때문에, 차별적인 식민지 정부에 의한 그 용어의 채택은 남아프리카 공화국의 흑인들이 그것을 사용하는 것을 피하게 했다. 비록 그 언어들이 공통된 기원에서 나왔을 가능성이 높긴 하지만, 최근의 학계는 반투어를 사용하는 공동체들이 상당한 공통된 민족사를 공유한다는 것에 의문을 제기해 왔다. 그러한 이유로, '반투'는 언어적 의미에서는 여전히 사용되지만, 민족적 표지로는 사용되지 않는다.

ethnic 형 민족의 coin 동 (용어를) 만들다
derive 동 가져오다, 이끌어내다 indigenous 형 토착의
umbrella term 포괄적 용어 homogenous 형 동질적인
ethnicity 명 민족성 foraging 명 수렵 anthropologist 명 인류학자
dispersal 명 확산 colonial 형 식민지의 dominate 동 지배하다
pastoralism 명 유목 breeding 명 번식 occupant 명 거주자
fuel 동 동력을 공급하다 elaborate 형 정교한
fall out of favor 인기를 잃다 temporarily 부 일시적으로
sentiment 명 정서 discriminative 형 차별적인
oppression 명 억압

1 지문의 단어 "homogenous"와 의미가 가장 비슷한 것은?

(A) 똑같은
(B) 체계적인
(C) 논쟁의 여지가 있는
(D) 다양한

2 1단락에 따르면, 다음 중 '반투'라는 단어에 관해 사실인 것은?

(A) 줄루족의 공통된 조상을 묘사한다.
(B) 아프리카인 언어학자에 의해 만들어졌다.
(C) 관계가 있는 언어들을 분류하기 위해 사용된다.
(D) 서아프리카의 한 민족 집단을 지칭한다.

3 지문의 단어 "this"가 가리키는 것은?

(A) 전파
(B) 문화
(C) 언어
(D) 대륙

4 지문의 단어 "dispersal"과 의미가 가장 비슷한 것은?

(A) 주입
(B) 추정
(C) 중요성
(D) 분산

5 3단락에서 글쓴이는 왜 반투 문명들의 소몰이에 관해 논하는가?

(A) 그들이 원시적인 삶의 방식을 가지고 있었다는 것을 보여주기 위해
(B) 그들이 정치적 힘을 얻는 데 도움을 준 것을 밝히기 위해
(C) 그들의 소고기의 우수한 품질을 강조하기 위해
(D) 그들이 목초지를 개간하기 위해 사용한 방법을 설명하기 위해

6 3단락에 따르면, 다음 중 1800년대 이전에 반투어를 사용했던 사람들에 관해 사실이 아닌 것은?

(A) 정교한 방어 시설을 건설했다.
(B) 그들의 영향력은 한 지역에 국한되어 있지 않았다.
(C) 아랍어로 의사소통할 수 있었다.
(D) 그들의 상업 활동은 귀중품의 무역을 포함했다.

7 아래 문장 중 지문 속의 음영된 문장의 핵심 정보를 가장 잘 표현한 것은? 오답은 문장의 의미를 크게 바꾸거나 핵심 정보를 생략한다.

(A) 학자들은 반투족들에게 어떠한 공통점이라도 있는지에 대해 의문을 제기한다.
(B) 연구자들은 반투족이 기원이 되는 언어를 공유하지만 공통된 민족성은 공유하지 않는다고 생각한다.
(C) 학자들은 반투어들이 단일 언어에서 유래했다고 생각한다.
(D) 연구는 반투족이 같은 조상을 갖지 않는다는 것을 보여준다.

8 영국의 지배하에 살았던 남아프리카 공화국의 흑인들에 관해 추론할 수 있는 것은?

(A) 반투어 대신 영어를 사용하도록 강요받았다.
(B) 1920년대 이전에는 일반적으로 그들 자신을 반투족이라고 지칭하지 않았다.
(C) 영국인들이 그들을 "토착민"이라고 지칭한 것에 불쾌감을 느꼈다.
(D) 1960년대 이전에는 영국 식민지의 일부가 되는 것에 만족했다.

9 네 개의 네모[■]는 다음 문장이 삽입될 수 있는 곳을 나타내고 있다.

이와는 반대로, '반투'는 관련된 언어를 사용하는 8천 5백만 명 이상의 수백 개의 서로 다른 부족들을 지칭한다.

이 문장은 어디에 들어가는 것이 가장 적절한가?

10 **지시**: 지문 요약을 위한 도입 문장이 아래에 주어져 있다. 지문의 가장 중요한 내용을 나타내는 보기 3개를 골라 요약을 완성하라. 어떤 문장은 지문에 언급되지 않은 내용이나 사소한 정보를 나타내므로 요약에 포함되지 않는다. **이 문제는 2점이다.**

> **반투는 원래 언어학적 개념으로 만들어졌다.**
> · (A) 반투어들은 서아프리카 사람들의 집단들에 의해 사용되었던 원형 반투어에서 유래했다.
> · (E) '반투'라는 용어는 영국의 지배 기간 동안 그것이 사용된 방식 때문에 부정적인 의미를 가지게 되었다.
> · (F) 반투 문명은 유럽의 식민지화 이전의 천 년 동안 아프리카의 넓은 지역에 걸친 주요한 세력이었다.

(B) 반투어를 사용하는 민족들과 이슬람교도들 사이의 상호작용은 거대한 국제 무역망의 발달로 이어졌다.
(C) 유럽 학자들은 종종 반투족들을 야만인으로 묘사했으며, 이는 반투족들 사이에 분노를 일으켰다.
(D) 약 기원전 100년부터 서기 1000년까지, 원형 반투어를 사용하는 사람들은 가족 단위로 나누어졌다.

iBT Reading Test 2

본문 p.24

1 (D)	2 (C)	3 (B)	4 (A)
5 (B)	6 (B)	7 (A)	8 (C)
9 (B)	10 (B), (C), (D)		

플라스틱 오염

1869년에, 미국인 기술자 존 하이엇은 셀룰로이드라고 명명된 최초의 상업적으로 이용 가능한 플라스틱을 생산했다. [2]이 물질은 실제로 환경 운동가들로부터 광범위한 인정을 받았는데, 이는 그것이 상아의 대체물 역할을 하도록 만들어졌기 때문으로, 그것은 이 물질의 유일한 원천이 심각하게 멸종 위기에 처한 코끼리라는 사실에도 불구하고 당구공과 다른 흔한 물건들을 만드는 데 사용되었다. 산업 회사들이 화석 연료 생산에서 나오는 폐기물을 쇼핑백, 냉장고 용기, 심지어 인공 신체 기관으로 바꿀 수 있다는 것을 발견함에 따라, 이어지는 세기는 플라스틱에 황금기였다. 인간은 20세기 후반이 되어서야 플라스틱의 보편성이 자연계를 질식시키고 있다는 것을 깨달았다.

사실상 부서지지 않는 플라스틱이 환경뿐만 아니라 세계의 매립지들에 쌓이면서, 그것들은 지구에 사는 생물들을 오염시키고 있다. 공장들은 1950년대부터 83억 톤의 플라스틱을 생산해왔고, 그것은 빠르게 분해되지 않는다. 설계상, 플라스틱 제품들은 내구성이 강한 탄소 대 탄소 결합에 의해 고정된 긴 분자들로 구성되어 있다. **그것들은 자연적으로 썩지 않으며, 그것들을 분해할 수 있는 어떤 유기체도 진화하지 않았다.** 그 결과, 새, 소 및 다른 동물들은 우리의 포장 음식에서 나온 소화할 수 없는 플라스틱 쓰레기를 섭취하고 결국 장폐색에 걸린다. 일부 플라스틱을 구성하는 화학물질들은 침출되어 인간의 혈류로 들어가 우리의 호르몬계에 오래 지속되는 손상을 입힌다.

버려진 플라스틱의 상태가 세계의 강과 바다보다 더 심각한 곳은 없다. 일부 수역은 플라스틱에 의해 완전히 잠겨 있다. 이탈리아 앞바다에서, 티레니아해는 현재 1제곱 피트당 186,000개의 미세 플라스틱 조각이 있다. 매년 수백만 톤의 플라스틱 잔해가 수역으로 씻겨 들어가며, 비록 그것의 일부는 결국 해저에서 멈추게 되지만, 일부는 여전히 해양 생물과 쉽게 마주칠 수 있는 수면이나 그 근처에 표류한다. 시간이 지남에 따라, 바닷물과 햇빛은 더 큰 물체들을 미세 플라스틱으로 분해하기 시작하고, 이는 고래에서 동물성 플랑크톤에 이르는, 먹이 사슬의 위쪽에서 아래쪽까지의 동물들이 체내의 미세 플라스틱 축적에 취약해지게 한다. [6]설상가상으로, 미세 플라스틱은 유기체의 지방 세포 속으로 흡수되어 그곳에서 오랜 동안 남아 있는 독성 화학물질을 함유하고 있다.

좋은 소식은, 그 문제에 대한 인식이 증가하고 있으며, 이것이 플라스틱 오염의 영향을 줄이기 위한 많은 시도들로 이어지고 있다는 것이다. [8B/8D]생분해성 플라스틱은 더 흔해졌고, 플라스틱 제조업체들은 점점 더 그것들의 제품을 수거하고 재활용하도록 강제되고 있으며, 더 위험한 플라스틱 중 일부는 금지되었다. [8A]많은 지방자치 단체들은 재사용 가능한 천 쇼핑백의 사용을 촉진하기 위해 쇼핑백 요금을 시행해오고 있다. 있어서는 안 되는 장소에 이미 퇴적된 모든 플라스틱을 제거하는 것은 실현 불가능하지만, 인류는 추가적인 오염을 최소화하는 방향으로 진전하고 있는 중이다.

viable 형 이용 가능한　endangered 형 멸종 위기에 처한
ensuing 형 이어지는　prosthetic 형 인공 기관의
ubiquity 명 보편성　virtually 부 사실상
indestructible 형 부서지지 않는　disintegrate 동 분해되다
molecule 명 분자　durable 형 내구성이 강한

undigestible 형 소화할 수 없는 intestinal blockage 장폐색
leach 동 침출되다 predicament 명 (곤경에 처한) 상태
discard 동 버리다 thoroughly 부 완전히 inundate 동 잠기게 하다
awareness 명 인식 biodegradable 형 생분해성의
compel 동 강제하다 municipality 명 지방자치 단체
implement 동 시행하다 unfeasible 형 실현 불가능한
contamination 명 오염 make strides 진전하다

1 지문의 단어 "ensuing"과 의미가 가장 비슷한 것은?
(A) 이전의
(B) 전체의
(C) 불운한
(D) 다음의

2 1단락에 따르면, 다음 중 셀룰로이드에 관해 사실인 것은?
(A) 기술자들의 집단에 의해 발명되었다.
(B) 환경 운동가들에 의해 받아들여지지 않았다.
(C) 상아의 사용을 대체하려 했다.
(D) 상업적 용도가 있는 것으로 생각되지 않았다.

3 지문의 단어 "disintegrate"와 의미가 가장 비슷한 것은?
(A) 모이다
(B) 분해되다
(C) 사라지다
(D) 재생되다

4 지문의 단어 "inundated"와 의미가 가장 비슷한 것은?
(A) 뒤덮인
(B) 검사된
(C) 연관된
(D) 격리된

5 3단락에서 글쓴이는 왜 고래와 동물성 플랑크톤을 언급하는가?
(A) 미세 플라스틱의 독성에 면역성이 있는 일부 해양 야생생물을 밝히기 위해
(B) 미세 플라스틱에 의해 위협받는 광범위한 유기체들을 강조하기 위해
(C) 세계의 바다에 있는 먹이사슬의 복잡성을 강조하기 위해
(D) 티레니아해에 서식하는 생물들의 예를 들기 위해

6 다음 중 3단락에서 미세 플라스틱에 관해 추론할 수 있는 것은?
(A) 적은 양으로도 해양 동물들에게 치명적이다.
(B) 유기체의 배설물을 통해 쉽게 배출되지 않는다.
(C) 물에 6개월 동안 노출된 후에도 사라지지 않는다.
(D) 햇빛에 노출되었을 때만 바닷물에서 분해된다.

7 아래 문장 중 지문 속의 음영된 문장의 핵심 정보를 가장 잘 표현한 것은? 오답은 문장의 의미를 크게 바꾸거나 핵심 정보를 생략한다.
(A) 존재하는 플라스틱을 완전히 제거하는 것은 불가능하지만, 인류는 추가적인 오염을 줄이기 위한 조치를 취하고 있다.
(B) 이미 잘못 퇴적된 모든 플라스틱은 추가적인 플라스틱이 더해지기 전에 제거되어야 한다.
(C) 인류가 플라스틱 오염을 최소화하려고 노력하고 있다는 사실에도 불구하고, 플라스틱 포장을 없애는 것은 실현 가능하지 않다.
(D) 너무 많은 플라스틱이 무책임하게 버려졌기 때문에, 존재하는 오염에 대해 인류가 무언가를 하는 것이 필요하다.

8 4단락에 따르면, 다음 중 플라스틱 오염을 줄이기 위한 전략이 아닌 것은?
(A) 재사용 가능한 쇼핑백 사용 장려하기
(B) 더 많은 생분해성 플라스틱 만들기
(C) 부적절하게 플라스틱을 폐기하는 회사에 벌금 부과하기
(D) 플라스틱 제조업체들에게 재활용 강요하기

9 네 개의 네모[■]는 다음 문장이 삽입될 수 있는 곳을 나타내고 있다.
그것들은 자연적으로 썩지 않으며, 그것들을 분해할 수 있는 어떤 유기체도 진화하지 않았다.
이 문장은 어디에 들어가는 것이 가장 적절한가?

10 **지시:** 지문 요약을 위한 도입 문장이 아래에 주어져 있다. 지문의 가장 중요한 내용을 나타내는 보기 3개를 골라 요약을 완성하라. 어떤 문장은 지문에 언급되지 않은 내용이나 사소한 정보를 나타내므로 요약에 포함되지 않는다. **이 문제는 2점이다.**

> **플라스틱은 다양한 산업적 목적에 있어 유용하지만, 그것들은 생태학적 위협을 제기한다.**
> · (B) 긍정적인 측면에서, 그 문제에 대한 높아진 인식으로 인해 플라스틱 오염의 영향을 줄이기 위한 상당한 노력이 기울여지고 있다.
> · (C) 플라스틱 오염 문제는 플라스틱이 해양 유기체들에 위협이 되는 세계의 다양한 수역에서 가장 심각하다.
> · (D) 많은 양의 플라스틱의 폐기와 제조는 동물과 인간에게 똑같이 유해한 영향을 초래하는 유독한 환경을 만든다.

(A) 인공 분자로 구성된 완전한 합성 플라스틱은 환경에 가장 큰 위협을 제기하는 플라스틱의 종류이다.
(E) 제조된 플라스틱의 화학적 결합은 매우 내구성이 강하기 때문에 플라스틱을 섭취하는 동물들에게 장 문제를 일으킨다.
(F) 세계의 바다에서 수행된 연구는 분석된 바닷물의 매 제곱피트에서 미세 플라스틱을 발견했다.

Vocabulary Review
본문 p.28

1 confidence		2 practitioner	3 undeniable
4 discriminative		5 consequent	6 tackle
7 (A)	8 (D)	9 (C)	10 (B)
11 (B)	12 (B)	13 (A)	14 (C)

CHAPTER 02
Reference

Example
본문 p.31

1 (C) 2 (D) 3 (A)

최초의 컴퓨터들

1930년대 후반, 존 아타나소프라는 이름의 물리학 교수는 많은 변수를 가진 방정식을 푸는 자동화된 방법을 고민하며 긴 시간을 보냈다.

복잡한 계산은 물리학의 문제에서 필수적이며, 그것들은 수행하는 데 시간이 오래 걸릴 수 있다. 아타나소프는 이러한 도전에 대한 디지털 방식 해결책을 생각해낸 최초의 사람이었다. 그와 대학원생 클리포드 베리는 대수 연산을 위해 280개의 진공관을 사용하는 700파운드 무게의 기계 장치를 조립했다. 아타나소프-베리 컴퓨터, 혹은 ABC는 현대 컴퓨터의 중요한 선구자였다. ABC는 15초마다 하나의 연산을 수행하는 속도로 29개의 변수를 가진 방정식을 풀 수 있었는데, 이는 그 기계가 완성되었던 1942년에는 빠른 것이었으나, 오늘날의 컴퓨터에 의해 수행되는 초당 수백만 개의 연산들 앞에서는 무색해진다. 또한, 후자와 달리, 아타나소프의 창작물은 선형 방정식만 풀 수 있었기 때문에 프로그래밍될 수 없었다.

ABC는 1947년에 법적 분쟁의 주제가 되었다. 또 다른 디지털 컴퓨터인 전자식 숫자 적분 및 계산기(ENIAC)의 발명가들은 특허를 신청했고, 이는 아타나소프가 ABC에 대해 하지 않았던 것이었다. 하지만, ENIAC 설계팀의 한 구성원이 아타나소프의 원래 설계를 모방했을 가능성이 있다는 것이 밝혀졌을 때, 판사는 그 새 기계의 특허 신청을 거부했고, 컴퓨터의 개념은 특허를 얻을 수 없다고 결정했다. 그것이 누구나 특허의 보호를 위반하지 않고 컴퓨터를 만들 수 있다고 판결함으로써 그 판결은 디지털 컴퓨터의 제조와 설계에 대한 선례를 남겼다.

ponder 동 고민하다　automate 동 자동화하다　equation 명 방정식
variable 명 변수　graduate student 대학원생
construct 동 조립하다　algebraic 형 대수의　precursor 명 선구자
pale in comparison to ~ 앞에서 무색해지다　linear 형 선형의
controversy 명 분쟁　patent 명 특허; 동 특허를 얻다
application 명 신청　precedent 명 선례

1 지문의 단어 "they"가 가리키는 것은?
(A) 방정식
(B) 변수
(C) 계산
(D) 문제

2 지문의 어구 "the latter"가 가리키는 것은?
(A) 29개의 변수를 가진 방정식
(B) 하나의 연산
(C) 그 기계
(D) 오늘날의 컴퓨터

3 지문의 단어 "it"이 가리키는 것은?
(A) 판결
(B) 선례
(C) 제조
(D) 설계

Reading Practice 1

본문 p.32

1 (A)　2 (C)　3 (C)　4 (D)　5 (D)　6 (A)

세계 최초의 도시

오늘날, 이라크의 수도 바그다드에서 남쪽으로 약 150마일 떨어진 우루크를 둘러싼 척박한 사막은 주요 도심지가 아니며 인간의 거주를 위한 매력이 거의 없다. 하지만 5,500년 전에 이 장소는 서쪽으로는 유프라테스강과 동쪽으로는 티그리스강으로 손쉽게 접근할 수 있는 비옥한 습지였다. [2A]질척한 토양은 너무 많은 밀과 보리를 생산해서 주민들은 그들의 모든 시간을 농사에 쏟을 필요가 없다는 것을 알게 되었다. [2B]강들에는 물고기가 풍부했고 물새들을 끌어들였다. 소, 양, 염소가 그곳에서 번성했고, 그 땅에는 대추, 무화과, 사과를 포함한 열매가 열렸다. [2D]기원전 3100년경, 메소포타미아의 이 모퉁이는 약 9만 명의 사람들의 고향이었고, 이는 우루크를 세계 최초의 주요 도시로 만들었다.

우루크에 매우 많은 사람들이 있게 되면서, 인류 역사상 처음으로 글자가 필수적인 것이 되었다. 점토판에 새기기 위해 갈대를 사용함으로써, 우루크 사람들은 그들의 가축 떼에 있는 양과 염소의 수뿐만 아니라 그들의 창고에 저장된 곡식의 양도 기록할 수 있었다. 원시적인 글자가 수를 센 물건을 나타내는 그림 문자에서 추상적인 숫자 기호로 발전하는 데 400년이 걸렸다. [3]설형 문자라고 알려진 문자를 개발한 후, 우루크 사람들은 또한 왕과 사제에서 직공과 보석상에 이르기까지, 그 도시 주민들에 의해 수행되는 전문적인 역할들을 기록했다.

인구가 증가함에 따라 정부의 필요성이 빠르게 부상했다. [5]처음에, 행정 업무들은 사제들에 의해 수행되었다. 그러나, 시간이 지나면서 주변 도시들이 부상했고, 땅과 자원들의 지배권에 대한 전쟁에 참여했으며, 결과적으로 우루크에서는 전사들이 더 큰 권력을 차지하기 시작했다. 결국, 그들은 한 명의 독재적인 왕에 의해 계승되었다. 우루크의 가장 유명한 왕은 길가메시였는데, 그는 기원전 3000년에서 2500년 사이의 어느 시점에 우루크를 통치했고 그 도시의 위엄 있는 외벽을 건설했다. 그는 그를 3분의 2의 신으로 묘사한 설형 문자 서사시에서 불멸성을 부여받았다. '길가메시 서사시'는 인류 역사에서 가장 오래된 문학 작품들 중 하나로 여겨진다.

바빌론과 니네베 같은 다른 메소포타미아 도시들이 서양인들에게 우루크보다 더 잘 알려져 있다는 사실은 부분적으로 성경에서 그 도시의 희박한 존재감으로 설명될 수 있는데, 성경은 오직 지나가는 말로만 우루크를 언급한다. 그럼에도 불구하고, 그 세계 최초의 도시는 그것이 남긴 물질 문화를 통해 고고학 역사에 지울 수 없는 흔적을 남겼다. 고고학자들은 대량 생산되어 오늘날의 이란과 튀르키예에 이르는 먼 곳까지 거래된 우루크 시대의 그릇들을 발굴했다. [6B/6C]다른 주목할 만한 유물들에는 최초의 인간 얼굴 묘사 중 하나인, 대리석으로 조각된 여성의 머리인 와르카의 가면과, 두 명의 남자가 창과 화살로 사자를 사냥하는 것을 보여주는, 이야기를 표현하는 조각인 사자 사냥 석비가 있다. [6D]고대 우루크는 또한 모자이크 디자인을 특징으로 하는 장식된 기둥을 갖춘, 벽으로 둘러싸인 기념비적인 건물들의 잔해가 있는 장소이기도 하다.

barren 형 척박한　habitation 명 거주　marshland 명 습지
soggy 형 질척한　devote 동 (시간·노력 등을) 쏟다
teem with ~이 풍부하다　waterfowl 명 물새
necessity 명 필수적인 것　inscribe 동 새기다
primitive 형 원시적인　pictorial 형 그림의　abstract 형 추상적인
cuneiform 명 설형 문자　weaver 명 직공
administrative 형 행정의　consequently 부 결과적으로
be succeeded by ~에 의해 계승되다　authoritarian 형 독재적인
immortalize 동 불멸성을 부여하다　scant 형 희박한
in passing 지나가는 말로　indelible 형 지울 수 없는
archaeological 형 고고학적인　unearth 동 발굴하다
artifact 명 유물

1 지문의 어구 "this place"가 가리키는 것은?

(A) 척박한 사막
(B) 우루크
(C) 바그다드
(D) 도심지

2 1단락에 따르면, 다음 중 우루크라고 알려진 메소포타미아의 모퉁이에 관해 사실이 아닌 것은?

(A) 그것의 토양은 특정 곡식들의 풍부한 생산을 뒷받침했다.
(B) 야생 생물이 풍부한 강들이 있었다.
(C) 그것의 주민들은 모든 시간을 농사에 쏟았다.
(D) 알려져 있는 최초의 주요 도시를 포함했다.

3 2단락에 따르면, 설형 문자 개발 이후 우루크 사람들이 하기 시작한 것은?

(A) 저장된 곡식의 규모 기록하기
(B) 가축 떼에 있는 동물들의 수 추적하기
(C) 다양한 전문적인 업무 기록하기
(D) 거래되는 상품의 수 세기

4 지문의 단어 "they"가 가리키는 것은?

(A) 사제들
(B) 도시들
(C) 자원들
(D) 전사들

5 3단락에 따르면, 우루크에서 사제들이 정치적 권력을 잃기 시작한 것은

(A) 메소포타미아 문화에서 종교가 덜 중요해졌기 때문이다
(B) 그들의 권위를 독재적인 왕에게 빼앗겼기 때문이다
(C) 그 도시가 주변의 침략자들에게 정복되었기 때문이다
(D) 영토 분쟁이 전사들의 권력을 증가시켰기 때문이다

6 4단락에 따르면, 우루크의 고고학적 유산의 일부가 아닌 것은?

(A) 이란과 튀르키예에서 수입된 그릇들
(B) 인간의 얼굴을 묘사하는 조각
(C) 사냥 장면이 담긴 조각
(D) 패턴으로 장식된 기둥들

Reading Practice 2

본문 p.34

1 (B) 2 (B) 3 (C) 4 (B) 5 (B) 6 (D)

이슬람 서예

이슬람교의 창시자인 선지자 마호메트가 "신이 처음으로 창조한 것은 펜이었다"라고 말했다고 전해질 정도로 이슬람교에서 문자는 중요한 역할을 한다. 그러한 정신에서, 7세기의 이슬람 확산은 중동과 남아시아를 가로지르는 영토에 아랍어 형태의 문자를 가져왔고, 민족 및 문화적으로 다양한 지역들에서 공통된 의사소통 수단을 제공했다. 이슬람 문자의 중요한 형태는 서예인데, 이는 글자를 아름다운 손글씨체로 쓰는 예술이다.

이슬람 서예의 아름다움은 주로 아랍어의 역동적인 특징에서 비롯된다. 그 문자는 이슬람 종교 자체만큼이나 오래되었는데, 그것은 아랍어 알파벳의 전신이었던 6세기 아랍어 방언인 나바테아어에서 파생되었다. [2]그것은 17개의 기본 글자로, 오른쪽에서 왼쪽으로 쓰여지지만, 단모음은 그 숫자에 계산되지 않으며, 대신 자음과 장모음의 위나 아래에 기호를 배치함으로써 형성된다. 서로 다른 글자들은 인접한 글자들에 붙여지는 데 있어 서로 다른 규칙들을 가지고 있다. 일부는 양쪽에 연결되는 데 반해, 다른 것들은 앞 글자에만, 또는, 그렇지 않으면, 뒤에 나오는 글자에만 연결된다. 이러한 독특한 연결은 아랍어 문자에 장식용 글씨체에 적합한 흐름을 제공한다.

이슬람 역사 초기에 서예가들에 의해 사용되었던 두 가지 주요 글씨체가 있다. 필기체는 편지 쓰기와 같은 일상적인 맥락에서 사용되었으며 엄격한 규칙의 적용을 받지 않았다. 한편, 메소포타미아에 있는 이슬람 도시의 이름을 딴 쿠픽체는 코란의 최초 사본들과 같은 종교 문서에 사용되었다. 이 글씨체는 필기체보다 훨씬 더 격식이 있었고, 어느 정도의 위엄을 나타냈다. 글자들은 컸으며, 이는 글이 페이지당 세 줄 이상을 차지하지 않게 했다. 쿠픽체는 11세기에 나스크체에 의해 대부분 대체되었는데, 그것은 여전히 아랍어 문자의 가장 인기 있는 형태로 남아 있다. [4]어느 정도까지, 그것은 필기체의 원래의 무질서함과 더 격식 있는 쿠픽체가 병합된 형태로 간주될 수 있으며, 양쪽 모두의 특성을 가지고 있다.

서예는 역사를 통틀어 이슬람 예술의 가장 두드러진 예들 중 일부에서 사용되어 강력한 효과를 낸다. 예를 들어, 이슬람 건축의 걸작인 인도의 타지마할은 벽옥에 쓰여지고 그 건물의 하얀 대리석 바닥에 새겨 넣어진 코란 구절들을 특징으로 한다. [6A/6B]건축에서의 서예는 보통 여러 가지 목적을 수행했는데, 이것들 중 첫 번째는 건물과 후원자의 이름, 건축 일자를 밝히는 것이었다. [6C]그것은 또한 힘을 보여주는 역할을 했으며, 후원자의 부와 신의 영광 둘 다에 대한 경외심을 불러일으켰다. 덜 기념비적인 규모에서, 서예는 보통 선의의 메시지가 새겨진 도자기나 청동 거울을 장식했다. 어떠한 경우든, 서예가 보통 언어적인 개념을 포함하긴 했지만, 새겨진 글귀는 때때로 기하학적인 패턴이나 추상적인 디자인에 더 가까웠기 때문에, 심지어 일부 글을 읽고 쓸 줄 아는 이슬람교도들조차 그것들을 읽을 수 없었다.

calligraphy 명 서예 fundamental 형 중요한 prophet 명 선지자
ethnically 부 민족적으로 script 명 글씨체 dialect 명 방언
precursor 명 전신 vowel 명 모음 placement 명 배치
consonant 명 자음 attachment 명 붙임 adjacent 형 인접한
preceding 형 앞의 alternatively 부 그렇지 않으면
distinctive 형 독특한 cursive script 필기체 majesty 명 위엄
free-for-all 명 무질서함 prominent 형 두드러진 jasper 명 벽옥
inlay 동 새겨 넣다 patron 명 후원자 evoke 동 불러일으키다
reverence 명 경외심 adorn 동 장식하다 goodwill 명 선의
geometric 형 기하학적인 abstract 형 추상적인
literate 형 글을 읽고 쓸 줄 아는

1 지문의 단어 "It"이 가리키는 것은?

(A) 이슬람 서예
(B) 문자
(C) 나바테아어
(D) 아랍어 방언

2 2단락에 따르면, 다음 중 아랍어에 관해 사실인 것은?

(A) 이슬람 종교보다 더 오래되었다.
(B) 일부 모음을 만들기 위해 기호를 사용한다.
(C) 그것의 글자들은 통일된 규칙을 가지고 있다.
(D) 그것의 언어적 기원은 여전히 알려져 있지 않다.

3 지문의 단어 "majesty"와 의미가 가장 비슷한 것은?

(A) 우선순위
(B) 자연스러움
(C) 위엄
(D) 공손함

4 3단락에 따르면, 다음 중 쿠픽체를 대체했던 글씨체에 관해 사실인 것은?

(A) 그것의 큰 크기는 페이지당 겨우 세 줄만을 허용했다.
(B) 격식 있는 양식과 일상적인 양식을 혼합했다.
(C) 11세기까지 사용되었다.
(D) 그것의 이름은 메소포타미아에 있는 한 도시에 의해 공유되었다.

5 지문의 단어 "them"이 가리키는 것은?

(A) 개념
(B) 새겨진 글귀
(C) 패턴
(D) 디자인

6 4단락에서, 다음 중 이슬람 건축에서 서예가 수행한 목적으로 언급되지 않은 것은?

(A) 건물이 언제 건축되었는지를 정확히 보여주는 것
(B) 건물의 이름을 알아보는 것
(C) 신에 대한 존경심을 불러일으키는 것
(D) 호의의 메시지를 보내는 것

Reading Practice 3 본문 p.36

1 (A) 2 (A) 3 (B) 4 (D) 5 (A) 6 (C)

아기새의 구걸 행위

[1]둥지를 틀고 사는 새들은 생존을 위해 전적으로 그것들의 부모에게 의존하기 때문에, 자연은 먹이가 필요하다는 신호를 보냄에 있어 매우 시끄럽게 울고 노골적인 것들을 선호해왔다. 그것들이 배고플 때, 대부분의 아기새들은 그것들의 머리를 하늘을 향해 돌리고 그것들의 부리를 활짝 벌려 오해의 여지가 없는 "나에게 먹이를 주세요"라는 메시지를 보낸다. 이에 대응하여, 부모 새들은 그 먹이가 역류된 더 일찍의 식사이든 갓 잡은 곤충이든, 먹이를 그것들의 새끼의 크게 벌린 턱에 떨어뜨린다. 때때로 새끼들 전체를 만족시키기에 충분한 먹이가 있으나, 없는 경우에는, 먹이를 주는 다 자란 새들은 어려운 선택을 해야 한다.

구걸 행위에 대한 부모의 반응은 종에 따라 다르다. 예를 들어, 녹색제비는 "삐걱거리는 바퀴가 기름을 얻는다."라는 옛 속담을 따르는데, 그것들은 조용한 형제들보다 가장 격렬한 구걸자들에게 먹이를 더 많이 먹인다. 대조적으로, 후투티 어미들은 구걸에는 전혀 관심을 기울이지 않으며 단순히 더 큰 아기새들에게 더 많은 먹이를 제공한다. 일부 종들에서, 아비 새들은 그것들의 암컷 동반자와 먹이 주는 임무를 공유하며, 먹이 공급 전략은 부모의 성별에 따라 달라질 수 있다. [3]금화조 어미들은 어떤 아기새들이 맨 앞줄에 있는지와 관계없이 그것들이 먹이고 싶은 새끼 새들을 골라 그 선택을 고수하는 경향이 있는 반면, 아비들은 선착순 기준으로 양식을 분배하는 경향이 있다. 한편, (남아프리카 종인) 집단길쌈새 가족에서는 부모의 성별이 구걸에 대한 부모의 반응에 거의 또는 전혀 영향을 미치지 않는다.

구걸 행위에 대한 한 연구는 부모의 먹이 주기 선택이 가족의 환경적 맥락에 달려 있다는 것을 밝혀냈다. 옥스퍼드 대학교의 한 팀은 143개의 서로 다른 새 종에 걸친 306개의 연구 결과들을 수집했다. 그들은 안정적인 먹이 공급이 가능한 이상적인 조건에서는 부모가 시끄러운 구걸자들을 선호한다는 것을 밝혀냈는데, 이는 아마 구걸을 더 큰 욕구의 신호로 받아들이기 때문이다. 하지만 불충분한 시기에는, 다 자란 새들이 더 큰 아기새들에게 영양분을 제공할 것이다. 이 결정은 전략적인 것으로 보이는데, 더 성숙한 아기들이 더 나은 생존 가능성을 가지고 있는 반면, 더 시끄럽고 더 작은 아기새들은 어쨌든 살아남지 못할 것이라는 가정에 기초하고 있다.

배고픈 어린 새들을 돌보는 것은 부모에게 무거운 부담을 지우는데, 그것은 주요 자전거 경주에서 사람에 의해 쏟아지는 것과 동등한 에너지를 요구한다. 그러한 이유로, 일부 새 종들은 자신의 새끼를 돌보는 힘든 과정을 완전히 포기한다. 예를 들어, 인디고새와 와이다같은 탁란조는 경쟁 종들의 둥지에 그것들의 새끼들을 두어, 그것들의 부모 임무를 사실상 외부에 위탁한다. 기생하는 아기들은 그 둥지를 소유한 종의 구걸 행위와, 심지어는 입 모양까지도 모방한다. 숙주 부모는 속아서 그 작은 침입자들을 마치 자신의 것처럼 키운다. **그러나, 이렇게 함으로써, 그것들은 사실 그것들의 새끼를 심각한 위기에 처하게 한다.** 탁란조들은 보통 더 빨리 자라며 다른 어린 새들을 둥지 밖으로 밀어낸다.

nestling 형 둥지를 틀고 사는 vocal 형 시끄럽게 우는
demonstrative 형 노골적인 unmistakable 형 오해의 여지가 없는
gaping 형 크게 벌린 regurgitate 동 역류시키다 brood 명 새끼들
adage 명 속담 squeaky 형 삐걱거리는 sibling 명 형제
avian 형 새의 provision 동 공급하다 stick 동 고수하다
compile 동 수집하다, 엮다 optimal 형 이상적인
presumably 부 아마 nourishment 명 영양분
assumption 명 가정 tend to ~을 돌보다
expend 동 (시간·에너지 등을) 쏟다 forgo 동 포기하다
taxing 형 힘든 brood parasite 탁란조
outsource 동 외부에 위탁하다 parasitic 형 기생하는
mimic 동 모방하다 intruder 명 침입자

1 1단락에 따르면, 다음 중 둥지를 틀고 사는 새들에 관해 사실인 것은?

(A) 언어 및 비언어적 신호를 이용해 배고픔을 나타낸다.
(B) 역류한 식사에 대한 확실한 선호를 보인다.
(C) 종종 다른 새끼를 위한 먹이를 훔친다.
(D) 곤충 같은 먹이를 사냥하는 방법을 빠르게 배운다.

2 지문의 단어 "vigorous"와 의미가 가장 비슷한 것은?

(A) 강력한
(B) 궁핍한
(C) 지나친
(D) 짜증 나게 하는

3 2단락에서, 글쓴이가 금화조의 먹이 주기 전략에 관해 묘사하는 것은?

(A) 조산의 아기새들에게 먹이를 더 먹이는 경향
(B) 성별에 기반한 접근법의 차이
(C) 대부분의 먹이 주기를 수행하는 아비들
(D) 시끄럽게 우는 아기들을 더 선호하는 어미새들

4 지문의 어구 "This decision"이 가리키는 것은?

(A) 과거 연구들을 수집하는 것
(B) 안정적인 먹이 공급을 제공하는 것
(C) 궁핍한 아기새들을 선호하는 것
(D) 더 큰 아기들을 먹이는 것

5 지문의 단어 "their"가 가리키는 것은?

(A) 탁란조
(B) 새끼들
(C) 둥지
(D) 경쟁 종들

6 네 개의 네모[■]는 다음 문장이 삽입될 수 있는 곳을 나타내고 있다.

그러나, 이렇게 함으로써, 그것들은 사실 그것들의 새끼를 심각한 위기에 처하게 한다.

이 문장은 어디에 들어가는 것이 가장 적절한가?

iBT Reading Test 1

본문 p.38

1 (D) 2 (C) 3 (B) 4 (B)
5 (B) 6 (D) 7 (D) 8 (C)
9 (C) 10 (A), (C), (E)

지구의 자기장

해수면 약 1,800피트 아래에서는, 태양의 표면만큼이나 뜨거운 온도에서 녹은 금속이 세차게 움직이며 소용돌이친다. 그 움직임은 시속 수천 마일의 속도로 수백 마일을 흐르는 전류를 만들어낸다. 그 전류는 지구의 밀도 높은 중심핵에서 방출되어, 그것의 내부를 완전히 통과해 뻗어나가고, 우주로 퍼져나가는 거대한 자기장을 만들어내며, 사실상 그 행성을 거대한 막대자석으로 바꾸어 놓는다. 지구의 가장 가까운 이웃들(수성, 금성, 화성)에는 없는 이 특징은 이 행성을 차지하고 있는 생명체들에게 매우 중요했다.

과학자들은 많은 야생생물 종들이 지구의 자기장을 이용하여 그들의 길을 찾는다고 믿는데, 그것은 북극과 남극을 둘 다 가지고 있다. [3A]예를 들어, 유럽 울새는 그것들의 윗부리에 그 새들이 지구의 자기장을 따라 길을 찾는 것을 돕기 위해 신경계와 함께 작동하는 자기 감각 기관을 가지고 있다. [3C]지구의 자전 축에 의해 결정되는 지리적인 극과 자극이 약간 다르다는 것을 알아두는 것은 중요하다. 자극은 심지어 지난 260만 년 동안 10번 그랬던 것처럼 북극이 남극이 되고 또 그 반대도 마찬가지가 되면서 완전히 반전될 수도 있다. **과학자들은 이러한 반전 동안 자기장의 세기가 90퍼센트만큼이나 약해졌다는 것을 밝혀냈다.** [3D]이는 이주를 위해 자기장에 의존하는 야생생물 종들에게 지장을 줄 수 있다.

우주는 생물들에게 위험으로 가득 차 있고, 지구의 자기장은 그중 많은 것들로부터의 보호를 제공한다. 태양의 상층 대기는 집합적으로 태양풍이라고 알려진, 전자, 양성자, 알파 입자를 포함하고 있는 전하를 띤 입자를 끊임없이 뿜어낸다. 자기장은 전하를 띤 입자들만 빗나가게 하며, 전하를 띠지 않은 무해한 태양 중성미자가 대기를 통과하도록 한다. [6]과학자들은 태양풍이 화성의 대기를 생명체가 생존하거나 자리잡을 수 없는 수준으로 저하시킨 원인이라고 믿는다. 태양은 또한 코로나 질량 방출이라고 불리는 위험한 플라스마와 자기성 구름을 방출한다. 더 나쁜 것은, 이 태양계 너머에서 오는 암을 유발하는 우주 방사선이 계속해서 지구를 폭격하고 있다는 것이다. 다행스럽게도, 지구의 자기장에 의해 생성된 자기권은 이러한 맹공격으로부터의 방어를 제공하며, 반 알렌대라고 불리는 한 쌍의 도넛 모양의 구역에 그것들을 무해하게 가두어 놓는다.

자기장의 보호가 없었다면, 고등 생명체들은 아마 결코 발달하지 못했을 것이다. 지구가 40억 년 전에 형성되었을 때, 그것의 중심핵에 있는 금속들은 아직 굳기 시작하지 않았었고, 따라서 자기장은 지금과 같이 강하지 않았다. 자기장이 아직 약할 때 생명체가 출현했지만, 수십억 년 동안 완강히 단세포 상태로 남아 있었다. 그것은 아마 우주에서 온 방사선 세례가 복합 생명체의 진화를 막았기 때문일 것이다. [8]약 5억 년 전이 되어서야 중심핵의 경화가 진화의 번성을 가능하게 했고, 지구의 강력한 자기장 때문에 생명체가 해로운 방사선으로부터 더 잘 보호받게 되었다.

magnetic field 자기장 churn ⓢ세차게 움직이다
electrical current 전류 emanate ⓢ방출되다 radiate ⓢ퍼지다
effectively ⓟ사실상 axis ⓝ축 reverse ⓢ반전되다
disruptive ⓗ지장을 주는 migration ⓝ이주
electron ⓝ전자 proton ⓝ양성자 deflect ⓢ빗나가게 하다
innocuous ⓗ무해한 neutrino ⓝ중성미자
penetrate ⓢ통과하다 degrade ⓢ저하시키다
take hold 자리를 잡다 expel ⓢ방출하다 cosmic ray 우주 방사선
bombard ⓢ폭격하다 magnetosphere ⓝ자기권
onslaught ⓝ맹공격 solidify ⓢ굳다 stubbornly ⓟ완강히
barrage ⓝ세례 hardening ⓝ경화 robust ⓗ강력한

1 지문의 단어 "radiates"와 의미가 가장 비슷한 것은?

(A) 분열되다
(B) 기어가다
(C) 흐르다
(D) 흩어지다

2 지문의 어구 "This feature"가 가리키는 것은?

(A) 녹은 금속
(B) 전류
(C) 거대한 자기장
(D) 밀도 높은 중심핵

3 2단락에 따르면, 다음 중 자극에 관해 사실이 아닌 것은?

(A) 그것들의 방향은 일부 종들의 감각 기관에 의해 감지될 수 있다.
(B) 지구가 중심으로 삼아 자전하는 지점들이다.
(C) 지리적인 극과 완전히 같지는 않다.
(D) 그것들의 반전은 동물의 이주를 방해할 수 있다.

4 지문의 단어 "innocuous"와 의미가 가장 비슷한 것은?

(A) 만성적인
(B) 무해한
(C) 단명하는
(D) 최고의

5 지문에서 글쓴이는 왜 "the magnetosphere"를 언급하는가?

(A) 코로나 질량 방출이 어떻게 비롯되는지 보여주기 위해
(B) 무엇이 우주 방사선을 지구에서 무해하게 만드는지 설명하기 위해
(C) 태양으로부터의 일부 방출이 암을 유발할 수 있다는 것을 강조하기 위해
(D) 우주에서 중성 전하를 가진 지역의 예를 들기 위해

6 다음 중 3단락에서 전하를 띤 입자들에 관해 추론할 수 있는 것은?

(A) 지구에 도달하기 전에 중성미자로 변한다.
(B) 화성의 대기에는 존재하지 않는 것처럼 보인다.
(C) 북극과 남극 사이에서 이동한다.
(D) 아마도 생명체의 생존에 해롭다.

7 지문의 단어 "That"이 가리키는 것은?

(A) 고등 생명체들의 발달
(B) 지구의 형성
(C) 자기장의 약함
(D) 단순한 생명 형태의 오랜 지속

8 4단락에 따르면, 복합적 생명체가 진화한 것은

(A) 단세포 생명체들이 멸종했기 때문이다
(B) 자기장이 세포 성장을 촉진했기 때문이다
(C) 자기장이 우주 방사선을 줄였기 때문이다
(D) 지구 표면에 있는 해로운 금속들이 물러났기 때문이다

9 네 개의 네모[■]는 다음 문장이 삽입될 수 있는 곳을 나타내고 있다.

과학자들은 이러한 반전 동안 자기장의 세기가 90퍼센트만큼이나 약해졌다는 것을 밝혀냈다.

이 문장은 어디에 들어가는 것이 가장 적절한가?

10 **지시:** 지문 요약을 위한 도입 문장이 아래에 주어져 있다. 지문의 가장 중요한 내용을 나타내는 보기 3개를 골라 요약을 완성하라. 어떤 문장은 지문에 언급되지 않은 내용이나 사소한 정보를 나타내므로 요약에 포함되지 않는다. **이 문제는 2점이다.**

> **지구의 자기장은 생명체들에게 이롭다.**
> · (A) 자기장이 없었다면 복합 생명체가 결코 존재하게 되지 않았을 가능성이 있다.
> · (C) 과학자들의 의견에 따르면, 다양한 생명체들이 길 찾기를 위해 자기장을 이용한다.
> · (E) 자기장은 우주에 존재하는 해로운 입자들로부터 보호함으로써 많은 생물들을 돕는다.

(B) 미래에 자극의 반전이 다시 발생한다면 지구에 서식하는 동물들은 위험에 처할 수 있다.
(D) 자기장 때문에 태양풍과 그것의 모든 전하를 띤 입자들은 지구 표면에서 빛나가게 된다.
(F) 지구가 처음 형성되었을 때 자기장이 없었음에도 불구하고 생명체는 어떻게든 발달할 방법을 찾았다.

iBT Reading Test 2

본문 p.42

1 (B) 2 (B) 3 (D) 4 (D)
5 (D) 6 (C) 7 (D) 8 (A)
9 (D) 10 (A), (C), (E)

불면증

수면은 외부 자극에 대한 감소된 반응과, 호흡 및 심장 박동 같은 무의식적 신체 기능이 느려지는 것으로 특징지어진다. 대부분의 의학 전문가들은 인간이 그들의 신체가 필수적인 세포 과정을 완료하기 위해 요구하는 휴식 시간을 얻지 못할 때, 그들이 깨어 있는 시간 동안 완전한 기능을 달성할 수 없다고 믿는다. [2]성인은 건강과 웰빙을 유지하기 위해 매일 밤 최소 7시간을 자야 하며, 그것이 없으면 신체가 "수면 빚"을 축적하는 것으로 나타났다. 이 빚의 전부는 아니더라도 일부는 예를 들어 주말 동안 휴식을 취하거나 장기적인 휴가를 보냄으로써 갚아질 수 있다.

하지만, 정상 상태로 돌아갈 수 없는 사람들은 계속해서 수면 부족의 상태로 산다. 지속적인 수면 손실의 주요 원인은 불면증으로, 이는 잠을 자지 못하거나 하루에 최소 4시간의 연속된 잠을 자지 못하는 것이다. 불면증은 2일이나 3일 동안만 지속되어 일시적일 수도 있고, 한 번에 몇 주나 몇 달 동안 지속될 수도 있다. 만성 환자들은 우울증이나 수면을 유도하기 위해 처방된 약에 대한 중독과 같은 다양한 신체 및 정신 건강 관련 문제를 겪는다. **그러므로, 이러한 심각한 사례들은 환자들이 구제받을 수 있도록 의학적 또는 정신 의학적 도움을 필요로 할 수 있다.**

의사들은 불면증의 원인이 되는 일반적인 요인들을 기록했는데, 그것들은 예측 가능한 범주들로 분류되는 경향이 있다. 생리적 원인은 카페인과 니코틴 같은 각성제들의 섭취와 관련이 있을 수 있는데, 이것들은 신경계 내의 특정 화학물질들의 수치를 변화시켜 뇌가 작동을 멈추고 적절한 수면 주기에 들어가는 것을 어렵게 한다. 인간의 수면과 깨어남의 자연스러운 타이밍인 하루 주기 리듬의 혼란 또한 불면증의 원인이 될 수 있다. 하루 주기 리듬의 혼란은, 예를 들어 사람이 구어체로 "시차증"이라고 지칭되는, 비행기를 타고 여러 시간대를 가로질러 여행한 후 새로운 환경에 적응해야 할 때, 혹은 직장이 불규칙한 패턴으로 일어나는 교대 근무를 필요로 할 때 일어날 수 있다.

그러나, 생리적 결정 요인들과는 대조적으로, 심리적 요인들은 장기적인 불면증의 원인이 될 가능성이 더 높은 것으로 나타났다. 여러 가지 원천에서 발생하는 스트레스와 불안의 감정들은 가장 잘 기록된 원인들이다. 예를 들어, 젊은 성인들은 학업적 책임, 방과 후 활동, 그리고 대인 관계의 균형을 유지하기 위해 심한 압박을 겪을 수 있다. [6]이것은 잠자리에 들기 전에 마음을 가라앉히고 성공적으로 잠드는 것을 어렵게 만들 수 있다.

불면증은 또한 외상 후 스트레스 장애와 같은 더 심각한 심리적 질병과 관련될 수 있다. [8C]이러한 경우, 잠들지 못하는 것은 불면증 환자가 과거 트라우마의 기억으로 인해 자주 고통을 받는 것과 관련이 있는데, 그것들은 악몽과 회상의 형태로 다시 떠오른다. [8B/8D]환자는 그러한 부정적인 반응을 방지하기 위해 수면을 완전히 피하거나, 쉬려고 하는 동안 계속해서 방해받을 것이다. 그나 그녀는 또한 신체의 활력을 되찾는 데 필요한 장시간의 지속적인 수면을 방해하는 과도한 놀람 반응을 발달시킬 수 있다.

insomnia 명 불면증 stimulus 명 자극 involuntary 형 무의식적인
accumulate 동 축적하다 deprivation 명 (필수적인 것의) 부족
uninterrupted 형 연속된 transient 형 일시적인
chronic 형 만성적인 addiction 명 중독 prescribe 동 처방하다
induce 동 유도하다 predictable 형 예측 가능한
physiological 형 생리적인 stimulant 명 각성제
nervous system 신경계 circadian rhythm 하루 주기 리듬
colloquially 부 구어체로 jet lag 시차증
psychological 형 심리적인 determinant 명 결정 요인
ailment 명 질병
post-traumatic stress disorder 외상 후 스트레스 장애
resurface 동 다시 떠오르다 flashback 명 회상 avert 동 방지하다
rejuvenate 동 활력을 되찾다

1 지문의 단어 "they"가 가리키는 것은?

(A) 전문가들
(B) 인간
(C) 시간
(D) 과정

2 1단락에 따르면, 밤새 잠을 자지 못하는 사람은
(A) 놓친 수면 시간을 되찾을 수 없다
(B) 휴식 시간의 결핍을 누적시킬 것이다
(C) 건강하지 못한 세포 과정을 발생시킨다
(D) 깨어 있는 동안 기능하지 못한다

3 지문의 단어 "transient"와 의미가 가장 비슷한 것은?
(A) 부적절한
(B) 비싼
(C) 집요한
(D) 잠깐 동안의

4 지문에서 글쓴이는 왜 "caffeine and nicotine"을 언급하는가?
(A) 섭취에 의해 체내로 들어가는 물질을 보여주기 위해
(B) 불면증으로 이어지는 주요 조건들을 분명히 하기 위해
(C) 신경계에 이로운 화학물질들을 보여주기 위해
(D) 수면 패턴에 영향을 미치는 물질들의 종류의 예시를 들기 위해

5 아래 문장 중 지문 속의 음영된 문장의 핵심 정보를 가장 잘 표현한 것은? 오답은 문장의 의미를 크게 바꾸거나 핵심 정보를 생략한다.
(A) 예측할 수 없는 근무 시간과 여행은 하루 주기 리듬을 해칠 수 있지만, 이것들은 피해질 수 있다.
(B) 비행기 여행 후에 시차증을 극복하는 것은 신체의 하루 주기 리듬을 다시 맞추기 위해 필수적이다.
(C) 하루 주기 리듬 혼란의 주요 원인은 불규칙적인 직장 일정이다.
(D) 시간대를 가로질러 여행하거나 표준적이지 않은 시간에 일하는 것은 하루 주기 리듬을 방해할 수 있다.

6 4단락에 따르면, 젊은 성인들은
(A) 사회적 압박을 극복하는 법을 배워야 한다
(B) 방과 후 활동을 제한해야 한다
(C) 잠들기 전에 마음을 가라앉히는 데 어려움을 겪을 수 있다
(D) 건강한 관계를 유지하기 위해 노력할 수 있다

7 지문의 단어 "rejuvenate"와 의미가 가장 비슷한 것은?
(A) 검사하다
(B) 보호하다
(C) 자극하다
(D) 생기를 되찾게 하다

8 5단락에서, 다음 중 외상 후 스트레스 장애와 관련이 있는 것으로 언급된 것이 아닌 것은?
(A) 수면 동안의 끝없는 꿈
(B) 완전한 수면 회피
(C) 과거의 잊을 수 없는 기억
(D) 지속적인 휴식 방해

9 네 개의 네모[■]는 다음 문장이 삽입될 수 있는 곳을 나타내고 있다.
그러므로, 이러한 심각한 사례들은 환자들이 구제받을 수 있도록 의학적 또는 정신 의학적 도움을 필요로 할 수 있다.
이 문장은 어디에 들어가는 것이 가장 적절한가?

10 **지시:** 지문 요약을 위한 도입 문장이 아래에 주어져 있다. 지문의 가장 중요한 내용을 나타내는 보기 3개를 골라 요약을 완성하라. 어떤 문장은 지문에 언급되지 않은 내용이나 사소한 정보를 나타내므로 요약에 포함되지 않는다. **이 문제는 2점이다.**

불면증은 일부 사람들에게 빈번한 수면 부족으로 이어진다.
· (A) 불면증과 관련된 장기적인 문제들은 아마 대부분 심리적인 요인들이 원인이다.
· (C) 불면증은 수면 부족의 주요 원인들 중 하나이다.
· (E) 불면증의 기록된 흔한 원인들 중에는 하루 주기 리듬에 혼란을 일으킬 수 있는 생리적 조건들이 있다.

(B) 의학 전문가들은 불면증이 장기간 지속될 수 있다는 것을 인정한다.
(D) 만성 불면증 환자들은 그들이 잠드는 것을 돕는 의학적 치료에 의지한다.
(F) 사람들은 휴식을 만회하기 위해 주말이나 긴 휴가를 사용함으로써 수면 빚을 극복할 수 있다.

Vocabulary Review 본문 p.46

1 scant		2 patented	3 outsource
4 precursor		5 abstract	6 literate
7 (B)	8 (D)	9 (B)	10 (C)
11 (C)	12 (A)	13 (D)	14 (A)

CHAPTER 03
Sentence Simplification

Example 본문 p.49

1 (C) 2 (B)

대수층

대수층은 지하수로 포화된 암석 또는 침전물의 층이다. [1]때때로 대수층은 투과성의 토양을 통해 직접 접근할 수 있으며, 이러한 경우 그것은 비피압 대수층이라고 지칭되지만, 다른 때에는 물이 침투될 수 없는 암석이나 점토의 두꺼운 층에 의해 갇힌다. 대수층은 음용이나 농업용 또는 산업용 물의 일반적인 공급원이기 때문에 이것은 중요한 차이이다. 비피압 대수층의 물이 더 쉽고 저렴하게 얻어질 수 있는 반면, 피압 대수층으로 구멍을 뚫는 데는 비용이 많이 들 수 있다.

피압 대수층은 종종 굳어지는데, 이는 물을 담고 있는 암석이 다공성이지만 함께 굳어진다는 것을 의미한다. 굳어진 대수층의 일반적인 물질은 사암, 혈암, 화강암, 현무암을 포함한다. 비피압 대수층은 굳어지지 않는 경향이 있으며, 모래, 점토, 미사와 같은 느슨한 침전물들로 구성된다. [2]비피압 대수층으로 구멍을 뚫는 것의 단점은 그것들이 잔디용 화학제품, 과적된 오수 정화조, 또는 산업 오염에 의해 쉽게 오염되며 그 후에 해로운 물질들이 급수로 스며든다는 것이다. 물이 침전물이

나 암석을 통과하면서 일정량의 자연적인 여과가 일어나지만, 일부 오염물질은 꼭 걸러지지 않을 수도 있다. 대수층을 다룰 때 고려할 또 다른 요인은 그것들이 종종 강수에 의해 채워지며, 이는 느리고 불안정한 과정일 수 있다는 것이다. 따라서, 물이 자연적으로 보충될 수 있는 것보다 더 빠르게 사용될 경우 대수층은 상당히 쉽게 고갈된다.

aquifer 명 대수층 sediment 명 침전물 saturated 형 포화된
permeable 형 투과성의 confine 동 가두다 penetrate 동 침투하다
consolidate 동 굳히다 porous 형 다공성의 shale 명 혈암
granite 명 화강암 basalt 명 현무암 silt 명 미사
downside 명 단점 overload 동 과적하다 septic tank 오수 정화조
filtration 명 여과 precipitation 명 강수 deplete 동 고갈시키다
replenish 동 보충하다

1 아래 문장 중 지문 속의 음영된 문장의 핵심 정보를 가장 잘 표현한 것은?

(A) 대수층이 투과성 토양을 통해 접근될 수 있는 경우, 그것은 비피압으로 간주된다.
(B) 대수층이 암석이나 점토의 두꺼운 층에 의해 갇히면, 그것에 직접 접근하는 것은 불가능할 수 있다.
(C) 대수층은 투과성의 토양을 통해 접근할 수 있거나 침투될 수 없는 층에 의해 둘러싸여 있다.
(D) 비피압 대수층으로 침투하는 것이 더 어렵기는 하지만, 두 종류의 대수층은 모두 잠재적으로 접근이 가능하다.

2 아래 문장 중 지문 속의 음영된 문장의 핵심 정보를 가장 잘 표현한 것은?

(A) 산업 오염이 너무 많은 비피압 대수층을 오염시켜서, 급수를 위해 그것들을 사용하는 것은 해롭다.
(B) 비피압 대수층으로 구멍을 뚫는 것에는 문제가 있는데, 이는 그것이 급수 오염을 초래할 수 있기 때문이다.
(C) 위험한 화학제품들은 비피압 대수층에 쉽게 침투할 수 있어서, 그것들로 구멍을 뚫는 것은 엄격히 금지된다.
(D) 비피압 대수층은 최대의 급수량을 포함하지만, 그것들에 구멍을 뚫는 것에는 단점도 있다.

Reading Practice 1

본문 p. 50

1 (B) 2 (D) 3 (D) 4 (B) 5 (D) 6 (D)

로코코 운동

로코코는 대략 1715년부터 1770년까지 프랑스의 회화, 건축, 디자인 및 문학을 지배했으며 유럽의 많은 부분으로 퍼져나간 예술 운동이다. [1]그 양식은 그들이 통제하는 국가 부의 90퍼센트를 불필요하고 퇴폐적인 것을 추구하는 데 사용한 엘리트 계층인 프랑스 귀족의 가볍고 쾌락적인 문화를 반영했다. 그 운동의 경박함을 경멸했던 사람들에 의해 사용된 조롱적인 명칭인 로코코 예술은, 우스꽝스러움, 허영, 그리고 부와 화려함에 대한 뚜렷한 표현을 지지하여, 18세기 초 동안 유럽 예술에서 번성했던 바로크 전통의 진지함과 웅장함에 대한 거부로 정의되었다.

로코코 회화는 유쾌하게 낭만적이고 목가적인 주제들에 몰두했다. [2]바로크 예술의 극적인 성경적 표현 대신에, 로코코 예술가들은 초목이 무성한 야외 배경에서 식사하고, 춤추고, 시시덕거리는 화려하게 차려입은 귀족들의 묘사를 보여주었다. 예를 들어, 장 오노레 프라고나르의 '그네'(1767)에서, 꽃이 만발한 숲속 풍경에서 윙크하는 아기 천사는 그네를 탄 여성이 비스듬히 기대어 있는 그녀의 애인을 유혹하는 것을 구경한다. 그들이 그렇게 나태한 여가 활동을 하며 하루를 자유롭게 보낼 수 있다는 사실뿐만 아니라, 그 남성과 여성의 복장은 그들이 사회적 엘리트 계층의 구성원임을 보여준다. [3]게다가, 서로에 대한 그들의 억압되지 않은 낭만적인 관심은 사회 예절의 많은 규칙들을 위반했기 때문에 동시대의 관람자들에게 다소 수치스럽게 보였을 것이다.

로코코 실내 디자인에서는 장식이 유용성보다 더 높게 평가되었다. 집의 중심은 응접실이었는데, 이곳은 남성들과 여성들이 복잡하게 장식된 환경에서 교제할 수 있는 방이었다. 로코코 응접실의 색상은 파스텔, 흰색 및 금색이 눈에 띄게 진열되어 밝고 화려한 경향이 있었다. 가구는 동식물의 무늬로 덮여 있었고, 마치 어울리기를 권하는 것처럼 벽에서 떨어져 있었다. 천장은 화려하고 구불구불한 몰딩과 현란한 샹들리에를 특징으로 했다. 귀족의 허영을 인정하는 의미로, 거울은 자유롭게 활용되었다. 모든 세밀한 디자인 선택에 있어 재미와 유쾌함이 강조되었다.

[6]1789년의 프랑스 혁명은 귀족들의 정치적 및 경제적 지배에 도전했으며 프랑스에서 로코코 시대를 종식시켰다. 그렇게 엄숙한 사건 이후에 그것의 유쾌한 양식은 하찮게 보였다. 한 19세기 건축가는 로코코를 "조개껍데기, 용, 갈대, 야자수, 그리고 다른 식물들의 우스꽝스러운 뒤범벅"이라고 묘사했다. 그러나 그 미적 가치관은 이미 유럽의 디자인에 그것의 흔적을 남겼고, 이탈리아, 바바리아, 프로이센과 같은 국가들에서 인기를 얻었다. 그것은 심지어 호화로운 호텔과 같은 특정 환경에서 유행하게 되면서 21세기에 부활했다. 비록 그 현대적인 운동의 화려한 장식들이 종종 풍자적인 의도로 만들어지지만, 17세기 프랑스 귀족의 유쾌한 즐거움은 부유하고 권력을 가진 오늘날의 엘리트들 사이에 여전히 호소력을 가지고 있다.

aristocracy 명 귀족 segment 명 계층 deploy 동 사용하다
decadent 형 퇴폐적인 designation 명 명칭 disdain 동 경멸하다
insincerity 명 경박함 grandeur 명 웅장함 vanity 명 허영
conspicuous 형 뚜렷한 preoccupied 형 몰두한
pastoral 형 목가적인 elaborately 부 화려하게 flirt 동 시시덕거리다
lush 형 초목이 무성한 cherub 명 아기 천사 entice 동 유혹하다
recline 동 비스듬히 기대다 attire 명 복장 indolent 형 나태한
uninhibited 형 억압되지 않은 intricately 부 복잡하게
ornamented 형 장식된 flora and fauna 동식물
mingling 명 어울리기 festivity 명 유쾌함 minute 형 세밀한, 작은
trivial 형 하찮은 solemn 형 엄숙한 jumble 명 뒤범벅
aesthetic 명 미적 가치관 resurrect 동 부활시키다
merriment 명 즐거움

1 아래 문장 중 지문 속의 음영된 문장의 핵심 정보를 가장 잘 표현한 것은?

(A) 이 예술 양식을 이용한 프랑스 예술가들은 큰 부를 가진 개인들의 후원에 의존했다.
(B) 이 예술 운동에는 그 국가의 부유한 상류층의 방종한 활동들이 묘사되어 있었다.
(C) 프랑스 귀족은 이 양식으로 창작된 예술 작품들에 의해 부도덕하고 어리석은 행동에 참여하도록 고무되었다.
(D) 대다수의 사람들은 이 예술 운동을 귀족들의 경솔한 취미라고 여겼다.

2 아래 문장 중 지문 속의 음영된 문장의 핵심 정보를 가장 잘 표현한 것은?

(A) 바로크 예술은 영성의 표현을 시사하여 사회 활동의 표현을 거부했기 때문에 많은 사람들에게 호소력이 있었다.
(B) 바로크와 로코코 예술가들의 주된 차이점은 그들이 귀족의 행동을 묘사하는 방식이었다.
(C) 귀족들이 로코코 작품들의 더 재미있는 주제를 선호했기 때문에 바로크 예술은 인기를 잃었다.
(D) 로코코 예술은 바로크 작품들의 진지한 종교적 주제보다는 부유하고 권력을 가진 한가한 사람들에게 초점을 맞췄다.

3 2단락에 따르면, 논란의 여지가 있다고 여겨진 '그네'의 요소는?
(A) 아기 천사의 행동
(B) 남성과 여성의 복장
(C) 장면의 자연 배경
(D) 그림 소재들의 관계

4 지문의 단어 "ornamented"와 의미가 가장 비슷한 것은?
(A) 위치해 있는
(B) 꾸며진
(C) 넘친
(D) 분열된

5 지문의 단어 "trivial"과 의미가 가장 비슷한 것은?
(A) 의식하지 못하는
(B) 즐거운
(C) 부조리한
(D) 하찮은

6 4단락에 따르면, 로코코 예술 운동이 인기를 잃었던 것은
(A) 화려함의 표현을 풍자로 간주한 새로운 예술 운동의 성장 때문이다
(B) 다양한 유럽 국가의 엘리트층 사이에서의 경쟁 증가 때문이다
(C) 프랑스 부자들이 지출을 줄이도록 강제한 경제적 불황 때문이다
(D) 귀족의 역할을 위협한 사회적 및 정치적 격변의 시기 때문이다

Reading Practice 2

본문 p.52

1 (D) 2 (C) 3 (C) 4 (A) 5 (C) 6 (A)

유아기 기억상실

심리학에서, 유아기 기억상실은 성인들에서의 생애 첫 몇 년 동안의 자전적 기억의 상대적 부재를 지칭한다. 최초의 영속적인 기억이 정확히 언제 형성되는지는 사람마다 다르지만, 그것이 유아기 이후에 일어난다는 것은 보편적이다. 사람들은 3세 무렵이 되어서야 그들에게 일어났거나 그들이 참여했던 일들에 대한 기억을 갖게 된다. 심리학자들은 100년 넘게 이 현상을 연구해왔지만, 그 해답은 여전히 알기 어렵다.

어린 시절의 기억에 대한 최초의 연구는 19세기로 거슬러 올라가지만, 진전은 비교적 느렸다. 1910년에, 지그문트 프로이트는 현대 심리학자들에 의해 여전히 사용되는 용어를 제공했다. [2]입 밖에 낼 수 없는 욕망에 관한 어린 시절의 난처함을 누르기 위해 성인들이 어린 시절의 사건을 잊어버린다는 그의 의견이 대부분의 심리학자들에게 더 이상 받아들여지지 않음에도 불구하고, 그들은 여전히 그가 만든 '유아기 기억상실'이라는 용어를 사용한다. [3A/3B]기억상실은 기억의 손실을 지칭하는 용어이지만, 20세기의 대부분 동안 심리학자들은 어린아이들이 실제로 유아기의 기억을 잊어버리는 것인지, 아니면 단지 발달 중인 아기의 뇌가 애초에 장기 기억을 간직할 능력이 없는 것인지에 대해 논쟁했다. 1980년대와 1990년대까지는 후자의 견해가 지배적이었는데, 이때 연구들은 아기들이 특정 기억들을 한 번에 몇 달 동안 유지할 수 있다는 것을 밝혀냈다. [3D]오늘날, 대부분의 연구자들은 유아들이 기억을 형성하지만 성인들보다 빨리 그것을 잊어버린다는 것에 동의한다.

2세 이전에 일어났던 일들에 대한 기억은 유아기에 빠르게 희미해지는 것으로 보인다. [4]대부분의 성인들은 3세나 4세 이전에 일어난 일들에 대한 기억이 없는 반면, 5세에서 9세까지의 아이들은 그 경계보다 앞서 일어난 일들을 기억한다. 한 연구는 3세부터의 급격한 기억 저하를 기록했는데, 6세의 아이들은 면담자가 질문한 일들에 대해 약 70퍼센트를 기억했지만 그들이 9세가 되었을 쯤에는 그것들의 약 절반을 잊어버린다는 것을 발견했다. 대조적으로, 기억은 20세에서 70세 사이에는 꽤 안정적이며, 최초의 성인 기억은 일관되게 4세 무렵에 일어난 일들인 경향이 있다.

유아기 기억상실의 원인에 대해서는 일치된 의견이 거의 없다. [6]일부 과학자들은 지속되는 기억을 형성하는 능력이 인지적 자아 의식의 발달이나 언어 습득과 동시에 일어난다고 믿으며, 이는 둘 다 과거의 경험을 정리하는 수단을 제공한다. 다른 이들은 자전적 기억을 형성하고, 정리하고, 저장하는 것을 담당하는 뇌의 부분인 해마의 뉴런 생성과 같은 신경학적 요인들에 초점을 맞춘다. 연구는 뉴런이 유아기까지 계속해서 형성되며 성인기에는 점점 줄어든다는 것을 보여준다. 이는 새로운 뉴런과 오래된 뉴런 사이의 경쟁이 기억 유지 저하를 야기할 수 있다는 것을 시사한다. 심리학자들과 신경학자들은 인간 정신의 가장 중요한 불가사의에 대한 해답을 찾기 위해 유아기 기억상실에 대한 연구를 계속하고 있다.

infantile amnesia 유아기 기억상실　absence 명 부재
autobiographical 형 자전적인　recollection 명 기억
phenomenon 명 현상　elusive 형 알기 어려운
infanthood 명 유아기　terminology 명 용어　repress 동 억누르다
unmentionable 형 입 밖에 낼 수 없는　embed 동 (기억 속에) 간직하다
predominant 형 지배적인　threshold 명 경계
dwindle 동 저하되다　consensus 명 일치된 의견
lasting 형 지속되는　coincide with ~과 동시에 일어나다
cognitive 형 인지적인　acquisition 명 습득
neurological 형 신경학적인　hippocampus 명 (뇌의) 해마
taper off 점점 줄어들다

1 지문의 단어 "phenomenon"과 의미가 가장 비슷한 것은?
(A) 인식
(B) 문제
(C) 결점
(D) 일어난 일

2 아래 문장 중 지문 속의 음영된 문장의 핵심 정보를 가장 잘 표현한 것은?
(A) '유아기 기억상실'은 사회적으로 용납되지 않는 욕망에 대한 기억을 차단하는 성인들의 경향에 대한 프로이트의 설명이다.
(B) 말할 수 없는 욕망들은 성인들에 의해 억눌러지지만, 아이들은 '유아기 기억상실'로 알려진 과정으로 그 욕망들을 기억한다.
(C) 사람들이 어린 시절의 난처한 기억들을 억누른다는 프로이트의 이론은 그가 그것을 묘사하기 위해 사용한 용어만큼 오래 지속되지 않았다.
(D) 성인들은 어린 시절의 난처한 일들을 잊어버리며, 프로이트는 그 난처함에 대한 용어를 개발했다.

3 2단락에 따르면, 다음 중 유아기 기억상실에 대한 설명으로 고려되지 않은 것은?

(A) 어린아이들은 유아기의 기억을 잊어버린다.
(B) 유아들은 기억을 형성하는 능력이 없다.
(C) 어린아이들은 유아기의 기억을 새로운 것들로 대체한다.
(D) 유아들은 기억을 형성하지만, 그것들을 상당히 빠르게 잊어버린다.

4 아래 문장 중 지문 속의 음영된 문장의 핵심 정보를 가장 잘 표현한 것은?

(A) 대다수의 성인들은 3세 때 일어난 일들을 기억하지 못하지만, 5세에서 9세 사이의 아이들은 기억한다.
(B) 수년 전의 일을 기억하는 것은 모든 연령대에서 일반적이지만, 9년 이상 지속된 기억은 어른들에게만 남는다.
(C) 많은 아이들은 4년보다 더 오래 지속되는 기억을 가지고 있지만, 성인들은 수년 내에 대부분의 것들을 잊어버린다.
(D) 5세에서 9세의 아이들은 성인들이 하는 것처럼 3세 때 그들에게 무슨 일이 일어났는지 기억할 수 있다.

5 지문의 단어 "them"이 가리키는 것은?

(A) 기억
(B) 아이들
(C) 일들
(D) 면담자

6 4단락에 따르면, 언어를 사용하여 의사소통하는 능력은

(A) 경험한 것을 구조화하는 방법으로서의 역할을 할 수 있다
(B) 개인의 자아 의식 발달로 이어질 수 있다
(C) 해마에서의 증가된 신경학적 활동을 자극할 수 있다
(D) 과거의 일들에 대한 기억이 상당히 바뀌게 할 수 있다

Reading Practice 3

본문 p.54

1 (D) 2 (A) 3 (B) 4 (B) 5 (B) 6 (A)

페름기 말 멸종 사건

과학자들은 지구 역사의 과정에서 발생한 5번의 대멸종 사건들을 확인했으며, 가장 잘 알려진 것은 6천 6백만 년 전에 공룡을 멸종시킨 백악기-팔레오기 멸종이다. 하지만, 공룡이 출현하기 전에, 훨씬 더 파괴적인 멸종 사건이 해양 종의 95퍼센트와 육상 척추동물의 70퍼센트를 멸종시켰다. 비공식적으로 대멸종이라고 알려진 페름기 말 멸종 사건은 약 2억 5천만 년 전에 일어났다. [1]그 피해는 아마 겨우 10만 년에 걸쳐 일어났을 것인데, 이는 특히 지구가 생물 다양성에 있어 잃어버린 것을 회복하는 데 천만년이 걸렸다는 점을 고려하면 지질학적인 시간에서는 겨우 눈 깜짝할 새이다. 하지만, 수백만 종의 소멸이 화석 기록으로 분명하게 기록되어 있는 반면, 페름기와 트라이아스기 사이의 멸종의 원인은 잘 알려져 있지 않다.

일부 과학자들은 위에 언급된 두 대멸종 사건의 원인이 동일했다고 믿는데, 이는 거대한 소행성들의 지구와의 충돌이다. 2004년에, 연대가 페름기 후기까지 거슬러 올라가는 75마일 크기의 분화구가 호주 앞바다에 묻혀 있는 것이 발견되었다. [2]이 베두 분화구는 공룡의 멸종이 소행성에 의해 일어났다는 주요 증거로 여겨지는 멕시코만의 칙술루브 분화구와 크기가 비슷하다. 이 정도 크기의 소행성 충돌은 수개월 동안 태양을 가려 기온이 떨어지게 했을 거대한 입자 구름들을 만들어 냈을 수 있다. 산성비가 뒤따랐을 것이고, 완전한 어둠, 갑작스러운 추위, 그리고 이것의 결합은 초식동물이 생존을 위해 필요로 하는 대부분의 식물들을 파괴했을 것이다. 결국, 초식동물의 죽음은 그것들을 먹은 육식동물의 죽음으로 이어졌을 것이다. [4]그러나, 다른 전문가들은 베두의 구조물이 어쨌든 충돌 분화구가 아니라고 주장하며 그 소행성 가설에 이의를 제기한다.

덜 극적인 설명은 페름기 동안 물속에서 형성된 암석 안의 산소 고갈 징후들을 기반으로 한다. 이 가설은 해양 생물의 대량 죽음이 극지방 빙원의 부재에 의해 야기된 얕은 바다의 낮은 산소 농도 때문이라는 것을 시사한다. **이것들은 세계의 바다 전체에 걸쳐 물을 순환시키는 대류에서 중요한 역할을 한다.** 페름기 바다에서 이산화탄소의 축적이 있었을 수도 있는데, 이는 점차 바다 생물을 해쳤을 것이다. 그러나, 산소 고갈 가설의 지지자들은 이러한 변화에 대한 촉매제에 대해 확신하지 못한다.

한 가지 잠재적인 촉매제는 오늘날의 시베리아에서의 광범위한 화산 활동이다. 다수의 분출하는 시베리아 화산들은 지구를 뜨거운 용암으로 뒤덮어 대기를 화산 가스로 채우고 소행성 시나리오에서와 마찬가지로 산성비를 만들어 냈을 수도 있다. 그 결과 발생한 화재와 부패는 대기를 온실가스로 채우고 세계의 동물들에게 알맞은 수준 이상으로 세계를 가열했을 것이다. 화산 이론은 대멸종에 대한 가장 대중적인 설명으로 남아 있다.

Permian 형 페름기의 extinction 명 멸종 Cretaceous 형 백악기의
Paleogene 형 팔레오기의 devastating 형 파괴적인
terrestrial 형 육상의, 육지의 vertebrate 명 척추동물
biodiversity 명 생물 다양성 disappearance 명 소멸, 사라짐
Triassic 형 트라이아스기의 asteroid 명 소행성
herbivore 명 초식동물 carnivore 명 육식동물
contest 동 이의를 제기하다 hypothesis 명 가설
contend 동 주장하다 dramatic 형 극적인 depletion 명 고갈
absence 명 부재 carbon dioxide 이산화탄소
proponent 명 지지자 deprivation 명 고갈 catalyst 명 촉매제
decay 명 부패 hospitable 형 (환경이) 알맞은

1 아래 문장 중 지문 속의 음영된 문장의 핵심 정보를 가장 잘 표현한 것은?

(A) 지구가 이전 수준의 생물 다양성 수준으로 되돌아가는 데 수백만 년이 걸렸다.
(B) 지질학적 구조에 끼친 피해 때문에, 그 사건의 영향은 수백만 년 동안 지속되었다.
(C) 파괴의 정도를 고려했을 때, 지구는 놀라울 정도로 빠르게 회복했다.
(D) 생물 다양성 회복 기간의 길이를 고려하면, 파괴의 기간은 매우 짧았다.

2 아래 문장 중 지문 속의 음영된 문장의 핵심 정보를 가장 잘 표현한 것은?

(A) 베두 분화구의 크기는 공룡 멸종과 연관된 소행성 충돌 현장의 분화구 크기와 비슷하다.
(B) 베두와 칙술루브 분화구는 둘 다 소행성의 충돌에 의해 만들어진 것으로 확인되었다.
(C) 칙술루브 분화구는 소행성의 결과였으므로, 베두 분화구가 동일한 기원을 가지고 있을 가능성이 높다.
(D) 칙술루브 분화구에 대한 연구는 베두 분화구의 가장 유력한 원인에 대한 통찰을 제공했다.

3 지문의 단어 "this"가 가리키는 것은?

(A) 태양
(B) 산성비
(C) 완전한 어둠
(D) 갑작스러운 추위

4 2단락에 따르면, 소행성 가설에 이의가 제기된 것은 일부 과학자들이

(A) 산성비가 그렇게 많은 동물을 죽일 수 있었다는 것을 의심하기 때문이다
(B) 베두 분화구가 소행성에 의해 야기된 것이 아니라고 주장하기 때문이다
(C) 멸종이 따뜻한 기후에 의해 야기되었다고 생각하기 때문이다
(D) 공룡이 소행성에도 불구하고 살아남을 수 있었을 것이라고 믿기 때문이다

5 네 개의 네모[■]는 다음 문장이 삽입될 수 있는 곳을 나타내고 있다.

이것들은 세계의 바다 전체에 걸쳐 물을 순환시키는 대류에서 중요한 역할을 한다.

이 문장은 어디에 들어가는 것이 가장 적절한가?

6 지문의 단어 "hospitable"과 의미가 가장 비슷한 것은?

(A) 생존 가능한
(B) 특정한
(C) 신선한
(D) 고통스러운

iBT Reading Test 1

본문 p.56

1 (A)	2 (B)	3 (D)	4 (B)
5 (C)	6 (C)	7 (B)	8 (B)
9 (B)	10 (A), (D), (F)		

뇌-컴퓨터 인터페이스

뇌-컴퓨터 인터페이스(BCI)는 인간의 뇌와 컴퓨터 사이에 직접적인 의사소통 채널을 만들기 위해 고안된 다양한 기술을 포함한다. BCI의 주요 목표는 인간이 뇌 신호만을 이용하여 장치나 도구를 제어하는 방법을 개발하는 것으로, 이는 과학자들이 인간의 뇌를 더 잘 이해하게 도울 뿐만 아니라 심각한 신체 장애가 있지만 정상적인 인지 기능을 가진 사람들에게 기회를 제공할 능력이다. 예를 들어, 자동차 사고로 마비된 사람은 그나 그녀의 팔과 손을 움직일 수 없음에도 불구하고 휠체어를 조작할 수 있을 것이다.

현재, 뇌-컴퓨터 인터페이스 시스템에는 비침습적과 침습적의 두 가지 주요 범주가 있다. 일반적인 비침습적 기술은 뇌전도(EEG)의 사용을 수반하는데, 이는 뇌파의 변화를 감지하는 검사이다. 이 방법에서는, 전극이라고 불리는 작은 금속 원반들이 두피에 부착되며, 뇌에서 나오는 전기 신호들이 측정되고 기록된다. 반대로, 침습적 BCI 시술은 신경외과 수술 동안 뇌에 작은 전극들을 직접 이식하는데, 이는 더 비싸며 환자에게 더 위험하다. [3]그러나, 장점은 각 전극이 단일한 뉴런을 대상으로 하기 때문에 침습적 전극들이 훨씬 더 높은 그래픽 해상도를 만들어내며 더 구체적이라는 것이다.

어느 경우이든, 전극은 처리를 위해 외부 컴퓨터에 연결되는데, 이것은 일반적으로 뇌의 전기 신호가 해석되고, 분류되고, 수학 공식을 이용해 변환되는 몇 가지 단계를 필요로 한다. [4A]이 처리는 실험 대상자가 어떤 종류의 정신 작업을 수행하고 있는지 알아내어 데이터가 디지털 방식의 명령으로 변환될 수 있도록 하기 위해 필요하다. **그 변환은 뇌파를 컴퓨터가 이해할 수 있는 프로그래밍된 명령으로 변환하는 특정한 알고리즘을 이용해 이루어진다.** [4D]일단 디지털 방식의 명령이 생성되면, 그것은 커서나 로봇 팔의 움직임과 같은, 상응하는 동작을 완수하기 위해 외부 장치로 전송된다. [4C]의도된 동작의 성공이나 실패는 장치에서 사용자에게 돌아가는 피드백에 의해 결정된다.

뇌의 뉴런 활동을 이용하는 개념은 1960년대까지 거슬러 올라가지만, BCI 기술의 실용적인 과학적 응용은 여전히 초기 단계에 있다. [7]한 가지 이유는 뇌의 전기 신호가 개인마다 달라서 보편적인 디지털 방식의 출력 명령을 만드는 것이 가능하지 않기 때문이다. 더욱이, BCI에서 처리는 단순히 뇌에서 외부 환경으로 가는 정보의 일방적인 흐름이 아니다. 사실, 뇌의 뉴런들은 유연하며 BCI 환경에 반응하여 적응해야만 한다. [6]각 실험 대상자는 여전히 전기 신호와 디지털 방식의 명령들이 의도된 작업을 성공적으로 완수할 수 있도록 특정한 방식으로 생각하는 법을, 종종 시행착오를 통해 배워야만 한다. 따라서, BCI에 대한 누구에게나 맞는 접근법은 결코 결실을 보지 못할 수 있으며, 실험 대상자와 컴퓨터 사이 제삼자의 조정은 여전히 중요하다. 이런 의미에서, BCI가 첨단 기술 프로젝트임에도 불구하고, 그 과정은 면허를 가진 물리치료사의 도움과 지도를 받아 재활을 진행 중인 부상당한 운동선수의 그것과 유사하다.

cognitive function 인지 기능　paralyzed 형 마비된
noninvasive 형 비침습적인　invasive 형 침습적인
entail 동 수반하다　electroencephalogram 명 뇌전도
electrode 명 전극　scalp 명 두피　conversely 부 반대로
implant 동 이식하다　neurosurgery 명 신경외과 수술
resolution 명 해상도　processing 명 처리
corresponding 형 상응하는　notion 명 개념　harness 동 이용하다
application 명 적용　infancy 명 초기 단계　feasible 형 가능한
malleable 형 유연한　trial and error 시행착오
one-size-fits-all 형 누구에게나 맞는　fruition 명 결실
mediation 명 조정　undertaking 명 프로젝트
rehabilitation 명 재활

1 아래 문장 중 지문 속의 음영된 문장의 핵심 정보를 가장 잘 표현한 것은? 오답은 문장의 의미를 크게 바꾸거나 핵심 정보를 생략한다.

(A) 만약 사람들이 생각만으로 기계를 조종할 수 있다면, 과학자들은 뇌에 관해서 더 많은 것을 배울 수 있고 신체 장애가 있는 사람들 또한 이익을 얻을 수 있을 것이다.
(B) BCI의 주요 목표는 과학자들에게 컴퓨터를 사용하여 사람들이 인지 및 신체 장애를 극복할 수 있게 도와 그들이 더 정상적인 삶을 살 수 있도록 하는 기회를 제공하는 것이다.
(C) 과학자들은 BCI의 사용을 통해 인간의 인지에 관한 많은 지식을 얻었으나, 그것의 실제적인 응용은 정신적 장애가 있는 사람들에게로 제한되어 왔다.
(D) 과학자들이 인간의 뇌가 어떻게 작동하는지에 관해 더 배우기 위해서는, 피실험자들은 반드시 원격 장치와 도구를 제어하는 신체 및 인지 능력을 결합해야 한다.

2 지문의 단어 "entails"와 의미가 가장 비슷한 것은?

(A) 방지하다
(B) 수반하다
(C) 설명하다
(D) 발전시키다

3 다음 중 2단락에서 BCI에서의 뇌전도 사용에 관해 추론할 수 있는 것은?

(A) 대안적인 BCI 방법보다 사용하기에 더 비싸고 더 위험하다.
(B) 현재 과학에서 가장 적게 시행되는 BCI 시술이다.
(C) 직접적인 전극 이식보다 더 포괄적인 데이터를 제공한다.
(D) 침습적 기술보다 덜 상세한 뇌 활동 이미지를 제공한다.

4 다음 중 3단락에서 전극과 뇌의 전기 신호 처리 과정의 일부로서 언급되지 않은 것은?

(A) 데이터를 디지털 방식 명령으로 변환하는 것
(B) 데이터를 도식화된 차트로 변환하는 것
(C) 장치에서 사용자에게 피드백을 제공하는 것
(D) 디지털 방식의 명령을 외부 기계로 전송하는 것

5 지문의 단어 "fruition"과 의미가 가장 비슷한 것은?

(A) 논란
(B) 시작
(C) 완료
(D) 승인

6 4단락에 따르면, BCI 장치 사용자들은 무엇을 하는 능력을 발달시켜야 하는가?

(A) 빠르게 변화하는 기술에 적응하기
(B) 다양한 형태의 전자 메시지를 인식하기
(C) 알맞은 신호와 명령으로 이어지는 생각을 형성하기
(D) 디지털 방식 장치들의 명령을 해석하기

7 4단락에 따르면, 보편적인 디지털 방식의 출력 명령을 만드는 것이 가능하지 않은 이유는?

(A) 정보의 흐름이 한 방향으로만 이동한다.
(B) 서로 다른 뇌의 전기 신호가 각기 다르다.
(C) 그것들을 생산하는 것의 비용이 막대하다.
(D) 뇌의 뉴런이 그것들에 느리게 적응한다.

8 4단락에서, 글쓴이는 왜 부상당한 운동선수의 신체 재활을 언급하는가?

(A) BCI가 최첨단 기술을 사용한다는 점을 강조하기 위해
(B) BCI가 수행되는 방식에 대한 비유를 제공하기 위해
(C) 치료에서 시행착오의 역할을 강조하기 위해
(D) BCI의 잠재적인 미래 응용의 예시를 제공하기 위해

9 네 개의 네모[■]는 다음 문장이 삽입될 수 있는 곳을 나타내고 있다.

그 변환은 뇌파를 컴퓨터가 이해할 수 있는 프로그래밍된 명령으로 변환하는 특정한 알고리즘을 이용해 이루어진다.

이 문장은 어디에 들어가는 것이 가장 적절한가?

10 **지시:** 지문 요약을 위한 도입 문장이 아래에 주어져 있다. 지문의 가장 중요한 내용을 나타내는 보기 3개를 골라 요약을 완성하라. 어떤 문장은 지문에 언급되지 않은 내용이나 사소한 정보를 나타내므로 요약에 포함되지 않는다. **이 문제는 2점이다.**

> **과학자들은 인간의 뇌와 컴퓨터 사이의 직접적인 의사소통을 가능하게 할 뇌-컴퓨터 인터페이스(BCI) 기술을 추구하고 있다.**
>
> · (A) 뇌 신호를 이용한다는 발상은 새로운 것이 아님에도 뇌-컴퓨터 기술의 유용한 응용은 여전히 상당히 개발되지 않았다.
> · (D) 비침습적 및 침습적 시술은 현재 사용 중인 BCI의 두 가지 주요 분류이다.
> · (F) BCI 처리 절차 동안, 유선 전극들은 외부 컴퓨터에 연결되며 뇌의 전기 메시지가 처리된다.

(B) BCI는 뇌에서 환경으로 가는 일방적인 의사소통 흐름을 통해 컴퓨터가 뉴런 신호를 이해하게 하는 과정이다.
(C) BCI의 중요한 응용은 마비된 사람들에게 손을 사용하지 않는 기계 작동의 가능성을 제공하고 있다.
(E) 과학자들은 BCI 기술에서 약간의 진전을 이루었지만, 피드백을 장치로부터 사용자에게 돌려보내지 못했다.

iBT Reading Test 2

본문 p.60

1 (D) 2 (D) 3 (B) 4 (D)
5 (C) 6 (D) 7 (A) 8 (B)
9 (D) 10 (A), (C), (F)

미국의 주간 고속도로 시스템

[3]1920년대에, 포드 자동차 회사는 더 많은 사람들이 자동차를 소유할 수 있도록 노동자 계층을 위한 저렴한 자동차를 선보였다. 이는 운전을 대중화했고, 그로 인해 고속도로 시스템의 확장에 대한 수요가 증가했다. 그러나, 고속도로에 대한 정부의 자금 지원은 한정되어 있었고, 민간 기업들이 그 수요를 충족시키는 것을 도왔다. 1940년에 개통된 민간 유료 도로인 펜실베이니아 유료 고속도로는 미국의 현대식 고속도로의 첫 번째 사례였다. 그것은 매우 수익성이 높은 노선으로 증명되었으며, 정치인들에게 고속도로의 경제적 가치를 보여주었다. 자동차가 일반적인 것이 되어가고 주간 여행에 대한 대중의 관심이 증대됨에 따라, 연방 정부는 대규모 주간 고속도로 프로젝트를 고려하기 시작했다.

계획된 주간 고속도로 시스템은 1950년대에 드와이트 D. 아이젠하워가 대통령이 된 이후 공식적인 지원을 받았다. [5]제2차 세계대전 동안, 아이젠하워는 전국에 걸쳐 뻗어 있는 다차선 고속도로인 거대한 독일 아우토반과 마주쳤었다. 이것들을 목격한 것은 그로 하여금 고속도로가 군사 수송을 신속하게 하는 데 필수적이라고 믿게 했다. 그래서, 1956년에 그는 연방정부 지원 고속도로법을 승인함으로써 주간 고속도로 시스템을 건설하기 시작했다. [4]이 법안을 통해, 의회는 프로젝트 비용의 90퍼센트에 대한 연방 자금 지원을 확보했고, 그것은 휘발유에 대한 세금으로 자금을 조달 받았다.

새로운 주간 고속도로 시스템을 이전의 것들과 다르게 만든 것은 꼼꼼한 계획과 규모였다. 모든 주간 고속도로들은 비슷한 방식으로 설계되었다. [6A]그것들은 각 방향으로 가는 두 개의 차선을 가지고 있었고, 이것들은 넓은 중앙분리대에 의해 분리되었다. [6B]그것들은 또한 각 측면에 넓은 우선 통행권이 있어서, 그것들 옆에는 어떠한 건물도 건설될 수 없었다. [6C]입구와 출구 경사로가 유일한 접근 지점이었기 때문에 주간 고속도로로의 접근은 고도로 통제되었다. 이러한 종류의 접근이 통제된 고속도로는 무료 고속도로나 고속화도로로 알려져 있다. 거의 75,000킬로미터 길이의 고속도로 건설은 역사상 가장 크고 가장 비싼 공공사업 프로젝트였다.

새로운 주간 고속도로 시스템은 미국에 상당한 경제적 영향을 미쳤다. 쓰여진 달러마다, 그 도로들은 경제에 추가적인 6달러를 가져왔다. 건설 하나만으로도 10년 동안 미국의 생산성에 연간 31퍼센트를 더했다. [7]이러한 혜택들뿐만 아니라, 전국에 걸쳐 화물이 빠르게 수송될 수

있었기 때문에 수송 비용이 감소했다. **이것은 대부분의 소비재의 가격을 감소시켰다.**

그러나, 고속도로가 만들어낸 혜택들에도 불구하고, 그것들은 또한 사회적 문제를 야기했다. 거의 80만 채의 건물이 부서졌고, 그들 중 많은 수가 아프리카계 미국인이었던 가족들이 그들의 주택 파괴에 대해 적절하게 보상받지 못했다. 뿐만 아니라, 아프리카계 미국인 가족들은 차를 소유하고 있을 가능성이 더 낮았다. 이는 그들이 대중교통에 크게 의존하며, 대중교통 자금 지원이 도로 건설로 전환되었을 때 고통받는다는 것을 의미했다. 게다가, 1962년에 인기 소설 '침묵의 봄'의 출판은 더 높은 환경 의식을 장려했다. 그것은 고속도로 건설이 환경에 끼치고 있는 피해를 지적했다. 대중은 고속도로 개발에 있어 환경에 대한 명백한 무시에 분노했는데, 이는 그것들이 자연보다는 건설 비용과 이동 시간을 우선순위로 계획되었기 때문이었다.

interstate 형 주간의 affordable 형 저렴한 fulfill 동 충족시키다
toll road 유료 도로 profitable 형 수익성이 높은
norm 명 일반적인 것 encounter 동 마주치다 witness 동 목격하다
expedite 동 신속하게 하다 legislation 명 법안
secure 동 확보하다 methodical 형 꼼꼼한 median 명 중앙분리대
right-of-way 명 우선 통행권 ramp 명 경사로
productivity 명 생산성 freight 명 화물 bulldoze 동 부수다
suitably 부 적절하게 compensate 동 보상하다
destruction 명 파괴 reliant on ~에 의존하는 outraged 형 분노한
apparent 형 명백한 disregard 명 무시

1 지문에서 글쓴이는 왜 "The Pennsylvania Turnpike"를 언급하는가?

(A) 동시대의 건설 방법을 나열하기 위해
(B) 연방 공무원들 사이에서 그것의 인기를 보여주기 위해
(C) 고속도로의 목적을 설명하기 위해
(D) 민간 프로젝트의 사례를 제공하기 위해

2 지문의 단어 "norm"과 의미가 가장 비슷한 것은?

(A) 후임자
(B) 경계
(C) 조건
(D) 표준

3 1단락에 따르면, 어떤 요인이 1920년대에 운전을 대중적으로 만들었는가?

(A) 포드는 매 구매에 무료 휘발유를 제공했다.
(B) 자동차가 대다수의 사람들에게 비싸지 않게 되었다.
(C) 고속도로로 인해 운전이 편리해졌다.
(D) 낮은 세금이 장거리 여행의 비용을 줄였다.

4 2단락에 따르면, 다음 중 연방정부 지원 고속도로법에 관해 사실인 것은?

(A) 전체 주간 고속도로 프로젝트 비용을 충당하기 위한 연방 자금을 제공했다.
(B) 군사 수송을 위한 특별한 고속도로 차선을 요구했다.
(C) 승인되기 전인 초기에 의회에 의해 거부되었다.
(D) 주간 고속도로 시스템에 자금을 조달하기 위해 주로 휘발유에 대한 세금을 이용했다.

5 2단락에서 드와이드 D. 아이젠하워 대통령에 관해 추론할 수 있는 것은?

(A) 주간 고속도로 프로젝트를 고려한 첫 번째 정치인이었다.
(B) 전쟁 때문에 독일에 대한 경멸이 생겼다.
(C) 독일 고속도로의 실용적인 유용성에 감명받았다.
(D) 납세자들이 고속도로의 가치에 대해 회의적일 것이라고 생각했다.

6 3단락에 따르면, 다음 중 주간 고속도로가 설계된 방법에 관해 사실이 아닌 것은?

(A) 넓은 중앙분리대가 차선들의 각 세트를 분리했다.
(B) 우선 통행권이 인접한 곳의 건물 건설을 막았다.
(C) 접근이 경사로의 안과 밖으로 엄격히 제한되었다.
(D) 차선들의 각 세트는 양방향 통행을 허용했다.

7 4단락에 따르면, 주간 고속도로 시스템은 화물에 어떤 영향을 미쳤는가?

(A) 수송 비용이 감소했다.
(B) 배송 비용을 없앴다.
(C) 트럭에 대한 세금이 제거되었다.
(D) 통행료를 낮추었다.

8 아래 문장 중 지문 속의 음영된 문장의 핵심 정보를 가장 잘 표현한 것은? 오답은 문장의 의미를 크게 바꾸거나 핵심 정보를 생략한다.

(A) 고속도로 건설은 환경적 우려보다는 폭과 길이에 초점을 맞추었다.
(B) 건설 중에 자연보다 비용을 우선시하는 것이 대중의 분노를 키웠다.
(C) 도로 건설은 환경적 압력에 영향을 받지 않았다.
(D) 고속도로 건설에 있어 환경적 영향은 편리성만큼이나 중요했다.

9 네 개의 네모[■]는 다음 문장이 삽입될 수 있는 곳을 나타내고 있다.

이것은 대부분의 소비재의 가격을 감소시켰다.

이 문장은 어디에 들어가는 것이 가장 적절한가?

10 **지시:** 지문 요약을 위한 도입 문장이 아래에 주어져 있다. 지문의 가장 중요한 내용을 나타내는 보기 3개를 골라 요약을 완성하라. 어떤 문장은 지문에 언급되지 않은 내용이나 사소한 정보를 나타내므로 요약에 포함되지 않는다. **이 문제는 2점이다.**

더 많은 사람들이 차를 소유하고 차로 이동함에 따라, 연방 정부는 주간 고속도로에 투자하기 시작했다.

- (A) 주간 고속도로는 그것들의 체계와 범위 때문에 이전의 것들과 달랐다.
- (C) 주간 고속도로 시스템이 현실이 된 것은 아이젠하워 행정부 때였다.
- (F) 주간 고속도로가 상당한 혜택들을 만들어 냈음에도 불구하고, 그것들은 또한 사회 및 환경 문제를 야기했다.

(B) 주간 고속도로 시스템은 미국 군대가 직면한 혼잡 문제를 해결했다.
(D) 고속도로 건설은 수십만 명의 퇴거를 수반했다.
(E) 아프리카계 미국인 가족들은 주간 고속도로 시스템을 이용할 가능성이 가장 낮은 소수 집단이었다.

Vocabulary Review

본문 p.64

1 replenished　2 terrestrial　3 predominant
4 indolent　5 methodical　6 malleable
7 (D)　8 (A)　9 (B)　10 (A)
11 (D)　12 (C)　13 (C)　14 (A)

CHAPTER 04 Fact

Example

본문 p.67

1 (C)　2 (D)

클로비스 퍼스트 이론

대부분의 과학자들은 현대 인류가 지구의 다른 지역으로 이주하기에 앞서 약 30만 년 전에 아프리카에서 처음 나타났다는 데 동의한다. 이 시점에 북아메리카와 남아메리카는 이미 다른 대륙들로부터 분리되어 있었기 때문에, 그것들은 마지막에 정착되었다. 그렇다면, 사람들은 언제 신세계에 도착했을까?

[1]수십 년 동안, 유력한 설명은 최초의 인류가 홍적세 후기에 알래스카와 시베리아를 연결하는 베링육교를 걸어서 건넜고, 그런 다음 지금의 캐나다인 영토 중앙의 얼음이 없는 좁은 통로를 통해 나아갔다고 제시하는 클로비스 퍼스트 가설이었다. 클로비스 퍼스트 이론가들은 최초의 정착민들이 1930년대에 뉴멕시코주의 클로비스에서 발견된 사냥 도구 더미를 능숙하게 만들었던 수렵 채집인들이라고 믿었다. 그 도구들은 약 11,000년이 된 것으로 방사성 탄소 연대 측정되었으며, 이는 그것들을 아메리카 대륙 인류에 대한 최초의 고고학적 증거로 만들었다.

그러나, 보다 최근의 증거는 클로비스 퍼스트 설명에 의문을 제기해 왔다. 알래스카 유콘의 블루피쉬 강을 끼고 있는 블루피쉬 동굴들의 발굴은 최대 18,000년이 되었을 수도 있는 도구들을 내놓았다. [2]게다가, 1985년에는 거대한 매머드 뼈가 도구로 쓰이기 위해 그것들에서 조각들이 제거된 채 발견되었다. 그 매머드 뼈는 24,500년이 된 것으로 연대 측정되었고, 이는 블루피쉬 동굴을 북아메리카에서 가장 오래된 인류 거주 유적지로 만들었다. 다른 연구들은 방사성 탄소, DNA 및 대형 화석 자료를 수집하였으며 얼음이 없는 그 통로가 클로비스 도구들이 만들어진 훨씬 후까지 통과할 수 없었다고 결론 내렸다.

migrate 동 이주하다　settle 동 정착하다　leading 형 유력한
Late Pleistocene 홍적세 후기　corridor 명 통로
hunter-gatherer 명 수렵 채집인　expertly 부 능숙하게
radiocarbon date 방사성 탄소 연대 측정하다
archaeological 형 고고학적인
cast doubt upon ~에 의문을 제기하다　excavation 명 발굴
yield 동 (증거 등을) 내놓다　flake 명 조각　amass 동 수집하다
macrofossil 명 대형 화석　impassable 형 통과할 수 없는

1 2단락에 따르면, 클로비스 퍼스트 가설은 아메리카 대륙 최초의 인류가
(A) 약 30만 년 전에 아프리카에서 그곳으로 이주했다고 제시한다
(B) 홍적세 후기 중에 알래스카에서 시베리아로 항해했다고 제시한다
(C) 현재의 캐나다에 있는 얼음이 없는 지역을 통과해 걸어갔다고 제시한다
(D) 그 대륙들이 분리되기 훨씬 이전에 그 지역에 도착했다고 제시한다

2 지문에 따르면, 다음 중 블루피쉬 동굴에 관해 사실인 것은?
(A) 클로비스 도구들이 만들어진 이후까지 인간에 의해 훼손되지 않았다.
(B) 1985년에 발굴되어 24,500년이 된 인간의 뼈를 드러냈다.
(C) 클로비스 도구들보다 더 최근에 만들어진 도구들을 포함했다.
(D) 그것들의 발굴은 인간에 의해 변형된 동물 뼈를 찾아냈다.

Reading Practice 1

본문 p.68

1 (D)　2 (B)　3 (B)　4 (C)　5 (B)　6 (C)

동일 과정설과 수성설

18세기 후반, 스코틀랜드 지질학자 제임스 허턴은 25년간의 성실한 관찰을 요약한 새로운 이론을 발표했다. 훗날 동일 과정설로 알려진 그것은 모든 지질학적 변화가 무한한 기간에 걸친 균일한 과정의 결과라고 주장했다. [1]그의 이론은 당대에 인기 있었던 수성설 이론과 대조되었기 때문에 매우 논란이 많았다. 이것은 모든 지질학적 구조가 홍수에서 온 물의 결과라고 주장했다. 반대에도 불구하고, 허턴의 이론은 과학계에서 점차 받아들여졌고, 그는 현대 지질학의 창시자로 여겨진다.

수성설 이론가들, 특히 독일 지질학자 아브라함 고틀로프 베르너는 지구가 처음에 물로 덮여 있었다고 주장했다. 그의 말에 따르면, 물을 많이 함유한 이 행성은 약 6천 년 전에 신에 의해 창조되었다. **그 시간 범위는 이 시대에 널리 받아들여졌던 열렬한 기독교적 믿음을 만족시켰다.** 게다가, 화석은 성경의 홍수로 죽은 동물들의 잔해라고 설명되었다. 수성설은 따라서 모든 지질학적 구조와 화석이 홍수와 침식의 결과라고 제시했다. 그것은 비록 왜 그러한 후퇴가 일어났는지는 설명하지 않았지만, 물의 바다로의 후퇴가 현재의 대륙들과 섬들을 만들었다고 주장했다.

허턴의 관찰은 수성설을 부정했다. 그는 절벽 위의 퇴적암과 물고기 화석이 후퇴하는 물이 아니라 융기하는 땅의 결과라고 주장했다. 증거를 위해, 허턴은 스코틀랜드 전역의 많은 장소를 방문했다. 그는 두 가지 상반된 형태의 지질학적 활동을 볼 수 있는 표면인 부정합을 찾기 위해 노출된 암석 표면들을 조사했다. [4]식카 포인트에서, 허턴은 위쪽의 적색 사암들이 수평으로 퇴적되어 있는 반면, 더 낮은 쪽의 실루리아기 암석들은 수직으로 향한 것을 알아챘다. 이 구조는 적색 사암들의 퇴적 이전에 실루리아기 암석들의 융기와 방향 전환을 통해 일어났는데, 이는 오랜 기간에 걸쳐 발달한 작용이다. 이 효과는 홍수를 통해서는 달성될 수 없었을 것이다. 그것은 지구 자체에서 나오는 엄청난 압력을 필요로 했다. 결과적으로, 그는 지형, 암석 및 광물이 무한한 침식의 과정과 내부 압력으로부터의 융기 과정을 통해 형성되었다고 믿었다. 그는 이 과정에 매우 오랜 시간이 걸렸다고 주장했고, 지구의 나이가 6천 년 보다 훨씬 더 많다고 가정했다.

[6]그러나, 허턴은 지질학적 변화가 균일하고 시간이 지남에 따라 변하지 않는다고 믿었다는 점에서 틀렸다. 지질학적 변화의 속도는 지구 중

심부의 대류 과정에 따라 달라질 수 있다. 따라서, 현대 지질학자들은 지구가 세 가지의 서로 다른 과정의 조합을 통해 형성되었다고 주장한다. 물은 퇴적암 생성의 원인이지만, 열과 융기는 화성암을 형성한다. 지질학자들은 홍수나 화산 폭발 같은 갑작스러운 재앙적 사건들이 지구를 형성하는 데 있어 각자의 역할을 한다고 주장해왔다. 그러나 이것들은 제한된 영향을 미치며 수성설이 시사했던 것처럼 지구의 전반적인 지질학적 구조의 원인이 되지는 않는다. 대신, 허턴에 의해 가정되고 후대의 과학자들에 의해 발전된 동일 과정설 이론은 전 세계 대부분의 지질학적 구조를 설명한다.

uniformitarianism 명 동일 과정설　Neptunism 명 수성설
diligent 형 성실한　infinite 형 무한한　contrast with ~과 대조되다
claim 동 주장하다; 명 주장　remnant 명 잔해　perish 동 죽다
erosion 명 침식　recession 명 후퇴　contradict 동 부정하다
sedimentary rock 퇴적암　recede 동 후퇴하다
unconformity 명 부정합　vertically 부 수직으로
deposit 동 퇴적하다　horizontally 부 수평으로　uplifting 명 융기
reorienting 명 방향 전환　immense 형 엄청난　emanate 동 나오다
postulate 동 가정하다　convection 명 대류　contend 동 주장하다
igneous rock 화성암　catastrophic 형 재앙적인　posit 동 가정하다

1　1단락에 따르면, 동일 과정설이 논란이 된 것은

(A) 아주 적은 관찰에 기초했기 때문이다
(B) 지질학적 과정이 일시적이라고 주장했기 때문이다
(C) 홍수의 영향에 관해 뒷받침되지 않은 주장을 했기 때문이다
(D) 당시의 지배적인 이론과 상충했기 때문이다

2　네 개의 네모[■]는 다음 문장이 삽입될 수 있는 곳을 나타내고 있다.

그 시간 범위는 이 시대에 널리 받아들여졌던 열렬한 기독교적 믿음을 만족시켰다.

이 문장은 어디에 들어가는 것이 가장 적절한가?

3　지문의 단어 "perished"와 의미가 가장 비슷한 것은?

(A) 물속에 잠겼다
(B) 죽었다
(C) 번성했다
(D) 발전했다

4　3단락에 따르면, 다음 중 적색 사암에 관해 사실인 것은?

(A) 점차 낮아지는 수위에 의해 형성되었다.
(B) 어떤 장소에서는 수직으로, 다른 곳에서는 수평으로 향했다.
(C) 허턴이 조사한 장소에서 실루리아기 암석들 위로 들어 올려져 있었다.
(D) 실루리아기 암석들보다 더 이른 시기에 퇴적되었다.

5　지문의 단어 "these"가 가리키는 것은?

(A) 주장
(B) 사건들
(C) 홍수
(D) 폭발

6　4단락에 따르면, 허턴의 이론의 주요한 결점은

(A) 파괴적인 자연 현상이 일어나는 힘과 관련되어 있었다
(B) 지구 내부 중심핵의 전반적인 구조와 관련되어 있었다
(C) 지질학적 과정이 일어나는 일관성과 관련되어 있었다
(D) 다양한 종류의 암석 생성에 필요한 시간과 관련되어 있었다

Reading Practice 2

본문 p.70

1 (A)　2 (C)　3 (C)　4 (A)　5 (D)　6 (A)

네페르티티 논쟁

[2]1912년에 있었던 이집트 파라오 아케나텐의 공식 궁중 조각가의 작업장 발굴 작업에서, 독일 고고학자 루드비히 보르하르트는 한 세기 이상 지속될 논쟁을 일으켰다. 그는 아케나텐의 왕비인 네페르티티 여왕의 3,000년도 더 된 흉상을 발견했다. 그 조각된 머리는 석회와 치장 벽토로 만들어졌고 원래 있던 석영으로 된 눈들을 붙이기 위해 밀랍이 사용되었으며, 그것은 높이가 19인치이고 무게는 44파운드이다. 이상하게도, 그 눈들 중 하나는 그때부터 실종 상태이다. 보르하르트는 그 흉상을 독일로 가져갔으며, 이집트 정부에게는 매우 불만스럽게도, 오늘날 그곳에 있다.

독일 측의 이야기는 보르하르트가 이집트인 관리로부터 소유권을 적법하게 수여받았다는 것이지만, 이집트인들은 보르하르트가 그 흉상의 가치를 축소했다고 주장한다. 문서 기록은 1913년에 보르하르트가 발굴된 유물을 그들 사이에서 나누기 위해 이집트인 관리와 만났다는 것을 보여준다. [3]그 관리는 실제 조각상 대신에 잘 나오지 않은 사진을 보았고, 보르하르트는 그것이 유명한 여왕을 묘사했다는 것을 숨긴 채 그것을 어느 공주의 석고 흉상이라고 설명했다. 1924년 이래로, 이집트인들은 독일의 그 습득을 약탈이라고 표현해 왔다.

비록 그 흉상이 현재 베를린에서 가장 인기 있는 박물관 전시품이긴 하지만, 이집트 당국은 이 상황을 받아들이기를 거부해 왔으며 그 예술품을 본국으로 송환하기 위해 수많은 시도를 해왔다. 이것이 가장 가깝게 일어났던 것은 1933년에 있었는데, 이때 독일 정부는 이집트 왕의 즉위 기념일을 축하하기 위해 그 조각상을 돌려주겠다고 약속했다. 안타깝게도, 아돌프 히틀러가 개입해서 독일이 절대로 그 흉상을 포기하지 않을 것이라고 선언했다. 제2차 세계 대전이 끝난 이래로, 독일 정부는 이집트로부터의 모든 요청을 거절했고, 그 물건은 오늘날까지 베를린 신 박물관에 전시되어 있다.

[6]2016년에, 두 명의 독일 예술가들은 독일 정부의 정책을 극적으로 거부하는 시위를 벌였다. 그들은 게임 시스템과 사용되도록 설계된 휴대용 3D 스캐닝 장치로 비밀리에 네페르티티 여왕 머리의 데이터 맵을 만들었다. 그 스캔은 방문객 무리 가운데서 박물관의 경비원들이 시선을 돌릴 때마다 그 흉상의 주위를 빙빙 돌면서 만들어졌다. 그들은 그 후에 3D 프린터로 그 조각상의 복제품 두 개를 만들었다. 첫 번째 복제품은 이집트의 사막에 묻혔고, 두 번째 것은 카이로에 있는 박물관에 기증되었다. 그 예술가들은 "문화적 기념물로서의 고고학적 유물들은 대부분 남반구의 저개발국에서 유래하지만, 엄청난 수의 중요한 물건들을 서양의 박물관과 개인 소장품에서 찾을 수 있다. 우리는 오늘날에도 식민지적 구조가 계속해서 존재한다는 사실을 직시해야 한다"라고 선언하는 성명을 발표했다. 그 예술가들의 3D 데이터를 무료로 다운로드하고 그 여왕의 머리 복제품을 만드는 것은 여전히 가능하다. 사람들의 이목을 끌었던 그 행동은 네페르티티 흉상의 소유권에 대한 논쟁에 새로운 관심을 불러왔다.

excavation 명 발굴　archaeologist 명 고고학자
set off 일으키다, 유발하다　bust 명 흉상　limestone 명 석회
stucco 명 치장 벽토　beeswax 명 밀랍　affix 동 붙이다
quartz 명 석영　reside 동 있다　dissatisfaction 명 불만
grant 동 수여하다　downplay 동 축소하다　artifact 명 유물
unflattering 형 (사진이) 잘 나오지 않은　gypsum 명 석고
conceal 동 숨기다　acquisition 명 습득　looting 명 약탈

repatriate 동 본국으로 송환하다
ascension to the throne (왕의) 즉위 intervene 동 개입하다
relinquish 동 포기하다 repudiation 명 거부, 부인
subsequently 부 그 후에 Global South 남반구의 저개발국
colonial 형 식민지적인 stunt 명 이목을 끄는 행동

1 지문의 단어 "it"이 가리키는 것은?

(A) 머리
(B) 석회
(C) 치장 벽토
(D) 밀랍

2 1단락에 따르면, 네페르티티 여왕의 흉상은

(A) 수많은 보석들로 장식되어 있었다
(B) 고대 통치자의 개인 거주지에 전시되어 있었다
(C) 이집트 예술가의 작업장에 있었다
(D) 독일로 운송되기 전에 판매되었다

3 2단락에 따르면, 이집트인들은 보르하르트가

(A) 조각상의 외관을 바꾸기 위해 어떤 물질로 그것을 덮었다는 사실에 불만이 있다
(B) 정부의 대표자와 만나기를 거부했다는 사실에 불만이 있다
(C) 물건이 덜 가치 있게 보이도록 왜곡했다는 사실에 불만이 있다
(D) 허가 없이 유적지에서 물품을 옮겼다는 사실에 불만이 있다

4 아래 문장 중 지문 속의 음영된 문장의 핵심 정보를 가장 잘 표현한 것은?

(A) 이집트 정부는 그 조각상에 대한 독일 박물관의 권리를 거부하며, 그것을 되찾기 위해 조치를 취해 왔다.
(B) 베를린의 박물관은 그 유물에 대한 그 국가의 권리와 관련하여 이집트의 대표자들과 협상 중이다.
(C) 베를린에서 그 조각상의 인기는 이집트 관리들로 하여금 그것이 최대한 빨리 반환되도록 요구하게 했다.
(D) 그 물건의 독일 소유권을 받아들이는 것에 대한 이집트 정부의 거부는 두 국가 간의 갈등을 초래했다.

5 지문의 단어 "relinquish"와 의미가 가장 비슷한 것은?

(A) 인정하다
(B) 입증하다
(C) 이해하다
(D) 포기하다

6 4단락에 따르면, 독일 예술가들이 그 흉상의 복제품을 만든 것은

(A) 그 조각상을 되찾을 이집트의 권리를 지지하기를 희망했기 때문이다
(B) 그 흉상의 복제품을 만들기 위한 청사진을 판매하기를 희망했기 때문이다
(C) 복제품을 독일의 박물관에 전시하기를 희망했기 때문이다
(D) 복제품을 둘 다 이집트 정부에 기증하기를 희망했기 때문이다

Reading Practice 3

본문 p.72

1 (A) 2 (C) 3 (C) 4 (C) 5 (B) 6 (B)

소 가축화의 역사

수 세기 전에 고대 인류가 그것들을 가축화한 이래로, 소는 고기, 우유, 가죽 및 수송을 포함한 많은 혜택들을 인간에게 제공해 왔다. 그것들은 또한 가장 흔하게는 신 또는 조상을 기리기 위한 제물로서 종교의식에서 중요한 역할을 해왔다. 솟과의 동물들은 인류의 역사와 불가분하게 관련되어 있다. 그러나 소 가축화의 정확한 연대표는 논쟁의 대상으로 남아 있다. [2A/2B]전통적으로, 연구자들은 화석과 고고학적 증거를 조사함으로써 솟과 종들의 역사에 관해 알게 되었다. [2D]보다 최근에, 학자들은 핵 DNA보다 더 오래 견디고 유기 세포에 더 풍부한 미토콘드리아 DNA를 분석함으로써 이 분야에 대한 이해를 확장할 수 있었다.

현대의 소는 오록스로 알려진 야생 소의 한 종에서 진화했다. 지금은 멸종된 이 풀을 먹는 동물들은 거의 코끼리만큼 키가 컸고, 현재의 후손들보다 몸집이 훨씬 더 컸으며, 31인치까지 자랄 수 있는 거대한 뿔을 특징으로 했다. 그것들은 약 1,170만 년 전에 아마도 아시아에서 처음 나타났으며 자연적 원인으로 인해 폴란드에서 마지막 오록스들이 죽었던 1627년까지 존재했다. [3]멸종은 그것들이 살았던 중앙 유럽의 삼림 파괴와 아시아 및 아프리카에서의 남획의 결과로 일어났다. 그러나 그 종의 쇠퇴가 시작되기 훨씬 이전에, 사람들은 이 동물들의 유용성을 발견했다.

오록스는 오늘날의 북부 이집트와 쿠웨이트뿐만 아니라 이라크, 시리아, 레바논, 팔레스타인, 이스라엘, 요르단에 의해 차지된 영토에 걸친 지역인 비옥한 초승달 지대에서 약 10,500년 전에 최초로 가축화되었다. [5]화석과 유전자 연구는 인간이 어떠한 종의 쓰임새를 발견할 때 보통 그러하듯이, 오록스가 점차 더 작아졌다는 것을 보여주었다. 이 변화를 기록하기 위한 노력으로, 한 연구는 식용 소와 젖소가 투우용 상대보다 훨씬 더 작은 뇌를 가지고 있다는 것을 발견했다. 이 동물들은 고대 오록스의 것과 크기가 비슷한 뇌를 가지고 있었다. 몸집이 작은 소는 약 기원전 6000년경 (티그리스와 유프라테스강 사이의) 메소포타미아의 화석 기록에서 나타나기 시작한다. 중세 시대까지, 오늘날의 더 작은 황소와 소는 확고히 자리를 잡았다.

비옥한 초승달 지대에서의 오록스 길들이기는 역사 기록에서의 유일한 가축화 사례가 아니다. 두 번째의 솟과 동물 가축화 사건은 약 7,000년 전에 오늘날 파키스탄의 인더스 계곡 지역에서 일어났다. 제부로 알려진 한 혹등 소 종의 미토콘드리아 DNA는 그 동물들이 전 세계에 14억 마리가 있는 현대의 풀을 먹는 소들과 직접적으로 관련이 있다는 것을 보여준다. [6]약 기원전 6500년경 이집트 남부에서 또 하나의 사건이 일어났을 수도 있지만, 이 지역들에서 처음 가축화된 소가 사실 비옥한 초승달 지대에서 기원했다는 DNA 증거가 이 가설에 의문을 제기한다. 인간과 지금껏 교류한 가장 유용한 동물로서 말에 필적하는 동물인 현대 소의 정확한 진화를 분명하게 정의하기 위해서는 지속적인 연구가 필요하다.

domestication 명 가축화 ritual 명 의식 sacrifice 명 제물
bovine 형 솟과의 inextricably 부 불가분하게
intertwined 형 관련되어 있는 archaeological 형 고고학적인
durable 형 오래 견디는 plentiful 형 풍부한 evolve 동 진화하다
grazer 명 풀을 먹는 동물 descendant 명 후손
overhunting 명 남획 Fertile Crescent 비옥한 초승달 지대
counterpart 명 상대, 대응물 comparable to ~과 비슷한
tame 동 길들이다 humped 형 혹등의 pin down 분명하게 정의하다
rival 동 필적하다 cross paths with ~과 교류하다

1 지문의 단어 "intertwined"와 의미가 가장 비슷한 것은?

(A) 얽혀 있는

(B) 대체된
(C) 확장된
(D) 관찰된

2 1단락에서, 다음 중 소의 가축화에 관해 알아내기 위해 연구자들에 의해 연구되는 것으로 언급되지 않은 것은?
(A) 동물의 유해
(B) 인간의 유물
(C) 문서 기록
(D) 유전자 물질

3 2단락에 따르면, 다음 중 오록스에 관해 사실인 것은?
(A) 초기의 코끼리들과 자원을 두고 경쟁했다.
(B) 현대의 후손들과 크기가 비슷했다.
(C) 서식지 손실과 남획의 결과로 멸종했다.
(D) 인간에 의해 이용되기에 부적합하다고 여겨졌다.

4 지문의 단어 "those"가 가리키는 것은?
(A) 소
(B) 상대
(C) 뇌
(D) 크기

5 3단락에 따르면, 가축화 과정은
(A) 전반적인 지능의 상승을 야기한다
(B) 몸집 크기의 감소를 야기한다
(C) 건강의 개선을 야기한다
(D) 유전적 다양성의 증가를 야기한다

6 지문에 따르면, 이집트 남부에서의 가축화에 논란의 여지가 있다고 여겨지는 것은
(A) 말과 같은 다른 가축화된 종들이 그 지역에 흔하지 않았기 때문이다
(B) 솟과 종에 대한 유전적 기원에 대한 연구가 그 결론을 뒷받침하지 않기 때문이다
(C) 현대의 소들이 초기의 제부 종들과 많은 특징을 공유하지 않기 때문이다
(D) 연구가 소들이 더 먼저 인더스 계곡에서 사육되었다는 것을 보여주기 때문이다

iBT Reading Test 1

본문 p.74

1 (D)	2 (D)	3 (B)	4 (A)
5 (D)	6 (C)	7 (D)	8 (D)
9 (D)	10 (A), (C), (E)		

사바나 초원 생물 군계

사바나 초원은 초목, 기후, 야생생물 및 토양에 따라 분류되는 큰 지역인 지구의 8대 주요 육지 생물 군계들 중 하나이다. 사바나는 풀, 관목, 그리고 넓게 흩어져 있는 나무들로 특징지어진다는 점에서 숲과 사막 둘 다의 특성을 공유한다. 적도 근처에 가장 흔하게 위치해 있는 사바나는 남극 대륙을 제외한 모든 대륙에서 발견되며, 이는 지구상 육지의 약 20퍼센트에 해당한다. 북아메리카와 아시아 같은 일부 대륙에서는 사바나가 상당히 작다. 사바나 초원들의 가장 큰 집단은 아프리카에 있는데, 그곳에서 이 독특한 생물 군계는 대륙의 약 절반인 5백만 제곱마일에 걸쳐 있다.

사바나의 기후는 대단히 건조한데, 사실, 오직 두 계절만 존재한다. 강우의 강도로 인해 계절성 우기라고도 알려진 우기는 약 6개월 동안 지속되며 일반적으로 약 20에서 50인치의 강우를 특징으로 한다. 나머지 연중 내내 계속되는 건기에는 기본적으로 비가 오지 않는다. 기온은 범위가 화씨 60도에서 100도에 이르며 두 계절 내내 꽤 일정하게 유지된다.

사바나의 식물은 연중 절반 정도를 많은 물이 없이도 살아남을 수 있어야 한다. 우기 동안 풀은 꽤 두껍고 키가 크게 자라며, 때로는 10피트 높이까지 자라기도 하지만, 그 후에 물이 부족할 때는 갈색으로 변한다. [6]건기에 번개가 종종 화재를 일으키기는 하지만, 풀은 그것의 뿌리에 물을 저장하여 줄기와 잎이 화염에 의해 파괴되더라도 이것들이 무사하도록 보호하기 때문에 살아남는다. 풀뿌리는 사실 오히려 반대로 다공성의 붉은 토양에 물을 공급한다. 이러한 조건에서 살아남을 수 있는 나무는 거의 없지만, 바오바브나무는 비가 올 때만 잎을 자라게 하고 그것의 두꺼운 몸통에 물을 저장하는 방식으로 적응해 왔다. [5B]아카시아나무는 뿌리를 매우 깊게 자라게 해서, 그것들은 토양을 지나 그 아래에 있는 지하수에 도달한다. 아카시아나무는 또한 동물들로부터 그것들의 잎을 보호하도록 진화해왔다. [5A/5C]이 나무의 잎은 날카로운 가시를 가지고 있고, 종종 침을 쏘는 개미로 뒤덮여 있으며, 기린이 그것들을 씹어먹는 것을 막는 독성 화학물질을 함유하고 있다.

야생생물 또한 극단적인 기후에 대처해야 한다. 많은 종들은 가뭄을 겪고 있지 않은 지역을 찾아 사바나의 도처로 이주하는 방식으로 이것을 해낸다. [8]그곳에서 번성하는 새, 곤충 및 포유류에게는 다행스럽게도, 가뭄은 종종 국지적이다. 일부 작은 동물들은 땅속으로 파고들어 건기 동안 활동하지 않는다. 아프리카에서, 코끼리는 그것들의 긴 코와 순전히 물리적인 힘을 이용하여 바오바브나무를 부수어 열고 그 나무의 몸통에서 물을 빨아들인다. 아프리카 사바나에서 서식하는 다른 동물들에는 얼룩말, 코뿔소, 타조, 치타, 하이에나, 표범이 있다. 이 생물들은 가뭄뿐만 아니라 불과도 싸워야 한다. **예를 들어, 땅속으로 파고드는 동물들은 열과 화염을 피하기 위해 땅속으로 더 깊게 파고들어 간다.** 하지만, 검은두견이는 타고 있는 곤충을 먹기 위해 일부러 불 속으로 날아들기 때문에 들불에서 이익을 얻는다. 사바나는 살아 있는 생물들이 가혹한 조건에 적응하는 놀라운 능력을 보여준다.

biome 명 생물 군계　vegetation 명 초목　shrub 명 관목
scattered 형 흩어져 있는　equator 명 적도
amount to ~에 해당하다　distinctive 형 독특한
exceptionally 부 대단히　intensity 명 강도　constant 형 일정한
scarcity 명 부족　unharmed 형 무사한　porous 형 다공성의
adapt 동 적응하다　trunk 명 몸통; (코끼리의) 코
poisonous 형 독성의　munch on ~을 씹어 먹다
cope with ~에 대처하다　accomplish 동 해내다　drought 명 가뭄
localized 형 국지적인　burrow 동 (땅속으로) 파고들다
inactive 형 활동을 하지 않는　brute 형 순전히 물리적인
contend with ~과 싸우다　deliberately 부 일부러

1 지문에서 글쓴이는 왜 "a forest and a desert"를 언급하는가?
(A) 적도 근처의 육지에 관한 설명을 제공하기 위해
(B) 사바나가 대부분 아프리카에서 발견되는 이유를 설명하기 위해
(C) 지구상에서 가장 흔한 생물 군계를 보여주기 위해
(D) 생태계 유형의 물리적 특징들을 소개하기 위해

2 지문의 단어 "intensity"와 의미가 가장 비슷한 것은?

(A) 깊이
(B) 분배
(C) 길이
(D) 힘

3 아래 문장 중 지문 속의 음영된 문장의 핵심 정보를 가장 잘 표현한 것은? 오답은 문장의 의미를 크게 바꾸거나 핵심 정보를 생략한다.

(A) 소수의 바오바브나무만이 물을 모으고 저장하는 능력을 발달시켰다.
(B) 바오바브나무의 신체적 적응은 다른 많은 것들이 생존할 수 없는 곳에서 그것이 생존할 수 있게 한다.
(C) 가혹한 조건을 견딜 수 있는 나무들은 일반적으로 수분이 있을 때만 잎을 생산한다.
(D) 나무 몸통의 두께는 그것이 충분한 물 공급을 유지할 수 있을지를 결정한다.

4 지문의 단어 "them"이 가리키는 것은?

(A) 잎
(B) 나무
(C) 가시
(D) 기린

5 3단락에 따르면, 다음 중 아카시아나무에 관해 사실이 아닌 것은?

(A) 침을 쏘는 곤충들로 가득하다.
(B) 길고 깊은 뿌리를 가지고 있다.
(C) 잎이 유독성이다.
(D) 몸통에 물을 저장한다.

6 3단락에 따르면, 사바나의 풀은 왜 화재에서 살아남을 수 있는가?

(A) 수분을 저장하기 위해 우기에 빨리 자란다.
(B) 화염에서 줄기 내부를 보호하기 위해 두껍고 커진다.
(C) 그것의 일부가 죽지 않도록 뿌리에 수분을 저장한다.
(D) 그것의 잎이 불에 덜 타도록 토양에서 물을 흡수한다.

7 지문의 단어 "deliberately"와 의미가 가장 비슷한 것은?

(A) 직접적으로
(B) 분명하게
(C) 즉시
(D) 의도적으로

8 4단락에 따르면, 사바나의 일부 동물들에게 이주가 실용적인 전략인 것은

(A) 강우가 사바나와 접한 지역들에서 더 흔하기 때문이다
(B) 가뭄이 특정 지역에서 더 규칙적으로 발생하기 때문이다
(C) 비가 일시적인 수역 생성을 가져오기 때문이다
(D) 물 부족이 사바나의 특정 지역에 한정되기 때문이다

9 네 개의 네모[■]는 다음 문장이 삽입될 수 있는 곳을 나타내고 있다.

예를 들어, 땅속으로 파고드는 동물들은 열과 화염을 피하기 위해 땅속으로 더 깊게 파고들어 간다.

이 문장은 어디에 들어가는 것이 가장 적절한가?

10 지시: 지문 요약을 위한 도입 문장이 아래에 주어져 있다. 지문의 가장 중요한 내용을 나타내는 보기 3개를 골라 요약을 완성하라. 어떤 문장은 지문에 언급되지 않은 내용이나 사소한 정보를 나타내므로 요약에 포함되지 않는다. **이 문제는 2점이다.**

사바나 생물 군계는 그곳에 서식하는 생물들에게 커다란 도전 과제를 제시한다.
- (A) 동물들은 극단적인 기후 조건에서 살아남기 위해 많은 신체적, 행동적 특성을 얻게 되었다.
- (C) 뚜렷한 우기와 건기의 존재는 연중 대부분 동안 강우가 발생하지 않는다는 것을 의미한다.
- (E) 이러한 종류의 생태계는 장기간의 가뭄 기간 동안 죽을 가능성이 낮은 식물들을 포함한다.

(B) 바오바브나무와 아카시아나무 둘 다 물이 있을 때 물을 이용하기 위한 독특한 방법을 발달시켰다.
(D) 사바나는 아프리카에서 가장 흔하며, 그것들은 그 대륙의 상당한 부분을 차지한다.
(F) 번개에 의한 화재의 위협은 우기보다 건기에 더 높다.

iBT Reading Test 2

본문 p.78

1 (B)	2 (C)	3 (D)	4 (D)
5 (A)	6 (D)	7 (C)	8 (A)
9 (C)	10 (C), (E), (F)		

해파리 개체수 증가 요인

해파리는 2천 종 이상의 젤라틴질 동물 플랑크톤을 포함하는 광범위한 해양 생물 집단이다. 이 특이한 생물들은 동물의 생존에 중요하다고 여겨지는 대부분의 필수적인 기관들이 없다. 하지만, 그것들의 단순한 생리는 그것들이 매우 다양한 조건에 적응하도록 해준다. 이러한 적응성은 오염과 기후 변화와 같은 요인들에도 불구하고 그것들의 숫자가 증가할 수 있게 해주었다.

과학자들은 이산화탄소(CO_2) 오염이 해파리 개체수 증가에 상당한 역할을 한다고 단정한다. 이산화탄소 배출은 지구 온난화를 통해 꾸준히 기온을 변화시켜왔다. [2]이 과정은 대기로부터의 열 방출을 제한하여 공기와 물을 따뜻하게 한다. 연구자들은 더 따뜻한 물이 많은 종류의 해파리 개체군의 크기 증가를 초래했다는 것을 발견했는데, 이는 그것이 해파리가 연중 더 오랜 기간 동안 번식하고 더 많은 새끼를 낳을 수 있게 해주기 때문이다. 게다가, 대기의 이산화탄소가 물에 용해되어 탄산을 형성함에 따라, 지구 온난화는 바다의 산성화 증가를 초래한다. 산은 물의 pH 지수를 많은 유기체들에게 치명적일 수 있는 수준으로 낮춘다. [3]예를 들어, 그것은 물고기 유생의 후각 능력을 제거하여 포식자에게 취약하게 만듦으로써 그것들의 생존율을 떨어뜨린다. 하지만, 해파리에게는 높은 산성도가 거의 영향을 미치지 않는 것으로 보이며, 다른 생물들의 멸종으로 인해 생물학적 다양성이 감소하면, 해파리는 그 생태계에서 지배적이 될 수 있다.

농작물에 과도한 비료 주기 또한 비료 유출물이 결국 수원으로 들어가는 것을 말하는 부영양화를 통해 해파리 개체수에 긍정적으로 영향을 미칠 수 있다. 이 과정에서, 지나치게 영양분이 풍부한 물은 신선한 질소의 공급원을 제공함으로써 밀집한 식물 생장을 만들어낸다. 이것은 수면에 조류 대증식을 유발할 수 있으며, 대규모의 조류 개체군이 번식하고 죽어서 해저로 가라앉을 때 문제를 일으킨다. [5]그 후에 비정상적인 양의 조류 분해는 산소 공급을 크게 감소시키고, 그렇게 함으로써 산소에 의존하는 종들을 질식시켜 데드 존을 형성한다. **이 지역들은 일반적으로 큰 강들이 바다로 들어가는 곳에 형성되며 많은 생명을 부양할 수 없는 해양 사막을 만들 수 있다.** 하지만, 해파리는 저산

소 조건에 높은 내성이 있으며 이는 그것들이 부영양화가 일어난 지역에서 살아남을 수 있음을 의미한다.

게다가, 물고기 남획은 해파리 개체수를 억제하고 그것들이 새로운 영역으로 퍼지는 것을 막는 고유한 포식과 경쟁을 감소시킨다. 상업적 낚시는 해파리의 주요 포식자인 많은 수의 큰 물고기를 계속 제거하고 있다. [8]그것은 또한 동일한 먹이 자원에 의존하기 때문에 해파리의 주요 경쟁자인 멸치와 같은 작은 물고기들을 수확한다. 이 종들의 제거는 해파리의 증식을 촉진한다. 예를 들어, 1980년대 흑해에서의 어업 산업은 그 지역에서 해파리를 먹고 사는 물고기인 고등어와 블루피쉬의 돌이킬 수 없는 감소를 초래했다. 이것은 해파리 수의 엄청난 폭발을 초래했는데, 사실, 흑해의 많은 해안 지역들이 연중 특정 시기에 수백만 마리의 해파리로 범람하는 것은 이제 흔한 일이다.

gelatinous 형 젤라틴질의 zooplankton 명 동물 플랑크톤
physiology 명 생리 adaptability 명 적응성 posit 동 단정하다
acidification 명 산성화 dissolve 동 용해되다
carbonic acid 탄산 vulnerable 형 취약한 die-off 명 멸종
dominant 형 지배적인 fertilization 명 비료 주기, 비옥화
eutrophication 명 부영양화 runoff 명 유출물
provoke 동 유발하다 abnormal 형 비정상적인
decomposition 명 분해 deplete 동 크게 감소시키다
suffocate 동 질식시키다 innate 형 고유한 predation 명 포식
keep ~ in check ~을 억제하다 anchovy 명 멸치
proliferation 명 증식 irreversible 형 돌이킬 수 없는
mackerel 명 고등어 inundate 동 범람시키다

1 아래 문장 중 지문 속의 음영된 문장의 핵심 정보를 가장 잘 표현한 것은? 오답은 문장의 의미를 크게 바꾸거나 핵심 정보를 생략한다.
(A) 물 산성도의 증가는 다른 해양 종들의 희생으로 해파리의 번식을 촉진한다.
(B) 해파리는 다른 유기체들과 달리 산성도의 증가에 거의 영향을 받지 않기 때문에 서식지에서 널리 퍼질 수 있다.
(C) 물 산성화의 환경적 영향은 생물학적 다양성 감소의 주요 요인으로 확인되었다.
(D) 높은 산성도에 대처할 수 없는 생명체들은 일반적으로 생태계를 떠나고, 이는 해파리가 번성하게 한다.

2 2단락에 따르면, 다음 중 이산화탄소에 관해 사실인 것은?
(A) 해양 순환을 제한할 수 있다.
(B) 해파리를 해칠 수 있다.
(C) 열을 가둘 수 있다.
(D) 물의 pH 수준을 증가시킬 수 있다.

3 2단락에 따르면, 산성도가 높은 물은 물고기 개체군에
(A) 중요한 자원을 이동시킴으로써 영향을 미친다
(B) 수온을 변화시킴으로써 영향을 미친다
(C) 새로운 생물학적 물질을 들여옴으로써 영향을 미친다
(D) 중요한 감각을 없앰으로써 영향을 미친다

4 지문의 단어 "provoke"와 의미가 가장 비슷한 것은?
(A) 입증하다
(B) 방해하다
(C) 설득하다
(D) 조장하다

5 다음 중 3단락에서 조류에 관해 추론할 수 있는 것은?
(A) 부패하면서 많은 양의 산소를 흡수한다.
(B) 죽으면 수면으로 떠 오른다.
(C) 일부 해파리 종들의 먹이 공급원 역할을 한다.
(D) 산소가 거의 없는 물에서 더 빠르게 번식한다.

6 지문의 단어 "irreversible"과 의미가 가장 비슷한 것은?
(A) 고의적인
(B) 점차적인
(C) 중요한
(D) 영구적인

7 4단락에서 글쓴이는 왜 흑해에 관해 논하는가?
(A) 토착종이 어떻게 물고기 남획으로부터 보호될 수 있는지 설명하기 위해
(B) 특정 해파리 종이 어떻게 전 세계에 퍼졌는지 보여주기 위해
(C) 관행이 어떻게 해파리 증가의 원인이 되는지 입증하기 위해
(D) 상업적 낚시 산업을 위한 잠재적 후보를 확인하기 위해

8 4단락에 따르면, 멸치는 왜 해파리의 개체군 크기를 관리하는 요소인가?
(A) 해파리와 동일한 영양 공급원에 의존한다.
(B) 상당한 양의 해파리를 섭취한다.
(C) 해파리가 선호하는 서식지를 차지한다.
(D) 해파리를 사냥하는 포식 종을 끌어들인다.

9 네 개의 네모[■]는 다음 문장이 삽입될 수 있는 곳을 나타내고 있다.
이 지역들은 일반적으로 큰 강들이 바다로 들어가는 곳에 형성되며 많은 생명을 부양할 수 없는 해양 사막을 만들 수 있다.
이 문장은 어디에 들어가는 것이 가장 적절한가?

10 **지시:** 지문 요약을 위한 도입 문장이 아래에 주어져 있다. 지문의 가장 중요한 내용을 나타내는 보기 3개를 골라 요약을 완성하라. 어떤 문장은 지문에 언급되지 않은 내용이나 사소한 정보를 나타내므로 요약에 포함되지 않는다. **이 문제는 2점이다.**

> **전 세계의 과학자들은 최근의 해파리 개체수 폭등 이면의 요인들을 이해하려고 시도하고 있다.**
> · (C) 지나치게 영양분이 풍부한 유출물에 의한 수질 오염은 해파리 문제의 원인이 되었다.
> · (E) 지구 기온의 상승은 해파리 번식 증가에 기여했다.
> · (F) 물고기 남획은 해파리 개체군의 자연적 위험과 제한을 줄인다.

(A) 해파리는 물고기 유생을 먹음으로써 포식의 위험을 피할 수 있다.
(B) 연구자들은 해파리가 산성도가 높은 물에서 재생할 수 있다는 것을 발견했다.
(D) 해파리의 많은 자연 포식자 및 경쟁자들은 상업적으로 수익성이 있다.

Vocabulary Review

본문 p.82

1 adaptability		2 expertly	3 inactive
4 vulnerable		5 downplayed	6 porous
7 (B)	8 (D)	9 (D)	10 (C)
11 (B)	12 (D)	13 (A)	14 (C)

CHAPTER 05
Negative Fact

Example

본문 p.85

1 (B) 2 (D)

미국 남북 전쟁 이후의 토지 개혁

토지 개혁은 국가 농업 자원의 재분배이며, 일반적으로 그 국가의 정부에 의해 시작된다. 미국 정부는 미국 남북 전쟁 이후에 토지 개혁을 시도했다. 1865년 1월, 전쟁은 아직 끝나지 않았지만 결과는 명확해졌고, 정부는 승리를 준비하기 시작했다. 해결되어야 할 문제들 중 가장 중요한 것은 해방될 예정이었던 무수한 아프리카계 미국인들의 운명이었다. 북부 연방의 윌리엄 셔먼 장군은 남부 연합 주 조지아에서 아프리카계 미국인 성직자 집단과 만났다. [1D]그 집단에서 의견이 일치된 것은 아프리카계 미국인들이 자유, 교육, 토지를 원한다는 것이었다. [1A/1C]4일 후에, 셔먼은 남부 연합의 지주들에게서 몰수된 40만 에이커의 땅을 4만 아프리카계 미국인 가정을 위해 확보해두라는 명령을 내렸다. 셔먼의 명령이 각 가정이 최대 40에이커의 토지를 받을 자격이 있다고 명시했고 일부 가족들은 육군의 남아 있는 노새도 받았기 때문에 그 계획은 "40에이커와 노새"로 알려지게 되었다.

그러나, 이 토지 개혁 시도는 성공하지 못했다. [2A]셔먼의 지시는 1865년 가을에 앤드루 존슨 대통령에 의해 뒤집혔는데, 그는 그 토지가 남부 연합의 소유주들에게 반환되어야 한다고 주장했다. [2B/2C]의회에 의해 승인된 1862년의 자영 농지법과 1866년의 남부 자영 농지법과 같은 다른 토지 개혁 계획들이 해방된 노예들에게 토지를 입수할 기회를 제공했을지 모르지만, 사실상 돈에 접근할 수 없는 사람들에게는 가격이 너무 높게 책정되어 있었다. 대신, 그 계획들에 의해 제공된 토지의 대부분은 백인들에게 돌아갔다.

agrarian reform 토지 개혁 American Civil War 미국의 남북 전쟁
redistribution 명 재분배 initiate 동 시작하다 resolve 동 해결하다
Confederate 형 남부 연합의 consensus 명 의견이 일치된 것
confiscate 동 몰수하다 eligible 형 자격이 있는
leftover 형 남아 있는 mule 명 노새 directive 명 지시
reverse 동 뒤집다 procure 동 입수하다 virtually 부 사실상

1 1단락에 따르면, 다음 중 "40에이커와 노새" 계획에 관해 사실이 아닌 것은?

(A) 과거의 노예 가정들에 토지를 제공했다.
(B) 각 아프리카계 미국인 가정이 노새를 받을 것을 제안했다.
(C) 북부 연방의 윌리엄 셔먼 장군에 의해 명령되었다.
(D) 아프리카계 미국인 성직자들과의 만남에서 영감을 얻었다.

2 2단락에 따르면, 다음 중 해방된 노예들이 토지를 얻지 못하게 한 것이 아닌 것은?

(A) 미국 대통령의 의지
(B) 정부에 의해 분배된 토지의 높은 가격
(C) 토지를 매입할 자금에 대한 접근 기회 부족
(D) 의회에 의해 통과된 차별적인 법안들

Reading Practice 1

본문 p.86

1 (B) 2 (C) 3 (D) 4 (D) 5 (B) 6 (A)

애팔래치아산맥의 지질학적 특징

세계에서 가장 오래된 산맥 중 하나인 애팔래치아산맥은 앨라배마에서 캐나다의 뉴펀들랜드까지 북아메리카의 해안 지방 2,000마일을 가로질러 뻗어 있다. 그 산맥은 다양한 시대와 형성 원인을 나타내는 다양한 암석들을 특징으로 한다. [1]이것들은 정말 오래된 암석의 노출부와, 가장 유명하게는, 산업 시대에 그 지역 경제의 많은 부분에 동력을 공급했던 풍부한 석탄층을 포함한다. 애팔래치아산맥의 오랜 격동의 지질학적 역사를 연구하는 것은 어떻게 지구의 대륙들이 형성되고 오랜 세월 동안 변형되어 왔는지 관찰할 기회를 제공한다.

넓은 의미에서, 애팔래치아산맥은 두 개의 뚜렷한 하위 범주로 나누어질 수 있다. [3A]북동쪽의 구 애팔래치아산맥은 11억 년에서 5억 4,100만 년 전 사이에 형성된 결정 구조 암석들로 구성되어 있다. [3C]지각에 격심한 변동이 있었던 그 선캄브리아기에는 격렬한 화산 활동이 극도의 압력과 열로 인해 즉시 변형된 암석들을 형성했다. [3B]이는 오늘날 미국과 캐나다에서 여전히 그것의 노출부가 발견될 수 있는 단단한 화강암뿐만 아니라 석영과 대리석을 만들어냈다. 이 암석들은 지구상의 동식물 생명체 출현보다 더 오래되었으며 너무 혹독한 조건에서 형성되어 어떠한 미생물의 흔적도 지니고 있지 않다.

더 남쪽에는 2억 5,200만 년에서 5억 4,100만 년 전의 고생대로 거슬러 올라가는 퇴적암으로 대부분 이루어진 신 애팔래치아산맥이 자리 잡고 있다. 이 지역의 암석들은 더 완만하고 느린 과정을 통해 형성되었으며 동식물과의 접촉이 많아 화석이 풍부하다. [4A]사암, 혈암, 석회암 같은 이 더 부드러운 퇴적암들은 해저나, 남아메리카와 아프리카를 비롯해 오늘날의 플로리다를 포함했던 대륙인 곤드와나 대륙으로부터 융기하는 북아메리카 대륙을 갈라놓은 얕은 바다의 가장자리에 같이 쌓인 다른 암석들과 유기 물질들이 축적된 것이다. [4B]바닷속 깊은 곳이었던 일부 지역에서는 특히 구리를 포함한 금속의 풍부한 광맥이 암석으로 융합되었다. [4C]그 기간의 후반에는, 바닷물이 후퇴함에 따라, 신 애팔래치아산맥의 많은 부분이 늪지 숲으로 뒤덮였다. 이것들은 엄청난 양의 유기물질을 축적했고 나아가 오늘날의 웨스트버지니아와 펜실베이니아에서 발견되는 풍부한 석탄층을 형성했다.

그러나 그것들의 암석이 화산, 습지, 혹은 해저에서 형성되었는지와는 상관없이, 애팔래치아산맥의 양쪽 끝은 대륙 충돌이라는 동일한 원인으로 인해 주변 땅으로부터 솟아올랐다. 먼저, 약 4억 년 전에, 구 애팔래치아산맥은 최초의 북아메리카가 최초의 유럽에 충돌하면서 솟아올랐다. 그런 다음, 신 애팔래치아산맥은 2억 5,000만 년 전에 곤드와나 대륙에 충돌하면서 솟아올랐다. [6]이 충돌들은 섭입 과정을 통해 산들이 들어 올려지며 판게아 초대륙을 결합시켰을 것이며, 이는 거대한 히말라야산맥을 형성한 것과 같은 힘으로, 사실 2억 년 전에 애팔래치아산맥은 비슷한 높이였을 것이다. 이와 같이 애팔래치아산맥은 침식의 힘의 예시일 뿐만 아니라 그것들 역사의 영구적 성질에 대한 증거이기도 하다.

outcropping 명 노출부 coal bed 석탄층 tumultuous 형 격동의
subcategory 명 하위 범주 crystalline 형 결정 구조의
Precambrian era 선캄브리아기 upheaval 명 변동
predate 동 더 오래되다 microorganism 명 미생물
sedimentary rock 퇴적암 Paleozoic age 고생대
sandstone 명 사암 shale 명 혈암 accumulation 명 축적된 것
vein 명 광맥 recede 동 후퇴하다 collision 명 충돌

soar 동 솟아오르다 supercontinent 명 초대륙
subduction 명 섭입 comparable 형 비슷한 testament 명 증거

1 1단락에 따르면, 애팔래치아산맥은 그 지역에 사는 사람들에게 유익한데, 왜냐하면 그것들이
(A) 해안을 따라 아주 긴 거리를 뻗어 있기 때문이다
(B) 많은 양의 석탄을 포함하고 있기 때문이다
(C) 전 세계에서 관광객들을 끌어들이기 때문이다
(D) 다른 어디에도 없는 암석층을 특징으로 하기 때문이다

2 지문의 단어 "predate"와 의미가 가장 비슷한 것은?
(A) 촉진하다
(B) 수용하다
(C) 먼저 발생하다
(D) 부추기다

3 2단락에 따르면, 다음 중 구 애팔래치아산맥의 결정 구조 암석들의 특징이 아닌 것은?
(A) 수억 년이 되었다.
(B) 다수의 국가들에서 발견된다.
(C) 화산 폭발에 의해 형성되었다.
(D) 생명체가 발달한 이후에 만들어졌다.

4 3단락에 따르면, 다음 중 신 애팔래치아산맥의 형성에 역할을 한 것이 아닌 것은?
(A) 해양 환경에 있는 물질들의 축적
(B) 금속의 암석층으로의 편입
(C) 해수면이 낮아진 후 초목의 성장
(D) 특정 지역에 있는 거대한 석탄층의 흡수

5 아래 문장 중 지문 속의 음영된 문장의 핵심 정보를 가장 잘 표현한 것은?
(A) 서로 다른 조건에서 형성된 암석들의 존재가 애팔래치아산맥 각 부분의 특징을 결정했다.
(B) 암석들의 원천과 관계없이, 대륙들의 충돌이 애팔래치아산맥이 솟아오르는 것을 야기했다.
(C) 대륙 충돌 때문에, 애팔래치아산맥은 다양한 높이에 있는 광범위한 암석들로 구성되어 있다.
(D) 대륙의 이동은 다른 힘들과 결합하여 애팔래치아산맥의 암석들을 그것들 주변 위로 높이 들어 올렸다.

6 4단락에 따르면, 다음 중 히말라야산맥과 애팔래치아산맥의 공통점은?
(A) 섭입을 통해 형성되었다.
(B) 동시에 형성되었다.
(C) 판게아가 나타났을 때 결합되었다.
(D) 원래 곤드와나 대륙의 일부였다.

Reading Practice 2

본문 p.88

1 (C) 2 (B) 3 (C) 4 (D) 5 (C) 6 (C)

야수주의

야수주의로 알려진 20세기 초의 예술 운동은 인상주의로부터의 밝게 채색된 독립 선언으로, 그 자체로서 오래 지속된 서양 예술 전통으로부터의 중요한 단절을 상징했다. 1870년대에, 일상적인 것들에 대한 인상주의 화가들의 주관적 묘사는 회화를 역사적, 종교적, 또는 신화적 맥락에서의 사실적 형태에 대한 구속에서 해방시켰다. [1]1880년대는 인상주의의 경계를 단지 주관적인 시각적 인식을 기록하는 것에서 그들이 본 것의 감정적 영향을 표현하는 실험으로 확장시킨 빈센트 반 고흐와 폴 세잔 같은 후기 인상주의 화가들을 발견했다. [6A]하지만, 1905년경에, 이전에는 둘 다 후기 인상주의 접근법의 추종자였던 앙리 마티스와 앙드레 드랭은 자연에서 나타나는 색과는 관계없이 튜브에서 바로 짠 혼합되지 않은 색들이 감정을 표현할 수 있다는 생각에 기반한 훨씬 더 대담한 실험을 할 준비가 되어 있었다.

그 두 젊은 화가는 지중해 연안의 작은 어업항에서 전통적인 이미지들 위에 충동적으로 기이한 색상을 뿌리며 공동 작업하며 여름을 보냈다. [3A]이 그림들이 파리의 살롱 도톤에 출품되었을 때, 대개는 진보적인 심사위원단은 그것들이 불쾌하다고 느꼈다. [3B]둘 중 연장자이며 더 뛰어났던 마티스는 부자연스러운 녹색, 보라색, 분홍색의 얼룩으로 묘사된 그의 아내의 초상화인 '모자를 쓴 여인'을 회수하라는 권고를 받았다. [3D]한 친구가 그 그림이 드랭의 마티스의 얼굴을 청록색으로 그린 초상화 옆에 걸리도록 해준 후, '모자를 쓴 여인'은 유명한 미국 작가 거트루드 스타인에 의해 구매되었는데, 그녀의 오빠인 레오는 그것을 "내가 본 것 중 가장 끔찍한 물감 얼룩"이라고 묘사했다. [6B]경악한 한 평론가는 그 화가들과 그들의 작품을 "야수"를 의미하는 폄하적인 프랑스어 표현인 'fauves'라고 지칭함으로써 그 예술 운동을 정의했고, 이것은 빠르게 그 새로운 예술 운동의 이름으로 차용되었다.

야수주의 그림들은 밝은색들로 구성된 대담한 색채의 범위로 특징지어진다. 본질적으로, 야수주의 화가들은 대상이 현실에서 어떻게 보이는지를 정확히 묘사하는 것보다는 강렬한 감정을 전달하기 위해 색의 잠재력을 활용하는 것에 관심이 있었다. 그들의 목표는 소재에서 색을 해방시키고, 대신에 그것을 관객의 감정적인 반응을 자극하는 데 사용하는 것이었다. 이를 달성하기 위해, 야수주의 화가들은 종종 의도적으로 충돌하는 색들을 나란히 배치하곤 했다. **어떤 경우에는, 그들은 색 스펙트럼의 반대쪽 양 끝에서 단 몇 가지 색조만 선택하여 그림의 색채 범위로 사용함으로써 여기에서 더 나아갔다.**

야수주의 운동의 강렬함은 그것의 짧은 지속 시간과 일치했다. 1908년까지, 이 예술 양식의 발전에 중요한 역할을 했던 예술가들 중 다수가 다른 시도들로 옮겨갔다. 예를 들어, 그의 야수주의 그림들이 반복되는 기하학적 모양을 포함했던 예술가 조르주 브라크는 스페인 예술가 파블로 피카소와 함께 입체파를 개척했다. [6D]그러나, 야수주의는 지속적인 영향을 미쳤는데, 특히 표현주의와 같은 많은 현대의 예술 운동은 색에 대한 야수주의의 관대한 접근 방식을 통합했고, 그것을 구성, 선, 형태와 같은 회화의 다른 요소들에 적용했기 때문이다.

Fauvism 명 야수주의 Impressionism 명 인상주의
long-standing 형 오래 지속된 subjective 형 주관적인
rendering 명 묘사 bondage 명 구속 mythological 형 신화적인
perception 명 인식 adherent 명 추종자
impulsively 부 충동적으로 outlandish 형 기이한
progressive 형 진보적인 withdraw 동 회수하다, 철회하다
splotch 명 얼룩 turquoise 형 청록색의 smear 명 얼룩
dismayed 형 경악한 disparaging 형 폄하적인
stimulate 동 자극하다 juxtapose 동 나란히 배치하다
brevity 명 (지속 시간의) 짧음 endeavor 명 시도
geometric 형 기하학적인 Cubism 명 입체파
incorporate 동 통합하다

1 1단락에 따르면, 반 고흐와 세잔은 어떻게 인상주의의 경계를 확장했는가?
(A) 신화적 기원을 가진 대상들을 포함했다.
(B) 시각적 자극의 해석을 표현하려 노력했다.
(C) 장면이 불러일으키는 감정을 전달하려 시도했다.
(D) 흔한 사물을 예술적 맥락에 배치했다.

2 지문의 단어 "outlandish"와 의미가 가장 비슷한 것은?
(A) 외부의
(B) 이상한
(C) 일관성 없는
(D) 의무적인

3 2단락에 따르면, 다음 중 마티스의 그림 '모자를 쓴 여인'에 관해 사실이 아닌 것은?
(A) 소개되었을 때 논란을 일으켰다.
(B) 마티스와 관계가 있었던 사람을 묘사한다.
(C) 처음에 마티스가 그린 자신의 초상화 옆에 전시되었다.
(D) 미국의 유명한 작가에 의해 구매되었다.

4 네 개의 네모[■]는 다음 문장이 삽입될 수 있는 곳을 나타내고 있다.
어떤 경우에는, 그들은 색 스펙트럼의 반대쪽 양 끝에서 단 몇 가지 색조만 선택하여 그림의 색채 범위로 사용함으로써 여기에서 더 나아갔다.
이 문장은 어디에 들어가는 것이 가장 적절한가?

5 지문의 단어 "stimulate"와 의미가 가장 비슷한 것은?
(A) 관리하다
(B) 무시하다
(C) 불러일으키다
(D) 떼어내다

6 다음 중 야수주의에 관해 언급되지 않은 것은?
(A) 그것을 발전시킨 사람들은 후기 인상주의 운동의 지지자들이었다.
(B) 그것의 이름은 평론가의 경멸적인 논평에서 유래되었다.
(C) 그것의 작품들은 현실을 더 정확하게 반영하기 위해 이례적인 색들을 포함했다.
(D) 그것의 전제는 그 이후의 예술 양식들에 의해 차용되고 확장되었다.

Reading Practice 3

본문 p.90

1 (B) 2 (C) 3 (D) 4 (B) 5 (C) 6 (A)

알렉산더 대왕의 제국

알렉산더 대왕은 기원전 336년에 그가 마케도니아의 왕이 된 거의 그 순간부터 군사 정복을 시작했다. 그 20세의 통치자는 아버지인 필립 2세에 의해 이미 연합되어 있었던 그리스 도시국가 무리를 상속받았고, 그 왕국을 넓히기를 열망했다. 어린 시절 그의 스승이었던 위대한 그리스 철학자 아리스토텔레스의 영향을 받아, 알렉산더는 전 세계 곳곳에 그리스 문화를 전파하기로 다짐했다. 하지만, 그는 그렇게 하기 위해서는 그가 정복한 국가의 문화를 존중해야 할 것임을 알고 있었다. [1]겉보기에는 상충하는 이 두 가지 목표의 균형을 맞춤으로써, 알렉산더는 그때까지의 세계에서 가장 광범위한 제국을 건설할 수 있었다.

필립 2세가 왕실 경호원에 의해 암살된 후, 알렉산더의 첫 번째 목표는 페르시아 제국을 제패하려는 아버지의 꿈을 실현하는 것이었다. [2D]페르시아인들은 발칸 반도에서 파키스탄에 이르는 넓은 영토를 지배했고 그리스 국가들을 점령하려고 시도했었다. [2B]기원전 334년, 알렉산더는 오늘날 튀르키예의 서쪽 부분에 있는 도시들을 침공하여 페르시아인들을 그들의 해군 기지와 단절시켰다. 이듬해에, 그는 심한 수적 열세에도 불구하고 현대의 시리아 근처에서의 전투에서 페르시아의 다리우스 3세를 물리쳤다. [2A]처음부터, 알렉산더는 페르시아의 옷을 입고, 페르시아의 관습들 중 다수를 차용하고, 패배한 지도자들이 일상적인 업무를 계속 수행할 권리를 인정함으로써 페르시아 문화에 대한 큰 존중을 보여주었다. 그는 적의 방식을 받아들이는 것에 너무 열심이어서 그의 일부 동료들은 그것 때문에 그를 원망하기 시작했다.

그러고 나서 알렉산더는 북아프리카로 진군하여 한때 세계에서 으뜸가는 세력이었던 이집트를 정복했다. 그는 파라오의 자리에 앉혀줄 것을 요청했고, 이는 그가 사제들뿐만 아니라 이집트 대중의 환심을 사게 해주었다. 자신의 문화를 전파하기 위해 이 정치적 자산을 이용하며, 그는 그리스식 도시인 알렉산드리아를 세웠는데, 그것은 그리스식 극장과 그리스식 경기장을 특징으로 했으며 그것의 어마어마한 그리스식 도서관으로 유명해졌다. 이것이 완료되자, 알렉산더는 그의 군대를 인도의 펀자브 지역으로 이동시켰다. 기원전 326년에, 그는 파우라바의 포루스 왕과 전투에서 만났다. 그 마케도니아 황제가 코끼리가 측면에 배치된 군대를 만난 것은 그것이 처음이었다. [4]그는 그 거대한 동물들을 창으로 공격하라고 명령했지만, 그것은 양쪽 군대가 모두 짓밟히는 혼란스러운 상황을 만들어냈을 뿐이었다. 그러나, 결국 포루스의 미숙한 병사들은 알렉산더의 능숙한 전사들에게 상대가 되지 못했다. 알렉산더는 포루스를 왕처럼 대우하는 것에 동의했고 그의 적들을 존중하는 태도를 취함으로써 다시 한번 정치적 이득을 얻었다.

[6B/6C/6D]그 위대한 전사왕은 아마도 말라리아나, 그의 제국을 차지하려는 경쟁자에 의한 암살, 또는 포도주 과음의 희생자가 되어 32세의 나이로 사망했으나, 알렉산더 대왕이 그에게 알려져 있던 세계의 먼 곳들로 가져다준 그리스의 영향은 수 세기 동안 지속되었다. 그는 자신의 군대로 정복한 영토들이 그것들의 본질적인 특성을 유지하도록 허용하는 동시에 그리스 사상을 전파한다는 주요 목표를 둘 다 성취했다.

conquest 명 정복 inherit 동 상속받다 city-state 명 도시국가
aspire 동 열망하다 conquer 동 정복하다 seemingly 부 겉보기에
conflicting 형 상충하는 expansive 형 광범위한
assassinate 동 암살하다 fulfill 동 실현하다 defeat 동 물리치다
take over 점령하다, 차지하다 cut off 단절시키다 naval 형 해군의
outnumber 동 수가 더 많다 acknowledge 동 인정하다
affair 명 업무 zealous 형 열심인 resent 동 원망하다
propagate 동 전파하다 encounter 동 만나다 javelin 명 창
chaotic 형 혼란스러운 trample 동 짓밟다
inexperienced 형 미숙한 overconsumption 명 과음, 과식

1 1단락에 따르면, 다음 중 알렉산더 대왕의 제국에 관해 사실인 것은?
(A) 대부분이 그의 아버지로부터 상속되었다.
(B) 그 당시의 세계 역사에서 가장 큰 것이었다.
(C) 전부 군사 정복을 통해 얻어졌다.
(D) 정복된 국가의 문화를 억압했다.

2 2단락에 따르면, 다음 중 페르시아인들에 관해 사실이 아닌 것은?

(A) 그들의 통치자들은 알렉산더의 승리 후에 권력을 유지했다.
(B) 오늘날 튀르키예의 일부인 지역에 군사 시설을 운영했다.
(C) 그들의 군대는 항상 알렉산더의 군대보다 작았다.
(D) 그리스인들에 의해 지배되는 영토를 정복하려고 노력했었다.

3 지문의 단어 "propagate"와 의미가 가장 비슷한 것은?
(A) 조사하다
(B) 무시하다
(C) 근절하다
(D) 퍼뜨리다

4 다음 중 3단락에서 포루스 왕에 관해 추론할 수 있는 것은?
(A) 마케도니아인들에게서 배운 전술을 이용하여 펀자브를 정복했다.
(B) 전투에서 코끼리를 사용하는 그의 전략은 비효율적인 것으로 증명되었다.
(C) 그의 군대는 마케도니아인들과 싸우기 전에 많은 전투에 참여했다.
(D) 전투에서 알렉산더에게 패배한 후 처형되었다.

5 지문의 단어 "their"가 가리키는 것은?
(A) 목표
(B) 사상
(C) 영토
(D) 군대

6 다음 중 4단락에서 알렉산더의 죽음에 대한 잠재적인 설명으로 언급되지 않은 것은?
(A) 전투에서 부상을 입었다.
(B) 질병에 걸렸다.
(C) 술을 너무 많이 마셨다.
(D) 정적에 의해 살해되었다.

iBT Reading Test 1

본문 p.92

1 (C) 2 (A) 3 (A) 4 (A)
5 (C) 6 (A) 7 (B) 8 (B)
9 (D) 10 (B), (C), (F)

유기 농업의 환경적 비용

전통적인 농업의 과잉에 대해 우려하는 환경에 관심이 있는 많은 소비자들의 마음속에서 유기농 제품은 "환경친화적인" 대안이다. 이러한 인식은 유기 농장이 토양을 손상시키고 지역 생태계의 생물 다양성을 감소시키며 수자원을 오염시키고 농부들의 건강을 해칠 수 있는 합성 농약이나 비료를 사용하지 않는다는 사실에 뿌리를 두고 있다. 따라서, 전통적인 제품들보다 훨씬 더 높은 가격에도 불구하고, 미국에서 유기농 제품 판매로 인한 수익은 2020년 523억 달러에서 2028년까지 950억 달러로 증가할 것으로 예상된다. 남아시아 국가 부탄은 심지어 2035년까지 100퍼센트 유기농으로 전환하는 것을 목표로 하고 있다. 그러나, 대부분의 소비자들은 유기 농업의 환경적 비용에 대해 알지 못한다.

유기 농장들은 사실 전통적인 농장들보다 우리 대기의 탄소 부담을 증가시키며, 그렇게 함으로써 기후 변화의 위험을 증가시킨다. 문제는 화학 살충제가 (인간을 포함하여) 많은 유기체들에게 잠재적으로 해롭기는 하지만 농작물 수확량을 증가시키는 데 실제로 효과적이라는 것이다. [4]유기 농장들은 곤충과 다른 해충들에게 농작물을 잃기 때문에, 그것들은 전통적인 농장들과 같은 양의 농작물을 재배하기 위해 더 많은 땅을 필요로 한다. 식량을 위한 더 많은 땅은 숲을 위한 땅이 줄어들게 하며, 그 결과로 초래되는 저장되는 탄소 양의 감소는 지구 온난화에 대한 직접적인 원인 제공자인데, 이는 대기에 더 많은 양의 온실가스가 축적되기 때문이다.

또한 우려되는 것은 유기농 농부들에 의해 사용되는 천연 농약과 비료 일부의 환경적 비용이다. [5]많은 유기 농장은 농작물을 먹는 생물들을 막기 위해 유황을 사용하는데, 이는 그것이 합성 화학물질로 만들어진 농약보다 독성이 덜하다고 여겨지기 때문이다. 이 물질은 비교적 덜 해롭기는 하지만, 여전히 그것의 사용과 관련된 심각한 문제들이 있다. 예를 들어, 유황을 다루는 농부들은 현장 작업 동안 자극을 피하기 위해 눈 및 피부 보호구를 반드시 착용해야 하며, 그것은 또한 해로운 산성비를 야기한다고 알려져 있다. 게다가, 거름이 천연 비료이기는 하지만, 거름에 의해 생산된 질소의 50퍼센트 미만이 농작물에 의해 흡수된다. **나머지는 지하수를 오염시키고 결국 온실가스로 대기에 들어가게 될 수 있다.** 어떤 물질이 자연적으로 생산되었다는 것이 반드시 그것이 환경에 해롭지 않다는 것을 의미하지는 않는다.

농업에 대한 유기농 접근에 의해 제기되는 환경적 우려를 해결하기 위해서는 다양한 해결책이 요구된다. 그것들이 대규모 농작물 수확량을 생산하는 데 덜 효율적이기 때문에, 유기 농장들은 온실가스 배출의 위험한 증가를 만들어내지 않고서는 향후 30년 동안 예상되는 전 세계 식량 수요의 59퍼센트 증가를 충족시키지 못할 수도 있다. [8A]따라서, 세계의 농업 산업은 유기 농업과 전통적인 농업 사이에서 균형을 이루어야만 한다. 환경적으로 해로운 농약과 비료 문제와 관련해서, 산업화된 국가들의 유기농 농부들은 인도 같은 개발도상국의 유기농 농부들로부터 배울 수 있다. [8C/8D]그곳에서, 유기 농장들은 자연적으로 해충을 억제하는 식물들을 재배하고 질소의 유기적인 공급원으로 거름이나 합성 비료 대신 콩과 식물을 사용함으로써 생물 다양성을 지속가능성을 위한 전략으로 이용한다.

conscious 형 관심이 있는 excess 명 과잉
conventional 형 전통적인 alternative 명 대안
perception 명 인식 synthetic 형 합성의
biodiversity 명 생물 다양성 contaminate 동 오염시키다
compromise 동 해치다 considerably 부 훨씬 revenue 명 수익
potentially 부 잠재적으로 sulfur 명 유황 deter 동 막다
irritation 명 자극 manure 명 거름 demand 명 수요
strike a balance 균형을 이루다 industrialized 형 산업화된
sustainability 명 지속가능성 inhibit 동 억제하다
legume 명 콩과 식물

1 지문의 단어 "conscious"와 의미가 가장 비슷한 것은?
(A) 주류의
(B) 신중한
(C) 관심이 많은
(D) 순응하는

2 1단락에서 글쓴이는 왜 부탄을 언급하는가?
(A) 유기 농업이 증가할 것으로 예상되는 정도를 강조하기 위해
(B) 유기 농업 방식이 미국 밖에서 유래했다는 것을 시사하기 위해
(C) 유기 농산물의 가격이 크게 오른 이유를 설명하기 위해
(D) 세계 각국 유기농 제품의 가치를 비교하기 위해

3 지문의 단어 "they"가 가리키는 것은?

(A) 농장들
(B) 농작물
(C) 곤충
(D) 해충들

4 2단락에 따르면, 다음 중 유기 농장들에 관해 사실인 것은?

(A) 전통적인 농장들보다 농작물 수확량이 적다.
(B) 전통적인 농장들보다 더 적은 땅을 사용한다.
(C) 전통적인 농장들보다 더 많은 탄소 배출을 포획한다.
(D) 환경적인 관점에서 전통적인 농장들보다 더 바람직하다.

5 3단락에 따르면, 유황의 사용은 왜 유기농 농부들에게 인기 있는 해충 방제 방식인가?

(A) 농장 노동자들에게 건강 문제를 일으키지 않는다.
(B) 식물에 대한 산성 강수의 영향을 중화시킨다.
(C) 인공적인 제품만큼 해를 끼치지 않는다.
(D) 다른 종류의 농약보다 훨씬 더 저렴하다.

6 아래 문장 중 지문 속의 음영된 문장의 핵심 정보를 가장 잘 표현한 것은? 오답은 문장의 의미를 크게 바꾸거나 핵심 정보를 생략한다.

(A) 증가하는 인구에게 공급하기 위해 수확량이 더 적은 유기 농장들에 의존하는 것은 온실가스 배출량 증가를 초래할 것이다.
(B) 온실가스가 증가해왔기 때문에 인구 증가는 유기 농장들이 적절한 수확량을 생산하지 못하게 할 수도 있다.
(C) 유기 농장들은 증가하는 인구에 의해 요구되는 식량을 생산하기에 충분한 땅을 가지고 있지 않다.
(D) 향후 30년 동안 식량에 대한 수요가 상승하면 온실가스는 증가할 것이다.

7 지문의 단어 "inhibit"과 의미가 가장 비슷한 것은?

(A) 암시하다
(B) 막다
(C) 해방시키다
(D) 관리하다

8 다음 중 4단락에서 잠재적인 해결책으로 언급되지 않은 것은?

(A) 유기농 기술과 전통적인 농업 기술을 둘 다 사용하기
(B) 대기로 질소를 방출하기 위해 콩과 식물 기르기
(C) 농약을 필요로 하지 않는 작물 선택하기
(D) 특정한 종류의 비료 사용 피하기

9 네 개의 네모[■]는 다음 문장이 삽입될 수 있는 곳을 나타내고 있다.

나머지는 지하수를 오염시키고 결국 온실가스로 대기에 들어가게 될 수 있다.

이 문장은 어디에 들어가는 것이 가장 적절한가?

10 **지시:** 지문 요약을 위한 문장이 아래에 주어져 있다. 지문의 가장 중요한 내용을 나타내는 보기 3개를 골라 요약을 완성하라. 어떤 문장은 지문에 언급되지 않은 내용이나 사소한 정보를 나타내므로 요약에 포함되지 않는다. **이 문제는 2점이다.**

> **파악된 유기 농업의 이점들에도 불구하고, 이 관행은 환경에 해를 끼치는 것으로 알려져 있다.**
>
> · (B) 감소된 농작물 생산은 더 많은 땅의 이용을 필요하게 만들며, 대기 탄소를 줄일 잠재력이 있는 나무를 더 적게 남겨놓는다.
> · (C) 유기 및 전통적인 농업 방식을 병행하고 덜 해로운 유기 농업 관행을 채택하는 것은 유망한 해결책이다.
> · (F) 유기농 방식의 해충 방제와 토양에 비료 주기는 대기와 수질 오염 모두에 일조한다.

(A) 농작물 수확량의 감소는 많은 유기농 농부들이 더 독성 있는 형태의 농약 사용을 시작하도록 이끌었다.
(D) 유기농 제품들의 전반적인 가치는 크게 상승해 왔으며, 이러한 추세는 가까운 미래에도 계속될 것으로 보인다.
(E) 개발도상국의 농부들은 환경 문제들을 해결하기 위해 더 발전된 유기농 기술들을 채택해야 한다.

iBT Reading Test 2

본문 p.96

1 (B) 2 (D) 3 (D) 4 (B)
5 (B) 6 (A) 7 (B) 8 (B)
9 (C) 10 (A), (C), (D)

계산기의 역사

[2A/2B]재능 있는 수학자이자 발명가인 블레즈 파스칼은 프랑스 남부 작은 마을 세금 징수원의 아들이었다. 아버지의 일을 돕기 위해, 그는 기어로 연결된 열 개의 번호가 매겨진 톱니바퀴로 구성된 간단한 계산기를 고안했다. 파스칼린이라 불린 이 최초의 기계식 계산기는 최대 8자리의 숫자들을 더하고 뺄 수 있었다. [2C]수동 계산에 비해 상당한 개선을 제공하기는 했지만, 그 기계는 비싸고 신뢰할 수 없는 것으로 간주되었으며, 그것이 오작동하는 경우 오직 파스칼 자신만이 필요한 수리를 할 수 있는 지식을 가지고 있었다. 게다가, 회계사들은 그들의 일자리를 잃을 것을 우려하여 그 기계의 사용을 막았다. 이러한 문제들에도 불구하고, 파스칼의 혁신적인 장치는 미래의 장치들을 위한 토대를 마련했고 현대 컴퓨터의 선구자였다.

발명가 윌리엄 수어드 버로스의 이름을 딴 버로스 계산기는 1885년에 제작되어 특허를 받았다. 이 계산기는 계산을 수행하기 위해 사용자가 손잡이를 당겨야 했다. 초보 사용자들은 그들이 그것에 가한 힘의 양에 따라 매우 다른 계산 결과를 얻었다. [5]초기 기계들의 설계상의 결함과 막대한 가격은 상업적인 실패로 이어졌고, 첫 50개는 회수되었다. 그러나 버로스는 유압 조속기 사용을 포함한 개선된 계산기에 계속해서 공을 들였다. 그 부품은 손잡이가 당겨진 방식과 관계없이 그 기계가 제대로 작동할 수 있게 해주었다. 그 기계는 사업체들에게 인기를 얻었고, 세기가 바뀔 무렵에는 매출이 극적으로 증가했다. **사실, 그 기계는 매우 성공적이어서, 버로스가 설립한 회사는 미국 최대의 계산기 제조업체가 되었다.** 이후 모델들에는 손으로 구동되는 손잡이를 대체할 전자 모터가 포함되었다. 이 2세대 모델에는 누를 수 있는 키들 또한 추가되었고, 그것의 계산 결과를 종이에 인쇄할 수 있는 기능이 있었다.

1887년에는 도르 펠트라는 이름의 젊은 기술자가 키보드를 이용하는 최초의 실용적인 계산기를 개발했는데, 이것은 컴토미터라고 명명되었다. [7]그의 설계는 키가 눌린 후 원래 상태로 돌아갈 수 있도록 하는 충분히 빠른 캐리 메커니즘과 계산 결과를 지우는 레버를 기반으로 했다. 이 기계들은 매우 빠르고 신뢰할 만했지만, 조작에 대해 특별히 훈련된 전문가에 의해서 사용되어야 했다. 그 기계는 그것의 독특한 능력 때문에 40년 넘게 생산되었고, 이 시기 중에 그것에 많은 개선이 이루어졌다.

[8C]안전장치가 되어 있는 키가 기계를 삼갔고, 이는 이전의 모델들에서 그랬던 것처럼 부분적인 누름이 오류를 발생시키는 것을 막았다. [8A]키가 무제한으로 눌러질 수 있었고, 이는 더 빠른 계산을 가능하게 했다. [8D]이중 설계라고 불리는 또 다른 기능은 첫 번째 톱니바퀴가 계속해서 덧셈을 하는 동안 두 번째 다이얼 톱니바퀴 세트에 누계를 가지고 있었으며, 또 언제든지 누계로 옮겨질 수 있는 소계를 가지고 있었다.

subtract 동 빼다 substantial 형 상당한
unreliable 형 신뢰할 수 없는 malfunction 동 오작동하다
innovative 형 혁신적인 groundwork 명 토대
precursor 명 선구자 patent 동 특허를 내다 execute 동 수행하다
novice 형 초보인 flaw 명 결함 prohibitive 형 막대한
commercial 형 상업적인 hydraulic governor 유압 조속기
catch on with ~에게 인기를 얻다 crank 명 손잡이
depressible 형 누를 수 있는 exceedingly 부 매우
fail-safe 형 안전장치가 되어 있는 partial 형 부분적인
duplex 형 이중의 subtotal 명 소계

1 지문에서 글쓴이는 왜 "the modern computer"를 언급하는가?

(A) 파스칼의 계산기가 매우 다양한 유용한 기능을 가지고 있었다는 것을 시사하기 위해
(B) 발명품이 이후 기술들의 개발에 미친 영향을 강조하기 위해
(C) 파스칼의 계산기가 그 당시의 다른 계산기들보다 진보적이었다는 것을 증명하기 위해
(D) 계산을 하기 위해 사용되는 서로 다른 종류의 장치들을 비교하기 위해

2 1단락에서, 다음 중 글쓴이가 블레즈 파스칼에 관해 언급하지 않은 것은?

(A) 그의 아버지는 정부 관리였다.
(B) 산수에 관해 아는 것이 많았다.
(C) 그의 계산기는 많은 결함을 가지고 있었다.
(D) 회계사 직업을 가지고 있었다.

3 지문의 단어 "execute"와 의미가 가장 비슷한 것은?

(A) 수정하다
(B) 내보이다
(C) 확인하다
(D) 수행하다

4 지문의 단어 "it"이 가리키는 것은?

(A) 기계
(B) 손잡이
(C) 계산
(D) 힘

5 2단락에 따르면, 다음 중 초기의 버로스 계산기에 관해 사실인 것은?

(A) 파스칼린의 설계를 면밀히 모방했다.
(B) 많은 구매자들을 끌어모으지 못했다.
(C) 대다수의 사람들에게 알맞은 가격이었다.
(D) 특허를 받는 데 실패했다.

6 아래 문장 중 지문 속의 음영된 문장의 핵심 정보를 가장 잘 표현한 것은? 오답은 문장의 의미를 크게 바꾸거나 핵심 정보를 생략한다.

(A) 그 장치는 그것의 생산기간 동안 개선되었는데, 그것의 특별한 기능들 때문에 그 기간은 상당했다.
(B) 그 장치가 제조된 긴 기간은 그것의 설계에 대한 여러 개선의 결과였다.
(C) 그 장치는 40년 넘게 사용되었지만, 그것의 기능에는 많은 변화가 있었다.
(D) 그것의 특이한 능력 때문에, 그 계산기는 예상되었던 것보다 훨씬 더 오래 사용되었다.

7 3단락에 따르면, 초기의 컴토미터는

(A) 여러 개의 키보드가 부착될 수 있게 하는 부품을 포함했다
(B) 키가 원래의 자리로 돌아갈 수 있게 하는 부품을 포함했다
(C) 조작자가 정확하지 않은 데이터를 입력하는 것을 방지하는 부품을 포함했다
(D) 레버를 사용해서 계산 결과를 지울 필요를 없애는 부품을 포함했다

8 4단락에 따르면, 다음 중 컴토미터에 대한 개선이 아니었던 것은?

(A) 계산 속도를 높이는 기능
(B) 오류를 삭제하는 메커니즘
(C) 안전장치가 되어 있는 키
(D) 두 세트의 다이얼 톱니바퀴

9 네 개의 네모[■]는 다음 문장이 삽입될 수 있는 곳을 나타내고 있다.

사실, 그 기계는 매우 성공적이어서, 버로스가 설립한 회사는 미국 최대의 계산기 제조업체가 되었다.

이 문장은 어디에 들어가는 것이 가장 적절한가?

10 **지시:** 지문 요약을 위한 도입 문장이 아래에 주어져 있다. 지문의 가장 중요한 내용을 나타내는 보기 3개를 골라 요약을 완성하라. 어떤 문장은 지문에 언급되지 않은 내용이나 사소한 정보를 나타내므로 요약에 포함되지 않는다. **이 문제는 2점이다.**

계산기는 수백 년에 걸쳐 여러 사람들에 의해 개발되었다.
- (A) 도르 펠트는 계산을 하기 위해 필요한 정보를 입력하는 키보드를 가진 최초의 유용한 장치의 발명가이다.
- (C) 비록 블레즈 파스칼에 의해 발명된 계산기가 상당한 문제점들을 가지고 있었지만, 그의 노력은 이후의 더 효율적인 장치들을 위한 토대를 마련했다.
- (D) 윌리엄 버로스가 그가 개발한 계산기의 설계에 대한 초기의 문제점들을 해결하자, 그것은 소비자들에게 인기를 얻었다.

(B) 블레즈 파스칼은 그의 아버지가 업무를 수행하는 동안 큰 액수를 계산하는 것을 보면서 계산기를 만드는 방법을 배웠다.
(E) 비록 도르 펠트의 장치가 조작자로 하여금 다른 기계들로 할 수 있었던 것보다 더 빠르게 계산을 수행할 수 있게 해주었지만, 그것은 매우 신뢰할 수 없었다.
(F) 여러 해 동안 파스칼과 함께 회계사로 일한 후, 버로스는 자신만의 스타일의 계산기를 설계하고 만들기 시작했다.

Vocabulary Review

본문 p.100

1 Adherents		2 testament	3 upheavals
4 confiscated		5 tumultuous	6 deter
7 (A)	8 (A)	9 (C)	10 (C)
11 (B)	12 (A)	13 (A)	14 (D)

CHAPTER 06
Inference

Example

본문 p.103

1 (A) 2 (C)

새의 깃털

깃털의 모양과 크기는 새의 종류에 따라 다르지만, 형성 과정은 모든 경우에 동일하다. 깃털은 피부 속에 있는 혈관으로부터 영양분을 받는 조직이 뻗어 나온 것이다. [1]깃털이 완전히 자라면, 혈액 공급이 중단되고 중간의 통로는 비게 된다. 만약 깃털이 털갈이라고 알려진 과정을 통해 떨어지거나 뽑히면, 새의 갑상샘에서 나온 분비물은 모낭을 자극하여 새로운 깃털이 성장하도록 한다.

깃털은 여러 목적을 수행한다. 새가 비행에 깃털을 사용하려면, 깃털은 매우 강해야 하지만 또한 가볍고 유연해야 한다. 무거운 깃털을 가진 새들은 공중에 뜰 수 없다. 깃털은 질서 있는 방식으로 몸 위에 배열되어 있다. 그것들은 서로 겹쳐 있으며 대부분의 경우 새 피부의 대부분을 덮고 있다. 곡선과 유선형으로 이렇게 겹쳐 있는 것은 비행에 안성맞춤이다. 깃털은 또한 다양한 형태의 표현과 위장을 위해 새들에게 유용하다. [2]예를 들어, 왕 극락조의 알록달록하고 나선형인 깃털은 그것이 짝을 찾는 것을 돕고, 앵무새의 밝은 녹색 깃털은 그것이 우림에서 그것의 주변 환경에 섞여 드는 것을 돕는다. 일부 기후에서, 새들은 추위와 비로부터의 단열을 위해 깃털을 필요로 한다. 예를 들어, 아비새는 대부분의 시간을 물에서 지내는데, 이는 그것들 깃털의 방수 특성을 필수적인 것으로 만든다.

outgrowth 명 뻗어 나온 것 tissue 명 조직 nourishment 명 영양분
blood vessel 혈관 halt 동 중단하다 shaft 명 통로
hollow 형 빈 molting 명 털갈이 secretion 명 분비물
thyroid gland 갑상샘 stimulate 동 자극하다 follicle 명 모낭
flexible 형 유연한 airborne 형 공중에 뜨는 overlap 동 겹치다
streamlined 형 유선형의 spiraling 형 나선형의
insulation 명 단열 waterproof 형 방수의

1 다음 중 1단락에서 깃털에 관해 추론할 수 있는 것은?
(A) 깃털은 완전히 자라기 전에 혈액을 포함하고 있다.
(B) 나이 든 새들은 털갈이 후에 새로운 깃털들을 만들어낼 수 없다.
(C) 새의 혈관은 모낭이 새로운 깃털을 자라게 하도록 자극한다.
(D) 깃털이 떨어지면, 새로운 모낭이 피부 속에서 자란다.

2 2단락에서, 글쓴이가 왕극락조에 관해 암시하는 것은?
(A) 깃털의 모양과 질감 때문에 비행이 불가능하다.
(B) 암컷에 의해 이용되는 표현 방식은 그들의 짝짓기 가능성을 높인다.
(C) 시각적인 모습이 수컷의 번식 성공에서 역할을 한다.
(D) 깃털의 특성이 위장을 효과적인 생존 방법으로 만든다.

Reading Practice 1

본문 p.104

1 (A) 2 (B) 3 (D) 4 (D) 5 (D) 6 (C)

인간의 활동과 침식

침식은 종종 물이나 바람에 의한 토양의 운반을 수반한다. 전자의 경우, 폭우나 범람한 강에서 나온 물이 지표면 위로 이동하면서 토양을 옮겨놓는다. 바람에 의한 침식은 강한 기류가 토양 입자를 들어 올려 그것들을 먼 거리로 운반할 때 발생한다. 방법과 관계없이, 최종 결과는 항상 같은데, 많은 양의 토양이 광대한 지역에 분산된다는 것이다. [1]침식이 자연적인 과정이긴 하지만, 그것은 농사와 벌목 같은 인간의 활동에 의해 악화된다.

토양은 농업 관행, 특히 기계식 밭갈이로 인해 침식에 취약해질 수 있다. 이 과정은 씨앗이 심어질 수 있도록 토양의 표면을 느슨하게 하는 트랙터의 사용을 수반한다. [3]안타깝게도, 그 무거운 기계들은 밑에 있는 토양을 압축시키는데, 이는 물이 쉽게 침투할 수 없다는 것을 의미한다. 그 후에 토양은 메말라져 바람에 매우 취약해진다. 이것의 주목할만한 예시는 1930년대 북아메리카의 더스트볼인데, 이때 미국 중부는 대기를 통해 수백만 톤의 표토를 운반하는 먼지 폭풍에 의해 강타당했다. 이 폭풍들은 많은 지역을 농작물을 기르기에 적합하지 않게 만들었고 많은 농업 노동자들이 이주하도록 강제했다. 그 사건은 부분적으로 미국 농업 산업의 빠른 기계화에 의해 촉발되었는데, 농부들은 그들의 새로운 동력화된 장비로 광대한 땅을 경작해서, 토양을 침식에 위태롭게 노출시켰다.

침식에 기여하는 또 다른 인간의 활동은 과도한 방목이다. [5]가축이 한 지역에서 장기간 지속적으로 야생 풀과 관목을 먹도록 허용되면, 그 식물들은 회복하지 못하며 땅에는 곧 초목이 부족해진다. 표토가 드러나면, 물과 바람에 의한 침식은 상당한 위험이 된다. 아마도 과도한 방목의 영향이 사헬에서보다 더 뚜렷한 곳은 없을 것이다. 대서양부터 홍해까지 뻗어 있는 아프리카의 이 지역은 사하라 사막과 더 먼 남쪽에 있는 더 비옥한 사바나 사이의 경계를 형성한다. 항상 홍수에 취약해 왔음에도 불구하고, 사헬은 오랫동안 농부들과 유목 생활을 하는 목자들을 부양했다. 그러나, 20세기 초반의 인구 증가는 늘어나는 수의 소와 양이 그 땅에 방목되는 결과를 낳았다. 아주 짧은 시간 안에, 이 지역의 많은 부분에 초목이 없게 되었으며 침식을 겪게 되었다.

벌목 작업은 침식과 관련한 또 하나의 중요한 요인인데, 이는 삼림벌채가 토양의 유동성에 직접적으로 기여하기 때문이다. 나무뿌리들은 토양을 제자리에 고정시키고, 이것들이 제거되면 침식의 위협이 상당히 높아진다. 이것은 1940년부터 1963년까지 우림의 약 50퍼센트를 잃은 코스타리카의 사례에서 잘 보여진다. [6]모순적이게도, 농사에 적합하게 만들기 위해 많은 땅이 개간되었지만, 그 과정은 연간 8억 6,000만 톤의 표토 유실을 초래했다. 침식된 토양은 강과 개울로 흘러들어 하류로 운반되어 바다로 들어갔고 그 땅이 이전보다 훨씬 덜 비옥해지게 했다.

erosion 명 침식 torrential rain 폭우 displace 동 옮겨놓다
disperse 동 분산시키다 exacerbate 동 악화시키다
logging 명 벌목 susceptible 형 취약한 tilling 명 밭갈이
loosen 동 느슨하게 하다 underlying 형 밑에 있는
penetrate 동 침투하다 vulnerable 형 취약한 batter 동 강타하다
unsuitable 형 적합하지 않은 mechanization 명 기계화
precariously 부 위태롭게 overgrazing 명 과도한 방목
vegetation 명 초목 prone to ~에 취약한
nomadic 형 유목 생활을 하는 herder 명 목자, 양치기
remarkably 부 아주 deforestation 명 삼림벌채
mobility 명 유동성 ironically 부 모순적이게도

1 1단락에 따르면, 다음 중 농사와 벌목 같은 인간의 활동에 관해 사실인 것은?

(A) 침식 과정을 악화시킨다.
(B) 풍부한 토양에 의존한다.
(C) 특정한 지역에 토양이 축적되게 한다.
(D) 자연적인 침식보다 더 많은 피해를 초래한다.

2 지문의 단어 "precariously"와 의미가 가장 비슷한 것은?

(A) 화가 나게
(B) 위험하게
(C) 점증적으로
(D) 시험적으로

3 다음 중 2단락의 농업에 관한 논의에서 추론할 수 있는 것은?

(A) 기계화된 농기구의 사용은 씨앗을 심는 비효율적인 방법이다.
(B) 압축된 토양은 강우가 부족한 기간 동안에만 메마를 것이다.
(C) 더 아래의 토양에 심어진 씨앗들은 농작물을 생산할 가능성이 더 높다.
(D) 과거의 밭갈이 방법은 현대적인 방법보다 토양을 압축시킬 가능성이 더 낮았다.

4 아래 문장 중 지문 속의 음영된 문장의 핵심 정보를 가장 잘 표현한 것은?

(A) 인구가 폭발적으로 증가하면서 동물은 중요한 식량원이 되었다.
(B) 식량을 찾기가 어려워지면서 가축 사육이 점점 더 어렵게 되었다.
(C) 사람들은 1900년대 초반에 농장의 동물들을 돌보는 데 더 많은 시간을 쏟았다.
(D) 사람들의 수가 증가하면서 더 많은 가축들이 방목되었다.

5 3단락에서 글쓴이가 암시하는 것으로, 가축 방목의 부정적인 영향은

(A) 가축을 매우 다양한 초목이 있는 지역에 있게 함으로써 방지될 수 있다
(B) 목자들이 그들의 동물을 농촌에 너무 가깝게 데려오지 못하게 함으로써 방지될 수 있다
(C) 서로 다른 종들의 혼합을 같은 지역에서 함께 방목함으로써 방지될 수 있다
(D) 동물들이 주기적으로 정해진 기간 동안 지역에 접근하지 못하게 함으로써 방지될 수 있다

6 4단락에 따르면, 코스타리카에서 삼림벌채가 일어난 것은 부분적으로

(A) 농업 분야에서 감소하는 수익을 증대시킬 필요성 때문이었다
(B) 우림에 대한 외국 벌목 회사의 관심 때문이었다
(C) 농작물을 기를 땅을 얻고자 하는 바람 때문이었다
(D) 홍수로 잃은 농장을 되찾으려는 욕망 때문이었다

Reading Practice 2

본문 p.106

1 (A) 2 (A) 3 (D) 4 (B) 5 (C) 6 (D)

무성 영화 시대의 종말

오디오 및 비디오의 재생은 둘 다 19세기 후반에 일어난 폭발적 발명으로 가능해졌다. 그러나, 토머스 에디슨과 다른 사람들의 노력에도 불구하고 소리와 영화가 공존할 수 없다는 것은 머지않아 일반적 통념이 되었다. 그리고 영화 산업은 소리를 필요로 하는 것처럼 보이지 않았다. 1900년대 초반에, 할리우드는 지역 극장 음악가들에 의해 제공되는 음악을 포함한 무성 영화 덕분에 그것이 오늘날 그러한 것처럼 문화 및 상업 중심지가 될 수 있었다.

인간 목소리의 이점 없이, 무성 영화는 폭넓고, 관중을 즐겁게 하는 볼거리로 특징지어지는 예술 형태로 발전했다. 비록 무성 영화가 대화나 설명을 포함한 타이틀 카드를 종종 포함하기는 했지만, 이것들은 화면 전체를 차지했고 동작을 느려지게 했다. [1]대중을 즐겁게 하기 위해, 무성 영화는 대부분 말이 없고 한눈에 파악될 수 있는 단순한 상황들로 가득했다. 말은 액션 모험 영화의 아슬아슬한 행위를 이해하는 데 꼭 필요한 것도, 코미디의 과장된 표정과 익살스러운 몸짓을 이해하는 데 필요한 것도 아니었다.

심지어 오디오 기술이 개선되었음에도, 대형 영화사들은 그들의 성공 공식을 바꾸기를 꺼렸다. 그래서 1926년에 최초로 인간의 목소리를 화면의 동작에 일치시킨 것이 상대적으로 덜 알려진 워너 브라더스 스튜디오였다는 것은 말이 된다. 그러나 워너 브라더스조차도 이것을 주로 음악과 코미디를 추가하는 방법으로 구상했다. 처음에는, 연예인이 카메라에 대고 직접 노래를 부르고 농담을 하는 짧은 보드빌 무대 공연을 보여주기 위해 그들이 웨스턴 일렉트릭으로부터 인가받은 소리 증폭 시스템인 비타폰이 사용되었으나, 이것들은 오직 무성 영화들 사이의 막간에만 상영되었다. [3]약간의 녹음된 음악과 몇 편의 대화를 포함한 장편 영화인 1927년의 '재즈 싱어'가 매표소에서 뜻밖의 성공으로 입증된 후에야 영화사들은 영화 내내 음성을 일치시키는 것을 고려했다.

1920년대 후반과 1930년대 초반의 꾸준한 생산 흐름에도 불구하고 소리를 포함한 영화, 혹은 그것들이 나중에 불리게 된 것처럼 '토키'는 시장을 빠르게 지배하지 못했다. 순수주의자들은 이 새로운 형태의 영화가 열등한 상품이며 싸구려 장치라고 주장했다. **그리고 그 새로운 기술과 관련하여 이 비판을 유효하게 만든 많은 중요한 문제들이 있었다.** 초기의 마이크들은 배우들이 화면에서 정지해 있을 것을 요구했다. 이는 동작이 거의 없는 생기 없는 장면들을 만들어냈으며, 그 문제는 카메라의 시끄러운 윙윙거리는 소리가 카메라 조작자들이 그 소리를 막기 위해 박스 안에 머물러 있어야 함을 의미한다는 사실에 의해 악화되었다. 그것은 또한 목소리가 외모와 어울리지 않았던 일부 인기 있는 배우들에게 직업상의 큰 장애물로 드러났다. [6]게다가, 혹사당한 영사기사들은 오디오가 일치되게 하기 위해 고군분투했는데, 이는 그들이 릴을 교체할 때 전축에 바늘을 떨어뜨려야 했고 그들의 타이밍이 맞지 않을 때마다 관중들이 야유를 쏟아냈기 때문이다. **토키가 영화관에서 무성 영화를 대체할 때까지 카메라 시스템, 마이크, 영사기 개선에 수년이 걸렸다.**

reproduction 명재생 conventional 형일반적인
incompatible 형공존할 수 없는 hub 명중심지
spectacle 명볼거리 dialogue 명대화 exposition 명설명
wordless 형말이 없는 at a glance 한눈에
death-defying 형아슬아슬한 exaggerated 형과장된
physicality 명몸짓 reluctant 형꺼리는 obscure 형덜 알려진
conceive 동구상하다 amplify 동증폭하다 license 동인가받다
interlude 명(영화·연극의) 막간 synchronize 동일치시키다
dominate 동지배하다 purist 명순수주의자 gimmick 명장치
primitive 형초기의 stationary 형정지해 있는 listless 형생기 없는
whir 명윙윙거리는 소리 baffle 동막다 obstacle 명장애물
projectionist 명영사기사

1 2단락에서 추론할 수 있는 것으로, 타이틀 카드는

(A) 필요할 때만 영화에 포함되었다
(B) 이야기의 속도를 늦추기 위해 이용되었다

(C) 새로운 장면이 시작하기 전에 화면을 가리기 위해 사용되었다
(D) 배우들 사이의 긴 대화를 나타내기 위해 보여졌다

2 지문의 단어 "these"가 가리키는 것은?
(A) 공연
(B) 연예인
(C) 노래
(D) 농담

3 3단락에 따르면, 다음 중 1927년의 영화 '재즈 싱어'에 관해 사실인 것은?
(A) 워너 브라더스에 의해 개봉된 오디오를 포함한 첫 영화였다.
(B) 잘 알려진 많은 연주자들을 특징으로 했다.
(C) 그 시대의 다른 영화들보다 명백히 더 길었다.
(D) 전반적인 티켓 판매 측면에서 예상을 뛰어넘었다.

4 네 개의 네모[■]는 다음 문장이 삽입될 수 있는 곳을 나타내고 있다.
그리고 그 새로운 기술과 관련하여 이 비판을 유효하게 만든 많은 중요한 문제들이 있었다.
이 문장은 어디에 들어가는 것이 가장 적절한가?

5 지문의 단어 "listless"와 의미가 가장 비슷한 것은?
(A) 들리지 않는
(B) 숨이 막히는
(C) 활기 없는
(D) 대담한

6 다음 중 4단락에서 초기의 영사기사들에 관해 추론할 수 있는 것은?
(A) 영화가 재생되는 동안 소리를 더하기 위해 다양한 방법들을 즉흥적으로 만들었다.
(B) 일부 극장에서 토키가 상영되는 것을 막기 위해 운동을 벌였다.
(C) 오디오와 비디오 녹음을 일치시키기 위해 관중들의 신호를 사용했다.
(D) 토키를 가능하게 만든 기술의 도입을 싫어했다.

Reading Practice 3

본문 p.108

1 (D) 2 (B) 3 (B) 4 (C) 5 (A) 6 (B)

균류

균류는 일반적으로 움직이지 않고 지표면이나 토양에서 자라기 때문에 한때 식물의 친척으로 여겨졌다. 그러나, 오늘날의 과학자들은 균류가 자신만의 계를 대표한다는 것을 인정한다. [2]균류의 구별되는 특징은 그것들이 광합성을 하는 식물처럼 탄소를 내부에서 만들기보다는 그것을 외부에서 흡수하는 방식이다. 그러나, 그것들은 섭취하기 전에 음식을 소화한다는 점에서 동물과 다르다. 모든 균류 종은 이동에 사용되는 채찍 같은 꼬리인 편모를 가진 단세포 유기체에서 진화했다고 여겨진다. 전체로서, 균류는 지구상의 거의 모든 서식지를 차지하는 약 15만 종의 매우 다양한 집단으로 구성되어 있다.

많은 균류 종들은 쓰러진 나무 같은 부패하는 유기물에 의존하며, 죽은 물질에 있는 셀룰로스와 리그닌을 당으로 전환함으로써 분해 과정에 도움을 준다. 그것들은 유기 분자를 분해하는 것을 돕는 효소를 방출함으로써 영양분을 얻고, 그 후에 균류의 복합 세포들은 그것들에서 남은 영양분을 흡수한다. 그것들의 활동의 결과로, 균류는 질소와 인 같은 영양분을 재활용하고, 그것들이 토양을 강화하고 새로운 식물들이 번성하는 것을 가능하게 하도록 땅으로 돌려보낸다. 분해자인 균류는 1차, 2차, 혹은 3차로 분류될 수 있다. 1차 분해자는 살아 있거나 죽어가는 유기체에서 살아남을 수 있고, 기생할 수도 있지만, 그것들은 대부분 죽은 물질을 먹고 그것을 퇴비로 바꾼다. [4]3차 분해자는 유기물이 이미 고도로 분해된 토양층 자체에서 살아남는 반면, 2차 분해자는 생존을 위해 이 퇴비에 의존한다.

균류의 생식은 매우 다양하며 무성 또는 유성일 수 있다. 무성 생식의 간단한 유형은 균사체라고 불리는 뿌리 같은 구조에서 발생한다. 균사체는 여러 방향으로 뻗어나가는 얇은 흰색 필라멘트로 이루어져 있다. 이 필라멘트들은 균사라고 불리며, 그것들이 조각나면 그 조각들 각각은 일부 식물의 잘린 뿌리가 새로운 싹을 만들 수 있는 방식으로 새로운 유기체를 만들어낸다. [5B]무성 생식은 또한 세포 측면에 불룩한 부분이 형성되고 궁극적으로 원래 핵의 일부와 함께 분리되어 새로운 세포를 만드는 출아를 통해 일어날 수 있다. [5C]또 다른 종류의 무성 생식은 하나의 부모가 포자를 방출하는 경우이다. [5D]이 방법들은 모두 복제 생물의 생성을 초래한다. 그에 반해서, 유성 생식은 두 개의 부모를 필요로 하며, 따라서 서로 다른 유기체들에서 나온 DNA를 결합한다. 일반적으로 그 과정은 원래 세포들 각각에서 나온 DNA의 완전한 세트를 포함하는 접합체를 만들기 위해 서로 다른 균류에서 나온 세포 두 개의 융합을 수반한다. [6]그 접합체는 그 후에 이 DNA의 서로 다른 조합을 가진 네 개의 새로운 세포로 분열된다. 이것들은 그 후에 포자에 의해 분산되어 새로운 균류를 형성한다. 유성 생식의 장점은 그것이 그 종의 전체적인 다양성을 증가시킨다는 것이다.

fungi 명 균류　immobile 형 움직이지 않는
distinguishing 형 구별되는　photosynthetic 형 광합성을 하는
flagellum 명 편모　locomotion 명 이동
collectively 부 전체로서, 집단적으로　decaying 형 부패하는
organic matter 유기물　decomposition 명 분해
phosphorus 명 인　fortify 동 강화하다　tertiary 형 3차의
parasitic 형 기생하는　compost 명 퇴비　asexual 형 무성의
mycelium 명 균사체　hypha 명 균사
fragment 동 조각내다; 명 조각　sever 동 자르다　budding 명 출아
bulge 명 불룩한 부분　detach 동 분리되다　nucleus 명 핵
spore 명 포자　fusing 명 융합　zygote 명 접합체

1 지문의 단어 "ingesting"과 의미가 가장 비슷한 것은?
(A) 완성하는
(B) 얻는
(C) 식별하는
(D) 섭취하는

2 1단락에 따르면, 균류가 식물과 다른 것은 그것들이
(A) 영양분을 위해 토양의 의존하지 않기 때문이다
(B) 외부의 원천에서 탄소를 얻기 때문이다
(C) 음식을 완전히 소화할 수 있기 때문이다
(D) 단세포 유기체에서 진화했기 때문이다

3 지문의 단어 "those"가 가리키는 것은?
(A) 효소
(B) 유기 분자
(C) 복합 세포들
(D) 영양분

4 다음 중 2단락에서 2차 분해사에 관해 추론할 수 있는 것은?

(A) 그것들 중 적은 수가 기생한다.
(B) 가장 흔한 분해자 유형이다.
(C) 1차 분해자 없이는 생존할 수 없을 것이다.
(D) 그것들 중 대다수는 토양층 안에서 산다.

5 다음 중 3단락에서 무성 생식에 관해 언급되지 않은 것은?

(A) 서로 다른 세포 두 개의 융합을 수반한다.
(B) 핵 일부의 분리를 수반할 수 있다.
(C) 하나의 부모가 포자를 생산할 때 일어난다.
(D) 복제 생물의 생성을 초래한다.

6 다음 중 3단락에서 접합체의 분열로 초래되는 세포들에 관해 추론할 수 있는 것은?

(A) 부모와 똑같은 자손을 만든다.
(B) 서로 유전적으로 다르다.
(C) 그것들이 분산되기 전에 DNA를 교환한다.
(D) 여러 개의 독특한 특징을 지닌 세포들로 분열된다.

iBT Reading Test 1

본문 p.110

1 (B) 2 (B) 3 (B) 4 (A)
5 (D) 6 (C) 7 (A) 8 (A)
9 (C) 10 (A), (E), (F)

백악관

백악관의 건설은 연방 정부가 포토맥 강가 지역에 위치할 것이라고 선언한 1790년의 의회 법령에서 기인했으며, 이는 1800년 뉴욕에서 워싱턴DC로의 대통령 관저 이전으로 이어졌다. [3]도시 설계자는 조지 워싱턴 대통령과 함께 관저를 위한 장소를 선택했다. 건축 설계를 위한 9개의 제안서가 제출되었고 아일랜드 태생의 건축가 제임스 호반의 것이 선택되었다. 그의 설계는 더블린에 있는 의회 건물인 렌스터하우스에서 영향을 받았는데, 이것은 결국 안드레아 팔라디오의 르네상스 건축에서 영향을 받았다. 비록 조지 워싱턴이 백악관의 건축을 감독했지만, 그는 결코 그곳에서 살지 못했다. 그곳의 첫 번째 거주자들은 미국의 2대 대통령인 존 애덤스와 그의 아내인 애비게일이었다.

[5]토머스 제퍼슨 대통령은 현관홀에 박물관을 만들었고, 또한 백악관을 공공 투어에 개방한 첫 번째 대통령이었다. 그것은 전시 중을 제외하고는 그 이래로 계속 개방되어 있었다. 제퍼슨은 독립기념일과 취임식과 같은 특별한 날에도 문을 개방했다. "민중의 사람"인 앤드루 잭슨이 1829년에 취임했을 때, 백악관은 2만 명이 넘는 일반 시민들로 넘쳐났고, 그들은 그들의 후보의 승리를 축하하기 위해 찾아왔다. 그 파티는 너무 크고 무질서해져서 잭슨은 안전한 호텔로 피신할 수밖에 없었다. 그 후, 그 관행은 바뀌었고, 백악관 앞에 대통령의 군대 사열을 위한 그랜드스탠드가 세워졌다. [6]이 행진은 오늘날의 공식 취임식 퍼레이드로 발전했다.

백악관은 수 세기에 걸쳐 상당한 보수와 변화를 겪어왔다. 1812년의 전쟁 중에, 영국군은 그 건물에 불을 질렀다. [7B]그 뒤에, 오직 몇몇 외벽들만 여전히 서 있었고, 이것들의 대부분이 교체되어야 했지만, 새 대통령인 제임스 먼로는 1년 후에 다시 돌아올 수 있었다. [7C]추가적인 보수공사는 체스터 아서가 스테인드글라스 창문을 포함하여 빅토리아 시대풍의 장식을 설치했던 1881년과, 시어도어 루스벨트가 그 건물 원래의 고전적인 스타일을 복원했던 1902년에 일어났다. **후자는 대통령 집무실을 관저 2층에서 그 건물의 새롭게 설치된 웨스트 윙으로 이전했다.** [7D]다음 미국 대통령인 윌리엄 하워드 태프트는 1909년에 그 유명한 오벌 오피스가 건설되게 했다. 1948년까지, 노후화된 백악관은 관리 소홀로 인해 붕괴될 위기에 처해 있었고, 많은 사람들로 하여금 그것을 완전히 철거하는 것을 장려하게 만들었다. 그러나, 영부인인 엘리자베스 트루먼은 그것의 역사적 중요성을 보존하기 위해 그것을 복구하자고 주장했다. **특히, 그녀는 영국군에 의한 훼손에서 살아남은 벽들을 미국 독립의 중요한 상징으로 보았기 때문에 그것들을 지키고 싶어 했다.** 이 개입은 백악관과 관련된 일에 있어 영부인의 역할을 공고히 했고, 재키 케네디와 힐러리 클린턴 같은 후속 영부인들은 백악관의 유산을 희생시키지 않으면서 그것을 새롭게 단장하는 데 주요한 기여를 했다.

relocation 명 이전 architectural 형 건축적인
parliamentary 형 의회의 oversee 동 감독하다
inaugurate 동 취임하다 be inundated with ~으로 넘치다
candidate 명 후보 disorderly 형 무질서한 flee 동 피신하다
review 명 사열, 검토 procession 명 행진 undergo 동 겪다
substantial 형 상당한 alteration 명 변화 tear down 철거하다
advocate 동 주장하다 intervention 명 개입
refurbish 동 새롭게 단장하다 sacrifice 동 희생시키다
legacy 명 유산

1 아래 문장 중 지문 속의 음영된 문장의 핵심 정보를 가장 잘 표현한 것은? 오답은 문장의 의미를 크게 바꾸거나 핵심 정보를 생략한다.

(A) 의회가 그 국가의 수도로 포토맥 강가에 있는 지역을 승인한 것은 1800년이었다.
(B) 대통령 관저의 이전을 요구하는 입법 조치가 백악관의 건설로 이어졌다.
(C) 의회 법령 통과 이후, 대통령의 관저는 뉴욕으로 옮겨졌다.
(D) 1790년에, 의회는 대통령의 관저를 워싱턴DC로 공식 이전했다.

2 지문의 단어 "oversaw"와 의미가 가장 비슷한 것은?

(A) 명령했다
(B) 감독했다
(C) 승인했다
(D) 제작했다

3 1단락에 따르면, 다음 중 백악관의 위치에 관해 사실인 것은?

(A) 1790년 의회 법령에 의해 결정되었다.
(B) 대통령과 도시 설계자에 의해 함께 선택되었다.
(C) 더블린시의 배치에서 영감을 받았다.
(D) 원래 뉴욕이 될 예정이었다.

4 지문의 단어 "disorderly"와 의미가 가장 비슷한 것은?

(A) 제멋대로의
(B) 감탄하는
(C) 폭력적인
(D) 품위 있는

5 2단락에 따르면, 다음 중 토머스 제퍼슨에 관해 사실인 것은?

(A) 그는 시민들이 적은 요금으로 백악관 박물관을 볼 수 있게 해주었다.
(B) 그는 백악관에서 살았던 첫 번째 미국 대통령이었다.

(C) 그는 전시 중에 백악관을 개방해 놓을 것을 요구했다.
(D) 그는 백악관 공공 투어를 제공하는 관행을 시작했다.

6 다음 중 2단락에서 백악관 앞에 있는 그랜드스탠드에 관해 추론할 수 있는 것은?

(A) 앤드루 잭슨의 취임식을 기념하기 위해 건설되었다.
(B) 대통령이 신변의 안전을 우려해 피신한 뒤에 임시 폐쇄되었다.
(C) 그것이 건설되었을 때 공식적인 취임식 퍼레이드는 열린 적이 없었다.
(D) 군대는 대통령 사열을 목적으로 오늘날에도 계속해서 그 옆을 행진한다.

7 3단락에 따르면, 다음 중 백악관에 이루어졌던 보수공사가 아닌 것은?

(A) 웨스트 윙의 확장
(B) 외벽의 교체
(C) 스테인드글라스 창문의 추가
(D) 오벌 오피스의 건설

8 3단락에서 글쓴이는 왜 1812년의 전쟁을 언급하는가?

(A) 백악관의 주요 보수공사를 초래한 사건을 강조하기 위해
(B) 백악관을 허물고 재건해야 했던 이유를 제시하기 위해
(C) 미국과 영국의 정치적 긴장이 매우 심각했던 이유를 설명하기 위해
(D) 애국적 상징으로서 백악관의 중요성을 강조하기 위해

9 네 개의 네모[■]는 다음 문장이 삽입될 수 있는 곳을 나타내고 있다.

특히, 그녀는 영국군에 의한 훼손에서 살아남은 벽들을 미국 독립의 중요한 상징으로 보았기 때문에 그것들을 지키고 싶어 했다.

이 문장은 어디에 들어가는 것이 가장 적절한가?

10 지시: 지문 요약을 위한 도입 문장이 아래에 주어져 있다. 지문의 가장 중요한 내용을 나타내는 보기 3개를 골라 요약을 완성하라. 어떤 문장은 지문에 언급되지 않은 내용이나 사소한 정보를 나타내므로 요약에 포함되지 않는다. **이 문제는 2점이다.**

18세기 후반 이래로, 백악관은 미국 대통령과 국가 자체의 영원한 상징이었다.
· (A) 백악관의 역사를 통틀어, 그것은 많은 변화를 겪었지만 그것의 역사적 유산은 그대로 남아 있다.
· (E) 조지 워싱턴 자신은 백악관 안에서 살지 못했지만, 백악관은 그의 임기 중에 구상되고 계획되었다.
· (F) 특히 제퍼슨과 잭슨의 것과 같은 각 대통령의 임기는 백악관에 대한 대중의 접근권 방침을 정했다.

(B) 비록 대통령들이 대부분의 관심을 받았지만, 영부인들 또한 백악관의 발전에 기여해왔다.
(C) 초기에 백악관은 대중에게 개방되어 있었지만 앤드루 잭슨의 당선 이후 대중의 접근권이 없어졌다.
(D) 의회는 모든 배경의 건축가들이 제안서를 제출하는 것을 허락했고, 결국 외국 태생 건축가의 설계가 선택되었다.

iBT Reading Test 2

본문 p.114

1 (C)	2 (B)	3 (D)	4 (B)
5 (C)	6 (D)	7 (D)	8 (B)
9 (D)	10 (A), (C), (E)		

얼룩말 홍합

얼룩말 홍합은 껍데기의 독특한 흑백 줄무늬 모양에서 이름을 얻은 민물 종이다. 외국 수원으로의 이 종의 유입은 많은 지역들에서 심각한 환경 파괴를 초래했다. 동유럽의 배수 유역에서 유래된 얼룩말 홍합 개체군은 해상 무역의 확장으로 여기에서부터 주요 항구들로 빠르게 퍼져나갔다. 1824년까지, 그것의 존재는 멀리 런던에서까지 발견되었다. 1세기 반이 넘은 후에, 이 종은 미국 오대호 지역의 세인트클레어 호에서 발견되었다.

얼룩말 홍합은 화물선의 밸러스트 탱크를 통해 운반되었다. 밸러스트 탱크는 수생 생물체로 가득 찬 물을 싣고, 이것들은 외국 항구에 도착하면 방출되며, 그 외래 종들을 갑자기 새로운 생태계에 내려놓는다. 만약 염분을 함유한 바닷물에 버려지면, 얼룩말 홍합은 소금물을 견디지 못하기 때문에 빠르게 죽는다. 그러나, 북아메리카의 담수호들은 이 생물체들의 원래 서식지와 아주 비슷하고, 그 때문에 그것들의 생존을 용이하게 한다. [4]또한, 이 호수들에는 청돔과 잉어를 포함한 동유럽의 흔한 수생 포식자들이 없다.

이 종의 빠른 확산은 많은 생태학적 문제들을 야기했다. 예를 들어, 얼룩말 홍합은 각각이 하루에 1리터의 물을 깨끗하게 할 수 있는 물 여과기이다. 자리를 잡은 군체는 오염물질과 미립자를 섭취함으로써 물의 투명도를 상당히 높일 수 있다. 이것이 유익해 보일 수 있지만, 투명도의 갑작스러운 변화는 햇빛의 투과를 증가시키고, 이는 조류 대증식을 초래한다. [6]이 미생물들이 죽을 때, 물 속 산소의 양이 감소한다. 얼룩말 홍합은 또한 토종 동물들에게 직접적인 영향을 미칠 수 있다. 단단한 표면에 달라붙는 그것들의 능력을 이용하여, 얼룩말 홍합은 종종 오대호의 토종 패류의 껍데기에 부착된다. 이러한 방법으로, 그것들은 그것들로부터 영양분을 훔치기 위해 좋은 자리를 차지한다. [7]성장하는 얼룩말 홍합은 껍데기 뚜껑을 부수고 그것을 열기에 너무 무겁게 만들며, 그 뒤에 다른 그 생물은 아사한다.

얼룩말 홍합의 존재는 또한 피해를 입는 인간 사회에 경제적 문제를 제기한다. 유생은 방해받지 않고 수도관에 들어가 위쪽으로 이동할 수 있다. 시간이 지남에 따라, 성체 껍데기는 관을 완전히 막을 수도 있다. 게다가, 썩어가는 홍합은 방문객들을 단념시키는 고약한 냄새를 내뿜는다. 이러한 이유로, 식당과 수상 스포츠 회사 같은 해안가의 사업체들은 수익의 감소를 겪는다.

국가 및 지역 기관들은 유생과 성체의 운반을 막는 방법에 대해 대중을 교육하기 위한 정보 소책자를 발행해 왔다. 주요 권장 사항은 새로운 수역에 들어가기 전에 모든 배와 낚시 장비를 세심하게 청소하고 건조시키는 것이다. 또한, 레저용이 아닌 모든 선박의 밸러스트 물의 화학적 처리를 규제하는 법률이 미국 해안경비대에 의해 시행되고 있다. 게다가, 전력 회사들은 그들의 파이프라인에서 그 조개류를 씻어내기 위해 액체 형태의 비료와 유기물 살충제에 투자해오고 있다. **그러나, 이러한 선택들은 새로운 화학물질을 수원에 유입시킴으로써 그 생태계에 더 큰 해를 끼칠 수 있다.**

derive 동 얻다, 이끌어내다　disruption 명 (환경) 파괴
drainage 명 배수　basin 명 유역　maritime 형 해상의
discharge 동 방출하다　abruptly 부 갑자기　deposit 동 내려놓다
exotic 형 외래의　saline 형 염분을 함유한

intolerable 형 견디지 못하는 facilitate 동 용이하게 하다
colony 명 군체 clarity 명 투명도 pollutant 명 오염물질
particulate 명 미립자 transparency 명 투명도
penetration 명 투과 mollusk 명 패류 starvation 명 굶주림
afflicted 형 피해를 입는 unimpeded 형 방해받지 않는
vessel 명 선박 biopesticide 명 유기물 살충제 flush 동 씻어내다

1 지문의 단어 "these"가 가리키는 것은?

(A) 외국 수원
(B) 많은 지역들
(C) 동유럽의 배수 유역
(D) 얼룩말 홍합 개체군

2 아래 문장 중 지문 속의 음영된 문장의 핵심 정보를 가장 잘 표현한 것은? 오답은 문장의 의미를 크게 바꾸거나 핵심 정보를 생략한다.

(A) 밸러스트 탱크는 수생 종을 운반하기 위해 설계된 장비이다.
(B) 수생 생물은 밸러스트 탱크를 통해 생태계 사이에서 우연히 수송된다.
(C) 밸러스트 탱크의 물은 선박 외부에서 수생 생물을 씻어내기 위해 사용된다.
(D) 수생 생물체는 이동 수단으로서 밸러스트 탱크에 의도적으로 들어간다.

3 지문의 단어 "intolerable"과 의미가 가장 비슷한 것은?

(A) 받아들여지는
(B) 매력적인
(C) 불쾌한
(D) 견딜 수 없는

4 2단락에 따르면, 북아메리카의 호수들은 왜 얼룩말 홍합의 성장에 유리한가?

(A) 번식에 치명적인 낮은 염도를 가지고 있지 않다.
(B) 홍합을 잡아먹는 생물을 포함하고 있지 않다.
(C) 유생에게 해로운 독소를 가지고 있지 않다.
(D) 홍합을 얼리는 쌀쌀한 날씨를 겪지 않는다.

5 지문의 단어 "penetration"과 의미가 가장 비슷한 것은?

(A) 모음
(B) 방해
(C) 입장
(D) 분산

6 다음 중 3단락에서 투명한 물에 관해 추론할 수 있는 것은?

(A) 보통 어떠한 화학적 오염물질도 포함하지 않는다.
(B) 대부분의 민물 종들에 의해 선호된다.
(C) 홍합이 서식하는 장소에서는 드물다.
(D) 모든 수생 종들에게 반드시 이로운 것은 아니다.

7 3단락에 따르면, 경쟁 조개류를 물리치기 위해 얼룩말 홍합에 의해 어떤 방법이 사용되는가?

(A) 조개류의 껍질을 부수어 연다.
(B) 조개류에서 물을 빼앗는다.
(C) 조개류의 산소 공급을 제한한다.
(D) 조개류의 먹이를 잡는 능력을 없앤다.

8 4단락에서 글쓴이는 왜 썩어가는 홍합에 관해 논하는가?

(A) 그것들이 수도관에 야기하는 피해를 설명하기 위해
(B) 그것들이 특정 사업체들에게 부정적으로 영향을 미치는 방식을 설명하기 위해
(C) 그것들이 인간의 건강에 해로울 수 있다는 것을 강조하기 위해
(D) 그것들의 경제적 사용의 예시를 제공하기 위해

9 네 개의 네모[■]는 다음 문장이 삽입될 수 있는 곳을 나타내고 있다.

그러나, 이러한 선택들은 새로운 화학물질을 수원에 유입시킴으로써 그 생태계에 더 큰 해를 끼칠 수 있다.

이 문장을 어디에 들어가는 것이 가장 적절한가?

10 **지시:** 지문 요약을 위한 도입 문장이 아래에 주어져 있다. 지문의 가장 중요한 내용을 나타내는 보기 3개를 골라 요약을 완성하라. 어떤 문장은 지문에 언급되지 않은 내용이나 사소한 정보를 나타내므로 요약에 포함되지 않는다. **이 문제는 2점이다.**

> **얼룩말 홍합은 그것들이 북아메리카 수로에 도착한 이래로 상당한 피해를 초래해 왔다.**
> · (A) 얼룩말 홍합은 무역선에 의해 새로운 지역들로 운반되었고, 여기에서 그것들의 개체군은 빠르게 증가했다.
> · (C) 얼룩말 홍합의 확산은 생태계에 있는 토착 종들에게 부정적인 영향을 미쳤다.
> · (E) 얼룩말 홍합의 존재는 영향을 받은 지역 사회에 경제적 비용을 발생시킨다.

(B) 얼룩말 홍합은 때때로 가시성이 좋지 못한 물의 수질을 향상시키기 위해 사용된다.
(D) 밸러스트 물이 사용되는 방법에 대한 정부의 규제는 최근 얼룩말 홍합 문제를 해결했다.
(F) 얼룩말 홍합이 매우 구체적인 물의 조건을 필요로 하기 때문에 그것들은 토종 홍합의 영역을 거의 침해하지 않는다.

Vocabulary Review

본문 p.118

1 locomotion		2 torrential	3 airborne
4 insulation		5 tertiary	6 inaugurated
7 (B)	8 (A)	9 (A)	10 (B)
11 (D)	12 (C)	13 (D)	14 (B)

CHAPTER 07

Rhetorical Purpose

Example

본문 p.121

1 (B) 2 (D)

벼의 기원

벼의 기원은 얼마간 논의되어 왔다. 중국 양쯔강 중류와 하류의 증거는 인간이 이미 기원전 12,000년에 그 지역에서 벼를 사용했다는 것을 보여준다. 기원전 8,000년으로 거슬러 올라가는 일부 고고학 유적지는 상당한 양의 벼를 포함하고 있었는데, 이는 그것이 그 지역 사람들

의 삶에서 필수적인 부분이 되었음을 시사한다. 그러나, 이 장소들에서 발견된 벼가 야생의 것인지 재배된 것인지는 알려져 있지 않다. 쿤산의 고고학 유적지에 있는 가장 오래된 것으로 확인된 논에서 발굴된 벼 낟알의 탄소 연대 측정은 벼 재배를 수천 년 후로 어림잡았다. 중국의 벼 재배 기술은 약 4,000년 전에 둘 다 야생 벼 종이 없었던 한국과 일본에 도달했고, 또한 동남아시아로 전파되었다. 이것 이전에, 벼 재배는 인도와, 그 후에는 아프리카에서도 독립적으로 이루어졌다.

성공적인 벼 재배의 전제조건은 씨앗이 떨어지기 전에 벼가 수확될 수 있도록 씨앗의 탈립을 통제하거나 줄이는 능력이었다. 탈립은 다 자란 씨앗이 확산을 위해 모체에 의해 방출되는 과정이다. 유전자 분석은 씨앗의 탈립을 줄이거나 없애는 돌연변이 유전자를 발견했다. 따라서, 초기의 벼 재배는 이러한 특성을 가진 벼를 선택하고 그것들을 매우 느리고 점진적인 과정으로 농업에 접목시키는 것을 포함했을 가능성이 높다. 더 상세한 유전자 배열과 향상된 기술을 이용하여, 전문가들은 가까운 미래에 이 과정에 대해 더 많이 배우기를 희망한다.

origin 명기원 archaeological 형고고학의 substantial 형상당한
integral 형필수적인 domesticated 형재배된
carbon dating 탄소 연대 측정 unearth 동발굴하다
independently 부독립적으로 prerequisite 명전제조건
shattering 명탈립 dispersal 명확산 mutant 형돌연변이의
trait 명특성 incorporate 동접목시키다 gradual 형점진적인
sequencing 명배열

1 지문에서 글쓴이는 왜 "Kunshan"을 언급하는가?
(A) 벼를 재배하기 위해 사용된 최초의 방법들을 설명하기 위해
(B) 최초라고 확인된 벼 재배 사례를 밝히기 위해
(C) 한국과 일본에 대한 벼 수출의 출처를 강조하기 위해
(D) 사람들이 처음으로 벼를 섭취했던 장소를 강조하기 위해

2 2단락에서 글쓴이의 주된 목적은?
(A) 초기 농부들이 문제를 극복한 방법 설명하기
(B) 식물이 번식하는 과정 묘사하기
(C) 농작물의 약점 지적하기
(D) 작물 재배를 위한 조건 밝히기

Reading Practice 1

본문 p.122

1 (A) 2 (B) 3 (D) 4 (C) 5 (D) 6 (B)

웜홀 이론

알베르트 아인슈타인 이전에, 아이작 뉴턴 경과 같은 과학자들은 우주가 평평하다고 잘못 추정했다. 그러나, 그의 일반 상대성 이론에서, 아인슈타인은 우주가 사실 역동적이며 고무나 플라스틱처럼 구부러지고, 늘어지고, 휘어질 수 있다고 주장했다. 이러한 우주관에서, 공간, 시간, 중력의 조합은 물질이 어디에 존재하며 다른 물체에 비하여 어떻게 움직이는지를 결정한다. 후에, 현대 천문학자들은 아인슈타인의 이론을 더 발전시켰고 물질이 우주에서 일반적으로 예상되는 것보다 훨씬 더 빠르게 먼 거리를 횡단하는 것이 가능할지도 모른다고 추측했다. 이것이 달성될 수 있는 방법은 웜홀이라고 알려져 있는데, 이는 다른 상황 아래에서라면 시간과 공간에서 서로 훨씬 멀리 떨어져 있는 두 점 사이의 가상의 지름길로 정의된다.

현대 과학에 따르면, 웜홀의 형성은 블랙홀와 화이트홀 사이의 관계에 달려 있는데, 전자는 빛을 전혀 방출하지 않고 그것으로부터 아무것도 빠져나갈 수 없는 매우 밀도가 높은 우주 공간이다. [4]덜 알려진 화이트홀은 정반대인데, 이는 그것이 매우 밝으며 물질이 그것으로부터 끊임없는 흐름으로 쏟아져 나온다는 것을 의미한다. 이론상으로, 웜홀은 이 두 존재들 사이에 형성되어 그것들을 연결하고 물체가 이동할 수 있는 포털을 만들 수 있다. 이것은 공간의 두 지점 사이에 길을 생성할 것이며 그것들이 웜홀 바깥의 일반적인 공간 및 시간에서보다 서로에게 훨씬 더 가깝게 있을 가능성을 허용할 것이다. 이를 시각화하기 위해, 두 끝이 평행이 되어 한쪽이 다른쪽 위에 있도록 구부러진 긴 종이 한 장을 상상해보라. 각 끝 근처에는 종이에 구멍이 나 있으며 이 구멍들은 짧은 관으로 연결되어 있다. 두 개의 구멍 사이의 거리는 구부러진 종이의 표면을 따라 측정되었을 때보다 그 관을 통해 측정되었을 때 더 짧다. 이 시나리오에서, 종이는 공간을, 구멍들은 블랙홀과 화이트홀을, 관은 웜홀을 나타낸다.

비록 웜홀 이론이 대단히 흥미롭고 수많은 천문학자들과 애호가들의 관심을 끌어오긴 했지만, 심각한 문제들이 없는 것은 아니다. 블랙홀과 화이트홀의 관측이 어려움으로 가득하다는 사실을 무시하더라도, 현재의 물리학 분석은 만약 웜홀이 가능하다면, 형성 후 매우 빠르게 사라질 것이라고 시사한다. [6]사실, 그것은 너무 빨리 소멸되어 아마 어떤 것이라도 통과해 지나가기에는 시간이 충분하지 못할 것이다. 그럼에도 불구하고, 일부 연구자들은 미래의 어느 시점에는 우주여행에 이용하기 위해 웜홀을 안정화시키는 것이 가능할 수도 있다는 이론을 세웠다. **그러나 정확히 어떻게 이것이 달성될 수 있는지는 알려져있지 않으며, 이는 이 제안에 대한 비평가들이 그것을 공상 과학으로 치부하게 만든다.**

wormhole theory 웜홀 이론 erroneously 부잘못
theory of general relativity 일반 상대성 이론 dynamic 형역동적인
bent 형구부러진 gravity 명중력 astronomer 명천문학자
surmise 동추측하다 traverse 동횡단하다
hypothetical 형가상의 shortcut 명지름길
contemporary 형현대의 lesser-known 형덜 알려진
pathway 명길 visualize 동시각화하다 parallel 형평행인
fascinating 형대단히 흥미로운 enthusiast 명애호가
be fraught with ~으로 가득하다 analytics 명분석
vanish 동사라지다 dissipate 동소멸되다
insufficient 형충분하지 못한 utilization 명이용

1 지문에서 글쓴이는 왜 "rubber or plastic"을 언급하는가?
(A) 과학자의 가설의 요소를 설명하기 위해
(B) 이론의 근본적인 문제를 지적하기 위해
(C) 아인슈타인과 현대 천문학자들의 연구를 비교하기 위해
(D) 우주에 관한 뉴턴의 믿음을 뒷받침하기 위해

2 지문의 단어 "surmised"와 의미가 가장 비슷한 것은?
(A) 불가능하게 했다
(B) 추측했다
(C) 선언했다
(D) 인정했다

3 2단락에서 글쓴이는 왜 구부러진 긴 종이 한 장을 논하는가?
(A) 완전히 반대되는 물체들의 모양을 비교하기 위해
(B) 공간의 두 지점 사이의 광대한 거리를 강조하기 위해
(C) 존재들이 어떻게 서로의 반사 이미지가 될 수 있는지 설명하기 위해

(D) 두 장소 사이의 거리가 달라질 수 있음을 보여주기 위해

4 2단락에 따르면, 다음 중 화이트홀에 관해 사실인 것은?

(A) 블랙홀보다 훨씬 더 밀도가 높다.
(B) 그것에 접근하는 모든 물체는 받아들여지지 않는다.
(C) 물질이 그것으로부터 끊임없이 흘러나온다.
(D) 우주에서 가장 희귀한 물체들 중 하나이다.

5 네 개의 네모[■]는 다음 문장이 삽입될 수 있는 곳을 나타내고 있다.

그러나 정확히 어떻게 이것이 달성될 수 있는지는 알려져있지 않으며, 이는 이 제안에 대한 비평가들이 그것을 공상 과학으로 치부하게 만든다.

이 문장은 어디에 들어가는 것이 가장 적절한가?

6 3단락에 따르면, 웜홀을 통과하는 물질의 통로에는 왜 문제가 있는가?

(A) 웜홀이 그것에 들어간 모든 물질을 파괴할 것이다.
(B) 웜홀이 거의 즉시 사라질 것이다.
(C) 웜홀의 크기가 매우 작을 것이다.
(D) 웜홀 두 개의 형성은 결코 동시에 일어나지 않을 것이다.

Reading Practice 2

본문 p.124

1 (D) 2 (C) 3 (A) 4 (A) 5 (B) 6 (B)

조로아스터교

현대 종교로서, 조로아스터교는 추정상 10만에서 20만 명의 신도들에 의해 실천된다. 세계 최대의 두 종교인 기독교와 이슬람교의 약 38억 명의 신도와 그것을 비교하면 선지자 조로아스터에 의해 창시된 그 4천 년 된 신앙은 현대 세계에 거의 영향을 미치지 않는 것처럼 보일지도 모른다. 그러나, 조로아스터교에서 기원한 것으로 보이는 많은 사상들은 이제 오늘날 전 세계적으로 매우 두드러지는 소위 아브라함 종교(유대교, 기독교, 이슬람교)들의 중요한 교리이다. 이러한 기준에서, 잘 알려지지 않은 것처럼 보이는 이 종교는 오늘날의 신봉자들과는 관계없이 역사상 가장 영향력 있는 종교들에 속한다.

일부 역사학자들은 조로아스터교를 세계 최초의 유일신 종교로 여긴다. [2B]학자들은 자라투스트라로도 알려진 선지자 조로아스터가 존재했던 정확한 시기에 대해 논쟁하지만, 그가 기원전 1500년과 1200년경에 오늘날의 이란과 아프가니스탄의 국경 근처 지역에서 살았음을 시사하는 상당한 고고학적 증거가 있다. [2A]그는 아마 다신교 부족의 일원이었을 것이다. 조로아스터교 신도들은 조로아스터가 하나의 진정한 신으로 받아들이게 된 아후라 마즈다의 신성한 존재와 마주했던 30세 때 이교도의 의식에 참여했다고 믿는다. [2D]그의 신앙은 결국 페르시아 제국의 국교가 되었고 그 후 중국, 중동, 유럽을 연결하는 그 유명한 실크 로드를 따라 아시아 전역으로 전파되었다.

그러나 유일신론이 조로아스터교와 아브라함 신앙들의 유일한 유사점은 아니다. 조로아스터의 메시지는 또한 천국과 지옥, 사탄, 그리고 최후의 심판일 개념을 특징으로 했다. [4]조로아스터교 신도들의 신앙은 바빌로니아인들에게 닿아 키루스 대제가 이끄는 페르시아인들에 의해 강화되었을 수 있는데, 그는 기원전 538년에 유대인들을 바빌로니아인들의 억류로부터 해방시켜 그들이 유대 왕국에 있는 그들의 고향으로 돌아가도록 허락했다. 한편, 조로아스터교는 기원후 7세기에 이슬람교도들이 페르시아를 정복할 때까지 그곳에서 지배적인 종교로 남아 있었다. 대부분의 이란인 조로아스터교 신도들은 그 후에 그들을 겨냥한 세금과 다른 이슬람 친화적인 정책들에 강요되어 이슬람의 신앙을 받아들였고, 오래된 신앙을 계속 실천했던 사람들 중 다수는 인도로 탈출하여 오늘날 조로아스터교의 특징을 유지하고 있는 파르시 종교를 창시했다.

비교적 적은 조로아스터교 신도들이 계몽주의 시대까지 남아 있었지만, 조로아스터교는 그 시기(1685-1815) 유럽의 가장 중요한 사상가들 중 일부에게 상당한 영향을 미쳤다. 프랑스 작가 볼테르는 페르시아인 조로아스터교 신도에 관한 철학 중편 소설인 '자디그'를 썼다. 얼마 지나지 않아, 독일 시인 요한 볼프강 폰 괴테는 '서동시집'에서 조로아스터교에 관해 썼다. 심지어 오스트리아 작곡가 볼프강 아마데우스 모차르트는 조로아스터교의 테마를 그의 오페라 '마술 피리'에 넣었다. [6]그 작품들과 다른 것들은 오늘날까지 존재하면서 비교적 잘 알려지지 않은 신앙의 울림을 서구 세계에 가져온다.

Zoroastrianism 명 조로아스터교 contemporary 형 현대의
practice 동 실천하다 faith 명 신앙 prophet 명 선지자
tenet 명 교리 obscure 형 잘 알려지지 않은
monotheistic 형 유일신의 considerable 형 상당한
archaeological 형 고고학적인 polytheistic 형 다신교의
pagan 형 이교도의 ritual 명 의식 divine 형 신성한
state religion 국교 reinforce 동 강화하다 liberate 동 해방시키다
captivity 명 억류 homeland 명 고향 dominant 형 지배적인
subsequently 부 그 후에 coerce 동 강요하다
philosophical 형 철학의 novella 명 중편 소설 echo 명 울림

1 지문에서 글쓴이는 왜 "Christianity and Islam"을 언급하는가?

(A) 특정한 신앙의 상대적인 수명을 보여주기 위해
(B) 신앙 체계가 점차 영향력을 상실해 왔음을 시사하기 위해
(C) 두 개의 서로 다른 종교 운동의 교리를 비교하기 위해
(D) 종교가 소수의 신봉자를 가지고 있다는 것을 보여주기 위해

2 2단락에 따르면, 다음 중 조로아스터에 관해 사실이 아닌 것은?

(A) 다신교 부족에서 자랐다.
(B) 오늘날의 이란이나 아프가니스탄에 살았다.
(C) 실크로드로 중국을 향해 여행했다.
(D) 그의 신앙은 제국의 국교가 되었다.

3 지문의 단어 "coerced"와 의미가 가장 비슷한 것은?

(A) 강요된
(B) 지정된
(C) 보상된
(D) 준비된

4 3단락에 따르면, 다음 중 키루스 대제에 관해 사실인 것은?

(A) 억류자들로부터 유대인들을 해방시켰다.
(B) 유대인들을 조로아스터교로 개종하려고 노력했다.
(C) 조로아스터교를 믿지 않는 사람들에게 세금을 부과했다.
(D) 7세기에 이슬람 전사들에게 패배했다.

5 지문에서 글쓴이는 왜 "*Zadig*"를 언급하는가?

(A) 볼테르가 조로아스터 종교의 신도였음을 시사하기 위해
(B) 조로아스터교의 영향의 예시를 들기 위해
(C) '자디그'가 '서동시집'보다 우월한 작품이었다고 주장하기 위해
(D) 조로아스터교와 계몽주의 사상을 대조하기 위해

6 다음 중 4단락에서 조로아스터교에 대한 계몽주의의 영향에 관해 추론할 수 있는 것은?

(A) 더 적은 사람들이 그 신앙을 실천하게 했다.
(B) 더 많은 유럽인들이 그 종교에 대해 알도록 했다.
(C) 많은 사람들이 조로아스터교로 개종하도록 영감을 주었다.
(D) 조로아스터교 문학의 번역본을 소개했다.

Reading Practice 3

본문 p.126

1 (A) 2 (C) 3 (B) 4 (C) 5 (C) 6 (B)

에니그마

제2차 세계대전 동안, 연합군과 추축군 세력은 둘 다 적이 그들의 메시지 내용에 대한 지식을 얻지 못하게 하는 효율적인 의사소통 방식을 개발하려고 시도했다. 성공적일 때, 이 전략은 군사 작전 세부 사항에 관한 메모를 안전하게 보내도록 해주었다. 일부 보안 조치에는 암호화된 메시지가 포함되었으며, 이것들 중 가장 유명한 것은 에니그마라고 불리는 암호화 장치와 함께 나치 독일에 의해 시행되었다. [1]그것이 마침내 해독되기 전에, 에니그마는 완전하게 안전한 의사소통 수단으로 여겨졌다.

비록 에니그마는 둘 이상의 디자인을 가지고 있었지만, 일반적인 것은 몇 가지 추가 기능을 가진 타자기라고 묘사될 수 있다. 위에서 보면, 장치 표면의 하단에는 키보드가 있었고, 각 키는 알파벳의 글자를 나타냈다. 키보드 위에는 전구 한 세트가 있었다. 이것들은 글자에 해당했으며, 글자들은 같은 배열로 놓여 있었다. 전구들 위에는 회전자라고 불리는, 엄지손가락으로 움직일 수 있는 세 개의 바퀴가 있었는데, 이는 오른쪽에서 왼쪽으로 빠르게, 중간, 느리게 지정되었다. [4D]각 회전자는 한쪽에 26개의 전기 접점을 가지고 있었고, 이것들은 나머지 한 쪽의 26개의 글자들에 연결되었으며, 각 회전자는 수동으로 언제든지 어떤 글자로든 설정될 수 있었다. [4A]조작자가 키를 누르면 오른쪽 회전자가 입력된 글자마다 전진하는 반면, 가운데 회전자는 26개 글자마다 한 번씩 전진했고, 왼쪽 회전자는 676개 글자마다 한 번씩 앞으로 전진했다. [4B]세 개의 회전자들 중 어느 하나라도 움직이면 알파벳의 글자들이 연속적으로 재배열되는 결과를 낳았고, 따라서 이 배열은 겉보기에는 가능한 출력의 무한한 조합을 만들어냈다.

전기 신호가 세 개의 회전자를 통해 이동하면서, 그것들은 전자 반사기와 마주쳤고 그것은 전류를 반대 방향에 있는 회전자로 돌려보냈다. 그러나, 배선은 전류가 별도의 경로를 통해 돌아가도록 설정되었다. 예를 들어, 만약 조작자가 'A'를 누르면, 신호는 'A', 'P', 'Z'를 통해 이동할 수 있었으며, 그 후에 반사기는 전류가 회전자를 통해 돌아가는 길에서 'Z', 'G', 'B' 접점을 통해 다시 전송할 수 있었다. 이 예시에서, 'B'는 'A'의 '암호문', 혹은 암호화된 문자 형태가 될 것이며 'B' 전구가 켜질 것이다. [5]만약 'A'가 두 번째로 눌리면, 다음 경로에 대한 완전히 다른 순서가 만들어질 것이다.

에니그마의 전기 회로는 완벽하게 대칭적이었다. 결과적으로, 동일한 방식으로 구성된 두 기계를 사용할 때, 메시지는 하나의 기계에서 암호화된 다음 다른 기계에서 쉽게 해독될 수 있었다. 수신자가 추가적인 변환이나 해석 없이 빠르게 메시지를 해독할 수 있었기 때문에 이 대칭성은 구성에 대한 키를 가지고 있는 누구에게나 편리했다. 그러나, 그것은 또한 에니그마를 더 취약하게 만들었으며, 이 약점은 결국 그것의 불가사의한 암호를 해독한 폴란드와 영국 연합군의 암호학자들에 의해 이용되었다.

coded (형)암호화된 implement (동)시행하다 encryption (명)암호화
decode (동)해독하다 typewriter (명)타자기
correspond to ~에 해당하다 layout (명)배열 rotor (명)회전자
designate (동)지정하다 contact (명)접점 manually (부)수동으로
reorder (동)재배열하다 boundless (형)무한한 reflector (명)반사기
current (명)전류 wiring (명)배선 sequence (명)순서
circuit (명)회로 symmetrical (형)대칭적인 identical (형)동일한
decrypt (동)해독하다 configuration (명)구성
decipher (동)해독하다 conversion (명)변환 vulnerable (형)취약한
exploit (동)이용하다 cryptographer (명)암호학자
ultimately (부)결국

1 1단락에서 에니그마에 관해 추론할 수 있는 것은?

(A) 독일인들은 가장 민감한 정보를 전달하기 위해 그것을 사용했다.
(B) 연합군 세력은 자신만의 암호를 만들기 위해 그것을 복제하고 싶어 했다.
(C) 군인들은 처음에 그것의 유용성에 대해 확신하지 못했다.
(D) 적의 의사소통은 그것을 이용해 쉽게 해독될 수 있었다.

2 지문의 단어 "boundless"와 의미가 가장 비슷한 것은?

(A) 대단히 귀중한
(B) 풍부한
(C) 무제한의
(D) 한정된

3 2단락에서 글쓴이는 왜 타자기를 언급하는가?

(A) 발명 이면에서 영감을 준 것을 명시하기 위해
(B) 장치의 기본적인 외관을 설명하기 위해
(C) 수동식 키보드가 있는 최초의 기계를 확인하기 위해
(D) 장치를 조작하기 위해 사용된 방법을 설명하기 위해

4 다음 중 2단락에서 에니그마의 회전자와 관련하여 언급되지 않은 것은?

(A) 오른쪽에 있는 회전자는 키를 누를 때마다 움직였다.
(B) 어떠한 회전자를 움직여도 알파벳이 재배열되었다.
(C) 가운데 회전자가 가장 느리게 움직였다.
(D) 각 회전자는 26개의 글자들에 연결되었다.

5 3단락에 따르면, 에니그마 조작자가 같은 글자를 두 번 누르면 어떤 일이 일어나는가?

(A) 전기 신호가 반대 방향으로 이동할 것이다.
(B) 그 글자를 나타내는 전구가 켜질 것이다.
(C) 두 번째 경로가 완전히 다른 순서를 가질 것이다.
(D) 암호화된 글이 같은 글자에서 끝날 것이다.

6 4단락에서 글쓴이의 주된 목적은?

(A) 독일의 장치를 연합군의 대응물과 비교하기
(B) 보안상의 결함으로 밝혀진 기능을 보여주기
(C) 생산된 암호를 해독하기 어려웠던 이유 설명하기
(D) 메시지를 암호화하는 방식에 대한 개선 제안하기

iBT Reading Test 1

본문 p.128

1 (D) 2 (C) 3 (C) 4 (B)
5 (D) 6 (B) 7 (C) 8 (C)
9 (D) 10 (B), (D), (F)

기후 변화와 해류

비록 과학자들이 지구 온난화의 정도와 영향에 대해 계속 논쟁하고 있지만, 그들은 모두 그 현상이 실재하며 세계의 해양에 상당한 영향을 미칠 것이라는 데 동의한다. 2A/2B가장 명백한 우려는 극지방 빙원의 용해가 해수면이 급격히 상승하도록 하면서 해안 지역에 홍수의 위험을 초래할 것이라는 점이다. 2D그러나, 훨씬 더 심각한 위협은 물을 지구 해양 곳곳으로 운반하는 해류 체계 중단에 대한 가능성이다.

해류는 두 가지의 주요 유형으로 나누어질 수 있는데, 이는 표층 해류와 심층 해류이다. 표층 해류는 주로 열대 및 극지방에서 지속적으로 동쪽으로 이동하는 기단들과 중위도 지역에서 서쪽으로 이동하는 것들과 같은 탁월풍에 의해 이끌린다. 심층 해류는 각각 "열"과 "염도"을 뜻하는 그리스어 'thermo'와 'haline'에서 유래된 용어인 열염분 순환으로 알려진 것의 결과이다. 그 이름이 시사하듯, 열염분 순환은 바닷물의 온도와 염분의 변화에 의존하는데, 바닷물이 더 차가워지고 염분이 더 많아질수록 물의 밀도는 높아진다. 어떤 지점에서, 그것은 해저로 가라앉아 아래에 있는 물을 대체할 것이다. 같이 작용하는 이 두 가지 유형의 해류는 방대한 양의 바닷물이 고정된 패턴으로 엄청난 거리를 이동하도록 야기하는데, 이는 해양 컨베이어 벨트라고 알려지게 된 과정이다.

이 해류 네트워크를 추적할 때, 과학자들은 일반적으로 매우 추운 온도가 얼음 형성을 야기하는 북대서양에서 시작한다. 7얼음은 소금을 포함하지 않기 때문에, 남아 있는 차가운 바닷물은 매우 높은 염도를 가지고 있으며, 그 결과, 밀도가 매우 높다. 필연적으로 그것이 가라앉을 때, 그것은 대서양 깊은 곳에 이미 존재하는 물을 그것이 남극 대륙에 도착할 때까지 남쪽으로 밀어내고, 대륙붕을 따라 동쪽으로 이동하기 시작한다. 결국, 이 물은 북쪽으로 흘러 인도양과 태평양으로 들어가는데, 그곳에서 그것은 더 따뜻하고 덜 짠 물과 섞이며 표면으로 떠오르기 시작한다. 이 시점에, 그것은 멕시코 만류 같은 풍류의 영향을 받게 되며, 다시 북대서양으로 운반되고, 그곳에서 그것은 전체 여정을 다시 시작한다.

8지속적인 이동과 따뜻하고 차가운 물의 섞임은 지구의 기후를 조절하고 해양 생물에게 필수적인 영양분을 운반하기 때문에, 해양 컨베이어 벨트는 지구의 전반적인 건강에 매우 중요하다. 안타깝게도, 지구 온난화가 이 해류 네트워크를 중단할 수 있을 상당한 가능성이 있다. 주요한 문제는, 계속 진행 중인 북반구 빙원의 용해가 북대서양으로 들어가는 대량의 담수가 된다는 것이다. **동시에, 상승하는 온도로 인해 새로운 해빙은 더 느린 속도로 형성되고 있다.** 이에 대응하여, 바닷물은 덜 짜지고, 따라서, 밀도가 낮아지고 있다. 만약 이것이 유입되는 바닷물이 더 이상 해저로 가라앉지 않을 정도까지 지속된다면, 열염분 순환이 없어져 해양 컨베이어 벨트가 완전히 허물어지게 할 수 있다.

extent 명정도 implication 명영향 phenomenon 명현상
dramatically 부급격히 coastal 형해안의 interruption 명중단
prevailing wind 탁월풍 air mass 기단 latitude 명위도
outcome 명결과 thermohaline circulation 열염분 순환
salinity 명염도 respectively 부각각 density 명밀도
sink 동가라앉다 displace 동대체하다 in unison 같이, 일제히
immense 형엄청난 fixed 형고정된 track 동추적하다
typically 부일반적으로 inevitably 부필연적으로
continental shelf 대륙붕 critically 부매우 vital 형필수적인

1 지문의 단어 "extent"와 의미가 가장 비슷한 것은?
(A) 신뢰성
(B) 결과
(C) 적용
(D) 규모

2 1단락에 따르면, 다음 중 지구 온난화와 관련된 문제가 아닌 것은?
(A) 지구의 북쪽과 남쪽 지역에 있는 얼음의 손실
(B) 지구 해양 표면 높이의 상승
(C) 홍수로 불어난 물이 바다쪽으로 이동함에 따른 해안선의 침식
(D) 먼 거리에 걸친 바닷물의 이동에 대한 방해

3 지문의 단어 "ones"가 가리키는 것은?
(A) 유형
(B) 해류
(C) 단
(D) 지방

4 아래 문장 중 지문 속의 음영된 문장의 핵심 정보를 가장 잘 표현한 것은? 오답은 문장의 의미를 크게 바꾸거나 핵심 정보를 생략한다.
(A) 열염분 순환은 바닷물의 온도 하락이나 그것의 염도 상승으로 인해 촉발될 수 있다.
(B) 온도가 떨어지고 염도가 상승함에 따라 물의 밀도가 상승하는 것은 열염분 순환의 근거이다.
(C) 열염분 순환이 없으면, 바닷물은 점점 더 차가워질 것이며 그것의 염도는 계속해서 상승할 것이다.
(D) 열염분 순환의 정도는 바닷물의 온도와 염도를 측정함으로써 밝혀질 수 있다.

5 지문의 단어 "inevitably"와 의미가 가장 비슷한 것은?
(A) 즉시
(B) 별도로
(C) 지속적으로
(D) 필연적으로

6 지문에서 글쓴이는 왜 "the Gulf Stream"을 언급하는가?
(A) 남극에서 온 물이 더 따뜻해지는 이유를 설명하기 위해
(B) 표면의 물을 움직이는 풍류의 예시를 제공하기 위해
(C) 풍류가 북대서양에 도달할 수 있다는 것을 입증하기 위해
(D) 바닷물의 움직임에 영향을 미치는 요인들의 수를 강조하기 위해

7 3단락에 따르면, 북대서양 바닷물의 염도를 상승시키는 것은?
(A) 얼음의 형성이 소금 침전물들이 덩어리로 합쳐지도록 한다.
(B) 바닷물의 온도가 하락함에 따라 그것의 밀도가 더 높아진다.
(C) 담수가 얼어붙음에 따라 해양에서 제거된다.
(D) 차가운 물이 가라앉음에 따라 소금이 아래로 밀려난다.

8 4단락에 따르면, 해양 컨베이어 벨트가 중요한 것은 그것이
(A) 영양물을 찾는 해양 동물의 이주를 용이하게 하기 때문이다
(B) 소금물과 담수 사이의 올바른 균형을 보장하기 때문이다
(C) 해양 생물에 의해 요구되는 먹이 자원을 순환시키기 때문이다
(D) 일부 지역에서 해빙이 용해되는 속도를 느리게 하기 때문이다

9 네 개의 네모[■]는 다음 문장이 삽입될 수 있는 곳을 나타내고 있다.

동시에, 상승하는 온도로 인해 새로운 해빙은 더 느린 속도로 형성되고 있다.

이 문장은 어디에 들어가는 것이 가장 적절한가?

10 지시: 지문 요약을 위한 도입 문장이 아래에 주어져 있다. 지문의 가장 중요한 내용을 나타내는 보기 3개를 골라 요약을 완성하라. 어떤 문장은 지문에 언급되지 않은 내용이나 사소한 정보를 나타내므로 요약에 포함되지 않는다. **이 문제는 2점이다.**

> 해양 컨베이어 벨트는 지구 해양의 건강에 필수적이지만 지구 온난화에 의해 위협받고 있다.
> · (B) 표층 풍류와 심해 열염분류는 결합하여 해양 컨베이어 벨트를 형성한다.
> · (D) 바닷물은 북대서양에서 남극 대륙으로 이동하며 그 후에 인도양과 태평양을 통해 되돌아온다.
> · (F) 기후 변화는 바닷물의 염도를 낮추고 있으며, 이는 심해의 해류를 방해할 수 있다.

(A) 지속적으로 한 방향으로 부는 바람은 해양의 표면을 따라 이동하는 해류의 원인이다.
(C) 북대서양 해저에 있는 물은 해양의 다른 부분에 있는 물보다 더 차갑고 염분이 더 많다.
(E) 온도 상승은 용해되는 얼음에서 세계의 해양으로 들어가는 담수의 양을 증가시켰다.

iBT Reading Test 2

본문 p.132

1 (C)	2 (B)	3 (D)	4 (A)
5 (A)	6 (A)	7 (A)	8 (C)
9 (C)	10 (A), (C), (D)		

부리의 진화

1만 종의 현존하는 새들이 공룡의 직계 후손이라는 가설은 과학계에서 더 이상 논쟁의 대상이 아니다. [2]생물학자 토머스 헨리 헉슬리가 그의 1870년 저서 '공룡 파충류와 새 사이의 유사성에 대한 추가 증거'에서 그것을 제안한 이후, 그 연관성은 수십 년 동안 논란이 되었지만, 그의 가설에 대한 모든 이의는 새로운 화석 발견에 의해 하나씩 해결되었다. [3A/3B]하늘을 나는 공룡, 차골을 가진 공룡, 세 개의 갈퀴 발톱을 가진 공룡, 그리고 넓은 움직임 범위를 가진 손목을 가진 공룡들이 있었다. [3C]1996년에, 한 중국인 농부가 깃털 달린 공룡인 '시노사우롭테릭스'를 발견하면서 사실상 그 논쟁을 끝냈다. 현재는 많은 공룡들이, 아마 거대한 티라노사우루스 렉스까지도 깃털을 가지고 있었다고 믿어진다. 그러나 과학자들은 공룡과 새의 한 가지 차이점에 대해 여전히 어리둥절해한다. 새는 어떻게 치아가 없는 부리를 발달시켰을까? 이 놀라운 다용도 구조물은 깃털에서 기생충을 꼼꼼하게 손질하는 것뿐만 아니라 먹이를 잡고, 끄집어내고, 찢을 수 있다. **이러한 기능들은 대부분의 공룡들을 특징짓는 치아가 있고 신축성 없는 주둥이로는 수행될 수 없었다.** 새의 치아 부재에 대한 설명은 생태학적 및 발달적의 두 가지 범주로 나누어지는 경향이 있다.

새의 부리 발달에 대한 가장 일반적인 생태학적 설명은 먹이 획득이 원동력이었다고 추측한다. 이 설명은 1830년대 찰스 다윈의 갈라파고스 섬으로의 여정으로 거슬러 올라간다. [5]그는 여러 섬에 있는 되새류들의 부리 모양에서 차이점들을 발견했고 부리가 새들이 구할 수 있는 씨앗을 담을 수 있도록 진화했다고 결론 내렸다. 동시대의 수많은 연구가 다윈의 가설을 뒷받침했지만, 새의 개별 종의 진화는 훨씬 더 넓은 규모로 부리의 발달을 추적할 때 모호한 중요성을 갖는다. [6]2016년, 데릭 라슨은 치아가 있고 새와 비슷한 수많은 공룡들이 백악기-팔레오기 대멸종에서 절멸했음을 입증했으며, 치아가 없는 새들이 살아남은 것은 육식성이면서 새와 비슷한 공룡들이 불행한 결말을 맞게 한 운석 충돌 이후에도 남아있었을 것으로 보이는 씨앗 은행에 의존했기 때문이라고 추측했다. 다시 말해, 새들은 그것들의 부리 때문에 견디었다. 그러나, 치아가 없는 일부 중생대의 새들은 그 대멸종으로 소멸했으며, 이는 생태학적 설명에 한계가 있음을 시사한다.

발달적 모델은 유전 과학과 화석 증거를 결합하여 부리가 어떻게 발달했는지 설명한다. 2017년, 중국 고생물학자 슈오 왕은 초기 새 화석의 내부를 정밀 검사하였으며, 이는 치아 손실의 단계적 진행을 관찰할 수 있게 했다. 새와 관련된 일부 공룡들은 성체 시기에 빠진 치아를 어릴 때는 가지고 있었다. 다른 것들은 치아가 없었지만 그것들의 턱에 치아 구멍을 유지하고 있었다. 현대의 새들에 대한 연구는 BMP-4로 알려진 유전 분자가 부리의 성장과 치아의 억제를 둘 다 조절한다는 것을 밝혀냈다. 그것은 또한 현대 새 종들의 공룡 조상들의 치아가 있는 턱에서 부리로의 점진적인 발달에 있어 중요한 역할을 했을 가능성이 높다.

hypothesis 명 가설　affinity 명 유사성　reptile 명 파충류
objection 명 이의　effectively 부 사실상　versatile 형 다용도의
pry 동 끄집어내다　fastidiously 부 꼼꼼하게　parasite 명 기생충
absence 명 부재　ecological 형 생태학적인　posit 동 추측하다
acquisition 명 획득　finch 명 되새류
accommodate 동 담다, 수용하다　dubious 형 모호한
significance 명 중요성　speculate 동 추측하다
outlast 동 더 오래 가다　doom 동 불행한 결말을 맞게 하다
carnivorous 형 육식성의　perish 동 소멸하다
paleontologist 명 고생물학자　progression 명 진행, 발달
molecule 명 분자　suppression 명 억제

1 지문의 단어 "fastidiously"와 의미가 가장 비슷한 것은?
(A) 마지못하여
(B) 기괴하게
(C) 꼼꼼하게
(D) 즉시

2 1단락에 따르면, 생물학자 토머스 헨리 헉슬리는
(A) 공룡이 새의 조상이라는 이론에 반대했다
(B) 두 종류의 유기체 사이의 관계를 시사했다
(C) 과학적 논쟁을 초래한 화석을 발견했다
(D) 현대 과학자들에 의해 거부된 제안을 했다

3 1단락에 따르면, 다음 중 새의 조상이 멸종한 공룡이라는 주장을 뒷받침하는 공룡의 특징이 아닌 것은?
(A) 발의 모양
(B) 관절의 유연성
(C) 깃털의 성장
(D) 뼈의 밀도

4 지문의 단어 "dubious"와 의미가 가장 비슷한 것은?
(A) 미심쩍은
(B) 과장된
(C) 부정확한
(D) 구식인

5 2단락에 따르면, 갈라파고스섬에서 다윈에 의해 관찰된 되새류들은

(A) 다양한 부리 형태를 보였다
(B) 같은 종류의 씨앗을 먹었다
(C) 한 섬에서 더 큰 집단으로 살았다
(D) 먹이를 찾아 정기적으로 이주했다

6 다음 중 2단락에서 백악기-팔레오기 대멸종 동안의 치아가 있고 새와 비슷한 공룡들에 관해 추론할 수 있는 것은?

(A) 생존하기에 충분한 양의 먹이에 접근할 수 없었다.
(B) 치아가 없는 새들과 동일한 자원을 놓고 경쟁했다.
(C) 운석 충돌의 영향에 크게 영향을 받지 않았다.
(D) 생존하기 위해 급격한 생리적 변화를 겪었다.

7 아래 문장 중 지문 속의 음영된 문장의 핵심 정보를 가장 잘 표현한 것은? 오답은 문장의 의미를 크게 바꾸거나 핵심 정보를 생략한다.

(A) 새의 점진적인 치아 손실과 관련된 데이터는 화석을 연구하는 중국인 과학자에 의해 수집되었다.
(B) 중국인 연구자에 의해 조사된 화석은 최초의 새들이 치아가 있는 턱을 가지고 있었음을 분명히 보여주었다.
(C) 중국인 고생물학자에 따르면 새의 치아 손실은 원래 생각했던 것보다 훨씬 더 일찍 일어났을 수도 있다.
(D) 중국인 전문가에 의해 연구된 새들은 시간이 지나면서 치아가 없도록 진화했기 때문에, 그것들 모두가 치아를 가지고 있었던 것은 아니다.

8 3단락에서 글쓴이는 왜 BMP-4에 관해 논하는가?

(A) 현대의 새들이 초기의 공룡들과 유사하다는 것을 보여주기 위해
(B) 일부 유기체가 노화로 인해 치아를 잃는 이유를 설명하기 위해
(C) 생리학적 전환의 가능한 원인을 식별하기 위해
(D) 많은 조류 종들이 밀접하게 연관되어 있음을 시사하기 위해

9 네 개의 네모[■]는 다음 문장이 삽입될 수 있는 곳을 나타내고 있다.

이러한 기능들은 대부분의 공룡들을 특징짓는 치아가 있고 신축성 없는 주둥이로는 수행될 수 없었다.

이 문장은 어디에 들어가는 것이 가장 적절한가?

10 지시: 지문 요약을 위한 도입 문장이 아래에 주어져 있다. 지문의 가장 중요한 내용을 나타내는 보기 3개를 골라 요약을 완성하라. 어떤 문장은 지문에 언급되지 않은 내용이나 사소한 정보를 나타내므로 요약에 포함되지 않는다. **이 문제는 2점이다.**

> **과학자들은 공룡으로부터 온 새의 혈통을 인정했지만, 부리의 발달에 관해서는 여전히 확신하지 못한다.**
> · (A) 부리의 발달에 대한 생태학적 설명은 먹이를 획득하는 데 있어서의 부리의 사용에 초점을 맞춘다.
> · (C) 전 세계적인 파괴를 초래한 사건은 부리를 갖는 것을 중요한 장점으로 만들었을 수 있다.
> · (D) 발달적 설명은 유전자 과학과 화석 연구 둘 다에서 파생된다.

(B) 갈라파고스섬으로의 여행 동안 다윈이 발달시킨 이론들은 더 최근의 연구에 의해 뒷받침된다.
(E) 치아가 없었음에도 불구하고 턱에 치아 구멍을 가지고 있는 일부 하늘을 나는 공룡들이 존재했다.
(F) 일부 새 종들이 깃털을 발달시켰을 때 새는 공룡으로부터 분리되어 진화하기 시작했다.

Vocabulary Review

본문 p.136

1 visualize		2 pried	3 unearthed
4 doomed		5 monotheistic	6 erroneously
7 (D)	8 (A)	9 (B)	10 (A)
11 (D)	12 (C)	13 (C)	14 (D)

CHAPTER 08
Sentence Insertion

Example

본문 p.139

1 (D) 2 (B)

흰머리독수리

미국인들이 항상 그들의 국조인 흰머리독수리에게 최고의 보호자였던 것은 아니며, 그 위엄 있는 포식자는 40년간 멸종 위기종 목록에 올라 있었다. 그것의 수는 사냥꾼들에 의해 줄어들었는데, 그들은 오락을 위해, 또 그 독수리가 너무 많은 물고기를 먹는 것을 우려하여 그 새에게 총구를 겨누었다. 그러나, 1940년대를 시작으로, DDT라고 불리는 합성 살충제가 흰머리독수리에 대한 가장 큰 위협으로서 사냥을 대체했다. 그 화학 물질은 그 새의 주요 식량원이었던 물고기들에게 스며들었고 독수리의 번식력에 파괴적인 영향을 미쳤다. **그것은 또한 더 얇아진 알 껍데기를 초래했고, 따라서 더 적은 수의 흰머리독수리가 성년기에 도달할 수 있었다.** 1970년까지, 비록 알래스카의 야생 영역에는 그것들이 풍부하게 남아 있긴 했지만, 더 아래쪽의 48개 주들에는 오직 400쌍의 독수리만이 남아 있었다.

흰머리독수리의 개체 수는 미국 정부와 환경 보호론자들에 의한 집중적인 노력 덕분에 1970년대 초에 반등하기 시작했다. 그 새의 확산에 있어 가장 중요한 요인은 1972년의 국가적 DDT 사용 금지였다. **그러나, 이것이 그 재기에 있어 역할을 한 유일한 요인은 아니었다.** 광범위한 흰머리독수리 서식지가 보존을 위해 지정되었으며, 이는 이전 수십 년간의 서식지 감소와 퇴화의 추세를 뒤집었다. 게다가, 설계 개선이 이루어진 후에는 더 적은 수의 독수리들이 전선에 의해 감전되었으며, 포획된 새끼 독수리들은 야생의 독수리 둥지에 넣어졌다. 2007년까지, 이러한 노력은 매우 크게 성과를 거두어서 그 국조는 그 국가의 멸종 위기종 목록에서 제외되었다.

caretaker 명 보호자　regal 형 위엄 있는　predator 명 포식자
endangered 형 멸종 위기의　synthetic pesticide 합성 살충제
supplant 동 대체하다　permeate 동 스며들다
devastating 형 파괴적인　rebound 동 반등하다
conservationist 명 환경 보호론자　proliferation 명 확산
designate 동 지정하다　preservation 명 보존　reverse 동 뒤집다
degradation 명 퇴화　electrocute 동 감전시키다
captive 형 포획된

1 1단락에서 네 개의 네모[■]는 다음 문장이 삽입될 수 있는 곳을 나타내고 있다.

그것은 또한 더 얇아진 알 껍데기를 초래했고, 따라서 더 적은 수

의 흰머리독수리가 성년기에 도달할 수 있었다.

이 문장은 어디에 들어가는 것이 가장 적절한가?

2 2단락에서 네 개의 네모[■]는 다음 문장이 삽입될 수 있는 곳을 나타내고 있다.

그러나, 이것이 그 재기에 있어 역할을 한 유일한 요인은 아니었다.

이 문장은 어디에 들어가는 것이 가장 적절한가?

Reading Practice 1

본문 p.140

1 (C) 2 (D) 3 (D) 4 (C) 5 (C) 6 (B)

북아메리카 토착 천문학

식민지화 이전 시대에, 천문학은 북아메리카 토착민들의 삶에서 중요한 역할을 했다. 그것은 실용적인 지혜와 그들 문화의 중요한 부분 둘 다의 원천이었다. 그리고 천문학에 관한 토착의 지식이 많이 소실된 반면, 그것을 보존하려는 노력은 별을 바라보는 많은 대안적인 방법들을 보여준다.

예를 들어, 대부분의 아메리카 원주민 부족들은 문자 언어가 없었지만, 그들은 다른 방법으로 천문학적 사건들을 추적했다. 만들어진 대부분의 기록들은 그림의 형태였다. 비록 그것들의 기원 연대는 알려져 있지 않지만, 대대로 전해져 내려온 동물 가죽 위의 그림들과 이야기들은 여전히 존재한다. 아메리카 원주민들의 기록들 중 역사적인 사건의 예시는 1833년에 일어났던 사자자리 유성우이다. **이 사건은 엄청난 인상을 남겨 그 유성우에 대한 연대순 기록이 수 족에 의해 동물 가죽에 남겨졌다.** [3]마리코파 부족은 그 사건을 기록했던 달력 막대를 보관했다. 막대에 새겨진 각 자국은 "별들이 떨어진" 이래로 흐른 1년을 나타냈다.

아메리카 원주민들이 유성과 혜성에 대해 가졌던 설명은 특정 부족들이 다양한 범위의 태도를 가지고 있었음을 보여준다. 일부는 거의 두려움을 보이지 않았지만, 다른 부족들은 천문학적 사건이 발생했을 때 엄청난 두려움을 느꼈다. [4A]두려움을 보이지 않았던 부족들은 유성과 혜성이 사후 세계로 여행하는 주술사들의 영혼이라고 믿었다. [4D]예를 들어, 캘리포니아의 루이세뇨족에게 이것들은 그저 움직이는 별들일 뿐이었다. [4B]그러나 일부 부족들은 유성과 혜성을 지구의 종말이나 거의 모든 생물의 파괴와 같이 그들이 일어날 것이라고 믿었던 사건들과 연관시켰기 때문에 일종의 불길한 예감을 느꼈다. **그러한 부족들은 화석화된 공룡 뼈의 발견 때문에 후자가 사실일 것이라고 강하게 믿었다.** 몇몇 부족들은 그러한 사건들을 주술사의 설명이 필요한 징조라고 여겼다.

심지어 오늘날에도, 별에 대한 각 부족의 지식은 그것 자신의 신화에 대한 지식을 반영한다. 유럽인들이 그리스 전설을 따서 별자리들의 이름을 지은 것처럼, 아메리카 원주민들은 별을 설명할 때 그들 자신의 전통을 활용했다. 예를 들어, 유럽 출신의 누군가는 하늘에서 가장 밝은 별 세 개를 보고 사냥꾼 오리온을 떠올린다. 북아메리카 오대호 지역 출신의 오지브웨족 사람들은 동일한 밝은 별들을 보고 곧 추운 날씨가 올 것이라는 징조인 윈터메이커를 떠올린다. 비슷하게, 스키디족 사람들은 북쪽왕관자리로 알려진 별자리에 큰 의미를 부여했다. 그들은 이 별들의 무리를 족장들의 의회라고 불렀다. [6]이 해석은 농업 계획을 위한 지침뿐만 아니라 원로 위원회에 의한 정부 모델을 제공했다. 이 별자리가 너무 중요해서 스키디족 사람들은 그들이 사랑하는 의회를 명확히 시야에 담을 수 있는 지붕이 열린 오두막에서 살았다. 오늘날, 아메리카 원주민들의 천문학은 그들의 고대 종교의 렌즈와 과학적 지식의 렌즈를 통해 동시에 천문학적 현상을 바라보는 "두 눈으로 보는 것"을 옹호하는 부족 지도자들에 의해 전해진다.

indigenous 형 토착의, 고유의 colonization 명 식민지화
preserve 동 보존하다 alternative 형 대안적인
astronomical 형 천문학적인 meteor shower 유성우
notch 명 자국 comet 명 혜성 varying 형 다양한
enormous 형 엄청난 apprehension 명 두려움
shaman 명 주술사 afterlife 명 사후 세계
foreboding 명 (불길한) 예감 destruction 명 파괴 omen 명 징조
mythology 명 신화 constellation 명 별자리 luminous 형 밝은
ascribe 동 (의미 등을) 부여하다 committee 명 위원회
open-topped 형 지붕이 열린 simultaneously 부 동시에
phenomenon 명 현상

1 지문의 단어 "it"이 가리키는 것은?

(A) 지혜
(B) 문화
(C) 지식
(D) 천문학

2 네 개의 네모[■]는 다음 문장이 삽입될 수 있는 곳을 나타내고 있다.

이 사건은 엄청난 인상을 남겨 그 유성우에 대한 연대순 기록이 수 족에 의해 동물 가죽에 남겨졌다.

이 문장은 어디에 들어가는 것이 가장 적절한가?

3 2단락에 따르면, 마리코파 부족이 달력 막대에 자국을 새긴 것은

(A) 1년을 서로 다른 달들로 나누기 위함이었다
(B) 동물들의 연례 이동에 대해 알기 위함이었다
(C) 1833년 이후의 정확한 일수를 계산하기 위함이었다
(D) 유성우의 기념일을 나타내기 위함이었다

4 3단락에 따르면, 다음 중 혜성과 유성에 대한 아메리카 원주민의 설명이 아닌 것은?

(A) 움직이고 있는 망자들의 영혼이었다.
(B) 임박한 비극적 사건의 징조였다.
(C) 거대한 생물들의 잔해였다.
(D) 이곳저곳으로 이동하는 별들이었다.

5 지문의 단어 "ascribed"와 의미가 가장 비슷한 것은?

(A) 영구화했다
(B) 경험했다
(C) 부여했다
(D) 직감했다

6 4단락에 따르면, 다음 중 북쪽왕관자리에 대한 스키디족의 생각에 관해 사실인 것은?

(A) 그것을 그들의 오두막 설계에 대한 모델로 간주했다.
(B) 정부와 농업을 위한 지침으로 보았다.
(C) 다가오는 겨울의 징조로 해석했다.
(D) 그것이 깊은 종교적 중요성을 가지고 있는 것으로 여겼다.

Reading Practice 2

본문 p.142

1 (B) 2 (C) 3 (C) 4 (D) 5 (D) 6 (C)

태평양 생태계

태평양은 다양한 지리적 영역을 가로지르는 넓은 공간뿐만 아니라 그것의 순수한 크기 때문에 지구상에서 가장 중요한 환경적 체계 중 하나이다. 남반구의 남극에서부터 북반구의 북극까지 뻗어 있는 태평양은 세계에서 가장 큰 수역이다. **사실, 그것은 다음으로 가장 큰 것, 즉 대서양의 크기의 거의 두 배이다.** 그것은 또한 생물학적으로뿐만 아니라 상업적으로도 중요한 매우 다양한 생태계를 포함하고 있다. 따라서, 야생 생물과 인구 둘 다를 유지하는 데 있어서 태평양의 역할은 매우 중요하다.

태평양은 육지와 인접한 지역에서 특히 엄청난 생물 다양성을 가지고 있다. 예를 들어, 북아메리카 서부와 남아메리카 서부 앞바다는 지구상에서 가장 풍부하고 수익성이 높은 어장의 일부를 가지고 있다. [2]이것의 이유 중 하나는 태평양이 매우 깊고, 육지와 바다의 연결이 종종 점진적이라기 보다는 급작스러운 깊이의 변화를 만들어내기 때문이다. 이 수중 지형은 깊고 영양분이 풍부한 물을 표면으로 가져오는 융기라고 불리는 과정에서 차가운 물과 따뜻한 물의 혼합을 촉진한다. 영양분의 재순환은 먹이사슬의 기초를 이루는 플랑크톤과 같은 미생물에게 지속적인 자양물 공급원을 제공한다. 차례로, 작은 물고기들은 플랑크톤을 먹고, 그것들은 더 큰 포식성 물고기와 해양 포유류들에게 먹이를 제공한다.

환태평양 화산대에서의 화산 활동 또한 상당히 다양한 생물이 사는 독특한 서식지를 형성해 왔다. 화산은 모래 해안과 달리 조수 웅덩이 같은 생태계를 부양하는 바위가 많은 해안선을 만들었다. [3]만조 때 바닷물이 바위가 많은 해안으로 흘러나오면, 물웅덩이가 형성되고 이것들은 그것들의 작은 크기치곤 생물 다양성이 매우 높다. 비슷하게, 바로 앞바다에서는 태평양의 차가운 물이 켈프 숲을 부양하는데, 이는 아마 어떠한 대양 군락 중에서도 가장 큰 식물과 동물의 다양성을 품고 있는 밀집된 식물 생장 지역이다. [4A]태평양의 더 외딴 지역에서는, 화산 활동이 많은 섬들을 생겨나게 했다. **태평양에는 25,000개 이상의 섬이 있으며 이는 어떠한 대양보다도 많은 것이다.** [4B/4C]이것들과, 산호초뿐만 아니라 해저 화산 근처에서 형성되는 환초는 그렇지 않으면 상대적으로 적은 생물이 사는 공해일 태평양 지역의 중요한 서식지이다.

게다가, 태평양의 심해는 그 자체로 생태계이다. 부피로는 다른 것들에 비해 훨씬 더 낮은 생물 다양성을 담고 있음에도 불구하고, 이 환경은 가장 거대하다. 킹크랩의 특정 종들과 같은 일부 심해 생물들은 그것들의 상업적 가치로 인해 잘 알려져 있지만, 많은 것들은 기이하며 대부분 수수께끼로 남아있다. 국립 해양 대기청에 의한 3년간의 광범위한 연구는 거의 60만 제곱킬로미터의 범위에 걸쳐 약 35만 개의 독특한 심해 생물들을 발견했다. [6]이것들 중 오직 20퍼센트만이 종 수준에서 식별이 가능했기 때문에, 과학자들은 태평양의 심해 환경에 대해 아직 배울 것이 많다.

ecosystem 명 생태계　sheer 형 순수한, 순전한
expanse 명 넓은 공간　geographical 형 지리적인
hemisphere 명 반구　biologically 부 생물학적으로
commercially 부 상업적으로　particularly 부 특히
tremendous 형 엄청난　biodiversity 명 생물 다양성
adjacent 형 인접한　prolific 형 풍부한　profitable 형 수익성이 높은
fishery 명 어장　abrupt 형 급작스러운　gradual 형 점진적인
topography 명 지형　upwelling 명 융기　sustenance 명 자양물
predatory 형 포식성의　tide pool 조수 웅덩이　high tide 만조
harbor 동 품나　coral atoll 환초　coral reef 산호초
peculiar 형 기이한　enigmatic 형 수수께끼 같은
identifiable 형 식별이 가능한

1 네 개의 네모[■]는 다음 문장이 삽입될 수 있는 곳을 나타내고 있다.
사실, 그것은 다음으로 가장 큰 것, 즉 대서양의 크기의 거의 두 배이다.
이 문장은 어디에 들어가는 것이 가장 적절한가?

2 2단락에 따르면, 아메리카 대륙 서쪽 바다에 있는 어장은 왜 풍부한가?
(A) 영양분의 재순환이 급작스럽기보다는 점진적이다.
(B) 수중 지형이 차가운 물이 표면으로 올라오는 것을 막는다.
(C) 해안이 종종 급격한 깊이 변화를 만들어낸다.
(D) 포식성 포유류의 수가 다른 지역보다 적다.

3 다음 중 3단락에서 조수 웅덩이에 관해 추론할 수 있는 것은?
(A) 세계의 모든 대양에서 흔하다.
(B) 많은 종들을 부양할 수 없다.
(C) 켈프 숲보다 더 적은 수의 종들을 부양한다.
(D) 주로 태평양의 외딴 지역에 존재한다.

4 3단락에 따르면, 다음 중 태평양의 외딴 지역의 특징이 아닌 것은?
(A) 많은 화산섬들
(B) 다양한 산호 서식지들
(C) 수면 아래의 화산들
(D) 주로 생명체가 살지 않는 환경들

5 지문의 단어 "peculiar"과 의미가 가장 비슷한 것은?
(A) 평범한
(B) 희귀한
(C) 희박한
(D) 이상한

6 4단락에 따르면, 다음 중 국립 해양 대기청에 의한 3년간의 연구에 관해 사실인 것은?
(A) 상당한 상업적 가치를 가진 생명체들에 초점을 맞췄다.
(B) 태평양 면적의 약 20퍼센트를 포함했다.
(C) 심해 생물에 대해 얼마나 잘 모르고 있는지 밝혀냈다.
(D) 멸종된 것으로 여겨졌던 몇몇 종들을 발견했다.

Reading Practice 3

본문 p.144

1 (B) 2 (A) 3 (C) 4 (D) 5 (B) 6 (C)

잡초와 침입성 식물

잡초와 침입성 식물 종 사이의 차이에 대해 종종 혼란이 생긴다. 둘 다 농부들, 지주들, 환경 보호론자들을 답답하게 만들 수 있지만, 그것들은 같은 것이 아니다. [6D]잡초는 침입성이거나 비침입성일 수 있고, 침입성 종이 반드시 잡초로 간주되는 것은 아니다. [6B]'잡초'는 과학적인 용어가 아니며, 그것은 단지 농부나 정원사가 원치 않는 식물을 가리키는 단어이다. 반면에, '침입성'이라는 용어는 생물학자들에게 매우 구체적인 의미를 지닌다. 그것은 그것들이 자라는 생태계에 이질적이며 토착

종들에게 해를 끼치는 식물들을 가리킨다.

[6A]두 용어 사이의 중요한 차이점은 침입성 종이 종종 특정한 목적을 위해 인간에 의해 도입되는 반면, 잡초는 결코 의도적으로 재배되지 않는다는 것이다. 바랭이와 민들레 같은 잡초는 농장, 잔디밭, 정원에서 사람의 개입 없이 자유롭게 싹을 틔운다. [2]그것들은 농업에 있어 특히 해로운데, 여기에서 식량과 생계를 위해 재배되는 농작물들은 공간, 햇빛, 습기, 영양분을 위해 잡초와 경쟁해야 한다. 대조적으로, 침입성 종은 때때로 의도적으로 심어지는데, 이는 그 식물이 이질적인 지역에 사는 사람들이 그것이 매력적이라고 느끼거나, 다른 원치 않는 종들과의 경쟁에서 이기게 하기 위해 도입되기 때문이다. 예를 들어, 안데스산맥에서 유래한 식물인 바나나 포카는 그것의 먹을 수 있는 과일과 예쁜 꽃 때문에 20세기 초에 하와이에 도입되었다.

잡초와 침입성 종의 또 다른 차이는 잡초가 항상 해롭지는 않다는 것이다. 일부 잡초는 심지어 토양을 비옥하게 하고 침식을 막는 데 도움을 준다. 그것들은 자발적으로 자라기 때문에 잡초로 간주되지만, 사실 그것들은 생태계에 유용성을 제공한다. 그러나, 침입성 종은 그 자체로 해롭다. 한 식물이 침입성이 아니면서 외래일 수 있다는 점에 유의해야 한다. 한 예로 시베리아에서 미국으로 건너왔으나 관리하기가 쉽고 미국 대초원의 토양 안정에 유용하다고 여겨지는 마초풀이 있다. 따라서, 많은 토착 식물 애호가들과 일부 환경 운동가들이 모든 외래 식물 종을 위협으로 간주함에도 불구하고, 외래 식물의 유용성은 무시되어서는 안 된다.

일단 도입되면, 두 종류의 식물 모두 심각한 경제적 피해를 야기할 잠재력을 가지고 있다. 농부들에게 잡초는 수확량을 줄이고 유지비의 원인이 됨으로써 곤충, 식물 병해 및 설치류와 사슴같이 풀을 뜯어 먹는 유해 동물보다 더 큰 총체적 피해를 입힌다. 침입성 종들 또한 문제의 주요한 원인이다. [5]한 예로, 부레옥잠이라고 불리는 남아메리카의 식물은 그것의 매력적인 꽃 때문에 우간다로 가져와졌고, 그것이 너무 빽빽하게 자라 배들이 그 나라의 가장 큰 호수를 통과할 수 없었기 때문에 결국 항구를 폐쇄하고 어부들을 파산시키게 되었다. 피해에 대한 잠재력이 너무 크기 때문에 잡초와 침입성 종을 다룰 때는 세심한 종 관리가 요구된다. **이것의 중요한 한 측면은 관련 당사자들에게 원치 않는 종이 장악하는 것을 막는 가장 좋은 방법을 가르치는 지역사회 교육 프로그램이다.**

weed 명 잡초 invasive 형 침입성의 frustrating 형 답답하게 하는
conservationist 명 환경 보호론자 intentionally 부 의도적으로
crabgrass 명 바랭이 dandelion 명 민들레 sprout 동 싹을 틔우다
intervention 명 개입 sustenance 명 생계
outcompete 동 경쟁에서 이기다 undesirable 형 원치 않는
edible 형 먹을 수 있는 enrich 동 비옥하게 하다 erosion 명 침식
unbidden 형 자발적인 detrimental 형 해로운
by definition 그 자체로 crested wheatgrass 마초풀
stabilization 명 안정 enthusiast 명 애호가 potential 명 잠재력
collective 형 총체적인 rodent 명 설치류
water hyacinth 부레옥잠 densely 부 빽빽하게

1 지문의 단어 "intervention"과 의미가 가장 비슷한 것은?
(A) 지시
(B) 간섭
(C) 판단
(D) 보호

2 2단락에 따르면, 잡초가 농업에 있어 문제인 것은 그것들이
(A) 다른 식물들이 자라는 데 필요한 자원을 이용하기 때문이다
(B) 심어진 초목을 파괴하기 때문이다
(C) 농부들이 그들의 농작물을 쉽게 수확하는 것을 막기 때문이다
(D) 경작되어야 하는 땅의 양을 증가시키기 때문이다

3 지문에서 글쓴이는 왜 "crested wheatgrass"를 언급하는가?
(A) 침입성 종의 경제적 위험을 규명하기 위해
(B) 일부 침입성 종이 의도적으로 도입되었다는 것을 보여주기 위해
(C) 외래 식물이 유익할 수 있다는 증거를 제공하기 위해
(D) 침입성 종이 도입된 이유를 보여주기 위해

4 네 개의 네모[■]는 다음 문장이 삽입될 수 있는 곳을 나타내고 있다.
이것의 중요한 한 측면은 관련 당사자들에게 원치 않는 종이 장악하는 것을 막는 가장 좋은 방법을 가르치는 지역사회 교육 프로그램이다.
이 문장은 어디에 들어가는 것이 가장 적절한가?

5 4단락에 따르면, 우간다의 부레옥잠 도입은
(A) 큰 수역의 전체적인 심미적 매력을 강화했다
(B) 수입을 위해 호수에 의존했던 사람들에게 어려움을 초래했다
(C) 많은 개인 소유 배들에 심각한 피해를 초래했다
(D) 해안 지역사회들이 항구 시설을 개선하도록 부추겼다

6 지문에 따르면, 다음 중 잡초와 침입성 종에 관해 사실이 아닌 것은?
(A) 침입성 종은 때때로 의도적으로 재배되지만, 잡초는 그렇지 않다.
(B) 잡초는 일반적으로 비과학적인 의미의 원치 않는 식물이다.
(C) 잡초는 항상 침입성 종만큼 해롭다.
(D) 침입성 종이 반드시 잡초인 것은 아니다.

iBT Reading Test 1

본문 p.146

1 (A) 2 (C) 3 (B) 4 (C)
5 (B) 6 (D) 7 (B) 8 (D)
9 (C) 10 (B), (C), (F)

수력의 역사

인류는 문명의 여명기부터 동력을 위해 흐르는 물을 이용해 왔다. 곡물을 갈고 농작물을 관개하는 데 사용된 물레방아는 기원전 4000년경에 처음 나타났다. 이것들은 기어 장치의 추가를 포함하여 몇 가지 개선을 거쳤지만, 19세기까지 동일한 기본 설계가 그대로 유지되었다.

1827년에 중요한 혁신이 일어났는데, 이때 프랑스 기술자 브누아 푸르네롱이 터빈을 발명했다. [3]그는 물속에 수평으로 놓인 두 세트의 휘어진 날을 이용했고, 이는 그의 터빈을 흐르는 강물을 기계적인 에너지로 바꾸는 데 전통적인 수직 물레방아보다 훨씬 효율적이게 만들었다. 그의 첫 번째 모델은 겨우 6마력을 만들어낼 수 있었다. 그러나, 1837년까지 그는 원래 설계를 크게 개선했고 60마력을 만들어내는 모델을 만들었다. 푸르네롱의 터빈은 제조업자들에게 인기가 있었고, 미국 전역에 걸친 도시에 있는 공장들, 특히 그 국가 북동부에서 급성장하는 섬유 산업 공장들에 동력을 공급하는 일에 투입되었다.

전기를 만들어내기 위한 수력의 사용은 19세기에 전 세계의 기술자들로부터 큰 관심을 끌었지만, 이 새로운 기술이 본격적으로 적용되기 시작한 것은 미국에서였다. 전국에 시설들이 지어졌고, 이것들 중 가장

인상적인 것 중 하나는 1985년에 문을 연 에드워드 딘 애덤스 발전소였다. 수로가 나이아가라강의 물을 깊은 수직 통로 아래로 운반하는 파이프로 우회시켰다. 이 통로의 바닥에는 떨어지는 물의 힘에 의해 빠르게 회전하는 거대한 터빈이 있었다. 5그 터빈은 열 개의 발전기에 연결되어 있었는데, 이는 강력한 자석을 포함하고 있으며 회전될 때 전류를 생산하는 장치였다. 이 발전소에 의해 만들어진 전기는 뉴욕주 전역에서 사용되었다.

전기에 대한 폭발적인 수요를 충족시키기 위해 건설되는 어느 때보다 거대해진 댐들을 이용하여, 수력은 20세기 내내 원동력으로 남아 있었다. 수력이 낮은 비용 대 동력 비율을 제공했기 때문에, 그것은 성장하는 중공업 부문에게 필수적이었다. 그 결과, 많은 사람들이 수력을 진보와 연관 짓기 시작했다. 예를 들어, 1935년에 콜로라도 강에 완공된 후버 댐은 미국인들에 의해 국력과 모든 시민들을 위한 더 나은 삶의 상징으로 여겨지게 되었다. 그러나, 1980년대 후반에, 미국 대중은 수력에 대한 환상에서 깨게 되었다. 7그들은 특히 큰 댐들의 건설 중에 유발된 홍수가 물고기와 동물의 서식지를 파괴함에 따라, 그것들이 지역 생태계에 막대한 손해를 끼친다는 것을 이해하게 되었다. 이러한 문제들에 대한 인식은 수력의 추진력을 일시적으로 멈추었다.

21세기에, 기후 변화에 대한 우려는 그것의 환경적 단점들에도 불구하고 수력이 다시 주목을 받도록 했다. 강의 흐름이 일정하기 때문에, 물은 바람이나 태양보다 훨씬 더 실용적인 재생 에너지원이다. 그것은 또한 더 비용 효율적이라는 것이 입증되었다. **사실, 풍력과 태양 에너지로 만들어지는 전기는 각각 약 70퍼센트와 170퍼센트 더 비싸다.** 그 결과, 세계적으로 수력 발전 시설에 의해 만들어지는 동력의 양이 크게 증가해왔다.

hydropower 명 수력　harness 동 이용하다　dawn 명 여명기
waterwheel 명 물레방아　irrigate 동 관개하다
undergo 동 거치다, 겪다　horizontally 부 수평으로
mechanical 형 기계적인　manufacturer 명 제조업자
burgeoning 형 급성장하는　in earnest 본격적으로
divert 동 우회시키다　shaft 명 통로　swiftly 부 빠르게
explode 동 폭발하다　heavy industry 중공업
disillusioned 형 환상에서 깬
wreak havoc on ~에 막대한 손해를 끼치다　induce 동 유발하다
awareness 명 인식　momentum 명 추진력　drawback 명 단점
renewable 형 재생 가능한　solar 명 태양
cost-effective 형 비용 효율적인

1 지문의 단어 "undergo"와 의미가 가장 비슷한 것은?
(A) 경험하다
(B) 수송하다
(C) 증가시키다
(D) 입증하다

2 지문의 단어 "those"가 가리키는 것은?
(A) 터빈
(B) 제조업자들
(C) 공장들
(D) 도시

3 2단락에 따르면, 푸르네롱 터빈의 두드러진 특징은
(A) 그것을 움직이기 위해 필요한 동력의 양이었다
(B) 물에 대한 그것의 방향이었다
(C) 그것의 날이 휘어진 정도였다
(D) 강에 의한 손상을 견디는 능력이었다

4 아래 문장 중 지문 속의 음영된 문장의 핵심 정보를 가장 잘 표현한 것은? 오답은 문장의 의미를 크게 바꾸거나 핵심 정보를 생략한다.
(A) 19세기 동안, 미국 전문가들은 다른 나라에서 미국으로 수력 발전 기술을 가져왔다.
(B) 전기를 생산하기 위한 수력의 이용은 미국에서 시작되었고 1800년대에 다른 나라들로 옮겨졌다.
(C) 수력 발전 동력의 생산은 원래 1800년대 미국을 중심으로 이루어졌지만, 이 분야에 대한 세계적인 관심이 있었다.
(D) 수력이 전류를 만들어 내기 위해 사용될 수 있다는 것은 19세기에 미국의 기술자들에 의해 처음 발견되었다.

5 3단락에 따르면, 에드워드 딘 애덤스 발전소에서 사용된 터빈은
(A) 땅속 깊은 구멍의 입구에 위치해 있었다
(B) 전기를 만들어내는 부품 여러 개에 부착되어 있었다
(C) 발전기에 의해 생산된 전류에 의존했다
(D) 나이아가라강 중심에 있는 시설에 설치되었다

6 4단락에서 글쓴이는 왜 후버 댐을 언급하는가?
(A) 미국 중공업의 중요성을 강조하기 위해
(B) 수력에 대한 수요가 증가하고 있었음을 시사하기 위해
(C) 새로운 동력원의 경제적 이익을 보여주기 위해
(D) 기술의 문화적 중요성을 설명하기 위해

7 다음 중 4단락에서 1980년 이전의 미국인들에 관해 추론할 수 있는 것은?
(A) 전기를 만들어 내기 위한 강 생태계 파괴를 기꺼이 허용했다.
(B) 수력의 부정적인 환경적 영향에 대한 지식이 부족했다.
(C) 댐이 야생동물 개체군이 작은 지역에만 건설되어야 한다고 주장했다.
(D) 여러 곳에 수력 발전소가 지어지고 있다는 것에 좌절했다.

8 지문의 단어 "drawbacks"와 의미가 가장 가까운 것은?
(A) 정책들
(B) 영향들
(C) 기준들
(D) 부정적인 면들

9 네 개의 네모[■]는 다음 문장이 삽입될 수 있는 곳을 나타내고 있다.
사실, 풍력과 태양 에너지로 만들어지는 전기는 각각 약 70퍼센트와 170퍼센트 더 비싸다.
이 문장은 어디에 들어가는 것이 가장 적절한가?

10 **지시**: 지문 요약을 위한 도입 문장이 아래에 주어져 있다. 지문의 가장 중요한 내용을 나타내는 보기 3개를 골라 요약을 완성하라. 어떤 문장은 지문에 언급되지 않은 내용이나 사소한 정보를 나타내므로 요약에 포함되지 않는다. **이 문제는 2점이다.**

> 19세기 이래로의 기술적 발전은 수력의 유용성을 크게 증가시켰다.
> · (B) 1827년 터빈의 발명은 수력을 기계적인 에너지로 전환하는 효율을 크게 향상시켰다.
> · (C) 수력이 전기를 생산하기 위해 사용될 수 있다는 발견은 미국 전역에 이러한 종류의 발전소를 건설하도록 이끌었다.
> · (F) 환경적인 문제들에도 불구하고, 수력 발전은 현재 재생 가능 에너지의 가장 좋은 형태이기 때문에 사용이 계속 확대되고 있다.

(A) 물레방아의 기어 시스템에 대한 변화는 이 기계들이 매우 다양한 용도로 사용되는 결과를 낳았다.
(D) 에드워드 딘 애덤스 발전소는 뉴욕 전역의 지역사회에 전기를 공급할 만큼 충분한 용량을 가지고 있었다.
(E) 서식지 파괴에 관한 우려는 많은 미국인들이 새로운 수력 발전 시설들의 건설 중단을 요구하도록 이끌었다.

iBT Reading Test 2

본문 p.150

1 (C) 2 (B) 3 (D) 4 (B)
5 (C) 6 (C) 7 (A) 8 (B)
9 (D) 10 (A), (B), (E)

예술의 본질

2천 년 이상, 예술가들과 예술 비평가들은 아리스토텔레스의 '시학'에서 제시된 예술 이론에 대해 논의하고 논쟁했는데, 여기에서 그 철학자는 예술을 "자연의 패턴을 따르는 것"이라고 묘사했다. (주로 "모방"으로 번역되는) 그리스어 단어 '미메시스'에 대한 아리스토텔레스의 해석은 논의의 중심에 있어왔다. 예술 비평가들 사이에 널리 퍼져 있는 가정은 아리스토텔레스가 미메시스를 진정한 예술은 자연을 모사해야 한다는 문자 그대로의 하나의 의미로 사용했다는 것이었지만, 이 관점은 그의 이론의 이중적 의미를 포착하는 데 실패하는데, 이는 그가 또한 어린이들의 공상을 예술가의 창조적 의도에 비유했기 때문이다.

그럼에도 불구하고, 많은 르네상스 예술가들은 두 명의 고대 그리스 예술가인 제욱시스와 파라시우스 이야기에 대한 그들의 애정에서 보이듯이 그리스어 미메시스에 대한 엄격한 해석을 물려받았다. 로마 철학자 대 플리니우스에 따르면, 제욱시스와 파라시우스는 그들 사이에 누가 더 위대한 예술가인지 결정하기 위해 시합을 열었다. 제욱시스가 그의 포도 그림을 공개했을 때, 새들이 하늘에서 내려와 그것들을 먹으려고 하기 시작했다. 따라서 그 새들은 과일의 사실적인 묘사에 속은 것이었다. [3]이 결과를 자랑스럽게 여긴 제욱시스는 곧장 파라시우스의 그림에서 장막을 제거해 줄 것을 요청했지만, 요청을 하자마자, 그는 장막이 그림의 일부임을 깨달았다.

이 이야기는 17세기 중에 네덜란드에서 유행했으며, 그것의 직접적인 영향이 그 시기의 몇몇 네덜란드 그림들에서 뚜렷이 드러난다. 예를 들어, 아드리안 반 데르 스펠트는 그의 그림 '커튼이 있는 정물화'에서 비슷한 주제를 사용했는데, 그것은 마치 그것의 뒤에 있는 그림을 드러내려고 하는 것처럼 캔버스의 한쪽으로 당겨져 있는 커튼을 사실적으로 표현했다. [5]다른 많은 네덜란드 정물화는 마찬가지로 실물 같았고, 그 당시에 유행했던 경향은 예술가들이 착시의 인지를 만들어내려 시도하는 것이었다. 평범한 관찰자에게는 대부분의 네덜란드 정물화들이 순수하게 모방적으로 보이겠지만, 더 자세한 관찰은 그것들이 상징적인 요소들을 포함했다는 것을 드러내 보인다. 비록 그림의 대상이 종종 유형의 물품들을 포함했지만, 그 사물들은 단지 자연의 묘사는 아니었다. 예를 들어, 타고 있는 초나 모래시계의 존재는 부, 재물, 그리고 삶 자체의 덧없는 본질을 상징했다. **심지어 꽃과 과일도 이러한 의미를 전달했는데, 그것들이 때때로 삶의 즐거움의 덧없는 본질을 전달하기 위해 희미해지거나 썩어가는 것으로 보여졌기 때문이다.**

현대사에서, 많은 예술가들과 예술 비평가들은 예술이 자연을 모방해야 한다는 개념을 거부해 왔다. 일부 예술가들은 예술을 개인적인 표현의 수단이나 심지어 추상적이고 비인격적인 요소로 보았다. 그들에 따르면, 사물의 자연적인 모습은 부차적인 관심사가 되어야 한다. 예를 들어, 바실리 칸딘스키는 추상화가 형식의 세계와는 관련이 없으며, 오직 순수한 경험의 세계와 관련이 있는 영원한 예술적 힘이라고 믿었다. [8]예술의 진정한 본질에 대한 정의와 상관없이, 학습된 모든 것과 마찬가지로, 예술은 예술가의 문화적 맥락 안에서 평가되며 예술적 직업에 관련된 모든 사람들은 그들이 문화의 제도, 전통, 기대의 범주 내에서 작업한다는 한 가지 공통점을 공유한다.

interpretation 명 해석 prevalent 형 널리 퍼진
assumption 명 가정 literal 형 문자 그대로의 genuine 형 진정한
replicate 동 모사하다 liken 동 비유하다 intent 명 의도
inherit 동 물려받다 unveil 동 공개하다 descend 동 내려오다
deceive 동 속이다 portrayal 명 묘사 promptly 부 곧장
motif 명 주제 still life 정물화 fashionable 형 유행하는
perception 명 인지 illusion 명 착시 imitative 형 모방적인
tangible 형 유형의 fleeting 형 덧없는 abstract 형 추상적인
impersonal 형 비인격적인 subordinate 형 부차적인
institution 명 제도

1 아래 문장 중 지문 속의 음영된 문장의 핵심 정보를 가장 잘 표현한 것은? 오답은 문장의 의미를 크게 바꾸거나 핵심 정보를 생략한다.
(A) 아리스토텔레스가 진정한 예술은 자연을 면밀히 모방해야 한다는 그의 견해를 특히 강조했음에도 불구하고, 많은 예술 비평가들은 그것을 무시했다.
(B) 아리스토텔레스는 예술 비평가들이 그의 이론을 단지 창조적인 의도를 발전시킨 예술가들에게만 적용되는 것으로 해석하는 것을 의도하지 않았다.
(C) 아리스토텔레스는 예술이 정확한 묘사와 자연에 대한 창조적인 해석을 모두 포함한다고 생각했지만, 많은 전문가들은 그가 내린 정의의 뒷부분을 무시한다.
(D) 비평가들에 의해 잘 이해되지 않은 아리스토텔레스 이론의 한 측면은 그가 자연의 모방보다 창조적인 표현을 선호했다는 것이다.

2 지문의 단어 "unveiled"와 의미가 가장 비슷한 것은?
(A) 촉진했다
(B) 드러냈다
(C) 거부했다
(D) 시작했다

3 다음 중 2단락에서 그리스 예술가 제욱시스에 관해 추론할 수 있는 것은?
(A) 그의 예술 작품은 파라시우스의 것보다 더 인기 있었다.
(B) 그의 이야기는 대 플리니우스에 의해 조작되었다.
(C) 결국 예술 시합에서 승리했다.
(D) 처음에 파라시우스의 그림에 대해 혼란스러워했다.

4 지문의 단어 "it"이 가리키는 것은?
(A) 주제
(B) 커튼
(C) 캔버스
(D) 그림

5 3단락에 따르면, 다음 중 1600년대 네덜란드 예술가들에게 유행한 목표로 언급된 것은?
(A) 완전히 새로운 예술 형식을 발명하려고 했다.
(B) 고전적인 그림들을 재현하기를 원했다.

(C) 착시의 감각을 만들어내려 시도했다.
(D) 특이한 대상을 묘사하려 애썼다.

6 3단락에서 글쓴이는 왜 타고 있는 초와 모래시계를 언급하는가?
(A) 네덜란드 예술가들이 그리스인들로부터 차용한 주제들을 보여주기 위해
(B) 대부분의 네덜란드 그림들이 얼마나 실물 같았는지를 강조하기 위해
(C) 네덜란드 예술이 상징적인 표현을 포함했다는 것을 설명하기 위해
(D) 네덜란드 예술에서 묘사된 주요 사물들을 강조하기 위해

7 지문의 단어 "subordinate"와 의미가 가장 비슷한 것은?
(A) 부차적인
(B) 주요한
(C) 진실된
(D) 경솔한

8 4단락에 따르면, 예술 작품의 평가는
(A) 예술가가 전통에 충실한 정도를 고려해야 한다
(B) 그것을 만든 사람의 환경을 고려해야 한다
(C) 대상 물질이 표현된 정확도를 고려해야 한다
(D) 그것의 다양한 구성 요소에 대한 솜씨를 고려해야 한다

9 네 개의 네모[■]는 다음 문장이 삽입될 수 있는 곳을 나타내고 있다.
심지어 꽃과 과일도 이러한 의미를 전달했는데, 그것들이 때때로 삶의 즐거움의 덧없는 본질을 전달하기 위해 희미해지거나 썩어가는 것으로 보여졌기 때문이다.
이 문장은 어디에 들어가는 것이 가장 적절한가?

10 지시: 지문 요약을 위한 도입 문장이 아래에 주어져 있다. 지문의 가장 중요한 내용을 나타내는 보기 3개를 골라 요약을 완성하라. 어떤 문장은 지문에 언급되지 않은 내용이나 사소한 정보를 나타내므로 요약에 포함되지 않는다. **이 문제는 2점이다.**

> **무엇이 예술의 진정한 본질을 구성하는가는 아리스토텔레스의 예술 이론에서 시작하여 오랜 세월 동안 숙고되어 온 주제이다.**
> · (A) 예술이 얼마나 사실적이 될 수 있는지를 보여주는 이야기는 네덜란드 예술가들에 의해 높이 평가되었는데, 그들은 그들의 작품에 매우 사실적인 대상들과 상징적인 요소들을 결합했다.
> · (B) 예술이 자연을 모방해야 한다는 생각을 받아들이기를 거부하면서, 많은 현대 예술가들과 비평가들은 더 다양한 형태의 예술적 표현으로 눈을 돌렸다.
> · (E) 아리스토텔레스의 이론이 모방적인 측면과 창조적인 측면을 둘 다 포함했음에도 불구하고, 많은 르네상스 예술가들은 예술이 자연을 밀접하게 따라야 한다는 것을 계속 받아들였다.

(C) 그리스 예술에 대한 깊은 존경심에도 불구하고, 르네상스 예술가들은 점차 아리스토텔레스가 장려한 예술 이론을 거부하기 시작했다.
(D) 추상화로 향하는 현대 미술의 경향은 예술과 자연 세계의 관계에 대한 아리스토텔레스의 견해의 가장 중요한 요소를 무시한다.
(F) 아드리안 반 데르 스펠트의 '커튼이 있는 정물화'는 네덜란드 정물화의 훌륭한 예시이지만, 이미 존재하는 주제를 사용한 것은 독창성과 거리가 멀다.

Vocabulary Review

본문 p.154

1 foreboding		2 disillusioned	3 diverted
4 predatory		5 astronomical	6 replicate
7 (A)	8 (D)	9 (C)	10 (B)
11 (A)	12 (C)	13 (B)	14 (C)

CHAPTER 09

Summary

Example

본문 p.157

1 (A), (C), (F)

1929년의 주식 시장 붕괴

뉴욕 증권 거래소는 1929년 10월의 마지막 며칠에 전례 없는 붕괴를 겪었는데, 그것은 한 주 사이에 그것의 가치의 3분의 1을 잃었다. 미국 주식 시장의 실적을 반영하도록 설계된 지수인 다우존스는 검은 목요일(10월 24일)에 11퍼센트 하락했고, 주식을 매수하려는 은행가들의 단결된 노력으로 인해 금요일에 소폭 회복했으나, 검은 월요일에 주식 시장이 다시 열렸을 때 13.47퍼센트 급락했다. 검은 화요일에, 당황한 투자자들은 기록적인 1,600만 주를 처분했다.

그 붕괴는 많은 주식의 가격이 4배로 뛰었던 1920년대 동안의 지속 불가능한 호황의 결과였다. 수백만 명의 사람들은 이 추세가 지속될 것이라고 믿었고, 시장이 붕괴하면 갚지 못할 빚을 져가며 투자할 돈을 빌렸다. 1929년에 주식 가격이 하락하기 시작하자 이 사람들은 파산을 면하기 위해 즉시 그들의 주식을 팔기 시작했다. 동시에, 그 국가의 금융 기관의 안정성에 대한 우려가 많은 사람들로 하여금 그들의 은행에서 자금을 인출하게 만들었고, 이는 그 상황을 더욱 악화시켰다.

뒤따르는 수개월, 수년 동안, 대공황이 그 국가를 뒤덮었고 경제적 어려움이 전 세계로 퍼져나갔다. 대량의 주식 매도는 수십억 달러의 손실을 초래했고 많은 미국인들이 일생 동안 모은 저축이나 사업을 잃었다. 1933년까지, 실업률은 30퍼센트에 달했고 국가의 거의 절반의 은행들이 문을 닫았다.

unprecedented 형 전례 없는 collapse 명 붕괴; 동 붕괴하다
index 명 (주가 등의) 지수 reflect 동 반영하다 concerted 형 단결된
plummet 동 급락하다 panicked 형 당황한 unload 동 처분하다
unsustainable 형 지속 불가능한 quadruple 동 4배로 뛰다
incur 동 (빚 등을) 지다 ruin 명 파산 stability 명 안정성
withdraw 동 인출하다 ensuing 형 뒤따르는 envelop 동 뒤덮다
hardship 명 어려움 sell-off 명 매도, 매각
life saving 일생 동안 모은 저축

1 지시: 지문 요약을 위한 도입 문장이 아래에 주어져 있다. 지문의 가장 중요한 내용을 나타내는 보기 3개를 골라 요약을 완성하라.
1929년 10월의 한 주 동안, 주식 시장은 갑자기 그것의 가치의 큰 부분을 잃었다.
(A) 투자자들이 하루 만에 수백만 주를 팔면서 주식 시장은 1929년에 엄청난 하락을 겪었다.

(B) 금요일에 시장이 잠시 회복됨에 따라, 주식 시장을 지속시키기 위한 계획적인 시도는 성공했다.
(C) 붕괴는 많은 사람들이 주식을 사기 위해 빚을 냈던 10년 간의 경제 성장에 의해 선행되었다.
(D) 많은 은행들은 고객이 계좌에서 인출할 수 있는 돈의 액수를 제한하도록 강요되었다.
(E) 대공황이 미국 경제를 망쳐 놓았지만, 그것의 세계적인 영향은 훨씬 더 제한적이었다.
(F) 1929년의 주식 시장 붕괴는 엄청난 손실을 초래했고 대공황으로 이어졌다.

Reading Practice 1

본문 p.158

1 (B)　2 (A)　3 (C)　4 (A)　5 (A), (C), (D)

유럽의 초기 기계식 시계

유럽 최초의 완전한 기계식 시계는 13세기에 개발되었고, 이것들 중 최초의 것은 '굴대와 폴리옷' 시계로 알려져 있었다. 굴대는 수직 막대였고 폴리옷은 굴대의 꼭대기에 부착된 수평 막대였다. 폴리옷의 각 끝에는 막대의 균형을 유지하고 그것이 이동하는 거리를 바꾸기 위해 조절 가능한 추가 배치될 수 있었다. [2B]이 초기 설계의 다른 주요 부분은 톱니 바퀴(기어 바퀴)로, 이것은 폴리옷이 수평 시소처럼 앞뒤로 움직임에 따라 회전했다.

일반적으로, 매달려 있는 추는 각 움직임과 함께 가속된다. [2D]그러나, 굴대와 폴리옷 시스템은 폴리옷이 느리고 일정한 속도로 움직일 수 있도록 이 자연적 가속을 막았다. 이것은 바퀴의 톱니가 일정한 간격으로 움직이도록 해주었고, 기어 바퀴의 각각의 릴리스, 즉 "탈출"은 시계의 한 번의 똑딱임과 동등한 것을 나타냈다. 기어 바퀴같이 간헐적으로 계수 장치를 지연시키고 놓아주기 위해 에너지를 전달하는 장치는 '탈진기'라고 알려져 있다. [2C]비록 굴대와 폴리옷 탈진기가 해시계와 같은 이전의 시간 측정 기술들에 비해 상당히 개선된 것이기는 했지만, 그것은 단지 시간을 표시할 정도로만 정확했다. 시계가 분과 초 단위에서 정확해지기 위해서는 개선이 이루어져야만 했다.

이 방향으로의 첫 번째 주요한 진보는 진자의 발명이었다. 진자는 추축에 부착된 수직 막대와 막대 바닥에 부착된 매달려 있는 추로 구성된다. 움직이게 되면, 진자는 스스로 계속해서 앞뒤로 흔들린다. [3]진자가 한 번의 완전한 순환을 하는 데 걸리는 시간은 그것의 '주기'이며, 그 주기는 추의 질량이 아니라 오직 막대의 길이에 의해서만 결정된다. 많은 진자시계에서 닻 구조 탈진기가 사용되었다. 그것은 배의 닻처럼 생겼기 때문에 그것의 모양을 따서 이름 붙여졌다. 닻 구조 탈진기의 꼭대기는 일반적으로 위아래가 뒤집어진 'V' 같은 모양이었고, "다리"의 각 끝에 급격히 안쪽으로 향하는 지점이 있었다. 중앙에는 진자가 붙어 있었으며, 진자가 흔들리면서 그 두 지점은 회전하는 기어 바퀴의 톱니를 번갈아 가며 잡았다가 놓았다.

시간이 지남에 따라, 시계 제작자들은 진자시계의 정확성을 지속적으로 높이기 위해 그것들을 개조하는 방법을 익혔다. 실험을 통해, 그들은 각 흔들림이 정확히 1초 동안 지속되도록 정확히 2초의 주기를 만들기 위해서는 진자의 길이가 0.994미터가 되어야 한다는 것을 발견했다. [4]또 다른 혁신은 금속 막대의 팽창과 수축으로 인해 진자시계가 여름에는 더 느리게 가고 겨울에는 더 빠르게 간다는 것을 깨달은 이후에 일어났는데, 이는 따뜻한 계절 동안 주당 최대 1초의 손실을 야기했다. 이것을 보완하기 위해, 금속 막대는 나무 막대로 교체되었다. 결국, 이것들과 다른 개선들은 연간 1초 정도만 변동하여 조정이 거의 필요 없는 진자시계의 개발로 이어졌다.

mechanical 형 기계식의　vertical 형 수직의　horizontal 형 수평의
affix 동 부착하다　adjustable 형 조절 가능한　weight 명 추
suspended 형 매달려 있는　accelerate 동 가속되다
uniform 형 일정한　interval 명 간격　equivalent of ~과 동등한
intermittently 부 간헐적으로　impede 동 지연시키다
escapement 명 탈진기　sundial 명 해시계
precise 형 정확한　pendulum 명 진자　pivot 명 추축
alternately 부 번갈아 가며　modify 동 개조하다
realization 명 깨달음　contraction 명 수축
compensate 동 보완하다　fluctuate 동 변동하다

1 지문의 단어 "impede"와 의미가 가장 비슷한 것은?
(A) 복사하다
(B) 억제하다
(C) 강요하다
(D) 개정하다

2 다음 중 굴대와 폴리옷 시계의 특징으로 언급되지 않은 것은?
(A) 시간을 표시하는 데 있어 해시계보다 덜 정확했다.
(B) 기어 바퀴의 움직임을 조절하기 위해 수평 막대를 사용했다.
(C) 분과 초를 나타낼 만큼 충분히 정확하지 않았다.
(D) 매달려 있는 추가 빨라지는 것을 막았다.

3 3단락에 따르면, 다음 중 진자가 순환을 완료하는 데 걸리는 시간을 결정하는 것은?
(A) 회전하는 기어 바퀴의 속도
(B) 탈진기의 모양
(C) 막대의 길이
(D) 추의 질량

4 4단락에 따르면, 금속 진자 막대는 왜 나무 막대로 교체되었는가?
(A) 금속 막대가 계절적 변동을 일으켰다.
(B) 금속의 무게가 움직임을 방해했다.
(C) 나무가 2초 주기를 가능하게 했다.
(D) 나무 막대가 생산하기에 더 효율적이었다.

5 **지시:** 지문 요약을 위한 문장이 아래에 주어져 있다. 지문의 가장 중요한 내용을 나타내는 보기 3개를 골라 요약을 완성하라.

유럽인들은 13세기에 완전한 기계식 시계들을 만들어내기 시작했고, 그것들의 개발은 시간이 지남에 따라 진화했다.

(A) 진자시계 제작자들은 진자의 길이에 통달하는 것과 막대를 만드는 데 사용되는 재료를 바꾸는 것과 같은 발전을 통해 점진적으로 그것들의 정확도를 높였다.
(B) 굴대와 폴리옷 탈진기의 중대한 개선인 닻 구조 탈진기는 시계 제작자들이 기어 바퀴를 앞뒤로 흔들리는 추가 달린 막대로 교체하도록 해주었다.
(C) 굴대와 폴리옷 시계는 최초의 완전한 기계식 시계였으며, 그것들은 시간을 맞추는 기어 바퀴를 조절하기 위해 상호작용하는 부품들을 사용했다.
(D) 진자의 발명은 주기적인 움직임을 만들어내기 위해 막대와 매달려 있는 추를 이용하는 시계의 개발로 이어졌다.
(E) 개량된 진자시계는 각 연간 주기에서 약 1초의 변동을 만들어냈기 때문에 거의 그것들을 조정할 필요가 없었다.

(F) 시계 제작자들은 진자가 움직이기 시작한 후 그것이 계속해서 흔들리게 하기 위해서는 에너지를 재활용하기 위한 일련의 기어 바퀴가 필요하다는 것을 마침내 깨달았다.

Reading Practice 2

본문 p.160

1 (D)　2 (B)　3 (B)　4 (B)　5 (B), (D), (F)

낭만주의

18세기 후반은 미국 및 프랑스 혁명과 같은 사회적, 정치적 격변이 서양인들이 그들의 사회와 세상을 보는 방식을 극적으로 변화시켰기 때문에 혁명의 시대로 알려져 있다. 군주들이 통치했던 수 세기들 이후에, 사람들은 더 민주적인 형태의 정부로 돌아섰다. 한 세대의 지식인들과 예술인들이 이전 세기들의 문학 및 예술 경향에 도전하기 시작했을 때 문학과 예술에서도 혁명적인 정신의 발전이 일어났다. 18세기 말부터 19세기까지, 이 세대는 낭만주의로 알려진 운동 이면의 사상들에 영감을 주었다.

낭만주의의 지지자들은 이성과 논리보다 상상력의 역할을 강하게 우선시했다. 그들은 상상력이 인간의 주된 창조적인 힘이며 우리 자신과 우리 주위의 세계를 이해하는 데 가장 필수적인 요소라고 믿었다. [1]영국의 낭만주의 시인 윌리엄 워즈워스의 말에 따르면, 인간은 세상을 인식할 뿐만 아니라 그것을 형성하는 데 도움을 준다. 이러한 의미에서, 무언가를 상상하는 인간의 능력은 우주를 창조하는 신 또는 신적 존재의 능력과 비슷하다. 상상력은 인간이 그들의 경험을 해석하는 방법이며, 그다음 이것에 기반하여 작품을 창조하는 것은 낭만주의 예술가나 작가에게 달려 있다.

낭만주의의 또 다른 중심적 특징은 주관적인 개인주의와 자유에 대한 집중이었다. 이러한 강조는 자유주의가 상당한 추진력을 얻고 있었던 당대의 혁명 정신과 분명하게 일치했다. **사회적이자 정치적 운동인 자유주의는 평등과 행복을 추구하며 그나 그녀의 선택에 따른 삶을 살 개인의 권리와 같은 사상에 중점을 두었다.** 예술과 관련해서, 이는 예술가나 작가가 관습의 구속에서 자유로워야 함을 의미했다. 따라서, 낭만주의는 신고전주의의 표준화된 아름다움에 대한 집착과 계몽주의의 이성에 대한 고집에 대한 강한 반대를 나타냈는데, 이는 그것이 주관성, 규칙 순응에 대한 경멸, 강력한 개인주의의 우월성을 강조했기 때문이다.

개인주의의 이상을 추구하기 위해, 많은 낭만주의자들은 더 큰 자기 인식과 더 강화된 자연과의 관계를 얻기 위해 사회로부터 떨어진 고독한 삶을 실험했다. 야외에서 명상을 하고, 글을 쓰고, 그림을 그리는 관행이 그 시기의 주요 유행이 되었다. 확실히, 낭만주의자들은 이전 세대들이 하지 않았던 방식으로 자연을 숭배했다. [4]산업혁명 시대 동안의 경향이었던 것처럼 환경에 대한 인간의 지배를 수동적으로 받아들이는 대신, 낭만주의 지식인들은 자연계를 더 높은 지위로, 심지어 인간의 것과 동등하거나 그것보다 더 높이 들어 올리려 시도했다. 낭만주의의 이러한 측면은 낭만주의에 더 깊은 영적, 도덕적 특징을 더한 초월주의와 같은 비슷한 운동들에 영감을 주었다. 헨리 데이비드 소로와 랠프 월도 에머슨 같은 초월주의자들은 신이 자연에서 발견될 수 있으며 신과 자연과 하나가 되려고 노력하는 인간의 영혼이 영적 성취의 가장 고귀한 형태라고 믿었다.

upheaval 명 격변　monarch 명 군주　democratic 형 민주적인
intellectual 명 지식인　prioritize 동 우선시하다　reason 명 이성
principal 형 주된　discern 동 인식하다　deity 명 신적 존재
subjective 형 주관적인　individualism 명 개인주의
liberalism 명 자유주의　momentum 명 추진력　restraint 명 구속
objection 명 반대　obsession 명 집착　standardized 형 표준화된
Neoclassicism 명 신고전주의　insistence 명 고집
disdain 명 경멸　conformity 명 순응　supremacy 명 우월성
solitary 형 고독한　meditate 동 명상하다　venerate 동 숭배하다
Transcendentalism 명 초월주의　attainment 명 성취

1 2단락에 따르면, 낭만주의 시인 윌리엄 워즈워스가 인간에 관해 말했던 것은?
(A) 그들의 경험을 항상 주관적인 방식으로 해석한다.
(B) 그들 주위의 세계를 결코 이해할 수 없다.
(C) 신과 신적 존재의 형태로 만들어져 있다.
(D) 세계를 인식하며 그것의 창조를 돕는다.

2 네 개의 네모[■]는 다음 문장이 삽입될 수 있는 곳을 나타내고 있다.
사회적이자 정치적 운동인 자유주의는 평등과 행복을 추구하며 그나 그녀의 선택에 따른 삶을 살 개인의 권리와 같은 사상에 중점을 두었다.
이 문장은 어디에 들어가는 것이 가장 적절한가?

3 지문의 단어 "disdain"과 의미가 가장 비슷한 것은?
(A) 소극성
(B) 경멸
(C) 논리
(D) 유연성

4 다음 중 4단락에서 낭만주의자들과 초월주의자들에 관해 추론할 수 있는 것은?
(A) 사회가 엄격한 도덕 규칙을 강요해야 한다고 믿었다.
(B) 산업 혁명의 일부 측면에 반대했다.
(C) 인간의 영혼이 신과 하나가 될 수 있다는 것을 부정했다.
(D) 신고전주의와 계몽주의 사상에서 영감을 받았다.

5 지시: 지문 요약을 위한 도입 문장이 아래에 주어져 있다. 지문의 가장 중요한 내용을 나타내는 보기 3개를 골라 요약을 완성하라.
한 세대의 사상가들과 예술가들은 낭만주의 운동 동안 전통적인 관점에 도전하고 새로운 표현 방식을 장려하기 시작했다.
(A) 낭만주의는 18세기 중에 번성하긴 했지만, 그것은 19세기 초반에 초월주의에 의해 대체되었다.
(B) 개인주의적 지식인들은 자연 및 그들 자신과 접촉하는 데 집중하기 위해 사회로부터 도피했다.
(C) 낭만주의 예술가들은 신고전주의의 격식에는 강하게 반대했지만, 아름다움에 대한 그것의 감상을 공유했다.
(D) 낭만주의 옹호자들의 이상 중에는 창의성에 대한 논리와 이성의 종속이 있었다.
(E) 낭만주의자들처럼, 초월주의자들은 영적 경험의 우월한 형태가 신과 직접적으로 의사소통하는 것이라고 믿었다.
(F) 당대의 혁명 정신과 평행하게, 낭만주의 사상가들은 개인주의, 자유, 그리고 평등의 가치를 옹호했다.

Reading Practice 3

본문 p.162

1 (B)　2 (D)　3 (A)　4 (C)　5 (A), (B), (D)

프리 라디칼

유산소 세포 호흡은 인간 및 다른 유기체들이 대기에서 얻은 산소를 에너지로 변환시키는 과정이다. 주로 폐와 피부를 통해 신체에 의해 흡수된 산소의 대부분은 물과 이산화탄소로 전환된다. [1]그러나 산소의 약 5퍼센트는 활성 산소 종(ROS)으로 알려진 폐기물을 생산한다. 이러한 독성 혼합물은 종종 프리 라디칼을 형성하거나 프리 라디칼이 되는데, 이것은 짝지어지지 않은 전자를 포함한다는 사실로 구별되는 원자나 분자이다. 전자는 보통 둘씩 이동하는데, 하나 혹은 그보다 많은 전자가 그것들의 짝으로부터 분리되면, 그것들을 포함한 원자와 분자는 불안정해진다. 프리 라디칼이 유기 세포에서 생성되면, 프리 라디칼이 이웃한 분자로부터 그것의 잃어버린 전자를 얻어 그것을 프리 라디칼로 전환시킴으로써 자신을 안정화시키는 연쇄 반응이 촉발된다. 프리 라디칼의 수가 증가함에 따라, 세포 손상이 일어난다.

프리 라디칼은 매우 다양한 인간 질병의 발달에서 역할을 하며 심지어 노화와 관련된 퇴행성 과정의 원인이 될 수도 있다. [2]이러한 문제들은 한 세포의 100조 개로 추정되는 원자들 중 프리 라디칼의 비율이 너무 커져 산화 스트레스라고 알려진 상태를 만들 때 일어난다. 신체의 세포, 단백질, 지질, 그리고 DNA는 산화 스트레스에 의해 위태로워진다. 손상된 분자는 때때로 돌연변이 하여 종양이 된다. 지질은 모양을 바꾸고 동맥에 갇히게 되어 심혈관 문제들을 일으킬 수 있다. 신체가 노화함에 따라 프리 라디칼의 비율이 증가하며, 이는 주름진 피부, 근육과 관절 통증, 그리고 기억력 감퇴와 같은 노화 관련 문제들에 일조한다.

프리 라디칼은 유산소 호흡 중에 신체에 의해 자연적으로 생성되지만, 그것들은 외부 요인에의 노출의 결과로 생성될 수도 있다. 프리 라디칼의 이러한 외부적 원인은 대기 오염물질, 오존, 담배 연기, 엑스레이, 튀긴 음식, 그리고 산업용 화학물질을 포함한다. 프리 라디칼은 신체 운동 중에도 생산된다. 그러나, 신체 세포에 대한 운동의 전체적인 효과는 여전히 긍정적인데, 이는 운동이 또한 산화 방지제를 생성하기 때문이며, 이것은 자신의 전자를 프리 라디칼에 제공하고, 그 제공으로 인해 불안정해지지 않고도 짝지어진 전자에 대한 그 불안정한 분자의 요구를 해결한다.

프리 라디칼의 상당한 파괴적 잠재력에도 불구하고, 과학자들은 그것들이 여러 생물학적 과정에서 유익한 역할을 한다는 것을 깨닫게 되었다. 가장 중요하게는, 많은 연구들이 인체의 면역 체계가 병원균을 파괴하기 위해 프리 라디칼을 적극적으로 사용한다는 것을 보여주었다. 박테리아나 세균이 감지되면, 대량의 프리 라디칼이 생성되어 병원균을 중화시키기 위해 그것으로 향할 것이다. 게다가, 세포 손상을 일으킬 수 있는 그것들의 잠재력은 방사선 치료에서 암을 치료하기 위해 이용될 수 있는데, 이것은 신체의 전략적으로 표적이 된 위치에 프리 라디칼을 생성한다. 프리 라디칼은 또한 세포의 성장과 죽음을 조절하는 데 유용하다.

aerobic 형 유산소의　cellular 형 세포의　respiration 명 호흡
reactive oxygen species 활성 산소 종　compound 명 혼합물
atom 명 원자　electron 명 전자　chain reaction 연쇄 반응
degenerative 형 퇴행성의　proportion 명 비율
oxidative stress 산화 스트레스　lipid 명 지질
compromise 동 위태롭게 하다　mutate 동 돌연변이 하다
tumor 명 종양　artery 명 동맥　cardiovascular 형 심혈관의
complication 명 문제　antioxidant 명 산화 방지제
destabilized 형 불안정한　salutary 형 유익한
pathogen 명 병원균　neutralize 동 중화시키다
harness 동 이용하다　strategically 부 전략적으로

1 1단락에 따르면, 다음 중 활성 산소 종에 관해 사실인 것은?

(A) 유산소 호흡에 의해 물과 이산화탄소로 전환된다.
(B) 에너지를 생산하는 생물학적 과정의 유해한 부산물이다.
(C) 다른 것들과 짝을 이루는 전자를 결코 포함하지 않는다.
(D) 다른 분자들에 전자를 방출하여 자신을 안정화시키려고 한다.

2 2단락에 따르면, 산화 스트레스는

(A) 프리 라디칼에 의해 손상된 분자들의 돌연변이로 인해 야기된다
(B) 퇴행성 장애에 의해 변형된 사람의 DNA로 인해 야기된다
(C) 신체 세포에 있는 과도한 양의 원자들로 인해 야기된다
(D) 개별 세포에 있는 프리 라디칼의 과잉으로 인해 야기된다

3 지문에서 글쓴이는 왜 "antioxidants"를 언급하는가?

(A) 운동이 건강상의 위험을 제기하지 않는 이유를 설명하기 위해
(B) 운동이 전적으로 이롭다는 일반적인 믿음을 반박하기 위해
(C) 프리 라디칼이 긍정적인 영향을 미칠 수 있음을 입증하기 위해
(D) 신체적 반응이 전자를 제거하지 않는다는 것을 보여주기 위해

4 지문의 단어 "harnessed"와 의미가 가장 비슷한 것은?

(A) 개발되다
(B) 적응되다
(C) 이용되다
(D) 조사되다

5 **지시**: 지문 요약을 위한 도입 문장이 아래에 주어져 있다. 지문의 가장 중요한 내용을 나타내는 보기 3개를 골라 요약을 완성하라.

프리 라디칼은 짝지어지지 않은 전자를 포함하는 불안정한 원자나 분자이다.

(A) 세포 손상은 체내의 너무 많은 프리 라디칼의 축적으로 인해 야기될 수 있다.
(B) 다양한 노화 관련 문제들은 프리 라디칼의 존재로 인해 야기된다고 알려져 있다.
(C) 흡연 및 건강에 해로운 다른 활동들은 신체 세포의 프리 라디칼 수를 증가시킬 수 있다.
(D) 내적 및 외적 요인들 모두 인체 내 프리 라디칼의 생성에 기여한다.
(E) 프리 라디칼은 암세포 형성의 원인이라기보다 암 치료법이다.
(F) 심혈관 문제는 프리 라디칼이 동맥 내 지질에 미치는 영향으로 인해 야기된다.

iBT Reading Test 1

본문 p.164

1 (A)	2 (B)	3 (C)	4 (C)
5 (B)	6 (C)	7 (D)	8 (C)
9 (B)	10 (A), (B), (E)		

블루마운틴의 산불 생태학

호주의 블루마운틴 국립 공원은 267,000여 헥타르의 땅에 걸쳐 있으며 무수한 종의 희귀한 나무, 식물, 야생동물을 포함하고 있다. 산불들은 블루마운틴의 다양한 생태학적 특징들의 발달에 많은 기여를 해왔다. 이것들은 또한 유칼립투스속 나무 같은 많은 식물 종들에 의한 적응을 가져왔다. 유칼립투스 나무들은 그들의 잎 속에서 매우 가연성이 높은 향유를 만들어내며, 이 특성은 그것들 아래에 있는 숲 바닥이 불에 매우 잘 타는 잎들로 덮이게 하는데, 이것들은 산불에 강력한 연료

를 제공한다.

대부분의 산불은 숲에 낙뢰가 더 빈번한 여름 중에 발생한다. [3]더 아래쪽의 산간 지역은 더 적은 강우량으로 인해 그곳의 공기가 더 건조하기 때문에 발화의 위험이 더 크다. 더 아래쪽의 지역은 더 빈번한 화재를 겪어 유칼립투스 나무의 불에 잘 타는 잎들이 숲 바닥에 쌓일 새가 거의 없기 때문에, 그 지역들에서는 화재의 강도가 비교적 낮다.

산불의 강도는 그 지역의 다양한 식물이 활기를 되찾게 하는 데 있어 중요한 요소이다. 그 국립 공원 내에 있는 약 250종의 서로 다른 식물 종들이 씨앗 발아를 일으키기 위해 불을 필요로 한다. [4]이 종들 중 다수에서, 씨앗은 불이 날 때까지 토양 속에서 휴면 상태로 있는다. 땅속에 씨앗을 보관하는 것은 토양 씨앗은행이라고 불린다. 이 씨앗들 중 일부는 활성화를 위해 단지 연기의 방출이나 목탄을 필요로 하는데, 다른 것들이 강한 열 이후에야 싹을 틔울 수 있는 반면, 이것은 낮은 온도에서도 달성될 수 있다.

경쟁을 피하기 위해, 토양 씨앗은행이 없는 식물 종들은 산불에서 살아남기 위한 다른 전략들을 발달시켰다. '페트로필'속의 상록수 관목들은 그것들의 가지 위에 있는 단단한 나무 원뿔에 씨앗을 보관하고 그 씨앗들은 불이 원뿔을 터뜨려 열 때 방출된다. 일부 초본종에서, 성숙한 식물들은 그것들이 완전히 타서 재가 되지 않으면 빠르게 다시 자라도록 진화해왔다. **특히, 풀과 난초는 빠르게 회복하여 거의 즉시 생식적으로 성숙하게 된다.** 한편, 다 자란 유칼립투스 나무들은 그것들의 두꺼운 보호 껍질이 나무의 몸통이 손상되지 않을 수 있게 하는, 불에 대한 독특한 적응 형태를 특징으로 한다. [6]불에 탄 후, 나무의 몸통은 새로운 나뭇가지들이 나게 할 수 있다. 이러한 보호는 유칼립투스 나무에 불에 손상을 입은 다른 나무들에 대한 경쟁 우위를 제공한다.

식물의 번식을 촉진하는 것 이외에도, 산불은 몇 가지 다른 이점을 제공할 수 있다. 플로리다의 톨 팀버 연구소에 의해 수행된 40년간의 긴 실험은 화재로부터 보호받은 숲이 식물 다양성에서 90퍼센트의 감소를 겪었다는 것을 밝혀냄으로써 불이 숲 생태계의 필수적 측면이라는 것을 입증했다. [8A]불이 도움이 되는 한 가지 방식은 경쟁 종의 제거를 통해서이다. 지배적인 식물 종들을 태워버림으로써 한 지역의 생물 다양성은 급증할 수 있는데, 이는 덜 지배적인 종들이 갑작스런 생태학적 공백에서 꽃을 피울 기회를 갖게 되기 때문이다. [8D]동시에, 연소는 썩어가는 식물 물질을 영양분이 풍부한 재로 바꾸어놓을 수 있다. 탄소와 질소를 포함한 이러한 영양분은 토양으로 돌려보내져 건강한 묘목 성장을 촉진한다. [8B]마지막으로, 불은 나무 및 다른 형태의 식물들에 해로운 많은 곤충들을 박멸하여 숲을 건강하게 유지시킨다.

ecology 명 생태학, 생태계 rare 형 희귀한 contribution 명 기여
genus 명 (생물 분류상의) 속 combustible 형 가연성의
attribute 명 특성 flammable 형 불에 잘 타는 potent 형 강력한
prevalent 형 빈번한 ignition 명 발화 intensity 명 강도
rejuvenate 동 활기를 되찾게 하다 germination 명 발아
transpire 동 일어나다 dormant 형 휴면의 charcoal 명 목탄
activation 명 활성화 sprout 동 싹을 틔우다; 나게 하다
evergreen 명 상록수 herbaceous 형 초본의
regrow 동 다시 자라다 protective 형 보호하는 limb 명 나뭇가지
propagation 명 번식 eradication 명 제거 surge 동 급증하다
seedling 명 묘목

1 지문의 단어 "These"가 가리키는 것은?
(A) 산불
(B) 기여
(C) 특징들
(D) 블루마운틴

2 지문의 단어 "attribute"와 의미가 가장 비슷한 것은?
(A) 변동
(B) 특성
(C) 개요
(D) 양

3 다음 중 2단락에서 고도와 산불의 관계에 관해 추론할 수 있는 것은?
(A) 더 아래쪽의 장소는 강한 화재를 겪는다.
(B) 더 위쪽의 지역에서는 천천히 형성되는 화재가 일어난다.
(C) 더 위쪽의 지역은 더 적은 수의 화재를 겪는다.
(D) 더 큰 화재는 더 작은 산에서 발달한다.

4 3단락에 따르면, 토양 씨앗은행에 관해 사실인 것은?
(A) 씨앗이 싹을 틔운 이후에 씨앗을 보존한다.
(B) 계절이 변할 때까지 씨앗을 보호한다.
(C) 환경이 발아를 촉발할 때까지 씨앗을 보유한다.
(D) 악천후 동안의 보존을 위해 씨앗을 저장한다.

5 4단락에서 글쓴이는 왜 상록수 관목들을 언급하는가?
(A) 씨앗은행의 변형이 많은 종들에 의해 이용된다는 것을 입증하기 위해
(B) 씨앗은행이 없는 종의 화재 생존을 위한 적응 형태의 예시를 제공하기 위해
(C) 일부 생식 방법이 씨앗은행보다 더 효과적이라는 것을 시사하기 위해
(D) 화재가 발생하기 쉬운 생태계에서 씨앗은행을 가진 서로 다른 두 식물 유형을 비교하기 위해

6 4단락에 따르면, 유칼립투스 나무들은 화재로부터 회복하기 위해 무엇을 하는가?
(A) 원뿔을 통해 토양 위로 새로운 씨앗을 방출한다.
(B) 미성숙한 상태로 땅에서 싹을 틔우기 시작한다.
(C) 나무 몸통으로부터 새로운 가지들을 기르기 시작한다.
(D) 생식 전략을 개시하기 위해 열을 이용한다.

7 아래 문장 중 지문 속의 음영된 문장의 핵심 정보를 가장 잘 표현한 것은? 오답은 문장의 의미를 크게 바꾸거나 핵심 정보를 생략한다.
(A) 플로리다에서의 실험은 생물학적 성장이 산불로 인해 감소할 수 있다는 것을 보여주었다.
(B) 플로리다에서의 연구는 산불의 부정적 영향이 보존을 통해 어떻게 예방될 수 있는지를 밝혀냈다.
(C) 연구는 보호된 숲이 많은 양의 식물을 유지할 수 없다는 것을 보여준다.
(D) 보호 지역에 대한 광범위한 연구는 화재를 없애는 것이 숲의 생물 다양성 감소를 초래한다는 것을 알아냈다.

8 5단락에 따르면, 다음 중 화재로 인해 숲이 누리는 이점이 아닌 것은?
(A) 매우 성공적인 종들이 제거되며, 이는 다른 것들이 번성할 수 있게 해준다.
(B) 해충들이 박멸되며, 이는 많은 식물들의 전반적인 건강을 향상시킨다.
(C) 식물의 성장에 필요한 화학물질들이 대기로 방출된다.
(D) 영양분이 풍부한 연소된 식물 잔해가 토양에 더해진다.

9 네 개의 네모[■]는 다음 문장이 삽입될 수 있는 곳을 나타내고 있다.

특히, 풀과 난초는 빠르게 회복하여 거의 즉시 생식적으로 성숙하게 된다.

이 문장은 어디에 들어가는 것이 가장 적절한가?

10 지시: 지문 요약을 위한 도입 문장이 아래에 주어져 있다. 지문의 가장 중요한 내용을 나타내는 보기 3개를 골라 요약을 완성하라. 어떤 문장은 지문에 언급되지 않은 내용이나 사소한 정보를 나타내므로 요약에 포함되지 않는다. **이 문제는 2점이다.**

> **호주 블루마운틴의 생태는 빈번한 산불의 영향을 받는다.**
> · (A) 그 지역의 많은 종들은 산불에서 살아남기 위해 독특하게 적응했다.
> · (B) 연구는 숲이 매우 다양한 식물 종들을 포함하도록 하기 위해 종종 불이 필요하다는 것을 보여주었다.
> · (E) 화재의 강도는 블루마운틴의 나무 씨앗의 발아를 결정하는 데 있어 중요한 측면이다.

(C) 산불은 숲 바닥에서 썩어가는 생물학적 쓰레기를 청소할 기회를 제공한다.
(D) 산의 더 위쪽 지역의 강우량 부족은 더 빈번한 산불을 야기한다.
(F) 블루마운틴의 위치는 그 지역의 높은 산불 가능성에 기여한다.

iBT Reading Test 2

본문 p.168

1 (C)	2 (B)	3 (D)	4 (B)
5 (B)	6 (B)	7 (D)	8 (C)
9 (B)	10 (A), (D), (E)		

아야 소피아

(그리스어로 "성스러운 지혜"를 뜻하는) 아야 소피아는 튀르키예 이스탄불에 있는, 세계에서 가장 위대한 기념물 중 하나로 여겨지는 돔형 건축물이다. 그것은 서기 6세기까지 거슬러 올라가는 비잔틴 양식 건축의 표본으로서뿐만 아니라 수 세기에 걸쳐 그 지역을 뒤흔들어온 중대한 정치적 및 종교적 변화를 반영하는 매우 다채로운 역사로도 주목할 만하다. 그것은 처음에는 기독교의 성당으로, 다음에는 이슬람교의 모스크로, 다음에는 박물관이자 인기 있는 관광 명소의 역할을 했으며, 다시 한번 이슬람교도들의 예배 장소가 되었다.

아야 소피아가 532년에 건립되었을 때, 오늘날의 이스탄불이 당시 불렸던 이름인 콘스탄티노플은 비잔틴 제국의 수도였으며, 그것은 거대한 주요 도시였다. 비록 서로마 제국이 약 반세기 전에 멸망했지만, 동쪽 부분은 비잔틴 제국으로서 유스티니아누스 대제의 통치하에서 번영했다. 532년에 콘스탄티노플에 있는 한 교회가 높은 세금과 정부의 부패에 분노한 사람들에 의한 폭동 중에 불탔다. 유스티니아누스는 옛 교회의 자리에 정교한 새 교회를 지음으로써 자신의 권위를 확고히 할 기회를 잡기로 결심했다. [4]이것이 아야 소피아였으며, 그것은 놀라운 속도로 건설되어 6년 내에 완공되었다.

[5A]아야 소피아는 아직 남아 있는 비잔틴 양식 건축의 가장 훌륭한 예이며, 그것은 기독교의 바실리카 양식으로 만들어졌다. [5D]그 교회의 중심적인 특징은 벽돌과 모르타르로 만들어진 107피트 길이의 돔이다. **이것은 그 교회의 주요 신도석, 즉 예배 구역보다 180피트 위로 올려져 있다.** [5C]돔 바로 아래에는 40개의 창문이 있으며, 이것들은 대리석 바닥을 햇빛으로 흠뻑 적신다. 유스티니아누스의 요청에 따라, 북아프리카에서 온 벽돌과 에베소와 이집트에서 온 104개의 기둥을 포함한 건축 자재들이 그 광대한 제국 전역으로부터 왔다.

1453년에 콘스탄티노플이 오스만 제국의 손에 넘어갔을 때, 그 도시는 이스탄불로 이름이 바뀌었다. 정복자 메흐메트는 이슬람교가 공식적인 종교가 될 것을 명령했고, 그 결과 아야 소피아는 모스크가 되었다. 이슬람 건축 양식과의 일관성을 유지하기 위해, 그 건축물의 모서리에 네 개의 200피트 길이의 뾰족탑이 더해졌다. [6]돔 내부에 있는 예수 그리스도의 이미지를 포함한 기독교 모자이크는 이슬람 서예로 대체되었다.

1935년, 터키 공화국의 초대 대통령이었던 케말 아타튀르크는 아야 소피아가 박물관의 역할을 해야 한다고 결정했다. 그 건물이 모스크의 역할을 하는 동안 가려져 있었던 바닥의 장식과 벽의 모자이크들을 복원하기 위한 상당한 보수 작업이 수행되었다. 게다가, 세계 유산 기금(WMF)과 같은 국제기구들은 그 큰 돔형 지붕이 수리되고 내부에 추가적인 개선이 이루어질 수 있게 해주는 보조금을 제공했다. 이 프로젝트들은 압도적인 성공으로 입증되었으며, 2014년까지 아야 소피아는 매년 약 320만 명의 관광객을 끌어모으고 있었다. 그러나, 아야 소피아는 2020년에 다시 모스크로 전환되었으며, 이는 이 귀중한 유적지의 보존에 대한 우려로 이어졌다.

domed 형 돔형의 monument 명 기념물
remarkable 형 주목할 만한 architecture 명 건축
profound 형 중대한 erect 동 건립하다 metropolis 명 주요 도시
thrive 동 번영하다 riot 명 폭동 corruption 명 부패
assert 동 확고히 하다 elaborate 형 정교한 astounding 형 놀라운
drench 동 흠뻑 적시다 consistency 명 일관성 minaret 명 뾰족탑
calligraphy 명 서예 function 동 역할을 하다 grant 명 보조금
overwhelming 형 압도적인 treasured 형 귀중한

1 지문의 단어 "profound"와 의미가 가장 비슷한 것은?
(A) 우연한
(B) 충동적인
(C) 중대한
(D) 의도적인

2 지문의 단어 "it"이 가리키는 것은?
(A) 아야 소피아
(B) 콘스탄티노플
(C) 이스탄불
(D) 비잔틴 제국

3 지문의 단어 "riot"과 의미가 가장 비슷한 것은?
(A) 실패
(B) 재앙
(C) 침략
(D) 시위

4 2단락에서 추론할 수 있는 것으로, 아야 소피아의 건축은
(A) 비잔틴 제국의 전 지역에 높은 세금을 부과할 것을 요구했다
(B) 이 정도 규모의 프로젝트에 일반적인 것보다 훨씬 더 적은 시간이 걸렸다
(C) 그것이 교회의 파괴를 야기했기 때문에 종교 관계자들을 화나게 했다
(D) 유니티니아누스 황제가 콘스탄티노플에 더 큰 관심을 갖도록 촉진했다

5 3단락에 따르면, 다음 중 아야 소피아에 관해 사실이 아닌 것은?

(A) 다른 기독교 예배당을 본떠서 만들어졌다.
(B) 전 세계에서 획득한 자재들을 포함하고 있다.
(C) 낮 동안 많은 자연광이 있다.
(D) 벽돌로 만들어진 돔으로 덮여 있다.

6 4단락에 따르면, 1453년에 아야 소피아는 어떻게 변했는가?
(A) 새로운 아랍어 이름을 얻었다.
(B) 돔에 있는 예술품들이 제거되었다.
(C) 뾰족탑이 기둥을 대체했다.
(D) 파괴된 뒤에 이슬람 양식으로 재건되었다.

7 아래 문장 중 지문 속의 음영된 문장의 핵심 정보를 가장 잘 표현한 것은? 오답은 문장의 의미를 크게 바꾸거나 핵심 정보를 생략한다.
(A) 보수된 모스크는 벽에 이전보다 더 적은 수의 예술품을 포함했다.
(B) 그 장소가 모스크로 사용되지 않게 되자 많은 새로운 이미지들이 바닥과 벽에 추가되었다.
(C) 그 건축물을 종교의식에 더 적합하게 만들기 위해, 개조 중에 많은 장식들이 제거되었다.
(D) 그 건물이 예배 장소였을 때 가려졌던 장식적 특징들이 다시 보이게 되었다.

8 지문에서 글쓴이는 왜 "the World Monuments Fund"를 언급하는가?
(A) 시설의 목적을 변경하기 위한 재정적 장려책을 밝히기 위해
(B) 건축물을 이용한 기구의 예시를 제공하기 위해
(C) 건물에 대한 일부 작업 수행이 가능했던 이유를 설명하기 위해
(D) 개조 프로젝트가 계획했던 것보다 더 광범위했음을 시사하기 위해

9 네 개의 네모[■]는 다음 문장이 삽입될 수 있는 곳을 나타내고 있다.
이것은 그 교회의 주요 신도석, 즉 예배 구역보다 180피트 위로 올려져 있다.
이 문장은 어디에 들어가는 것이 가장 적절한가?

10 지시: 지문 요약을 위한 도입 문장이 아래에 주어져 있다. 지문의 가장 중요한 내용을 나타내는 보기 3개를 골라 요약을 완성하라. 어떤 문장은 지문에 언급되지 않은 내용이나 사소한 정보를 나타내므로 요약에 포함되지 않는다. **이 문제는 2점이다.**

아야 소피아는 수 세기에 걸쳐 그 지역의 역사를 반영하는 방향으로 변화해 왔다.
- (A) 원래 교회는 비잔틴 제국의 수도에 있는 더 이전 것의 장소 위에 건설되었다.
- (D) 15세기에, 아야 소피아는 모스크가 되었으며 그것의 새로운 역할 때문에 중요한 변화들을 겪었다.
- (E) 지금은 다시 모스크이긴 하지만, 그 건물은 현대에 복원되어 박물관으로 전환되었다.

(B) 비잔틴 제국의 다양한 곳에서 온 건축가들은 그 새로운 종교 시설을 설계하기 위해 함께 작업했다.
(C) 콘스탄티노플이 오스만 세력에 의해 정복되었을 때 아야 소피아는 많은 피해를 입었다.
(F) 보수 작업 프로젝트 완료 이후 아야 소피아를 방문하는 관람객들의 수가 크게 늘었다.

Vocabulary Review

본문 p.172

1 adjustable		2 prioritized	3 alternately
4 interval		5 quadrupled	6 unsustainable
7 (A)	8 (D)	9 (D)	10 (B)
11 (D)	12 (A)	13 (A)	14 (B)

CHAPTER 10
Category Chart

Example

본문 p.175

1 Alkaline: (A), (E), (F) Lithium-Ion: (B), (D)

알칼리와 리튬 이온 배터리

배터리는 21세기 사람들의 삶의 점점 더 많은 측면에 동력을 공급하고 있다. 오늘날 시중에는 두 가지의 주요 배터리 유형이 있는데, 이는 알칼리와 리튬 이온 배터리이다. 두 종류의 배터리 모두 화학 에너지를 저장하며, 그 후에 음극 단자, 즉 음극에서 양극 단자, 즉 양극으로 전자와 이온을 보냄으로써 그 에너지를 전기 에너지로 변환한다. 전자는 배터리의 회로를 통해 이동하며, 이온은 두 단자 사이에 위치해 있는 전해액이라고 불리는 화학 분리막을 통해 이동한다.

대부분의 알칼리 배터리는 전해액을 통해 이온을 오직 한 방향으로만 이동시킨다. 더 많은 이온이 음극으로 이동할수록, 배터리에 공급될 수 있는 전압은 더 줄어드는데, 이는 그것이 만들어내는 전기의 양이 감소한다는 것을 의미한다. 모든 이온이 이동되면, 일반적인 알칼리 배터리는 다 닳게 되며 재충전될 수 없다. 이산화망간이 양극의 역할을 하는 한편, 일반적인 알칼리 배터리의 음극은 아연으로 만들어진다. 대조적으로, 리튬 이온 배터리는 그것들의 이온을 배터리의 한쪽에서 다른 쪽으로 앞뒤로 이동시키며, 이는 그것들을 재사용 가능하게 만든다. 사용자는 재충전이라고 알려진 과정에서 사용된 리튬 이온을 금속 산화물 양극에서 다공성 탄소 음극으로 이동시키기 위해 배터리를 전원에 연결하기만 하면 된다. 알칼리 배터리와 달리, 리튬 이온 배터리의 전기 출력은 일정하다.

power ⓢ동력을 공급하다 electron ⓜ전자 terminal ⓜ단자
anode ⓜ음극 cathode ⓜ양극 circuit ⓜ회로
divider ⓜ분리막 electrolyte ⓜ전해액 voltage ⓜ전압
recharge ⓢ재충전하다 zinc ⓜ아연
manganese dioxide 이산화망간 reusable ⓗ재사용 가능한
porous ⓗ다공성의 constant ⓗ일정한

1 지시: 주어진 선택지에서 적절한 문장을 선택하여 관계있는 배터리에 연결하시오.

선택지	알칼리
(C) 이온이 배터리의 회로를 통해 보내진다. (G) 배터리가 세 개의 단자를 갖는다.	· (A) 일반적인 형태는 재충전할 수 없다. · (E) 사용됨에 따라 전압이 줄어든다. · (F) 이산화망간이 양극으로 사용된다.
	리튬 이온
	· (B) 이온이 양방향으로 이동한다. · (D) 전기 출력이 일정하다.

Reading Practice 1

본문 p.176

1 (D) 2 (D) 3 (B) 4 (D)
5 Sunni Muslims: (F), (G) Shia Muslims: (A), (D), (E)

수니파와 시아파 무슬림

이슬람교는 전 세계적으로 20억 명 이상의 신도가 있는, 세계 최대의 종교 중 하나이다. 그러나, 이슬람교 사람들이 흔히 불리는 이름인 무슬림들은 통합되어 있지 않다. 사실, 이슬람교는 수니파와 시아파라는 두 주요 종파로 나누어져 있다. 이 집단의 구성원들은 수백 년 동안 서로 밀접하게 접촉하며 살아왔고, 그들의 공유된 많은 역사 동안 평화롭게 공존했다.

이러한 이유 중 하나는 그 두 집단 간의 신학적 차이가 작다는 것이다. 둘 다 이슬람교의 경전인 쿠란을 천사 가브리엘을 통해 하나님으로부터 선지자 무함마드에게 전하는 신성한 전언으로 여긴다. 게다가, 각 종파의 신도들은 이슬람교의 기본적인 교리를 고수하기 위해 동일한 단계를 밟는데, 이는 종교적 축제일인 라마단 동안 금식하고, 메카 성지로 순례하고, 매일 다섯 번의 기도를 하고, 가난한 사람들에게 베풀고, 그 신앙의 주요 교의를 받아들이겠다고 공개적으로 선언하는 것이다. [2]이 교리들과 관련하여 작은 차이들이 있는데, 가령, 수니파 무슬림들은 다섯 번의 분리된 기도 시간을 갖는 반면, 시아파 무슬림들은 세 번의 기도 시간에 다섯 번의 기도를 하지만, 두 집단은 모두 전반적으로 동일한 기본적인 종교적 관습을 유지하고 있다.

주요한 차이는 각 종파의 신도들이 종교 지도자들을 인식하는 방식에 있다. 시아파 무슬림들은 이맘으로 알려진 그들의 성직자들을 지구상에 있는 하나님의 대표자들로 여기며, 그들이 성자가 될 잠재력을 가지고 있다고 믿어, 그들을 쿠란 속의 선지자들과 같은 수준에 놓는다. **이는 이맘이 하나님에게 직접 받은 권위를 지니기 때문이다.** 대조적으로, 수니파 무슬림들은 그들의 이맘을 단지 모스크와 공동체의 지도자가 된 학식 있는 사람들로 여긴다. 수니파 교도들은 이슬람교에 대한 이맘들의 지식과 헌신 때문에 그들에 대한 큰 존경심을 품지만, 그들이 하나님에 의해 선택되었다고 생각하지 않는다.

영적 권위에 대한 이 서로 다른 견해는 이슬람 신앙을 확립한 선지자 무함마드가 세상을 떠난 서기 632년으로 거슬러 올라갈 수 있다. 시아파 무슬림들은 무함마드가 그의 딸과 결혼하기도 했던 그의 사촌 알리를 이슬람교의 지도자 자리를 넘겨받도록 임명했다고 믿는다. 결과적으로, 그들은 한 개인이 이 혈통일 때만 종교적 권위를 가질 수 있다고 주장하며, 이 유산에 대한 자격을 가진 이맘만을 인정한다. 시아파 무슬림들이 이 요구조건에 두는 가치는 그 종파의 원래 이름인 'Shia't-Ali'에 반영되어 있는데, 이는 "알리의 신도"라는 의미이다. 그러나 수니파 무슬림들은 무함마드가 결코 후계자를 선택하지 않았고, 따라서 이맘은 단지 공동체 구성원들에 의해 지위에 선출된 학식 있는 사람이어야 한다고 주장한다. 이 접근법은 시아파의 더 엄격한 접근법보다 더 큰 매력을 가지고 있는 것으로 보이며, 무슬림의 15퍼센트만이 시아파인 반면, 약 85퍼센트는 수니파이다.

sect 명 종파 coexist 동 공존하다 theological 형 신학적인
divine 형 신성한 prophet 명 선지자 adhere 동 고수하다
tenet 명 교리 fasting 명 금식 pilgrimage 명 순례
profess 동 선언하다 perceive 동 인식하다 cleric 명 성직자
saint 명 성자 devotion 명 헌신 divergent 형 서로 다른
spiritual 형 영적인 appoint 동 임명하다 heritage 명 유산

1 지문의 단어 "divine"과 의미가 가장 비슷한 것은?
(A) 개인적인
(B) 효과적인
(C) 비언어적인
(D) 신성한

2 2단락에 따르면, 시아파와 수니파 무슬림들은
(A) 종교적 축제일 동안 금식할 필요성에 관해 의견이 다르다
(B) 메카 성지 방문의 가치에 관해 의견이 다르다
(C) 불우한 사람들을 지원해야 한다는 요구조건에 관해 의견이 다르다
(D) 매일 열리는 기도 시간의 수에 관해 의견이 다르다

3 네 개의 네모[■]는 다음 문장이 삽입될 수 있는 곳을 나타내고 있다.
이는 이맘이 하나님에게 직접 받은 권위를 지니기 때문이다.
이 문장은 어디에 들어가는 것이 가장 적절한가?

4 지문에서 글쓴이는 왜 "*Shia't-Ali*"를 언급하는가?
(A) 운동의 주요 인물을 식별하기 위해
(B) 오랜 전통에 의문을 제기하기 위해
(C) 종교적 갈등의 기원을 설명하기 위해
(D) 종파에서 혈통의 중요성을 강조하기 위해

5 **지시**: 주어진 선택지에서 적절한 어구를 선택하여 관계있는 종파에 연결하시오.

선택지	수니파 무슬림
(B) 쿠란의 선지자들이 선출되었다고 생각한다 (C) 무함마드의 딸이 종교적 권위를 지녔다고 주장한다	· (F) 무함마드가 후계자를 임명하지 않았다고 주장한다 · (G) 무슬림 인구의 대다수를 차지한다
	시아파 무슬림
	· (A) 이맘이 성자가 될 수 있다고 주장한다 · (D) 친척이 무함마드의 뒤를 이었다고 믿는다 · (E) 이맘이 반드시 이슬람교의 창시자와 관계가 있어야 한다고 주장한다

Reading Practice 2 본문 p.178

1 (D)　2 (A)　3 (C)　4 (C)
5 William the Conqueror: (A), (F)
Harold II of England: (B), (E), (G)

정복자 윌리엄

1066년은 앵글로색슨의 영국 지배 시대의 종말과 현재 영국 왕족 혈통의 시작을 나타낸다. 노르망디의 정복자 윌리엄이 헤이스팅스 전투에서 앵글로색슨 왕 해럴드 2세를 물리친 후, 영국 섬들의 언어, 건축, 사회 조직은 급격하게 변화했다. 역사학자들은 윌리엄의 결과적인 잉글랜드 정복이 순전히 군사적 우월성에 기반했는지, 아니면 그가 왕위에 대한 정당한 권리를 가지고 있었는지에 대해 오랫동안 논쟁해왔다. 이 중요한 사건이 현대 영국의 궁극적인 수립에서 수행한 역할을 고려하면, 그가 정당한 영국 군주였다는 윌리엄의 주장의 유효성을 입증하는 데 많은 관심이 쏠린다.

영국 왕위에 대한 윌리엄의 권리는 그의 전임자가 그를 잉글랜드의 왕으로 만들 것을 구두로 약속했다는 그의 주장에 근거했다. 1051년, 윌리엄은 앵글로색슨의 참회왕 에드워드를 만났다고 전해지며, 그는 남성 후계자가 없는 신앙심 깊은 통치자였다. [2B/2C]윌리엄은 프랑스 왕국에 속했던, 유럽 본토에 있는 영토인 노르망디의 강력한 공작이었으며, 그는 프랑스 왕에게 충성했다. [2D]그는 참회왕 에드워드의 먼 사촌이기도 했다. 그들의 만남에서, 윌리엄은 왕으로서의 복무에 자원했다. 구전에 따르면, 에드워드는 윌리엄을 그의 후계자로 임명하는 데 동의했다.

그러나, 왕위를 차지하려는 또 다른 경쟁자가 있었다. 해럴드 고드윈슨은 웨섹스 백작의 지위로 이미 잉글랜드 남부를 지배하고 있었다. 비록 그가 왕의 혈족은 아니었지만, 해럴드의 여동생이 에드워드와 결혼했으며, 이는 그에게 상당한 정치적 힘을 부여했다. [3]당시의 노르만 역사학자들에 따르면, 해럴드는 윌리엄과 매우 가까운 친구여서 잉글랜드 왕위에 대한 자신의 권리를 포기하겠다고 약속했다. 윌리엄에게 했다고 주장된 두 서약에도 불구하고, 1066년 1월 에드워드의 임종에 참석한 사람은 윌리엄이 아니라 해럴드였다. 해럴드는 에드워드와의 가까움을 죽어가는 왕이 자문 위원회에게 그의 후계자로 해럴드를 선택할 것을 추천하는 것으로 바꾸어 놓을 수 있었다.

이러한 구두의 맹세가 실제로 입 밖으로 내어졌는지를 확인할 방법은 없다. 역사학자들이 알고 있는 것은 윌리엄이 9개월 후에 수많은 군인들을 뒤에 데리고 잉글랜드의 남동부 해안에 도착했다는 것이다. 헤이스팅스 전투가 뒤따랐다. [4]새로운 앵글로색슨 왕 해럴드 2세는 이 전투에서 사망했다. 결과적으로, 윌리엄은 크리스마스에 왕위에 올랐으며 그 이후로 그의 가문은 잉글랜드를 통치해오고 있다. 일부 역사학자들은 그것을 단지 강력한 통치자가 정당한 자신의 것을 차지한 것으로 보는 반면, 다른 사람들은 그것을 프랑스에 의한 잉글랜드의 식민지화에 이르게 된, 주권을 가진 국가에 대한 정당한 이유 없는 침략 행위라고 주장하는 등 윌리엄의 군사적 정복은 해석의 대상으로 남아있지만, 그의 행동이 영국 역사에 끼친 오래 지속되는 영향에 대해서는 논란의 여지가 없다.

lineage 명 혈통　consequential 형 결과적인
superiority 명 우월성　legitimate 형 정당한　pivotal 형 중요한
validity 명 유효성　assertion 명 주장　rightful 형 정당한
monarch 명 군주　predecessor 명 전임자　verbal 형 구두의
successor 명 후계자　contender 명 경쟁자　capacity 명 지위
substantial 형 상당한　pledge 동 약속하다　renounce 동 포기하다
alleged 형 주장된　deathbed 명 임종　proximity 명 가까움
council 명 자문 위원회　oath 명 맹세　utter 동 입 밖으로 내다
in tow (사람을) 뒤에 데리고　ensue 동 뒤따르다
interpretation 명 해석　unprovoked 형 정당한 이유 없는
sovereign 형 주권을 가진　colonization 명 식민지화

1 지문의 단어 "legitimate"과 의미가 가장 비슷한 것은?
(A) 형식적인
(B) 악명 높은
(C) 정확한
(D) 유효한

2 2단락에서, 다음 중 정복자 윌리엄에 관해 언급되지 않은 것은?
(A) 그의 땅을 물려받을 아들이 없었다.
(B) 잉글랜드에 위치해 있지 않은 땅을 통치했다.
(C) 영국인이 아닌 군주에게 충성했다.
(D) 그가 대체한 통치자의 친척이었다.

3 3단락에 따르면, 노르만 학자들은 해럴드 고드윈슨이
(A) 사실 영국 왕의 친척이 아니었다고 주장했다
(B) 불법적인 수단으로 백작의 자리를 얻었다고 주장했다
(C) 왕국에 대한 그의 권리를 포기하겠다고 제안했다고 주장했다
(D) 에드워드가 세상을 떠났을 때 참석하지 않았다고 주장했다

4 4단락에 따르면, 헤이스팅스 전투는
(A) 영국의 프랑스 침략에서 비롯되었다
(B) 원래 계획했던 것보다 더 적은 수의 전투원을 포함했다
(C) 영국 군주의 사망으로 이어졌다
(D) 정복자 윌리엄에게 심각한 부상을 입혔다

5 **지시:** 주어진 선택지에서 적절한 어구를 선택하여 관계있는 사람에게 연결하시오.

선택지	정복자 윌리엄
(C) 높은 수준의 종교적 신념을 보였다 (D) 1066년 이전에 잉글랜드 북부의 많은 부분을 통치했다	· (A) 1051년에 에드워드왕과 만났다 · (F) 대군을 거느리고 잉글랜드를 침략했다
	잉글랜드의 해럴드 2세
	· (B) 에드워드왕의 처남이었다 · (E) 군주가 죽을 때 함께 있었다 · (G) 일 년 미만 동안 군주 역할을 했다

Reading Practice 3 본문 p.180

1 (A)　2 (B)　3 (B)　4 (A)
5 Greek: (A), (B), (G)　Roman: (D), (F)

그리스와 로마의 극장

연극은 고대 세계에서 중요한 문화적 표현 수단이었다. 그리스인들은 기원전 6세기에 종교의식의 파생물로서 그 예술 형태를 발명했으며, 그들이 희극을 상연하긴 했지만, 비극이 연극의 가장 고귀한 형태로 여겨졌다. [2]로마인들은 연극에 대해 훨씬 덜 진지했으며, 그 예술 형태에 대한 그들의 가장 큰 공헌은 희극 장르에 있었다. 그럼에도 불구하고, 로마인들은 대부분의 문화적 분야에서 그리스인들에게 결코 갚을 수 없는 막대한 빚을 지고 있었다. 극장 건축도 예외는 아니었다. 둘 다 동일한 세 가지의 독특한 구성 요소로 공연 공간을 건설했다.

연극을 관람하는 것은 두 문명 모두에서 인기 있는 활동이었기 때문에, 극장은 충분한 좌석을 필요로 했다. 표준적이고 고전적인 그리스의 '테아트론', 즉 좌석 공간은 15,000명에서 17,000명의 관객을 수용할 수 있었지만, 사람들은 여전히 돌려보내졌다. 기원전 5세기경, 그리스인들은 종교 축제에 참석하려는 엄청난 수요를 통제하기 위해 입장료를 부과하기 시작했다. 연극을 대중오락의 형태로 여겼던 로마인들은 그들의 극장에 훨씬 더 많은 좌석을 포함했다. 평균적인 (로마식 테아트론인) '카베아'는 25,000명의 관중을 수용했다. 그리스와 로마 극장 모두에서, 후원자들은 공연 공간을 마주 보는 커다란 반원형으로 배열된 벤치들의 열인 관람석에 앉았다. [3]그리스 극장에서, 관람석은 각 열이 그것 앞에 있는 것보다 약간 더 높도록 언덕의 경사에 배치되었고, 이는 모든 참석자들이 공연을 볼 수 있게 했다. 로마 극장에서, 관람석은 같은 효과를 얻기 위해 콘크리트로 만들어진 거대한 구조물을 따라 올라갔다.

두 국가 모두의 설계자들은 관객 앞에 '오케스트라'를 배치했다. [4]그리스 극장에서, 오케스트라는 배우들이 공연하는 원형 무대였고, 그것의 중앙에는 아마도 제물로, 그리고 연극의 사건에서 일종의 소품으로 사용되었을 제단이 있었다. 로마의 오케스트라는 반원 모양을 하고 있었으며 다른 목적을 수행했다. 배우들은 폭이 최대 300피트이고 지상에서 몇 피트 위로 올라와 있는 직사각형 무대에 등장했다. 공연이 상연될 장소를 제공하는 대신, 오케스트라는 정치 지도자들을 앉히기 위해 사용되었다.

그리스와 로마 극장의 뒤에 있는 배경은 그리스어로는 '스케네'라고 불리고 라틴어로는 '스카이나'라고 불리는 배경 건물이었다. 그리스식은 소품과 의상을 보관하기 위해 사용되었다. 스케네는 처음에 나무로 만들어졌고 마침내는 돌로 만들어졌다. 게다가, 그것은 아마도 그리스 궁전처럼 보이도록 설계된 무대 장치의 역할을 했다. 로마식은 더 정교했고 보통 2층이나 3층 높이였다. 그것의 앞면은 기둥과 문으로 장식적으로 설계되었다. 희극의 경우, 그것은 로마의 거리를 나타냈지만, 비극이 상연되는 경우 궁전으로서 역할을 할 수도 있었다. 때때로 스카이나 앞에 그림이 그려진 배경이 배치되기도 했다.

offshoot 명 파생물　ritual 명 의식　comedy 명 희극
tragedy 명 비극　contribution 명 공헌　incalculable 형 막대한
repay 동 (빚을) 갚다　ample 형 충분한　spectator 명 관객
overwhelming 형 엄청난　onlooker 명 관중　bleacher 명 관람석
ascend 동 올라가다　altar 명 제단　offering 명 제물
prop 명 소품　backdrop 명 (무대의) 배경　elaborate 형 정교한
ornately 부 장식적으로

1 지문의 단어 "incalculable"과 의미가 가장 비슷한 것은?
(A) 헤아릴 수 없는
(B) 남아 있는
(C) 증가하는
(D) 영속하는

2 1단락에서 추론할 수 있는 것으로, 비극은
(A) 로마 극장에서 결코 상연되지 않았다
(B) 그리스인들에게보다 로마인들에게 덜 인기 있었다
(C) 그리스의 종교 당국에 의해 반대되었다
(D) 두 문명 모두에서 세련되지 못한 것으로 간주되었다

3 2단락에 따르면, 다음 중 고대 그리스 극장의 관람석에 관해 사실인 것은?
(A) 큰 언덕 옆에 배치되었다.
(B) 자연 지형 위에 지어졌다.
(C) 직선의 열로 배열되었다.
(D) 콘크리트 구조물에 붙여졌다.

4 3단락에 따르면, 그리스 오케스트라의 목적은
(A) 배우들에게 공연 장소를 제공하는 것이었다
(B) 무대 장치들이 빠르게 교체되게 하는 것이었다
(C) 중요한 사람들에게 특별한 좌석을 제공하는 것이었다
(D) 음악가들과 그들의 악기를 수용하는 것이었다

5 지시: 주어진 선택지에서 적절한 문장을 선택하여 관계있는 극장의 종류에 연결하시오.

선택지	그리스식
(C) 관람석이 점토로 만들어졌다. (E) 비극은 제단에 있는 제물을 특징으로 했다.	· (A) 극장이 종교 축제를 위해 사용되었다. · (B) 배우들이 원형 무대에서 공연했다. · (G) 스케네가 의상을 보관하기 위해 사용되었다.
	로마식
	· (D) 배우들이 직사각형 연단에서 공연했다. · (F) 때때로 극을 위해 배경에 그림이 그려졌다.

iBT Reading Test 1

본문 p.182

1 (B)　2 (A)　3 (C)　4 (A)
5 (C)　6 (B)　7 (D)　8 (B)
9 (A)　10 Butterflies: (A), (B), (E)　Moths: (C), (G)

나비와 나방

대부분의 나방과 나비는 외양만으로 쉽게 구별할 수 있다. 그러나, 이 곤충들은 많은 공통점을 가지고 있고, 그것들의 차이는 보이는 것처럼 뚜렷하지 않다. 둘 다 그리스어로 "비늘 날개"를 의미하는 나비목에 속하며, 이는 그것들의 날개, 다리, 몸에 있는 빽빽한 비늘 층에 대한 인정이다. 과학자들에 따르면, 그 놀랍도록 다양한 곤충 목은 (16만 종의 나방과 1만 1천 종의 나비가 있다) 심지어 오늘날 나방과 나비 둘 다가 먹고 사는 개화 식물이 진화하기도 전인 3억 년 전에 출현한 공통된 조상의 후손이다. 이 공통된 조상은 그것들이 둘 다 세 부분으로 분할된 몸, 세 쌍의 다리, 한 쌍의 더듬이, 하나의 외골격을 가지고 있다는 사

실을 포함하여 그들의 많은 유사성들을 설명한다. 게다가, 나비와 나방이 애벌레에서 번데기로, 번데기에서 날개 달린 곤충으로 변하기 때문에 두 종류의 곤충의 생애 주기는 거의 같다.

나비목은 약 1억 년 전에 별개의 두 계열로 나뉘었으며, 낮에 나는 나비들은 야행성인 나방의 더 큰 집단에서 진화했다. **나방과 나비 사이의 차이점들 중 다수는 그것들 각각의 깨어 있는 시간과 수면 시간의 결과이다.** 다른 많은 알록달록한 동물들처럼, 나비는 낮의 포식자들에게 그것들이 불쾌한 맛이 나는 화학물질을 포함하고 있다고 믿게 하기 위해 밝은 색소를 발달시켰다. 알록달록한 날개는 그것들이 알록달록한 꽃들 사이를 날아다닐 때 나비를 위장하는 것을 돕는다. 대조적으로, 나방은 낮 동안 그것들이 위에 앉아서 쉬는 나무껍질에 섞여 들 수 있도록 베이지색, 갈색이나 회색 같은 더 칙칙한 색을 특징으로 하는 경향이 있다. [4]일부 나방들은 그것들 날개의 비늘이 실제로 음향 에너지를 흡수하는, 음향 위장으로 알려진 기술을 사용함으로써 그것들의 가장 위험한 야행성 포식자인 박쥐를 피한다. 이것은 박쥐가 반사된 음파를 이용하는 사냥 기술인 반향 위치 측정을 사용하여 그것들을 찾는 것을 방지한다.

그것들의 색깔에 더하여, 나방과 나비 사이에는 주목할 만한 다른 신체적 차이점들이 있다. 나비가 끝에 동그란 부분이 있는 가느다란 곤봉 모양의 더듬이를 가지고 있는 반면, 나방은 털로 덮인 더듬이를 가지고 있다. [5]나방의 앞날개와 뒷날개는 비행 중에 날개 가시라고 불리는 뻣뻣한 구조에 의해 고정되며, 이는 나비가 보이지 않는 특징이다. 심지어 나방과 나비가 성충기에 이르기 전에도 둘 사이에는 중요한 신체적 차이점들이 있다. 예를 들어, 접용이라고 불리는 나비의 번데기가 단단하고 부드러운 껍데기를 형성하는 반면, 나방의 번데기는 실 고치에 의해 보호된다.

나방과 나비는 너무나 밀접하게 관련되어 있어서 심지어 이러한 차이점들에도 예외가 없는 것은 아니다. [7]예를 들어, 일반적으로 나비의 날개들을 나방의 그것들과 구별 짓는 화려한 색깔을 특징으로 하지 않는 일부 나비들이 있다. 플로리다산 멸종 위기 나비 종인 샤우스 스왈로우테일은 칙칙한 갈색 날개를 가지고 있다. 마찬가지로 나방의 색이 한결같이 칙칙할 것이라고 기대할 수 없다. [8]혜성 나방은 붉은 점이 있는 밝은 노란색 날개를 가지고 있다. 그것은 심지어 주행성인데, 이는 그것이 낮 동안 활동적이라는 것을 의미한다. 최근 수년간, 일부 연구자들은 나비가 별개의 집단이 아니라 나방의 하위 집단으로 분류되어야 한다고 주장해 왔으며, 그들은 이 재분류에 대해 과학계에서 천천히 지지를 모으고 있다.

stark 형 뚜렷한 order 명 (동식물 분류상의) 목
Lepidoptera 명 나비목 acknowledgment 명 인정
feed on ~을 먹고 살다 segmented 형 분할된
exoskeleton 명 외골격 pupa 명 번데기 diverge 동 나뉘다
nocturnal 형 야행성인 pigmentation 명 색소
camouflage 동 위장하다 dull 형 칙칙한 acoustic 형 음향의
echolocation 명 반향 위치 측정 bulb 명 동그란 부분
bristly 형 뻣뻣한 frenulum 명 날개 가시 chrysalis 명 접용, 번데기
spectacular 형 화려한 endangered 형 멸종 위기의
diurnal 형 주행성의 subgroup 명 하위 집단
reclassification 명 재분류

1 지문의 단어 "stark"와 의미가 가장 비슷한 것은?

(A) 경솔한
(B) 분명한
(C) 일반적인
(D) 약화된

2 아래 문장 중 지문 속의 음영된 문장의 핵심 정보를 가장 잘 표현한 것은? 오답은 문장의 의미를 크게 바꾸거나 핵심 정보를 생략한다.

(A) 수많은 나방과 나비의 종은 그것들의 현재의 생존 수단이 진화하기도 전에 단일 종에서 진화했다.
(B) 나방은 나비보다 더 많지만, 그것들이 같은 종에서 진화했기 때문에 같은 종류의 식물을 먹는다.
(C) 그것들이 둘 다 꽃을 먹고 산다고 해도, 공통된 조상에서 진화했다고 하기에는 너무 많은 나비와 나방의 종이 있다.
(D) 개화 식물은 나방과 나비를 둘 다 낳은 곤충 종의 출현 직전에 진화했다.

3 지문에서 글쓴이는 왜 "foul-tasting chemicals"를 언급하는가?

(A) 나비가 야생에서 거의 사냥 당하지 않는 이유를 설명하기 위해
(B) 나비가 분비하는 물질을 설명하기 위해
(C) 나비가 포식자를 피하는 방법을 설명하기 위해
(D) 나비의 먹이의 예시를 제공하기 위해

4 2단락에 따르면, 나방의 특정 종들은

(A) 그것들의 날개에서 소리가 반사되는 것을 방지함으로써 박쥐를 피한다
(B) 탐지될 수 있는 소음을 내는 것을 피함으로써 박쥐를 피한다
(C) 나무 외부의 색깔에 조화됨으로써 박쥐를 피한다
(D) 밤에 보기 어려운 비늘을 가짐으로써 박쥐를 피한다

5 3단락에 따르면, 다음 중 나방에 관해 사실인 것은?

(A) 그것들의 더듬이는 나비 더듬이보다 더 가늘다.
(B) 실을 함유하지 않은 단단한 고치를 형성한다.
(C) 그것들이 날 때 그것들의 날개는 서로 연결된다.
(D) 그것들의 더듬이 끝에 동그란 부분을 가지고 있다.

6 지문의 단어 "they"가 가리키는 것은?

(A) 년
(B) 연구자들
(C) 나비
(D) 나방

7 4단락에 따르면, 샤우스 스왈로우테일은

(A) 플로리다 생태계에서의 풍부함으로 인해 주목할만하다
(B) 밤에 활동적인 성향으로 인해 주목할만하다
(C) 나비와 나방 둘 다로의 분류로 인해 주목할만하다
(D) 특이하게 밝지 않은 색으로 인해 주목할만하다

8 다음 중 4단락에서 혜성 나방에 관해 추론할 수 있는 것은?

(A) 그것의 날개 색깔은 포식자들을 피할 때 단점이 된다.
(B) 그것을 나비와 구별하기 위해서는 자세한 조사가 필요하다.
(C) 그것이 나방으로 잘못 분류되었는지에 관한 논의가 진행 중이다.
(D) 밤 동안 활동적일 수 있는 능력은 먹이에 대한 그것의 접근성을 높인다.

9 네 개의 네모[■]는 다음 문장이 삽입될 수 있는 곳을 나타내고 있다.

나방과 나비 사이의 차이점들 중 다수는 그것들 각각의 깨어 있는 시간과 수면 시간의 결과이다.

이 문장은 어디에 들어가는 것이 가장 적절한가?

10 **지시:** 주어진 선택지에서 적절한 어구를 선택하여 일반적으로 관계 있는 곤충에 연결하시오. **이 문제는 3점이다.**

선택지	나비
(D) 밤의 포식자들을 피하기 위해 반향 위치 측정을 사용한다 (F) 날개를 발달시킨 다음에 접용에 들어간다	· (A) 낮 동안 활동적이다 · (B) 개화 식물들 사이에서 찾아내기 쉽지 않다 · (E) 끝에서 넓어지는 가느다란 더듬이를 가지고 있다
	나방
	· (C) 낮 동안 내내 나무 위에 숨어있는다 · (G) 그것들의 최종 생애 주기 이전에 실 고치를 만든다

iBT Reading Test 2

본문 p.186

1 (B) 2 (C) 3 (C) 4 (B)
5 (A) 6 (B) 7 (D) 8 (D)
9 (D) 10 Natural Fertilizers: (A), (E), (F)
Chemical Fertilizers: (D), (G)

천연 비료와 화학 비료

천연 비료는 퇴비화를 통해 얻어지는데, 이는 음식 찌꺼기와 거름 및 골분을 포함한 동물 부산물의 결합물이다. 이 과정에서, 미생물과 육안적 생물은 부패하는 유기물을 필수적인 에너지원으로 활용한다. [2D]동시에, 이 유기체들은 암모니아 같은 귀한 부산물을 토양으로 배설한다. 예를 들어, 지렁이는 매일 영양적으로 풍부한 외피를 버리는데, 이것은 식물에게 질소, 칼슘, 인의 공급원이다. [2A]그것들은 또한 분해되고 있는 식물 물질을 통과해 기어가면서 토양 통기를 증가시키며, 그렇게 함으로써 배수를 개선한다. [2B]게다가, 유기체들은 토양과 물속의 오염물질을 줄임으로써 해로운 병원균으로부터 식물을 보호해준다. 그 결과, 생물학적 유기체의 노력을 통해 토양의 비옥도와 농작물의 생산성이 향상된다.

그러나, 천연 비료를 만들어 내는 데 사용되는 찌꺼기의 분해는 시간이 오래 걸리는 과정이기 때문에 그것들은 산업 규모에서 아주 비싸다. 게다가, 유기체에 의한 영양분의 복구는 매우 가변적이며, 이는 천연 비료의 구성을 불규칙적으로 만든다. 그러므로, 일부 천연 비료는 토양 내의 결핍을 대체하지 못할 수도 있다. [3]이러한 예측할 수 없는 변화 때문에, 천연 비료는 농부들에 의해 농작물 수확량을 늘리는 데 신뢰할 수 없는 것으로 여겨진다.

대조적으로, 화학 비료는 일련의 신뢰할 수 있는 화학적 반응을 통해 제조된다. 이 비료들은 주로 인, 칼륨, 질소로 구성된다. 인산은 반응기 내에서 황산, 물, 인암의 혼합을 수반하는 습식 과정을 통해 얻어진다. [4]결과로 얻어지는 산 형태는 식물이 성장에 필요한 효소와 단백질을 생성하도록 촉진한다. 마찬가지로, 농축된 칼륨은 염소와 결합하여 염화칼륨을 만드는데, 이것은 물 흡입을 조절하고 식물 단백질 형성을 촉진한다. 마지막 화합물인 질소는 하버법을 통해 얻어지는데, 그것에서 대기 질소는 수소와 금속 촉매에 노출된다. **이것은 액체 무수 암모니아를 만드는데, 이는 손쉽게 토양에 사용될 수 있는, 질소 함유량이 높은 물질이다.**

화학 비료는 명백하게 부정적인 환경적 영향을 미친다. 과도하게 비료를 준 토양은 비료 연소를 초래할 수 있는데, 이것은 유독성 소금의 과포화와 함께 식물을 죽인다. 그 화학물질은 또한 토양에 있는 육안적 생물 및 미생물에게 기여하지 않으며, 많은 경우에, 그 이로운 유기체들을 몰살시킨다. 게다가, 화학 비료는 화학물질을 너무 빠르게 방출할 수 있는데, 이는 식물의 잎이 무성한 부분에는 영양분을 강화하지만 약한 뿌리를 초래하여, 전염성 질병의 잠재적인 위험을 증가시키고 열매 생산성을 낮춘다. 마지막으로, 이 위험한 화학물질들이 강과 연못을 포함한 수원으로 흘러드는 것은 심각한 생태학적 피해를 야기해 왔다.

화학 비료의 사용과 관련된 위험들이 있지만, 그것들은 농작물 성장을 최적화하는 가장 효율적인 방법이다. 팽창하는 세계의 인구가 어느 때보다도 많은 양의 식량을 필요로 함에 따라 그것들은 점점 더 필수적이다. 인구에게 식량을 공급하기 위해 세계의 농작물 생산은 2050년까지 두 배가 되어야 할 것으로 현재 추정된다. [8]안타깝게도, 이러한 증가는 농업의 효율성을 증대시키는 화학 비료의 활용 없이는 달성될 수 없는데, 이는 환경에 추가적인 피해를 초래할 것이다. 따라서, 지구에 미치는 화학 비료의 부정적인 영향을 줄이기 위해 더 많은 노력을 들여야 한다.

fertilizer 명 비료 composting 명 퇴비화 byproduct 명 부산물
manure 명 거름 bone meal 골분
macroorganism 명 육안적 생물 excrete 동 배설하다
casing 명 외피 phosphorus 명 인 aeration 명 통기
pathogen 명 병원균 contaminant 명 오염물질
prohibitive 형 아주 비싼 variable 형 가변적인 deficiency 명 결핍
unpredictable 형 예측할 수 없는 undependable 형 신뢰할 수 없는
potassium 명 칼륨 sulfuric acid 황산 phosphate rock 인암
enzyme 명 효소 chlorine 명 염소 intake 명 흡입
catalyst 명 촉매 undeniably 부 명백하게
oversaturation 명 과포화 exterminate 동 몰살시키다
infectious 형 전염성의 optimize 동 최적화하다

1 지문의 단어 "excrete"와 의미가 가장 비슷한 것은?
(A) 지탱하다
(B) 내보내다
(C) 대체하다
(D) 흡수하다

2 1단락에 따르면, 토양 기반 유기체들이 수행하지 않는 행위는?
(A) 토양의 배수 증가
(B) 오염물질 제거
(C) 부패한 물질 분리
(D) 영양분 공급

3 2단락에 따르면, 농부들이 천연 비료 사용을 선호하지 않는 것은
(A) 생산하는 데 많은 노력을 요하기 때문이다
(B) 원료로 인해 만들기에 비싸기 때문이다
(C) 일관되지 않은 양의 영양분을 함유하고 있기 때문이다
(D) 특정 종류의 농작물에 해롭기 때문이다

4 3단락에 따르면, 인은 토양에서 어떤 기능을 하는가?
(A) 하버법을 개시되게 하여 질소를 생산한다.
(B) 식물을 성장시키는 세포의 생성을 촉진한다.
(C) 식물이 물 흡입을 촉진하도록 자극한다.
(D) 식물을 해치는 산성 화합물을 흡수한다.

5 지문의 단어 "exterminate"와 의미가 가장 비슷한 것은?

(A) 파괴하다
(B) 유인하다
(C) 주다
(D) 바꾸다

6 아래 문장 중 지문 속의 음영된 문장의 핵심 정보를 가장 잘 표현한 것은? 오답은 문장의 의미를 크게 바꾸거나 핵심 정보를 생략한다.

(A) 자주 사용되는 화학물질은 식물을 성장시키고, 지속적으로 식물 뿌리의 길이를 늘린다.
(B) 빠르게 활용된 영양분은 성장 불균형을 야기하고, 식물 건강의 악화를 초래한다.
(C) 빠르게 흡수된 화학물질은 광범위한 식물 성장을 야기하고, 결과로 얻어지는 열매의 품질을 높인다.
(D) 성급하게 방출된 영양분은 성장 잠재력을 저해하고, 식물의 열매가 질병을 발달시키도록 야기한다.

7 5단락에서 글쓴이는 왜 세계의 농작물 생산이 두 배가 되는 것을 언급하는가?

(A) 농작물 생산이 확대되어 온 방법을 설명하기 위해
(B) 천연 비료의 중요성을 보여주기 위해
(C) 비료가 사용되는 방법의 예시를 제공하기 위해
(D) 화학 비료의 필요성을 보여주기 위해

8 다음 중 5단락에서 화학 비료에 관해 추론할 수 있는 것은?

(A) 기술이 천연 비료를 향상시켰기 때문에 중요성이 감소했다.
(B) 그것들과 관련된 수확량은 이후 세대의 필요를 맞추기에 불충분하다.
(C) 그것들의 해로운 환경적 영향을 줄이려는 노력은 대체로 성공적이었다.
(D) 농작물 산출을 증가시키는 데 있어 그것들의 효능은 환경적 문제점을 뛰어넘는다.

9 네 개의 네모[■]는 다음 문장이 삽입될 수 있는 곳을 나타내고 있다.

이것은 액체 무수 암모니아를 만드는데, 이는 손쉽게 토양에 사용될 수 있는, 질소 함유량이 높은 물질이다.

이 문장은 어디에 들어가는 것이 가장 적절한가?

10 **지시**: 주어진 선택지에서 적절한 어구를 선택하여 관계있는 비료의 종류에 연결하시오. **이 문제는 3점이다.**

선택지	천연 비료
(B) 환경적 이점과 신뢰할 수 있는 수확량 증가로 인해 선호된다 (C) 수확량을 줄이는 토양의 결핍을 초래한다	· (A) 음식 찌꺼기와 동물 부산물로 만들어진다 · (E) 생산되는 데 일부 농부들에게 실용적인 것보다 더 오래 걸린다 · (F) 토양에 사는 유기체들과의 상호 작용을 필요로 한다
	화학 비료
	· (D) 신뢰할 수 있는 화학적 반응을 통해 생산된다 · (G) 근처의 수원을 오염시키는 것으로 알려져 있다

Vocabulary Review

본문 p.190

1 consequential		2 theological	3 divergent
4 diurnal		5 lineage	6 optimize
7 (A)	8 (D)	9 (B)	10 (A)
11 (D)	12 (B)	13 (A)	14 (A)

Actual Test 1

Passage 1

본문 p.192

1 (B)	2 (B)	3 (C)	4 (A)
5 (D)	6 (A)	7 (D)	8 (A)
9 (D)	10 (B), (C), (E)		

태양 광도와 온실가스

물체에 의해 방출되는 빛의 양은 광도로 측정된다. [2]별에서, 최대의 광도는 수십억 년 후 그것의 수명이 끝에 달할 때 나타난다. 태양은 46억 년 동안 존재해 왔고 그것이 고갈될 때까지 10억 년마다 계속해서 10퍼센트씩 밝아질 것이다. 지구가 45억 년 전에 처음 형성되었을 때, 태양의 광도는 그것의 현재의 세기보다 약 30퍼센트 더 낮았다. 태양 복사, 즉 햇빛은 초기의 지구를 결빙 온도 이상으로 덥히기에 충분하지 않았다. 그러므로, 영상의 온도를 유지하기 위해서는 지구 대기의 특정한 가스들이 필요했다. 특히, 원시 미생물은 막대한 양의 메탄을 방출했는데, 이는 태양 복사를 가두는 큰 용량을 가지고 있다. 그 결과, 태양으로부터의 열은 지구에 저장되었고, 액체 바다를 유지할 만큼 충분히 따뜻한 온도를 유지했다.

메탄으로 데우는 방법은 25억 년 전까지 계속되었는데, 이때 시아노박테리아는 광합성 하는 능력을 발달시켰다. 산소는 광합성의 부산물이다. 그러나, 산소의 작은 분자들이 적은 양의 태양 복사만을 가둘 수 있는 반면 메탄은 더 많은 양을 흡수한다. 산소가 메탄을 생산하는 박테리아에게 유독했기 때문에, 산소의 증가는 대기 중 메탄 양의 급격한 감소를 초래했다. 유지를 위한 메탄이 없어지자, 태양으로부터의 열은 다시 우주로 흩어졌다. **열의 손실은 빙하 작용을 야기하여 전 지구의 바다를 얼렸을 것이다.** 다행히도, 탄소 생산 유기체들의 진화를 통해 대기에 이산화탄소가 생성되기 시작했다. 수백만 년 후에, 대기의 이산화탄소는 태양 복사로부터의 열을 가두는 데 요구되는 양에 도달했고, 이는 지구가 녹고 더 큰 생명체들의 진화에 적합하게 되도록 해주었다.

태양의 증가하는 광도는 10억 년 이내에 지구를 사람이 살기 힘들게 만들 것이다. 그 시점 이전에, 지구는 1843년 독일 천문학자 새뮤얼 슈바베에 의해 발견된 11년 태양 활동 주기 내내 태양 발광의 변동을 겪을 것이다. 이것은 태양에 의해 내뿜어지는 태양 복사의 양에 영향을 미친다. 과학자들은 강렬한 자기 활동 영역인 태양의 흑점이 더 높은 복사 수준과 직접적으로 연관되어 있다는 것을 밝혀냈다. 태양의 흑점은 태양의 가장자리 근처에서 나타나며 11년의 기간에 걸쳐 중심으로 이동한다. [7]태양 흑점의 태양 활동 주기에서의 변화와 그 이후의 광도 변화는 지구의 온도에 영향을 미칠 수 있다.

전문가들은 인간 활동의 결과로서 대기에 들어오는 비정상적으로 많은 양의 이산화탄소 및 메탄과 함께, 증가된 태양 광도가 결국 폭주 온실 효과라고 알려진 것을 초래할 것을 우려한다. 이 현상은 지구 대기에 있는 열을 가두는 가스의 양이 태양으로부터의 열이 빠져나가는 것이 완전히 제한되는 지점까지 증가할 때 발생할 것이다. 8D이것은 지구의 대기와 표면이 둘 다 비교적 짧은 기간에 극적으로 가열되게 할 것이다. 8B가두어진 열로부터 온도가 상승함에 따라, 산소와 질소를 생산할 수 있는 유기체들은 하나씩 죽어갈 것이다. 대조적으로, 이산화탄소와 메탄을 방출하는 미생물들은 이러한 극단적인 조건 하에서 생존할 수 있을 것이며, 따라서 그것들의 수는 변화하는 기후에 의해 영향받지 않을 것이다. 8C증발하는 바다가 훨씬 더 많은 이산화탄소를 대기에 더하는 동안, 그것들은 꾸준히 이 두 가스를 생산할 것이다. 결국, 지구는 금성과 닮게 될 것인데, 이것은 96퍼센트 이상이 이산화탄소인 두꺼운 대기에 둘러싸여 있으며, 이는 섭씨 약 462도의 온도를 초래한다. 인간은 온실가스 배출량을 상당히 줄임으로써 이 결과를 지연시키거나 심지어 방지할 수 있다.

solar 형 태양의 luminosity 명 광도 give off 방출하다
peak 형 최대의 deplete 동 고갈시키다
inadequate 형 충분하지 않은 requisite 형 필요한
primitive 형 원시의 microbe 명 미생물 discharge 동 방출하다
photosynthesize 동 광합성하다 byproduct 명 부산물
molecule 명 분자 retention 명 유지
inhospitable 형 사람이 살기 힘든 fluctuation 명 변동
luminescence 명 발광 emit 동 내뿜다, 배출하다
sunspot 명 태양의 흑점 correlated 형 연관된
abnormally 부 비정상적으로 runaway 형 폭주하는
die off 하나씩 죽어가다 unaffected 형 영향을 받지 않는

1 지문의 단어 "requisite"과 의미가 가장 비슷한 것은?
(A) 대체된
(B) 필요한
(C) 유지된
(D) 회복된

2 1단락에 따르면, 별은 언제 가장 밝은가?
(A) 그것이 존재하기 시작할 때
(B) 그것의 소멸이 가까웠을 때
(C) 40억 년 후에
(D) 그것의 수명 중반에

3 지문에서 글쓴이는 왜 "cyanobacteria"를 언급하는가?
(A) 태양 복사가 대기에 나타나기 시작한 방법을 설명하기 위해
(B) 광합성의 여러 단계를 묘사하기 위해
(C) 초기의 산소 생산 배후에 있는 유기체를 확인하기 위해
(D) 다양한 종류의 미생물을 구별하기 위해

4 아래 문장 중 지문 속의 음영된 문장의 핵심 정보를 가장 잘 표현한 것은? 오답은 문장의 의미를 크게 바꾸거나 핵심 정보를 생략한다.
(A) 이산화탄소가 태양열을 가둘 만큼 충분히 풍부해짐에 따라, 더 큰 생명체들이 지구에서 진화할 수 있었다.
(B) 지구에서의 진화는 대체로 이산화탄소의 형성으로 인해 가능해졌다.
(C) 열의 일부가 이산화탄소에 손실되었음에도 불구하고, 태양 복사는 지구에서 더 큰 생명체들이 진화하도록 해주었다.
(D) 녹은 물은 증가된 이산화탄소의 양을 초래했고, 이는 더 큰 생명체들이 지구에 나타날 수 있도록 했다.

5 지문의 단어 "This"가 가리키는 것은?
(A) 태양
(B) 지구
(C) 발광
(D) 주기

6 지문의 어구 "correlated to"와 의미가 가장 비슷한 것은?
(A) ~과 연관된
(B) ~으로 구분되는
(C) ~으로 구성된
(D) ~에 부착된

7 3단락에 따르면, 태양의 흑점은
(A) 태양 복사의 속도를 변화시킴으로써 지구의 기상 조건을 형성한다
(B) 자기 활동의 방향에 영향을 미침으로써 지구의 기상 조건을 형성한다
(C) 태양 복사의 구성 요소를 변화시킴으로써 지구의 기상 조건을 형성한다
(D) 태양의 광도에 영향을 미침으로써 지구의 기상 조건을 형성한다

8 4단락에 따르면, 다음 중 폭주 온실 효과의 결과로서 일어나는 것이 아닌 것은?
(A) 메탄을 분비하는 미생물들이 소멸될 것이다.
(B) 일부 유기체들이 하나씩 죽어갈 것이다.
(C) 바다가 증발할 것이다.
(D) 온도가 상승할 것이다.

9 네 개의 네모[■]는 다음 문장이 삽입될 수 있는 곳을 나타내고 있다.
열의 손실은 빙하 작용을 야기하여 전 지구의 바다를 얼렸을 것이다.
이 문장은 어디에 들어가는 것이 가장 적절한가?

10 지시: 지문 요약을 위한 도입 문장이 아래에 주어져 있다. 지문의 가장 중요한 내용을 나타내는 보기 3개를 골라 요약을 완성하라. 어떤 문장은 지문에 언급되지 않은 내용이나 사소한 정보를 나타내므로 요약에 포함되지 않는다. **이 문제는 2점이다.**

지구의 기후는 20억 년 동안 약한 태양 발광과 메탄가스의 영향을 받았다.
- (B) 지구에서 충분한 이산화탄소가 생산되자, 태양으로부터의 열은 대기에 가두어지기 시작했다.
- (C) 태양의 흑점으로 인해 규칙적으로 일어나는 태양 발광의 변화는 지구의 온도에 상당한 영향을 미친다.
- (E) 태양 광도와 배출되는 온실가스의 양의 증가는 지구가 많은 생물 형태에게 거주할 수 없는 곳이 되도록 야기할 수 있다.

(A) 태양의 더 낮은 광도는 처음에 지구의 온도가 빙점 위로 상승하는 것을 방지했다.
(D) 태양의 흑점의 형성을 좌우하는 11년 주기는 1843년에 독일 천문학자에 의해 발견되었다.
(F) 금성의 대기가 주로 이산화탄소로 구성되어 있기 때문에, 그 행성은 지구보다 훨씬 더 높은 평균 온도를 가지고 있다.

Passage 2

본문 p.196

11 (C) 12 (A) 13 (B) 14 (C)
15 (C) 16 (C) 17 (D) 18 (B)
19 (B) 20 (C), (D), (F)

영국의 봉건 제도

봉건 제도는 로마 제국의 쇠퇴에 이어 유럽에서 발달한 경제적, 법적 통치 방식이었다. 이 제도는 왕에 의해 지휘되는 고도로 계층화된 사회를 강조했다. 영국에서의 봉건 제도의 정확한 시작에 관해 많은 학문적 논란이 있지만, 역사학자들은 봉건 계약이 그 왕국이 1066년에 윌리엄 1세에 의해 정복된 이후까지 영국 사회에 완전히 통합되지 않았다는 데 대개 동의한다.

영국을 침략하기 전에, 노르만 통치자 윌리엄 1세는 영국 왕좌에 대한 그의 권리를 지지하는 대가로 귀족들에게 '봉토'라고 알려진 토지 수여를 약속했다. 이 봉토들에는 특정한 조건이 붙었는데, 이는 봉건 계약에 의해 유지되었다. [12]봉건 계약은 군주와 신하, 혹은 더 높은 계급의 귀족과 더 낮은 계급의 귀족 사이의 계약이었는데, 그것을 통해 후자는 토지 권리를 대가로 전자에게 충성의 맹세를 했다. [13]왕좌를 얻은 이후, 윌리엄 1세는 영국 토지의 약 20퍼센트를 자신을 위해 보유했으며, 추가의 25퍼센트를 교회에 주었고, 그것의 나머지를 정복에 기여했던 170명의 귀족들 사이에서 나누었다. 왕으로부터 직접 토지를 받은 귀족들은 남작이라고 알려졌다.

가장 높은 단계의 봉건 계약은 왕과 그의 직계 봉신인 남작들 사이에서 이루어졌다. 그 계약은 각 당사자의 책무를 명시했다. 남작들은 왕의 요청에 따라 기사와 병사를 공급할 것을 약속했는데, 이 요구에 따른 군대는 매우 비싼 정규 군대에 대한 필요성을 낮추었기 때문에 왕에게 이로웠다. 결과적으로, 봉건 계약은 남작들에게 매우 이득이 되었는데, 이는 그들 또한 그것을 사용해 사회적 지위에서 그들 아래에 있는 사람들의 영주가 될 수 있었기 때문이다. 사실, 남작들이 왕에게 공급했던 자원은, 비싸기는 했지만, 봉건 제도에서 더 낮은 계급의 사람들이 남작에게 진 빚에 비하면 아주 적은 비용이었다. 그러므로, 남작들은 더 낮은 계급의 귀족들에게 그들의 사유지를 분배함으로써 힘들이지 않고 부를 창출할 수 있었는데, 그들은 봉건 계약을 통해 남작들의 봉신이 되었다. 종종, 봉신은 농업에 그 토지를 사용했고, 토지 사용의 대가로 남작에게 기사, 농작물 수확량의 일부, 현금 지급을 약속했다.

더 낮은 계급의 봉신은 차례로 그들의 토지 중 일부를 작은 조각으로 나누어 봉건 계약을 통해 농노와 자유민들에게 임대했으며, 그렇게 함으로써 스스로 영주가 되었다. [16]농노들은 일주일에 5일 동안 영주의 토지에 농사를 짓고 자신을 위해 농지의 작은 부분과 집을 받았던 사실상의 하인이었다. 더 낮은 계급의 약 10퍼센트를 차지했던 자유민들은 단지 농지를 대여했다. 그러나, 두 집단 모두 그들의 영주에게 식량의 형태로 많은 세금을 지불하도록 요구받았다.

이 제도가 수백 년이 지난 후에, 봉건 계약은 심각하게 격하되었다. 남작들은 스스로 엄청나게 강력해졌다. [18C]게다가, 왕은 자신의 군대를 감당할 만큼 부유했고 남작들의 군대에 의존하지 않았다. [18A]이 불균형은 남작들이 더 많은 권력과 왕으로부터의 자유를 추구함에 따라 13세기에 전쟁을 초래했다. 더욱이, 집합적으로 흑사병이라고 알려진 일련의 치명적인 전염병들이 영국을 통해 확산되었다. **이 질병은 쥐 같은 설치류에서 발견되는 벼룩에 의해 전염되었다.** 즉각적인 결과는 농업 노동력의 부족이었다. [18D]농노들과 자유민들이 둘 다 더 나은 기회를 가진 지역들로 이동함에 따라 수많은 마을들이 완전히 사라졌다. 봉신들 봉신들은 더 이상 그들의 상급자들에게 의존하거나 충성을 다하지 않았고, 이는 봉건 제도의 모든 계층에서의 불안정을 초래했다.

feudalism 명 봉건 제도　governance 명 통치
stratified 형 계층화된　head 동 지휘하다　scholarly 형 학문적인
invasion 명 침략　nobleman 명 귀족　fief 명 봉토
throne 명 왕좌　uphold 동 유지하다　monarch 명 군주
subject 명 신하　oath 명 맹세　conquest 명 정복
baron 명 남작　vassal 명 봉신(봉토를 받은 신하)
on-demand 형 요구에 따른　parcel 동 분배하다
pledge 동 약속하다　degrade 동 격하하다
immensely 부 엄청나게　imbalance 명 불균형
collectively 부 집합적으로　consequence 명 결과
shortage 명 부족　instability 명 불안정

11 지문의 단어 "stratified"와 의미가 가장 비슷한 것은?
(A) 폭력적인
(B) 정제된
(C) 계급에 따른
(D) 구식인

12 2단락에 따르면, 영국의 봉건 계약은 항상
(A) 토지 사용에 대한 대가로 충성의 약속을 포함했다
(B) 더 높은 귀족 계급으로의 승격에 대한 보장을 포함했다
(C) 국왕의 신하로서의 일부 책무에 대한 면제 제의를 포함했다
(D) 동등한 계급의 개인들 사이의 충성 선언을 포함했다

13 다음 중 2단락에서 윌리엄 1세에 관해 추론할 수 있는 것은?
(A) 그가 얻은 영국 토지의 대부분을 자신을 위해 보유했다.
(B) 종교적 기관의 지원을 받기를 희망했다.
(C) 봉토에 대한 그의 추종자들의 많은 요청을 거절했다.
(D) 교회 관계자들에게 귀족들과 같은 권리를 줄 것을 거부했다.

14 지문에서 글쓴이는 왜 "on-demand army"를 언급하는가?
(A) 남작들에 의해 누려진 장점을 강조하기 위해
(B) 왕이 많은 돈을 필요로 했다는 것을 강조하기 위해
(C) 왕이 봉신을 갖기 원했던 이유를 설명하기 위해
(D) 영국 군사 제도의 혁신을 보여주기 위해

15 아래 문장 중 지문 속의 음영된 문장의 핵심 정보를 가장 잘 표현한 것은? 오답은 문장의 의미를 크게 바꾸거나 핵심 정보를 생략한다.
(A) 사회적 지위가 남작보다 낮은 사람들은 남작보다 높은 사람들보다 돈을 덜 지불했다.
(B) 왕은 남작들이 금전적 지급을 통해 그에게 충분히 보상할 것을 요구했다.
(C) 남작들은 왕에게 빚을 진 것보다 더 많은 부를 그들의 봉신들로부터 받았다.
(D) 가난한 사람들은 남작에게 정기적으로 많은 액수의 돈을 지불할 것으로 기대되었다.

16 4단락에 따르면, 다음 중 농노에 관해 사실인 것은?
(A) 시장에서 식량을 거래함으로써 그들의 세금을 지불했다.
(B) 영주의 농지에서 매일 일했다.
(C) 그들의 영주로부터 토지의 구역을 수여받았다.
(D) 더 낮은 계급의 소수 집단을 구성했다.

17 지문의 단어 "degraded"와 의미가 가장 비슷한 것은?
(A) 증대된

(B) 깊이 밴
(C) 변형된
(D) 약화된

18 5단락에 따르면, 다음 중 봉건 제도가 쇠퇴한 이유가 아닌 것은?

(A) 남작들과 왕의 관계가 악화되었다.
(B) 부자들이 가난한 사람들과의 관계를 유지하는 데 무관심했다.
(C) 남작들의 봉사가 왕에게 덜 중요해졌다.
(D) 질병의 확산이 더 낮은 계층의 증가된 유동성을 초래했다.

19 네 개의 네모[■]는 다음 문장이 삽입될 수 있는 곳을 나타내고 있다.

이 질병은 쥐 같은 설치류에서 발견되는 벼룩에 의해 전염되었다.

이 문장은 어디에 들어가는 것이 가장 적절한가?

20 **지시:** 지문 요약을 위한 도입 문장이 아래에 주어져 있다. 지문의 가장 중요한 내용을 나타내는 보기 3개를 골라 요약을 완성하라. 어떤 문장은 지문에 언급되지 않은 내용이나 사소한 정보를 나타내므로 요약에 포함되지 않는다. **이 문제는 2점이다.**

봉건 계약은 노르만의 정복 이후 영국에서의 통치 제도를 유지하기 위해 사용되었다.
- (C) 윌리엄 1세는 봉건 계약을 체결한 귀족 집단에게 영국의 많은 부분을 분배했다.
- (D) 봉건 계약을 통한 토지 수여자들은 그들의 영주를 위해 수행해야 하는 특정한 책무들이 있었다.
- (F) 많은 요인들이 13세기 영국 봉건 제도의 몰락을 초래했다.

(A) 서기 1066년 노르만의 침략 이전에 영국에는 잘 수립된 봉건 제도의 형태가 존재했다.
(B) 윌리엄 1세가 달리 그의 군사 지도자들에게 보상할 수 없었기 때문에 봉토가 제공되었다.
(E) 농노와 자유민들에게 제공된 구역은 보통 어떠한 형태의 농업 활동에도 적합하지 않았다.

Passage 3

본문 p.200

21 (C) 22 (D) 23 (A) 24 (A)
25 (B) 26 (C) 27 (A) 28 (A)
29 (D) 30 (A), (B), (D)

화산과 기후 변화

주요 화산 분출은 수년간 기후 패턴에 영향을 미칠 수 있다. [22A]화산 활동과 기후 변화 사이의 최초의 명확한 연관성은 1784년 미국인 외교관 벤저민 프랭클린이 파리에 주재해 있는 동안 지어졌다. 그는 그가 이례적인 기상 상태라고 믿었던 것에 관한 많은 관찰을 기록했다. [22B/22C]이것들은 끊임없이 지속되는 안개가 북아메리카와 유럽의 많은 부분의 상공에 머물렀던 몹시 추운 겨울로 이어진 추운 여름을 포함했다. 이러한 현상들이 아이슬란드에서의 일련의 화산 분출과 연관되었을 수 있다는 그의 견해는 옳았다. 8개월 동안, 아이슬란드 라키 열극계의 거대한 분출은 용암, 화산재, 가스를 주변 환경으로 분출했다. 지역적으로, 엄청난 양의 이산화황, 염화수소 및 다른 유독 가스들이 가축과 작물을 죽인 산성비를 초래했고 엄청난 기근을 야기했다. 그 분출로 인해 아이슬란드 인구의 약 25퍼센트가 죽었다. [23]게다가, 화산 구름의 순환은 북반구 전역에 걸쳐 작물과 사람들의 생존을 위협한 더 낮은 기온을 야기했다. **심지어는 멀리 떨어진 일본에서도 쌀농사가 실패함에 따라 그 영향을 받았으며, 이는 그 국가 역사상 최악의 기근을 초래했다.**

화산을 지구의 기후에 있어 중요한 요소로 만드는 것은 물질들을 지표면 위로 높이 뿜어내는 그것들의 잠재력이다. 대기의 가장 낮은 부분은 땅에서부터 지표면 위 약 10킬로미터까지 뻗어 있는 대류권이다. 이 범위 내에서, 뿜어져 나온 가스와 고체는 대기 오염을 만들어내지만, 보통 그것들 자신의 무게로 인해, 혹은 비와 결합되었을 때 지표면으로 떨어진다. [24]그러나, 대류권을 넘어 성층권으로 들어가는 입자와 화학물질을 뿜어내는 대규모의 분출로부터 장기적인 영향이 야기된다. 화산 기둥에서 유황산은 흔하게 존재하며, 대기 높은 곳에서 그것들은 대부분 유황산으로 구성된 작은 방울인 황산 에어로졸로 전환된다. 이 작은 입자들은 분출 이후 수년간 성층권에 머무르며 지구를 순환할 수 있는 에어로졸 구름을 만든다.

에어로졸 구름은 지표면에서 나가는 지구의 복사와 태양으로부터 들어오는 복사에 영향을 미치기 때문에 기후에 이중적인 효과를 미친다. 과학자들은 이 복사 균형의 변화를 '복사 강제력'이라고 부른다. 복사 강제력의 정도는 에어로졸 입자의 크기와 연관된 것으로 보이며, 만약 그것들이 2미크론보다 크면, 그것들은 햇빛은 들어오게 하면서 지구의 복사가 빠져나가는 것은 막는 경향이 있는데, 이는 지구 온난화를 촉진한다. [25]만약 그것들이 더 작으면, 반대의 패턴이 발생하는 경향이 있다.

현대에, 과학자들은 여러 대규모 분출을 면밀히 연구할 기회가 있었다. 이것들 중 가장 주목할 만한 것은 1991년 필리핀 피나투보산의 분출이었다. 피나투보는 약 2천만 톤의 잔해와 가스를 대기 중으로 35킬로미터까지 뿜어냈다. 위성 사진은 기록된 역사상 가장 큰 이산화황 구름을 드러냈고, 그것은 그다음 3년간 지표면의 전반적인 냉각을 야기했다. 그러나, 복사 강제력은 과학자들이 조사한 대기나 지표면의 위치에 따라 복잡한 패턴을 만들어냈다. 그 패턴을 더 잘 이해하기 위해, 연구자들은 그들이 두 개의 모델을 비교한 컴퓨터 시뮬레이션에 데이터를 입력했는데, 한 개는 피나투보가 만들어낸 에어로졸이 존재하는 것이었고, 한 개는 그것들이 없는 것이었다. 그 조사 결과는 대류권이 냉각된 반면 성층권은 따뜻해졌음을 입증했지만, 대류권에는 지표면의 기온에 영향을 미친 계절적 변동이 존재했다. 특히, 연구자들은 전반적인 지구 냉각에도 불구하고 북반구에서는 겨울 동안 지표면 대기의 명확한 온난화가 있었음을 발견했다.

volcanism 명 화산 활동　station 동 주재시키다
anomalous 형 이례적인　frigid 형 몹시 추운
persistent 형 끊임없이 지속되는　contention 명 견해, 주장
sulfur dioxide 이산화황　hydrogen chloride 염화수소
famine 명 기근　hemisphere 명 반구　eject 동 뿜어내다
troposphere 명 대류권　stratosphere 명 성층권　plume 명 기둥
sulfate 명 황산　two-fold 형 이중적인　terrestrial 형 지구의, 육상의
radiation 명 (열·에너지 등의) 복사　radiative forcing 복사 강제력
debris 명 잔해　presence 명 존재　corroborate 동 입증하다

21 지문의 단어 "anomalous"와 의미가 가장 비슷한 것은?

(A) 보통의
(B) 불쾌한
(C) 특이한
(D) 어려운

22 다음 중 벤저민 프랭클린에 관해 언급되지 않은 것은?

(A) 파리에 있는 미국인 공무원이었다.

(B) 추운 여름과 겨울을 관찰했다.
(C) 오래 가는 안개의 존재에 주목했다.
(D) 분출 동안 아이슬란드에 있었다.

23 1단락에 따르면, 라키 분출 이후에 북반구 전역에 걸쳐 작물과 인간의 생명을 위험에 빠뜨렸던 것은 무엇인가?

(A) 기온 변화
(B) 산성비
(C) 유독 가스
(D) 용암과 화산재

24 2단락에 따르면, 화산 분출이 기후에 장기적인 영향을 미칠 것인지를 결정하는 것은?

(A) 뿜어져 나온 물질들이 상승하는 고도
(B) 황산 구름 속 입자들의 크기
(C) 화산 물질 속 가스와 고체의 비율
(D) 분출 직후에 내리는 비의 양

25 다음 중 3단락에서 에어로졸 입자에 관해 추론할 수 있는 것은?

(A) 대부분이 2미크론보다 훨씬 더 크다.
(B) 작은 것들은 기온이 떨어지도록 야기한다.
(C) 모두 복사가 대기를 빠져나가는 것을 막는다.
(D) 일부는 들어오거나 빠져나가는 에너지에 영향을 미치지 않는다.

26 지문의 단어 "corroborated"와 의미가 가장 비슷한 것은?

(A) 반박했다
(B) 시사했다
(C) 확인했다
(D) 깨달았다

27 아래 문장 중 지문 속의 음영된 문장의 핵심 정보를 가장 잘 표현한 것은? 오답은 문장의 의미를 크게 바꾸거나 핵심 정보를 생략한다.

(A) 전 세계적 기후 경향에 대한 특정 지역에서의 계절적 이상이 과학자들에 의해 관찰되었다.
(B) 지구의 기온 하락은 다른 지역에서보다 북반구에서 더 확연했다.
(C) 과학자들은 냉각 과정이 겨울에 세계의 일부 지역에서 가속화되었음에 주목했다.
(D) 비록 겨울에 북반구의 기온이 떨어졌지만, 연중 다른 때에는 상승했다.

28 4단락에서 글쓴이는 왜 필리핀에서의 분출에 관해 논하는가?

(A) 화산 활동과 기후 변화에 관한 최근 조사 결과의 예를 들기 위해
(B) 인간의 활동이 화산에 의한 지구 온난화에 미치는 영향을 기록하기 위해
(C) 화산과 기후 사이의 관계에 논의의 여지가 있다고 여겨진다는 것을 보여주기 위해
(D) 대류권이 성층권에 비해 화산 활동에 다르게 반응한다는 것을 입증하기 위해

29 네 개의 네모[■]는 다음 문장이 삽입될 수 있는 곳을 나타내고 있다.

심지어는 멀리 떨어진 일본에서도 쌀농사가 실패함에 따라 그 영향을 받았으며, 이는 그 국가 역사상 최악의 기근을 초래했다.

이 문장은 어디에 들어가는 것이 가장 적절한가?

30 **지시:** 지문 요약을 위한 도입 문장이 아래에 주어져 있다. 지문의 가장 중요한 내용을 나타내는 보기 3개를 골라 요약을 완성하라. 어떤 문장은 지문에 언급되지 않은 내용이나 사소한 정보를 나타내므로 요약에 포함되지 않는다. **이 문제는 2점이다.**

> **매우 큰 화산 분출은 상당한 지역적 영향을 미치며, 수년간 지구의 기후에도 영향을 미칠 수 있다.**
> · (A) 피나투보산의 분출은 과학자들에게 큰 분출이 기후에 영향을 미치는 방식을 측정할 기회를 주었으며, 그들은 유용한 데이터를 만들기 위해 컴퓨터 시뮬레이션을 사용했다.
> · (B) 18세기 말의 화산 분출은 화산 활동이 지구의 기후 패턴에 미치는 영향에 대한 초기의 단서를 제공했으며, 지역적인 피해가 단지 파괴적인 영향의 일부라는 것을 보여주었다.
> · (D) 기후에 대한 화산의 영향은 대기의 높은 곳으로 물질을 뿜어내는 그것들의 능력에서 비롯되며, 그곳에서 그 물질은 땅과 태양에서 오는 복사에 영향을 미친다.

(C) 태양으로부터 오는 복사의 많은 양이 지구의 대기에 들어오지만, 지표면으로부터의 에너지는 다시 우주로 방출된다.
(E) 거대한 화산 사건은 드물기 때문에, 과학자들은 화산 구름이 대기에 영향을 미치는 방식에 대해 자세히 연구할 기회가 거의 없었다.
(F) 피나투보산 분출에 관해 주민들에게 통지할 경고 시스템이 없었기 때문에, 사실상 근처의 모든 사람들이 목숨을 잃었다.

Actual Test 2

Passage 1

본문 p.204

1 (C)	2 (D)	3 (A)	4 (C)
5 (D)	6 (B)	7 (C)	8 (B)
9 (D)	10 (A), (C), (E)		

켈즈의 서

서기 8세기나 9세기에 만들어진 켈즈의 서는 이름의 색인 및 다른 보충 자료들과 함께 성경의 구절들을 포함하고 있는 채색된 필사본, 즉 삽화를 포함하고 있는 손으로 쓴 작품이다. 그 책 본문의 내용은 이 시기 가톨릭교회의 대표자들에 의해 제작된 다른 많은 것들에서 발견되는 것과 비슷하지만, 그것의 시각적 요소는 그것을 눈에 띄게 한다. 현재 더블린의 트리니티 대학에 전시되어 있는 그 책은 중세 시기 유럽 예술의 가장 중요한 작품 중 하나이다.

켈즈의 서가 어디에서 만들어졌는지는 확실히 알려져 있지 않지만, 대부분의 역사학자들은 둘 중 하나의 이론에 동의한다. 첫 번째는 그 책이 아일랜드의 북동쪽 지역에 위치한 켈즈 수도원에서 제작되었다는 것이다. 이는 켈즈의 서에 관한 최초의 언급이 울라 편년사에 있기 때문이다. 이 문서는 그 책이 서기 1007년에 바이킹의 습격 도중에 켈즈 수도원에서 도난되었으나 결국 되찾아졌다고 기록한다. [5]그러나, 일부 전문가들은 이 수도원이 9세기 초에 스코틀랜드에 있는 아이오나 수도원으로부터 수도사의 유입을 받았다는 것을 지적한다. 그 스코틀랜드 수도원이 책 제작의 오랜 전통을 가지고 있었기 때문에, 수도사들이 이동했을 때 켈즈의 서가 그곳에서부터 켈즈 수도원으로 이동되었다고

주장된다.

누구든 켈즈의 서를 만든 사람은 그것이 예술 작품으로서 눈에 띄게 만든 많은 특징들을 통합했다. 이것들 중 하나는 서예의 우수성이다. 켈즈의 서에 관한 분석은 세 명의 필경사들이 성경 구절과 다른 글 전부를 옮겨 적었음을 밝혀냈다. 7A각각은 시각적으로 매력적이면서 읽기에도 쉬운 인슐라체라고 알려진 독특한 서예 형태를 이용했다. 또 다른 주요 특징은 정교한 삽화이다. 7B켈즈의 서의 매 페이지는 가톨릭의 상징과 복잡하고 서로 맞물린 기하학적 모양의 켈트 예술 양식을 혼합하는 매우 상세한 장식적 요소들을 포함하고 있다. 켈즈의 서는 또한 종교적 인물들과 성경의 장면들을 묘사하는 33페이지의 전면 이미지를 포함하고 있다. 이것들 모두는 그 자체로 주목할 만한 삽화이다. 7D삽화에서의 선명하고 다양한 색상의 사용은 켈즈의 서의 또 다른 중요한 특징이다. 화가들은 많은 서로 다른 색조의 색깔 잉크를 만들기 위해 매우 다양한 천연 소재를 이용했다. 예를 들어, 보라색 색소는 조개류의 한 종류에서 추출되었고, 파란색 잉크는 중동에서 수입된 준보석인 청금석을 이용해 제작되었다. **당시 이 재료들은 둘 다 구하기 어려웠으며 엄청나게 비쌌다.**

켈즈의 서의 시각적 측면에 쏟아진 분명한 노력을 고려해볼 때, 대부분의 역사학자는 그 작품이 성경을 연구하기 위한 수단이라기보다는 전시물로서 기능하도록 의도된 것이라는 데 동의한다. 아마, 그 책은 교회에서 눈에 잘 띄게 전시되었을 것이며, 그 후 의식 행사 도중에만 낭독되었을 것이다. 이 주장은 켈즈의 서에 있는 글의 배치에 의해 뒷받침된다. 8복음서의 특정 부분을 빠르게 찾기 위해 필요한 장의 표제는 장식을 위한 더 많은 공간을 위해 생략되어 있다. 게다가, 페이지 위에 글자의 균일한 사각형 덩어리를 만들기 위해 때때로 단어와 심지어 문장 전체가 반복된다. 이는 교회 공직자가 켈즈의 서를 "낭독"했을 때, 그 책이 전시를 위해 참석한 사람들을 향해 들어 올려진 동안 그는 아마 암송을 했을 것임을 시사한다.

illuminated 형 채색된 manuscript 명 필사본
supplementary 형 보충의 representative 명 대표자
medieval 형 중세의 subscribe to ~에 동의하다 abbey 명 수도원
raid 명 습격 monastery 명 수도원 influx 명 유입
superiority 명 우수성 calligraphy 명 서예 scribe 명 필경사
appealing 형 매력적인 elaborate 형 정교한
interlocking 형 서로 맞물린 geometric 형 기하학적인
noteworthy 형 주목할 만한 pigment 명 색소 lapis lazuli 청금석
semiprecious 형 준보석의 showpiece 명 전시물
in all likelihood 아마 prominently 부 눈에 잘 띄게 layout 명 배치
recite from memory 암송하다

1 지문의 단어 "supplementary"와 의미가 가장 비슷한 것은?
(A) 무관한
(B) 의무적인
(C) 주변의
(D) 자발적인

2 아래 문장 중 지문 속의 음영된 문장의 핵심 정보를 가장 잘 표현한 것은? 오답은 문장의 의미를 크게 바꾸거나 핵심 정보를 생략한다.
(A) 교회에 의해 두어진 제한은 그 책의 내용이 다른 출판물의 것과 달라지는 것을 막았다.
(B) 이미지와 글의 결합은 이 책을 일반적으로 교회 공직자에 의해 제작된 것들과 구분 짓는다.
(C) 그 책이 종교적 출처에서 복사된 글 자료들을 포함하고 있기 때문에, 삽화가 그것의 유일한 흥미로운 특징이다.
(D) 그것의 글 내용이 다른 종교적 글의 것과 비슷하기 때문에, 그 책을 구별 짓는 것은 삽화이다.

3 지문의 어구 "subscribe to"와 의미가 가장 비슷한 것은?
(A) ~에 동의하다
(B) ~을 알아내다
(C) ~으로 정하다
(D) ~을 준비하다

4 지문에서 글쓴이는 왜 "Annals of Ulster"를 언급하는가?
(A) 같은 시기의 두 가지 역사적 기록을 비교하기 위해
(B) 기관이 책 제작의 오랜 역사를 가지고 있었음을 보여주기 위해
(C) 작품의 기원에 관한 주장에 대한 증거를 제공하기 위해
(D) 예술품이 처음에 생각되었던 것보다 나중에 만들어졌음을 시사하기 위해

5 2단락에 따르면, 아이오나 수도원의 수도사들은
(A) 많은 다른 왕국들로 책을 수출했다
(B) 스코틀랜드에 새로운 시설을 건설했다
(C) 아일랜드 수도사들에게 책 제작 기술을 가르쳤다
(D) 다른 지역에 있는 수도원으로 이주했다

6 지문의 단어 "these"가 가리키는 것은?
(A) 모양
(B) 이미지
(C) 인물들
(D) 장면들

7 3단락에 따르면, 다음 중 켈즈의 서의 독특한 특징이 아닌 것은?
(A) 글자체의 양식과 품질
(B) 각 페이지의 복잡한 이미지
(C) 종교적 지도자에 대한 정확한 묘사
(D) 밝은 색상의 다양한 조합

8 4단락에 따르면, 켈즈의 서에서 정보의 위치를 찾기가 힘들었던 것은
(A) 복음서의 순서가 바뀌었기 때문이다
(B) 부분의 제목이 생략되었기 때문이다
(C) 장의 이름이 반복되었기 때문이다
(D) 글의 배치가 일관성이 없었기 때문이다

9 네 개의 네모[■]는 다음 문장이 삽입될 수 있는 곳을 나타내고 있다.
당시 이 재료들은 둘 다 구하기 어려웠으며 엄청나게 비쌌다.
이 문장은 어디에 들어가는 것이 가장 적절한가?

10 **지시:** 지문 요약을 위한 도입 문장이 아래에 주어져 있다. 지문의 가장 중요한 내용을 나타내는 보기 3개를 골라 요약을 완성하라. 어떤 문장은 지문에 언급되지 않은 내용이나 사소한 정보를 나타내므로 요약에 포함되지 않는다. **이 문제는 2점이다.**

켈즈의 서는 중세 예술의 중요한 작품으로 여겨지는 채색된 필사본이다.
- (A) 대부분의 연구자들은 그 책이 아일랜드의 켈즈 수도원이나 스코틀랜드의 아이오나 수도원에서 만들어졌다는 것에 동의한다.
- (C) 켈즈의 서는 그것의 시각 예술 작품으로서의 전반적인 가치를 크게 상승시킨 여러 주목할 만한 특징들을 가지고 있다.

· (E) 성경을 연구하는 데 적합하지 않았기 때문에, 그 책은 눈에 잘 띄게 전시되기 위해 제작되었을 가능성이 가장 높다.

(B) 그 책에 대한 최초의 글로 된 언급은 11세기 바이킹의 수도원 공격에 대한 묘사 안에 있다.

(D) 켈즈의 서에 있는 삽화를 만들기 위해 사용된 색깔 잉크는 다양한 출처로부터의 색소를 포함한다.

(F) 그 책의 글은 많은 배치 오류를 포함하고 있는데, 이는 그것이 교회 의식에 사용된 적이 있는지를 의심스럽게 만든다.

Passage 2

본문 p.208

11 (B) 12 (A) 13 (B) 14 (A)
15 (B) 16 (A) 17 (C) 18 (A)
19 (C) 20 (B), (C), (E)

멸종에 대한 우려

생태계는 제한된 양의 자원을 위해 서로 경쟁하는 종들로 구성되어 있으며, 이 경쟁은 진화 이면의 주요 원동력인 종의 적응을 필요하게 만든다. 성공적인 종들은 살아남아 번식하지만, 변화하는 조건이나 다른 것들의 경쟁에 적응하지 못하는 것들은 멸종된다. 멸종은 또한 지진, 화산 분출, 홍수 같은 대 격동의 사건들에 의해 초래될 수 있다. **그러한 멸종은 보통 한 종이 제한된 지리적 범위를 가지고 있을 때 일어난다.** 진화 이론에 따르면, 멸종은 자연적이며 필연적이다. 사실, 그것들은 수백만 년 동안 일어나왔다. 그러나, 만약 멸종이 단지 지구에서의 삶의 자연적 측면이라면, 사람들은 왜 그것에 대해 걱정할까?

멸종이 자연적인 현상이긴 하지만, 그것들은 최근에 증가된 속도로 일어나오고 있다. 자연, 혹은 배경 멸종률은 화석 기록을 연구하고 수백만 년 동안의 평균을 계산하여 추산된다. [12]육지와 해양의 화석 집단을 둘 다 고려하여, 과학자들은 단일 종의 평균 수명이 약 백만에서 천만 년이라고 추산하지만, 그것은 생물의 종류에 따라 변한다. 예를 들어, 포유류 종들은 백만 년의 평균 수명을 가지고 있으며 그것들의 배경 멸종률은 2백년 당 한 종이다. 그러나, 지난 400년 동안, 89종의 포유류가 멸종된 것으로 공식적으로 등록되었으며, 그러므로, 포유류는 그것들의 자연적인 속도보다 40배 이상의 속도로 사라지고 있다. 현재 겨우 약 5,400종의 살아 있는 포유류가 존재하기 때문에 이 숫자는 특히 걱정스럽다. [13]같은 기간 동안, 알려진 조류 약 10,000종 가운데 128개의 조류 종이 사라졌으며, 추산 상 10퍼센트의 조류가 심각하게 멸종 위기에 처한 것으로 등록되었다.

최근 멸종의 가속화에 대한 주요 원인은 인간의 활동이다. 생물들에게 증가하는 압력을 가함으로써, 인간은 무심코 많은 종들의 멸종을 야기해 왔다. [15A]두 개의 주목할 만한 예시는 역사적으로 고기의 공급원으로서 지속이 불가능한 수로 포획된 조류인 도도와 화식조이다. 마찬가지로, 카리브해몽크물범은 20세기 중반에 멸종에 이를 때까지 사냥당했으며 그 해양 포유류의 마지막으로 확인된 목격은 1952년에 있었다. 전 세계의 우림에서 일어나고 있는 전례 없는 삼림 파괴는 오늘날의 생물들에 대한 가장 큰 위협 중 하나이다. [15C/15D]지구의 종 3분의 1 이상의 서식지인 아마존 유역은 벌목과 농사로 인해 빠르게 붕괴되고 있는 우림 생태계의 전형적인 예이다. (그중 35개가 동물인) 무려 130개의 종들이 매일 세계의 우림에서 멸종되고 있는 것으로 추정된다.

그럼에도 불구하고, '뭐 하러 생물 다양성을 보존할까?'라는 의문점이 남는다. [18]세계의 약의 상당 부분이 식물 추출물을 함유하고 있다는 것은 잘 알려져 있으나, 지구 식물군의 아주 작은 부분만이 약용 물질을 위해 심사되었다. 따라서, 서식지 파괴로 소실된 모든 검증되지 않은 종은 잠재적으로 치유력이 있는 속성을 가진 화학물을 발견할 잃어버린 기회에 해당한다. 알려진 약용 특성을 가진 현존하는 식물이 소실될 위험도 있다. 그러나, 생물 다양성의 직접적인 가치를 넘어서, 사람들은 지구의 책임감 있는 관리인으로서 행동해야 한다. 후세를 위해 지구의 풍요로움을 최대한 보존한다는 이 도덕적 의무는 모든 시민 사회의 위대한 사상가들에 의해 강조되어 왔다. 심지어 개인적인 자유와 행복의 추구에 대한 글로 유명한 정치 철학자 존 로크조차도 인간이 다음의 세대들을 위해 그들이 자신을 위해 취한 것만큼 많이 남겨두어야 한다고 말했다. 다시 말해서, 자유는 책임과 균형이 유지되어야 한다.

extinction 명 멸종　necessitate 동 필요하게 만들다
adaptation 명 적응　driving force 원동력
cataclysmic 형 대 격동의　inevitable 형 필연적인
terrestrial 형 육지의　critically 부 심각하게
endangered 형 멸종 위기에 처한　exert 동 (힘 등을) 가하다
inadvertently 부 무심코　unsustainable 형 지속이 불가능한
unprecedented 형 전례 없는　prime 형 전형적인
degrade 동 붕괴시키다　pharmaceutical 명 약　fraction 명 부분
flora 명 식물군　screen 동 심사하다　medicinal 형 약용의
curative 형 치유력이 있는　steward 명 관리인　imperative 명 의무
posterity 명 후세　successive 형 다음의

11 아래 문장 중 지문 속의 음영된 문장의 핵심 정보를 가장 잘 표현한 것은? 오답은 문장의 의미를 크게 바꾸거나 핵심 정보를 생략한다.

(A) 진화는 같은 서식지에 사는 다양한 집단의 생물 사이에 자원에 대한 경쟁을 위한 자극을 제공한다.
(B) 생태계를 구성하는 생물들의 자원을 위한 경쟁은 생물들의 적응을 강요하는데, 이는 진화의 주요 결정 요인이다.
(C) 개별 생물들의 적응은 다양한 자원을 위한 종들 간의 증가된 경쟁을 촉진한다.
(D) 종들은 부족한 자원을 위해 서로 경쟁하며, 이 경쟁은 그것들의 진화에 있어 주요한 역할을 한다.

12 다음 중 2단락에서 포유류에 관해 추론할 수 있는 것은?

(A) 다른 많은 종류의 동물들보다 빠르게 멸종된다.
(B) 해양 환경에서 살면 멸종할 가능성이 더 낮다.
(C) 먼 과거에 그랬던 것보다 지금 더 긴 수명을 가지고 있다.
(D) 화석 기록을 조사할 때 확인하기 어렵다.

13 2단락에 따르면, 약 10퍼센트의 조류 종들은

(A) 지난 두 세기 동안 멸종했다
(B) 완전히 멸종할 임박한 위협에 직면했다
(C) 과학계에 의해 아직 확인되지 않았다
(D) 그것들의 생존에 대한 어떠한 중대한 위험에도 직면하지 않고 있다

14 지문의 단어 "exerting"과 의미가 가장 비슷한 것은?

(A) 가하는
(B) 완화하는
(C) 관리하는
(D) 무시하는

15 3단락에서, 다음 중 멸종을 야기하는 인간 활동의 구체적인 예시로 언급되지 않은 것은?

(A) 식량을 위해 동물을 죽이는 것
(B) 댐으로 수로를 막는 것
(C) 목재를 얻기 위해 나무를 수확하는 것
(D) 농업을 위해 땅을 개간하는 것

16 지문의 단어 "curative"와 의미가 가장 비슷한 것은?

(A) 치유하는
(B) 자극하는
(C) 뛰어난
(D) 본질적인

17 지문에서 글쓴이는 왜 "the political philosopher John Locke"를 언급하는가?

(A) 개인적 자유와 환경 보호주의 사이의 관계를 보여주기 위해
(B) 환경 운동의 오랜 역사를 강조하기 위해
(C) 자연을 보호할 의무에 관한 주장을 뒷받침하기 위해
(D) 이기심이 자연 세계 보호에 대한 장애물임을 시사하기 위해

18 글쓴이가 주장하는 것으로, 많은 종의 식물은

(A) 인간을 위한 건강상의 이익이 있는 물질들을 포함한다
(B) 정기적으로 잠재적으로 위험한 화학물질을 흡수한다
(C) 그것들의 서식지가 변할 때 새로운 속성을 발달시킨다
(D) 멸종의 위협을 감소시키는 특성들을 드러낸다

19 네 개의 네모[■]는 다음 문장이 삽입될 수 있는 곳을 나타내고 있다.

그러한 멸종은 보통 한 종이 제한된 지리적 범위를 가지고 있을 때 일어난다.

이 문장은 어디에 들어가는 것이 가장 적절한가?

20 지시: 지문 요약을 위한 도입 문장이 아래에 주어져 있다. 지문의 가장 중요한 내용을 나타내는 보기 3개를 골라 요약을 완성하라. 어떤 문장은 지문에 언급되지 않은 내용이나 사소한 정보를 나타내므로 요약에 포함되지 않는다. **이 문제는 2점이다.**

> **최근의 멸종률 변화는 대체로 인간의 행동에 기인한다.**
> · (B) 지난 400년 동안의 멸종률은 자연적인 멸종률을 훨씬 넘어섰다.
> · (C) 식물의 약용 가치는 잘 알려져 있으나, 세계 식물 종의 많은 수가 아직 검증되지 않았다.
> · (E) 서식지 파괴는 세계 생물들의 상당 부분에 위협이 된다.

(A) 최근 멸종으로 소실되는 육지 및 해양 생물의 수는 역사적 기록의 어느 시점보다도 높았다.
(D) 과도한 사냥이 여러 주목할 만한 멸종을 직접적으로 초래하긴 했지만, 그것은 더 이상 한때 그랬던 것과 같은 만연한 문제가 아니다.
(F) 그것들의 아름다움 때문이든, 인간을 위한 풍부한 삶의 경험을 만들어내는 역할 때문이든, 생물들은 보호되어야 한다.

Passage 3

본문 p.212

21 (C) 22 (B) 23 (B) 24 (D)
25 (D) 26 (B) 27 (B) 28 (A)
29 (C) 30 Civil Law: (A), (C) Common Law: (B), (E), (G)

대륙법과 영미법

성문법 체계는 약 4천 년 전 그것들의 시작 이래로 훨씬 더 복잡하고 다양해져 왔지만, 그것들은 일반적으로 여전히 대륙법과 영미법이라는 두 개의 넓은 범주에 들어간다.

[22]대륙법은 7세기 초의 로마 황제 유스티니아누스까지 거슬러 올라갈 수 있으며, 전 세계에서 가장 일반적인 법 체계에 해당한다. 그것은 고도로 성문화된 법을 지칭하며, 이는 그것이 지속적으로 갱신되는 포괄적인 법규를 포함하고 있음을 의미한다. 대륙법은 입법 기관에 의해 수립된 법률인 법령에 주로 의지한다. [23A/23C]법령은 판사들로 하여금 소송 사건의 사실들을 빠르게 검토하고 그 후에 법령의 관련 조항을 정확하게 적용하도록 해준다. [23D]일단 판사가 피의자가 법을 위반했는지를 결정하면, 법령은 그나 그녀의 절차와 처벌에 대한 해석을 상당히 간단하게 만든다. 대륙법 법정에서의 소송 사건 이전과 도중에, 변호사들은 의뢰인을 대표하고, 법의 세부 사항에 관해 그들에게 조언하고, 그들이 법적인 서류를 준비하는 것을 돕도록 허용된다. 그러나, 법정 소송 절차 동안 그들의 역할은 매우 제한적이다. 판사는 최고 수사관처럼 기능하며, 사실을 수립하고 증인들을 심문하는 데 있어 주도권을 잡는다.

영미법은 일반적으로 영국 및 영국의 법적 전통에 의해 강하게 영향을 받은 국가들과 연관되어 있다. 이 국가들에는, 성문화된 법령들 또한 존재하긴 하지만, 판례법이 대단한 중요성을 갖는다. 판례법은 주목할 만한 소송 사건에서 판결을 내리고 그 결과 법적 선례를 수립한 특정 판사들의 공개된 의견으로 구성되어 있으며, 법적 선례는 유사한 소송 사건에 적용될 수 있는 사법적 판단이다. 이 선례들은 많은 권위를 가지고 있으며 미래의 사법적 판결에 강하게 영향을 미친다. **예를 들어, 미국 대법원의 판사들은 종종 이전의 대법원 판결을 뒤집는 것을 매우 꺼린다.** 영미법 하의 형사 법정 소송 절차는 의뢰인을 대표하는 데 있어 변호사의 역할을 강조한다. 변호사들은 판사 앞에, 가끔은 배심원단 앞에 서며, 고소인이나 피의자의 유죄나 무죄뿐만 아니라 법률적 논점에 관해 그들을 설득하려고 애쓴다. 판사들은 대개 중재자일 뿐이다. 이러한 역학 때문에, 판례법에서의 형사 소송 절차는 스포츠 행사와 유사한데, 여기에서 변호사와 의뢰인은 팀에 해당하며 판사는 심판이다. [25]배심 재판의 경우, 배심원이라고 불리는 보통 시민들은 피고의 유죄나 무죄를 결정하고, 판사는 대부분의 경우 그들의 결정을 받아들인다. 그러나, 배심원단에 의한 유죄 평결의 경우, 처벌은 판사의 단독 결정이다.

실제로는, 많은 법 체계는 대륙법과 영미법 둘 다의 측면들이 사용되는 방식으로 작동한다. 미국은 연방과 주 수준 둘 다에서 포괄적인 성문화된 법을 가지고 있다는 점에서 이것의 완벽한 예시이다. 미국 법전은 그 국가 전체를 위한 법령의 공식적인 모음이다. 그것은 모든 미국 시민에게 적용되며, 따라서 사실상 대륙법의 보편적인 형태로 기능한다. 게다가, 각 주는 오직 그 주의 거주자나 방문자들에게 적용되는 자신만의 법령 모음을 가지고 있다. [27]미국을 영미법 국가로 만드는 것은 법을 형성하는 데 있어 판사들의 중심적인 역할이다. [28]예를 들어, 연방 및 주의 대법원은 그것들의 판사들이 연방 또는 주의 입법 기관에 의해 만들어진 법을 유지하거나 거부할 수 있기 때문에 엄청난 권력을 갖는다. 따라서, 혹시라도 그 둘이 충돌하면 결국 영미법이 대륙법보다 우세하며, 대법원 소송 사건에서 판사들은 입법 기관에 의해 제정된 법이 미국 헌법에 대한 그들의 해석과 일치하는지를 결정할 수 있다.

civil law 대륙법 common law 영미법 sophisticated 형 복잡한 inception 명 시작 prevalent 형 일반적인 codified 형 성문화된 statute 명 법령 legislature 명 입법 기관 provision 명 조항 accused person 피의자 straightforward 형 간단한

attorney 명 변호사 proceeding 명 소송 절차 rule 동 판결을 내리다
precedent 명 선례 judicial 형 사법적인 guilt 명 유죄
innocence 명 무죄, 결백함 accuser 명 고소인
moderator 명 중재자 dynamic 명 역학 referee 명 심판
jury trial 배심 재판 juror 명 배심원 verdict 명 평결
practically 부 사실상 uphold 동 유지하다 accordant 형 일치하는

21 지문의 단어 "inception"과 의미가 가장 비슷한 것은?

(A) 혁신
(B) 발견
(C) 출현
(D) 감지

22 2단락에 따르면, 다음 중 대륙법에 관해 사실인 것은?

(A) 엄격한 처벌을 내리는 경향이 있다.
(B) 가장 흔한 법 체계이다.
(C) 오직 몇몇 국가에서만 사용된다.
(D) 오래된 법적 선례에 의존한다.

23 2단락에 따르면, 법령이 판사가 하도록 돕지 않는 것은?

(A) 소송 사건의 세부 사항들을 빠르게 검토하기
(B) 법적 개념들을 분명하게 설명하기
(C) 관련 조항들을 정확하게 적용하기
(D) 절차와 처벌을 간단히 해석하기

24 3단락에서 글쓴이는 왜 스포츠 행사를 언급하는가?

(A) 법정에서 변호사들이 그들의 의뢰인들과 상호 작용하는 방법을 묘사하기 위해
(B) 형사 소송 사건에서 변호사의 중요성을 강조하기 위해
(C) 판사들이 무죄와 유죄를 결정하기 위해 사용하는 방법을 설명하기 위해
(D) 특정한 법적 절차가 작동하는 방법에 대한 비유를 제공하기 위해

25 다음 중 3단락에서 배심원단의 결정에 관해 추론할 수 있는 것은?

(A) 범죄에 대한 처벌을 결정한다.
(B) 모든 배심원 간의 합의를 요구한다.
(C) 소송 사건의 변호사에 의해 승인되어야 한다.
(D) 가끔 판사에 의해 뒤집힌다.

26 지문의 단어 "accordant"와 의미가 가장 비슷한 것은?

(A) 명백한
(B) 일관된
(C) 일반적인
(D) 자연스러운

27 4단락에 따르면, 성문화된 법을 가지고 있음에도 미국이 영미법 국가로 간주되는 것은

(A) 연방 법령이 모든 주에 적용되기 때문이다
(B) 법을 형성하는 데 있어 판사들이 중요한 역할을 수행하기 때문이다
(C) 각 주가 자신의 법 모음을 가지고 있기 때문이다
(D) 입법 기관이 지속적으로 법령을 갱신하기 때문이다

28 4단락에 따르면, 다음 중 연방 및 주 대법원에 관해 사실인 것은?

(A) 법령을 승인하거나 기각할 수 있다.
(B) 법을 제정할 권력을 가지고 있다.
(C) 그들 자신의 판사를 임명할 수 있다.
(D) 입법 기관보다 힘이 약하다.

29 네 개의 네모[■]는 다음 문장이 삽입될 수 있는 곳을 나타내고 있다.

예를 들어, 미국 대법원의 판사들은 종종 이전의 대법원 판결을 뒤집는 것을 매우 꺼린다.

이 문장은 어디에 들어가는 것이 가장 적절한가?

30 **지시:** 주어진 선택지에서 적절한 문장을 선택하여 관계있는 법 체계에 연결하시오. **이 문제는 3점이다.**

선택지	대륙법
(D) 변호사들은 법정 소송 사건 이전에 판사에게 증거를 제출한다. (F) 형사 소송 사건은 항상 배심원단 앞에서 다투어진다.	· (A) 법정에서 변호사의 역할은 매우 제한적이다. · (C) 판사는 형사 소송 절차 동안 최고 조사관으로 기능한다.
	영미법
	· (B) 판사들의 이전에 공개된 견해가 강조된다. · (E) 형사 소송 사건에서 판사의 역할은 중재자의 그것이다. · (G) 변호사들은 그들의 의뢰인을 대신하여 판사를 설득하려고 시도한다.

MEMO

MEMO

MEMO

HACKERS

APEX READING for the TOEFL iBT®

Advanced